76/-

N

COMMUNITY STRUCTURE
AND DECISION-MAKING:
COMPARATIVE ANALYSES

CHANDLER PUBLICATIONS IN
ANTHROPOLOGY AND SOCIOLOGY
LEONARD BROOM, GENERAL EDITOR

SOCIOLOGY
CHARLES M. BONJEAN, EDITOR

 Science Research Associates, Inc., 259 East Erie Street, Chicago, Illinois 60611
A Subsidiary of IBM   Distributors

COMMUNITY STRUCTURE
AND DECISION-MAKING:
COMPARATIVE ANALYSES

Edited by

TERRY N. CLARK

The University of Chicago

CHANDLER PUBLISHING COMPANY
124 Spear Street, San Francisco, California 94105

Previously published and copyrighted materials are reprinted with the permission of authors, publishers, or copyright owners as listed below:

"Power and Community Structure," by Peter H. Rossi, reprinted from *Midwest Journal of Political Science* (November 1960), copyright 1960 by Wayne State University Press. Used by permission of the publisher and the author.

"Rancorous Conflict in Community Politics," by William A. Gamson, reprinted from *The American Sociological Review*, Vol. 31, No. 1 (February 1966), copyright © 1966 by the American Sociological Association. Used by permission of the publisher and the author.

"The Process of Decision-Making within the Context of Community Organization," by Paul A. Miller, reprinted from *Rural Sociology*, Vol. 17, No. 2 (1952), copyright 1952, by the Rural Sociological Society. Used by permission of the publisher and the author.

"Institutional and Occupational Representations in Eleven Community Systems," by William V. D'Antonio, William H. Form, Charles P. Loomis, and Eugene C. Erickson, reprinted from *The American Sociological Review*, Vol. 26, No. 3 (June 1961), copyright © 1961 by the American Sociological Association. Used by permission of the publisher and the authors.

"Reputation and Resources in Community Politics," by William A. Gamson, reprinted in *The American Journal of Sociology* (September 1966), copyright 1966 by the University of Chicago. Used by permission of The University of Chicago Press and the author.

"A Comparative Study of Decision Making in Rural Communities," by Kenneth Kammeyer, reprinted in *Rural Sociology*, Vol. 27, No. 1 (1962), copyright, 1962, by the Rural Sociological Society. Used by permission of the publisher and the author.

"Community Power and Urban Renewal Success," by Amos H. Hawley, reprinted from *The American Journal of Sociology* (January 1963), copyright 1962, 1963 by the University of Chicago. Used by permission of The University of Chicago Press and the author.

"Purposive Community Change in Consensus and Dissensus Situations," by Roland L. Warren and Herbert H. Hyman, reprinted from *Community Mental Health Journal*, Vol. 2, No. 4 (Winter 1966), © 1966 by Behavioral Publications, Inc. Used by permission of the publisher and the authors.

Book designed by Joseph M. Roter

CONTENTS

VI. POWER, RESOURCES, AND DECISION-MAKING

ACKNOWLEDGMENTS

About half of the material contained in this volume appears here for the first time. However, by special arrangement with Charles Bonjean, sociology editor for Chandler Publishing Company as well as editor of the *Southwestern Social Science Quarterly*, a few articles prepared for the present volume appeared in almost the same form in an issue of the *Quarterly* (December 1967) on Community Politics. The reader should note, however, that the articles by Claire W. Gilbert and myself, published in the *Quarterly*, have almost no overlap with those appearing here.

For commenting on sections of the volume signed by myself, I wish to thank Bernard Barber, Robert L. Crain, Robert A. Dahl, William J. Goode, Raymond Glazier, Terence K. Hopkins, Morris Janowitz, Juan J. Linz, Nelson W. Polsby, David Rogers, Peter H. Rossi, Immanuel Wallerstein, and Raymond E. Wolfinger. Students at Columbia and the University of Chicago acted as generally radical and occasionally constructive critics. Fred E. Duffell served as a remarkably tolerant and thoroughly professional typist.

Financial support from Columbia University, the National Institute of Mental Health, and the National Science Foundation (GS–1904) is gratefully acknowledged.

Substantial portions of these first five chapters were initially circulated as *Power and Community Structure*, Columbia University, September, 1964. Four articles were then adapted from this first manuscript: "Power and Community Structure: Who Governs, Where, and When?" presented at the 1965 annual meeting of the American Sociological Association, Chicago, Illinois, published in revised form with the same title in *The Sociological Quarterly*, Summer, 1967, Vol. 8, No. 3, pp. 291–316; "The Sixteen Faces of Power," mimeographed, Columbia University, 1965, published in revised form as "The Concept of Power: Some Overemphasized and Underrecognized Dimensions," *Southwestern Social Science Quarterly*, December, 1967, Vol. 48, No. 3, pp. 271–286; "A Respecification of the Concept of Social Stratification with Special Reference to Community Power Studies," dittoed, Columbia University, 1965; "Community or Communities—A Dilemma for Studies of Community Power," *Kansas Journal of Sociology*, Winter, 1967, Vol. 3, No. 1, pp. 1–11. The sections from these earlier articles, which are incorporated in the present manuscript, are reprinted with the permission of the publishers.

I

INTRODUCTION

INTRODUCTION

❷

The patterns by which men organize their relationships with one another are ancient topics of discussion and debate. Chronicles have detailed the ways of war lords, despots, and democratic states. Ideologues and philosophers have constructed systems to celebrate and, perhaps, explain these diverse types of social arrangements. An omnipresent theme has been power, or, conceived dynamically, decision-making—in a given social unit, who tends to have his way? Most conspicuous as subjects of attention have been the heads of states and their entourage, for they have traditionally handed down the most important decisions. For centuries, documentation of the affairs of state was a matter of reporting the rise and fall of royal houses, or a mere handful of individuals. There were, however, more sophisticated inquiries into the patterns by which decisions may be taken, and which led to typologies of leadership—such as Aristotle's influential categories of Monarchy, Aristocracy, and Democracy. Still others were concerned with explaining the underlying conditions that led a particular society to a given leadership pattern. Montesquieu pointed to the constraints on men's activities exercised by geography and climate. Marx analyzed the impact of the economic structure. Pareto and Mosca called attention to culture and personality. Weber penetrated the subtleties of religion and values.

These are some of the writers who have provided a fund of basic ideas, a set of conceptual tools for the analysis of power and decision-making, which have informed much of contemporary work. Patterns of power and decision-making characteristic of entire national societies remain the most glamorous areas for speculation and debate, and there has been no dearth of such studies in recent decades.[1]

---

[1] Some of the most discussed—often critically—have been Robert Brady, *Business as a System of Power*; David Riesman, *The Lonely Crowd*; C. Wright Mills, *The Power Elite*; Floyd Hunter, *Top Leadership U.S.A.*; Raymond A. Bauer, Ithiel de Sola Pool, and Lewis Dexter, *American Business and Public Policy*; and most recently, Arnold Rose, *The Power Structure*. Except for Brady's volume, these studies all focus on the United States. Analogous studies outside the United States seem fewer in number. See, however, Raymond Aron, "Social Structure and the Ruling Class," *British Journal of Sociology* (1950), pp. 1–116, 126–143.

But it is extraordinarily difficult to carry out a systematic study of a topic so vast as power or decision-making in a national society. To portray the over-all pattern on a single canvas is ambitious if not foolhardy, and the great majority of studies have focused on only a single narrow area—the role of a particular interest group, a few decisions in congress, the operation of one governmental agency, and the like. Yet even to study such topics as these demands interviewing, or attempting to interview, large numbers of persons, who, even if they do have time for an interview, are seldom at liberty to offer more than a partial view of what they know. Essential documents are inevitably secret. Newspaper accounts and memoirs of central actors, to which one must have recourse in order to supplement first-hand information, are egregiously vague, superficial, and misleading. Then, in order to generalize, international comparison is almost essential; but to investigate more than one national system compounds these problems enormously.

In addition, while there has been recent progress, power and decision-making remain frightfully general and diffuse matters. Much further conceptual and methodological progress is necessary before it will be possible to measure complex decision-making processes rapidly and precisely.

Confronted with these substantive, conceptual, and methodological problems of studying power at the national level, many have sought more manageable research animals. A favorite choice has been the local community, for many purposes a delightful sort of fruitfly: large in number and variety, far less complex than national societies, reasonably accessible, they are often flattered at being studied—although they can bite. But communities are not simply fruitflies. They are composed of living persons not always inordinately different from the researcher himself, and he has often found it enjoyable to talk with them and even to participate actively in their political, economic, and social affairs. While such complete immersion can provide a rich taste of community life and lead to many insights, it can also limit and distort the observer's perspective—particularly, as is generally the case, when he becomes immersed only in a single community.

Such total immersion was and, in fact, continues to be the principal research method for many community studies. But since the 1950's and the application of sociometric techniques and various other research tools to the local community, total or partial immersion has generally been accompanied by other more formal procedures.

The 1950's and early 1960's produced a rich harvest of case studies of individual communities. And while these frequently drew inspiration from one another, the research methods of earlier studies were almost never replicated with sufficient precision to permit systematic comparison of results. These years were also marked by bitter controversies over political ideology, conceptualization of power and decision-making, and research methods. In their passion and rhetoric, the debates occasionally seemed to resemble more closely the fluoridation battles and urban renewal controversies they sought to describe than the rational discourse generally expected of scientists.

After about 1960, however, it gradually came to be recognized that in order to transcend the narrow confines within which so much of the discussion had become locked, systematic comparative research on community decision-making was imperative. And so comparative studies of two, four, five and more communities were gradually undertaken. Much of the discussion still dealt, however, with questions initially raised by the case studies, but which the case studies never adequately answered. Only at the present time is the impact of the new, comparative perspective coming to be experienced by the field as a whole. If the late 1950's witnessed the Pluralist Revolution, it would seem that for studies of community decision-making, the late 1960's are destined to become the period of the Comparative Revolution.

This volume has been prepared in an effort to synthesize the most important findings emerging from research based on a comparative perspective. It is the first full-length volume published to be fully devoted to the analysis of community decision-making in large numbers of communities. And, to a large degree, the various articles no longer raise solely the question of "Who Governs?" as it was posed by Hunter, Dahl, and their followers; they are predominantly concerned with answering "Who Governs, Where, When, and with What Effects?" They no longer seek simply to describe the structure of decision-making processes, but attempt to specify as precisely as possible the types of community structures, under varying conditions, which give rise to different patterns of decision-making, and how these patterns in turn influence the actual outcomes of community decisions in one direction or another.

To answer these questions, it is necessary to investigate decision-making and related processes in a variety of communities characterized by differences in basic demographic, economic, legal-political, and cultural characteristics; by differences in leadership and decision-making patterns; and by differences in outputs. Comparison is essential, but comparison of significantly contrasting patterns is imperative if meaningful generalizations are to be formulated. For these purposes, cross-national studies are particularly valuable, as they practically force the researcher to transcend his national ethnocentrisms. There has been an attempt to include cross-national studies in the present volume, and the reason that more are not to be found in the following pages is that they have simply not been conducted—although, as discussed in the concluding chapter of the volume, many are now in progress.

Section II presents certain basic conceptual and methodological issues, and attempts a brief synthesis of research in the field. The first chapter offers a general framework for the comparative study of community decision-making based on ten sets of fundamental variables. *Inputs to the community* are closely related to *national societal characteristics*. But inputs are also shaped by basic community structural characteristics: *demographic characteristics,* and structures related to the performance of the four Bales-Parsons functional imperatives, *adaptation—economic-characteristics, goal attainment—legal political characteristics, integration —political parties and voluntary organizations, latent pattern-maintenance and tension-management—cultural characteristics.* Largely structured by these first sets of variables are the *leadership characteristics* of the community as well as its *decision-making structure,* and, finally, the *community outputs.*

Chapter 2 presents some basic dimensions of social stratification, and then elaborates a four-fold typology of stratification systems and associated decision-making patterns, emphasizing vertical and horizontal differentiation. Differentiation, however, implies integration; hence five mechanisms for integration are suggested: the institutionalized general value system, norms relating to the performance of specific roles, bureaucracy, the juridical system, and interchange between subsystems.

Chapter 3, on the concept of power, reviews the "individualistic" and "dyadic" approaches to power, and suggests as an alternative a "systemic" orientation. Power is distinguished from both influence and decision-making, and power structures are contrasted with decision-making structures. Then, in an effort to arrive at a conceptual synthesis of the power and communications approaches to decision-making, some essentials of an exchange theory are elaborated. The theory calls attention to the characteristics of resources controlled by various actors in a system, and the importance of various resources for exercising power, gaining prestige, and institutionalizing norms and values. Characteristics of resources examined are *generality* (broken down into *buying power, selling price,* and *exchange value*) ; *prestige value; institutionalization importance; power value; general applicability; resource expendability;* and *durability.* Some basic resources are quantified in terms of several of these characteristics. The importance of various resources at the separate stages of a decision are considered, and characteristics of issue areas and decisional outcomes examined. Methods for measuring decision-making patterns are analyzed briefly.

Chapter 4 presents a functional approach to the concept of community, discussing the community and the "community complex" as social units characterized by varying degrees of functional autonomy. A functional scheme classifies communities according to the degree to which they perform each of the AGIL functional imperatives, and operational procedures are suggested for measuring the level of performance of each function.

In Chapter 5, a number of the distinctions and classifications discussed earlier are brought together in a series of propositions which relate the ten sets of variables of the framework presented in Chapter 1 to one another. Five general formulations are offered at outset which focus on structural differentiation, leadership characteristics, functional orientation, distribution and generality of resources, and sectoral variations of communities. Largely by combining these general formulations, and applying them to various community institutions, 38 more specific propositions are elaborated.

Section III focuses on community structure and centralization of decision-making. The article by Rossi, originally published in 1960, is a landmark for emphasizing the importance of comparative studies and for presenting specific propositions relating such variables as homogeneity of the population, governmental arrangements, and voluntary organizations to centralization of decision-making.

The Gilbert article reports briefly on an ambitious project in which the results of individual studies of 166 communities were coded and analyzed for patterns of variables associated with centralized decision-making structures. The tabular presentation of the basic findings will no doubt serve as a valuable reference for future comparative studies.

Section IV relates community structures to various "styles" of decision-making. Interrelationships between certain cultural and structural variables are illuminated as Wolfinger and Field examine the Banfield-Wilson concepts of "public-regardingness" and "private-regardingness," and question their validity as explanatory variables for community decision-making. Their review of population characteristics, governmental structures, and such outputs as city planning and urban renewal expenditures in American cities forcefully emphasizes the importance that should be assigned to the historical context of immigration in different regions of the United States in determining the styles of decision-making that have evolved.

Studies of such issues as fluoridation and urban renewal have pointed to the importance of the level of conflict as a central variable in altering the decisions reached by a community. Gamson examines the correlates of community conflict in eighteen New England towns in his "Rancorous Conflict" article, and finds recent changes in the pattern of political control to be associated with conflict. However, several variables frequently hypothesized as conducive to conflict—such as participative governmental structures and the salience of community subgroups—were not found to be related to conflict. Conflicts dividing established sectors of the community were, however, more often rancorous than those which did not.

Crain and Rosenthal present a suggestive classification of community structures based on degree of executive centralization and participativeness of community members. Examining decisions to adopt fluoridation processes in American cities, they suggest that political structures which centralize decision-making in the hands of a few governmental officials and minimize citizen participation are most likely to achieve a higher level of adoption.

In a study of 37 suburbs of St. Louis, Missouri, Downes isolates four general types of communities, classified mainly by type of governmental expenditures: (1) High Expenditure Suburbs, which were more wealthy, Republican communities where decisions were often taken in covert fashion. (2) High for Selected Service Suburbs, which had high expenditures for such items as police protection and park facilities, were not so affluent and had a large proportion of young adults. (3) Low Except for Selected Service Suburbs which spent little except for police and fire protection and whose residents were generally older, affluent persons. Population size and growth rates were rather small. (4) Low Expenditure Suburbs which were less affluent, smaller, more rapidly growing communities, with larger numbers of young adults. Downes also contrasts governmental structures and Council decision processes in each type of suburb.

In his study of Poona and Agra, India, Rosenthal emphasizes some of the functions performed by their political systems, which, while to some degree present, are somewhat less salient in American cities. The greater importance of the governmental bureaucracy renders negotiation with bureaucratic officials an important activity; correspondingly, local political officials play an essential role in acting as intermediaries between the general public and the bureaucracy. Symbolic battles, especially among caste groups, take on greater importance than in the United States, resulting in an interesting form of "status politics." The greater integration of local politics into the national system also seems to lead more individuals to become involved in local affairs as a possible stepping-stone for a career at higher levels.

The two studies in Section V contrast community structures and patterns of leadership. Both also consider general cultural variables associated with communities in different regions of the United States, and in England and Mexico. Examining data on hospital decision-making from a total of 218 American communities, Miller points to striking differences between the patterns of leadership in the Northeast and Southeast of the United States. Northeastern hospitals were more often privately owned, and hospital leadership was frequently drawn from the more affluent business and professional sectors of the community. In contrast, Southeastern hospitals were generally created at the initiative of political or governmental officials, and financed and managed by governmental (often county) institutions. Despite more intensive efforts to win support for hospital projects from community citizens in the Northeast, many projects failed. In the Southeast, even with less activity designed to enlist citizen support, the backing of leading governmental officials frequently led to successful projects.

Comparing patterns of leadership in eleven English, Mexican, and American cities, D'Antonio, Form, Loomis, and Erickson document impressive regional and national differences. Government, labor, and religious groups were much more strongly represented in the leadership of the English city than elsewhere. In cities in the southwestern United States, on the other hand, businessmen were far more frequently named as leaders. Businessmen were also important in Mexican cities, but governmental officials were listed more often than in any other country, while professional, religious, and labor leaders were seldom named.

Section VI contains two studies which explore the process of converting resources for power into actual influence. Gamson suggests that the reputation for power is, if nothing else, an extremely valuable resource in decision-making situations. Comparing 52 decisions in 18 New England communities, he shows that active and united reputational leaders, when they support an issue, are very frequently on the winning side. This result does not appear to be a consequence of their simply supporting the more active side, however, for they often win even when supporting the less active side.

The Nuttall, Scheuch, and Gordon study, also concerned with reputed influence, presents a useful four-fold typology of influentials based on whether or not they actually enjoy access to resources, and on whether or not they are reputed to have access to these resources. They then develop a number of propositions relating these four types of leadership to involvement in decisions at various stages and to selected community characteristics, exemplifying the propositions with results from their study of decision-making in Cambridge, Massachusetts.

The three articles in Section VII are particularly concerned with the outcomes of decisions, and work back from outcomes to community characteristics that help explain differences in types of outcomes. Kammeyer examines decisions of communities to consolidate their schools in 110 small towns in Iowa. He finds three major factors associated with the decision to consolidate: high assessment value of property, large proposed high school size, and large community population—all of which predispose a community to decide against consolidating its schools with those of neighboring communities.·

Focusing on the success of urban renewal programs in American cities, Hawley argues that centralized decision-making structures are positively associated with urban renewal success. His measure of centralization—the proportion of managerial personnel in a community—is no doubt controversial. But, terminological matters aside, both his method and findings are provocative.

Warren and Hyman are concerned with the success of various action programs emerging from consensus or dissensus situations. Examining findings regarding 35 published efforts at purposive community change, they found that more collaborative strategies were employed in consensual situations, and contest strategies in dissensual situations. Dissensual action environments were more characteristic of larger communities, and of programs under governmental auspices. Warren and Hyman attempt to integrate these findings with more general theories on consensual as opposed to dissensual situations for decision-making.

Section VIII includes two articles dealing with inter-community relationships and associated decision-making processes. Williams criticizes international relations and power structure models as explanations of types and intensity of inter-community relationships. He proposes, instead, a model based on municipal life style. Similar in some respects to Clark's Chapter 4, the article emphasizes that communities vary in the style of life they support, and in the degree to which they are specialized. Particularly in larger and older metropolitan areas and in states with legislation granting extensive community autonomy, specialization of communities tends to be advanced. And the more specialized the communities in a given area, the less likely the development of numerous and intensive inter-community relationships.

Analyzing the results from previously published studies of 55 communites, Walton finds absentee ownership, adequate economic resources, satellite city status, and competitive political parties to be positively associated with decentralized decision-making structures. He suggestively argues that all five of these factors are associated with integration into national economic, political, and social structures. Thus, as vertical integration of communities into national structures advances, increasing competition between various subsectors of the community is likely, particularly at the time of change, and a more decentralized decision-making structure tends to emerge.

Section IX concludes the volume by considering perhaps the central problem of present and future comparative community studies: the question of comparability. Increasing numbers of comparative studies are being undertaken; indeed fourteen major studies are presently in progress, several of them cross-national. Most of these studies are similar in focusing on community demographic composition, economic structure, legal-political organization, and decision-making processes. Some studies are also tapping cultural variables by collecting information on the values of community leaders and of the general population. A consensus on the use of various research methods is gradually emerging. In an attempt to help coordinate various comparative studies, and to further comparability among them, the Committee for Comparability in Community Research was formed. Its activities, as well as plans for the creation of a Community Research Data Archive are described briefly.

The selections in this volume illustrate the diversity and complexity of the burgeoning body of research on community power and decision-making. But while they exemplify the accomplishments of past investigation, they also point to areas that demand closer study. By presenting some of what has been accomplished and showing how much remains to be done, these various studies help survey the path and provide some roadsigns for future investigations.

II

COMMUNITY STRUCTURE, POWER, AND DECISION-MAKING

II

1

WHO GOVERNS, WHERE,
WHEN, AND
WITH WHAT EFFECTS?

☯

Speculation on men's relations with one another within the context of the community can be traced back to Plato's *Republic*, but modern, systematic analysis of the community by social scientists generally is traced to the Lynds' study of Muncie, Indiana—better known as *Middletown*—first published in 1929.[1] *Middletown in Transition*,[2] their important reanalysis, appeared in 1937.

The series of investigations directed by Warner,[3] published after 1941, differed both from the Lynds' studies as well as from many subsequent works in that the primary focus was on the distribution of prestige while the problem of power was relatively ignored.[4]

The most influential single post-war study on community power is unquestionably Hunter's *Community Power Structure*, published in 1953.[5] Hunter concluded that Regional City (Atlanta, Georgia) was dominated to a large degree by a small number of business leaders who constituted a

---

[1] Robert S. Lynd and Helen M. Lynd, *Middletown* (New York: Harcourt, Brace, & World, 1929).

[2] Robert S. Lynd and Helen M. Lynd, *Middletown in Transition* (New York: Harcourt, Brace, & World, 1937).

[3] W. Lloyd Warner and Paul S. Lunt, *The Social Life of a Modern Community* (New Haven: Yale University Press, 1941) was the first of the five-volume Yankee City series. A one-volume abridged edition of the entire series is W. Lloyd Warner, ed., *Yankee City* (New Haven and London: Yale University Press, 1963).

[4] That power relationships were completely neglected by Warner is certainly incorrect; scattered throughout the Yankee City volumes are numerous remarks relating to the power dimension. Nevertheless, the difficulty in constructing a systematic conception of the distribution of community power from the Yankee City series is demonstrated by Polsby's diligent but relatively unfruitful efforts. See Nelson W. Polsby, *Community Power and Political Theory* (New Haven and London: Yale University Press, 1963), pp. 23–30.

[5] Floyd Hunter, *Community Power Structure* (Chapel Hill: University of North Carolina Press, 1953; Garden City: Doubleday Anchor Books, 1963). All page references are to the Anchor edition.

power elite. Although it could hardly be said that Hunter's work received
the uncritical acclaim of social scientists,[6] it was not until 1961, with the
publication of *Who Governs?*, Robert Dahl's carefully executed study,
that an alternative to Hunter's theoretical interpretation appeared in the
literature.[7] Dahl's central thesis was that a "pluralistic" conception of community power—where several competing groups vie with one another for
control of community resources in various areas—is more useful than the
power elite model. From both theoretical and methodological standpoints,
Who Governs? is the most incisive and challenging community power
study of recent years.

The works of Hunter and Dahl have served as opposite poles in the
heated discussions on community power stimulated by their influential
contributions. Much of the initial exchange tended to be uncompromising
in character and acrimonious in tone; with time, however, the intensity of
the cross-fire seems to be diminishing. This volume is based on the
assumption that enough of the smoke has cleared to enable a reevaluation
of the present situation in the field and to move forward once again.

A thesis central to this work is that previous investigation of community power started by asking if not the wrong questions, at least not the
most challenging ones. To inquire first, as Dahl argued, "Is there a power
elite?" is certainly an important question that must be satisfactorily
answered before one should attempt to ask, following Hunter, "Who constitutes the power elite?" Nevertheless, as intimated in the writings of
virtually all students of the problem, there have been different types of
power and decision-making structures in different communities under different conditions. To admit that there can be a variety of legitimate
answers to the question "Who Governs?" depending on the community
studied, suggests a reformulation of the problem in less absolutist terms.

This work proposes to analyze the series of questions "Who Governs,
Where, When, and with What Effects?"[8] Or, to be more precise, what
kinds of interrelationships exist among three general categories of variables: (1) basic structural characteristics of communities (demographic,
economic, and the like), (2) characteristics of the leadership and

---

[6] Two important early critiques of the study were Herbert Kauffman and Victor
Jones, "The Mystery of Power," *Public Administration Review*, XIV (Summer, 1954),
205–212 and Robert A. Dahl, "A Critique of the Ruling Elite Model," *American
Political Science Review*, LII (1958), 463–469. The degree to which Hunter's formulations should be referred to as "power elitist" will not be considered here.

[7] Robert A. Dahl, *Who Governs?* (New Haven: Yale University Press, 1961).

[8] The range of questions has thus been extended from the earlier formulation in
Terry N. Clark, "Power and Community Structure: Who Governs, Where, and When?"
The Sociological Quarterly (Summer, 1967), Vol. 8, No. 3, 291–316.

decision-making structure, and (3) community outputs, especially in the form of concrete decisions. Generally, the first set of variables is considered independent; the second, intervening; and the third, dependent. The basic relationships among the variables are represented schematically in Figure 1.

Over time, however, none of these sets of variables is independent; for this reason, lines have been drawn connecting the community outputs to other sets of variables. The community may be conceived, to a certain degree, as an autonomous system (this idea is developed further in Chapter 4). The present scheme provides an outline of community system characteristics which may be analyzed using a cybernetic model.[9] Work is presently under way to quantify the parameters involved to permit computer simulation of such a model. However, only with the systematic collection of information on all of these variables over time in a sample of communities—following essentially a panel design of data collection—will it be possible to assign empirically meaningful values to those arrows returning from the community outputs to the other variables. Nevertheless, for the study of a community at any one point in time, the lines running from left to right in the scheme indicate the general directions of the most useful types of analysis.

VARIABLES IN COMMUNITY DECISION-MAKING

[1]   First are the *inputs to the community*. While some community decisions are hardly influenced by inputs from outside the community, for many others, the amount and type of community inputs largely determine the outputs. The degree to which the outputs are determined by inputs is inversely related to community autonomy. Thus, in societies where local communities are less autonomous than in the United States—and this includes most countries of the world—it is particularly important to consider the variables determining the level and type of inputs into the local community. Because most of the literature on community decision-making has focused on American communities, neither community inputs themselves, nor the variables determining their nature and quantity, have been systematically examined. The work on public administration constitutes an important body of research in this area which needs to be integrated with research on community decision-making. Steps in this direction are being

---

9 On cybernetic models, see, among others, Norbert Wiener, *Cybernetics* (Cambridge: M.I.T. Press, 1948) ; and Karl W. Deutsch, *The Nerves of Government* (New York: The Free Press of Glencoe, 1963).

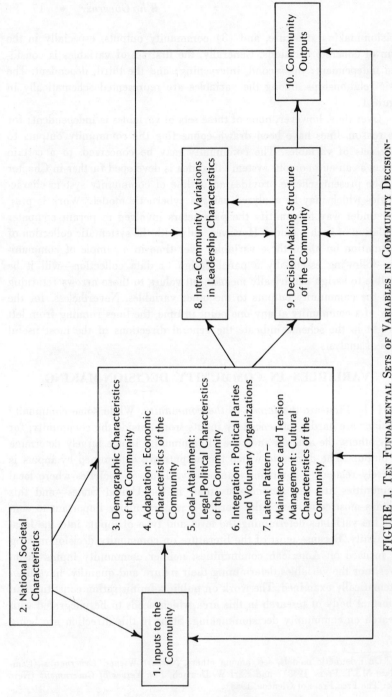

FIGURE 1. TEN FUNDAMENTAL SETS OF VARIABLES IN COMMUNITY DECISION-MAKING

taken by researchers who have begun systematic investigation of local community decision-making in countries outside the United States.[10]

[2] A major variable—or, more precisely, cluster of variables—to be dealt with when considering factors related to community inputs is the *characteristics of the national society.* However, it is difficult to evaluate systematically the impact of national characteristics without comparing several different societies, and as studies of community decision-making are only now entering the phase of systematic *intra*-national comparisons, it may be some time before this level is reached. The work of the International Studies of Values in Politics represents an important initial effort in this direction.

[3] *Demographic characteristics of communities*—such as size of the population, rate of population growth or decline, educational level, and religious and ethnic composition of the population—generally have been neglected variables in case studies of community decision-making. A major reason, no doubt, is that a single community does not provide sufficient variation in these characteristics to warrant special attention. To some extent, this same observation applies to all community structural characteristics which, however, in comparative studies, tend to remain at the center of analysis.

[4] Fourth are those community structures most related to the performance of the *adaptation function,* centered principally in *the economy.*[11]

Community economic characteristics, such as the number and importance of various community industries, generally have been discussed in more detail than demographic characteristics—in part, one might hypothesize, because of the latent (or sometimes not so latent) bias toward economic determinism present in much of the earlier community decision-making literature. Since the mid-1950's, local versus absentee ownership of major community industries has usually been reported, but

---

[10] This includes such projects as that of Michel Crozier and his colleagues in France (see "L'Administration face aux problèmes du changement," special issue of *Sociologie du Travail,* Vol. III [July–September, 1966]); the International Studies of Values in Politics in Poland, India, Yugoslavia, and the United States (discussed in Terry N. Clark, "Present and Future Research on Community Decision-Making: The Problem of Comparability," this volume); and the research reported on by Donald B. Rosenthal in this volume.

[11] The adaptation, goal attainment, integration, and latent pattern-maintenance and tension management functions discussed in the following paragraphs are adapted from the work of Bales and Parsons. One general exposition is Talcott Parsons, "An Outline of the Social System," in Parsons *et al.,* eds., *Theories of Society* (Glencoe: The Free Press, 1961), I, 30–79.

systematic data on such matters as the average income of community residents; ratio of primary to secondary and tertiary activities; and location of markets has been absent more often than not. When such information is not reported in a community study, and where the situation is further complicated by carefully concealing the community's true name, it is extremely difficult to return to census sources for additional information, and later researchers who might like to reanalyze the original data are thereby discouraged from doing so.

[5]   Fifth are those characteristics of communities related to the *goal-attainment* function; these are primarily the political structural characteristics. In contrast to most other countries, there is significant variation in legal-political structures at the local community level in the United States. Among the most widely recognized are such legal structural differences as partisan or non-partisan elections, representation from distinct geographical constituencies or from the community at large, and mayor versus city-manager form of government.[12]

[6]   Sixth are the structures associated with the *integration function*. At the local community level, these are primarily the *political parties and voluntary organizations* that serve to mediate relationships among the various subgroups within the community. The complex interrelationships between the formal-legal structures of government and the political parties and voluntary organizations have been a focus of no little attention in community decision-making literature. Extensive empirical detail, however, is too often a substitute for systematic classification or analysis, although efforts toward developing a general theory of community decision-making are perhaps more advanced in this area than elsewhere.[13]

[7]   The functions of *latent pattern-maintenance and tension management* are most closely associated with the *cultural activities* of communities. Community values and norms are inculcated and reinforced through educational, religious, and other cultural institutions. These values and norms, in turn, structure the processes through which decisions are reached and circumscribe the range of outputs acceptable to the community. Community values and norms are perhaps best measured through survey questionnaires administered to the general population, although other indicators can and have been used to this same end (culturally illuminating events, size of membership in organizations with distinctive ideologies, and the like).

---

[12] These characteristics have been studied in several articles contained in the present volume. See especially those by Gilbert, Wolfinger and Field, Rosenthal and Crain, and Downes.

[13] See Chapter 5.

[8] The "intervening" variables considered in box 8 of the schematic diagram are the *intra-community variations of the characteristics of community leaders.* Here are included not only the general social background characteristics of leaders—father's occupation, education, religious affiliation, ethnic group membership, and so forth—but also general values and normative beliefs. Data of this sort provide answers to such questions as how do communities with relatively even mixes of Republican and Democratic leaders differ from more homogeneous ones, and how do communities with high-status business leaders and low-status governmental officials differ from communities led by low-status businessmen and high-status governmental officials as to the kinds of decisions they reach. In the past, general social background characteristics of community leaders have been reported more frequently than the more difficult to measure cultural characteristics of leadership. The International Studies of Values in Politics represent a pathbreaking effort to collect extensive data on the values and beliefs, as well as general social background, of community leaders. It seems likely that future studies will focus more on such cultural characteristics than has generally been the case in the past.

[9] The ninth variable has been the focus of controversy in past research on community power and decision-making. Even its proper designation has been the subject of much debate. Hunter popularized the term "community power structure" in the title of his widely read study of Atlanta; Dahl and some of his students objected to its continuing use, arguing that it implied the existence of a "power elite." More recently, the popular press has taken over the term and frequently used it, as when speaking of "the white power structure" in segregationist Southern towns, to imply that a sector of a community is firmly entrenched in a position of domination. Occasionally the term "power structure" will be used here, but only for the restricted purposes specified in Chapter 3.

The vast bulk of the literature on community power and decision-making has been concerned with specifying the conceptual dimensions of this ninth variable and attempting to better operationalize and measure "power" or "decision-making" structures of communities. While this activity is certainly important, it has come to be an acknowledged weakness of the field as a whole that it has not investigated sufficiently the other types of variables necessarily associated, whether as causes or effects, with decision-making. Utilization of the framework presented here forces the researcher to take other sets of variables into account.

It is helpful to delimit at the outset the range of phenomena under consideration when speaking of community decision-making. *"Community decisions"* include *choices made by actors within the community among alternative goals relating to the maintenance or modification of institutions or facilities that involve the majority of community residents.*[14] That community decisions are *choices* suggests that they must not be dictated entirely by the demands of the situation; there must be left open a minimal number of alternatives from which it is possible to choose. The decision-makers are actors *within the community*, and although they will be influenced by extra-community factors, the stipulation conveyed by this phrase excludes decisions which are taken outside the community and then administered at the community level. Finally, the condition that the decisions influence institutions involving the *majority of community residents* excludes decisions restricted to very narrow subsectors of community life.

[10] *Community outputs* are the tenth and last variable in this scheme. These outputs in particular require explanation. They represent the actual results, the specific goals, that some communities successfully attain and others do not; for example—what type of mayor is elected? Is there an urban renewal program in a community, and of what size and nature? How large is the budget of a community, in absolute size and per capita, and what percentage of it is allocated to different areas? By contrasting communities in the degree to which their actual outputs differ, this scheme focuses on variations in the other nine sets of variables, attempting to explain some of the most salient causes for differences in this final variable. While in some cases it is necessary to collect information on community outputs through original research, in many other instances such information is centrally recorded—in the census, industrial manuals, handbooks of such professionals as city managers and health officials, and similar sources.[15] Unfortunately, this wealth of information seldom has been investigated carefully by students of community decision-making.

Most of the literature varies greatly as to the amount of attention given to the ten earlier sets of variables in this scheme. The economic structure, the political parties, and voluntary organizations generally have been the primary areas of concern, along with, of course, the decision-making structure. It seems likely, however, that as the comparative orientation becomes more widely adopted, the other sets of variables will take on

---

[14] This formulation is similar to Peter Rossi's in "Community Decision-Making," *Administrative Science Quarterly*, Vol. I (March, 1957), but differs in that it is not restricted to decisions by authoritative persons; it focuses on modifying as well as maintaining institutions; and it specifies that the decisions must be sufficiently important to influence institutions that involve the majority of community residents.

[15] See Clark, "Present and Future Research . . . ," this volume. In one sense, outputs may refer to decisions flowing out of a community. But here the term is used to refer to all decisions flowing from the community decision-making structure, whether they affect matters inside or outside the community's boundaries.

greater importance—often until two or more communities are compared and contrasted, these variables remain relatively "invisible." Thus, community inputs, demographic and cultural characteristics, as well as the intra-community variations in types of leadership and community outputs will probably receive more attention in future comparative analyses. But just as important, if not more important, is the possible need to reformulate some accepted views about the three sets of variables that have been most popular in the past—economic characteristics, political parties and voluntary organizations, and decision-making structures—as new insights emerge from re-examining these variables in terms of a comparative perspective.

The next three chapters elaborate a conceptual framework and formulate a series of propositions that permit filling in the ten boxes of variables more completely and specifying more precisely the nature of the relationships among them. Chapter 2 deals first with certain general dimensions of social stratification, then formulates four types of stratification systems and decision-making structures, and finally elaborates some basic mechanisms for integrating differentiated social structures.

Chapter 3 examines the concept of power, and suggests a means for integrating the communications and authority approaches to the study of decision-making through an adaptation of exchange theory. Imbalances in communication and exchange are conceptualized as leading to an imbalance in various types of resources which may be augmented or restructured by norms and values. A number of the properties of resources are examined: generality, buying power, selling price, exchange value, prestige value, institutionalization importance, power value, general applicability, and expendability. Procedures for quantifying these properties are explored. The concept of issue area is then re-examined, and a series of properties of issue areas and decisional outcomes considered. Finally, various procedures for measuring power and decision-making processes are analyzed.

In Chapter 4, a functional approach is followed in developing a typology of communities. Procedures for measuring the different types of functions are suggested.

Then, in Chapter 5, a number of the distinctions, classifications, and typologies elaborated in earlier sections are brought together in a series of propositions that relate characteristics of communities, of stratified social units, and of power and decision-making to community outputs.

2

SOCIAL STRATIFICATION, DIFFERENTIATION, AND INTEGRATION

☯

Stratification is one of the most vehemently attacked (and defended) of all concepts in discussion of community power. It has been employed so widely and with such diverse meaning that the entire matter has become obscured for want of a precise definition.[1] These differences in meaning necessitate a brief review of some basic aspects of the concept of stratification.

The argument in this chapter is three-fold and quite straightforward. First, a large variety of empirical types of stratification systems have existed in the past and continue to exist today. Second, these empirical types may be ordered along a number of underlying dimensions. Third, some theories and models of stratification are better adapted than others to different empirical types of stratification systems. A review of some of the

---

[1] Polsby's use of the term "stratification," as nearly synonymous to a "power elite" conception of community decision-making, seems particularly objectionable. While the present writer is as firmly opposed as Dahl, Polsby, and their associates to the *a priori* adoption of a power elite view of community decision-making and, correspondingly, is sympathetic to the general direction of analysis presented in Polsby's *Community Power and Political Theory*, he nevertheless dissents strongly with the practice of constructing a general conceptual framework for the stratification of power and ascribing it to earlier community studies. Many of the earlier works, such as *Elmtown's Youth* and the Warner *Yankee City* series simply did not provide a sufficiently elaborated conception of stratification insofar as it relates to power and decision-making to make it possible to speak legitimately of their "stratification theory."

Second, Polsby presents essentially a "power elite" view of community decision-making and argues that the view derives from what he terms "the stratification theory." Certainly the variety of writings by persons concerned with the general phenomenon of social stratification is sufficiently rich to contradict the assertion that there is any one "stratification theory" or that social stratification theories inevitably imply an elitist view of decision-making. See Nelson W. Polsby, *Community Power and Political Theory* (New Haven: Yale University Press, 1963); and Terry N. Clark, William Kornblum, Harold Bloom, and Susan Tobias, "Discipline, Method, Community Structure and Decision-Making: The Role and Limitations of the Sociology of Knowledge," *The American Sociologist* (forthcoming, June 1968).

basic dimensions of social stratification will be followed by a discussion of several ideal-types of stratification systems and their applicability to different empirical cases. Varying types of decision-making structures, and their articulation with the different types of stratification systems will be discussed next; and, finally, five mechanisms of integration will be presented.

DIMENSIONS OF SOCIAL STRATIFICATION SYSTEMS

Eight major dimensions underlying most analyses of social stratification can be distinguished. They are the unit ranked, vertical differentiation, the shape of the hierarchy, horizontal differentiation, values for ranking, interrelationships of hierarchies, autonomy of the system, and social mobility. Each can be viewed as dimensions in terms of which various social systems such as national societies, local communities, or small groups can be considered. Each dimension will be examined in turn.

The Unit Ranked

What precisely is stratified? It is generally agreed that stratification refers to the differential ranking of units within a social system in terms of some value.[2] Theorists differ, however, as to the unit ranked, some preferring to rank families (nuclear or extended);[3] others, individuals;[4] and still others, some culturally-defined unit of social behavior, such as role or status.[5] One useful approach, seldom considered, is to focus on a cluster of statuses related to a particular functional subsystem of society, such as the polity. Here the relevant units are political actors, best conceived of not as individuals, but as sectors of status sets[6]—such as Republican, member of

---

[2] See Harold W. Pfautz, "The Current Literature of Social Stratification: Critique and Bibliography," *American Journal of Sociology*, LVIII (January, 1953), 391–418; Bernard Barber, *Social Stratification* (New York: Harcourt, Brace, & World, 1957), Chapters i–v.

[3] For example, Max Weber, "Class, Status, Party," in Hans Gerth and C. Wright Mills, *From Max Weber: Essays in Sociology* (New York: Oxford University Press, 1958), pp. 180–195; Joseph Schumpeter, *Imperialism and Social Class* (New York: Meridian Books, 1951); Talcott Parsons, "An Analytical Approach to the Theory of Social Stratification," in *Essays in Sociological Theory* (rev. ed.; Glencoe: The Free Press, 1954), pp. 67–88.

[4] For example, Richard Centers, *The Psychology of Social Classes* (Princeton: Princeton University Press, 1949); Milton M. Gordon, *A System of Social Class Analysis*, "Drew University Studies," No. 2 (Madison, N.J.: Drew University Bulletin, 1951).

[5] For example, Kingsley Davis and Wilbert E. Moore, "Some Principles of Stratification," *American Sociological Review*, X (April, 1945), 242–249.

[6] See Robert K. Merton, *Social Theory and Social Structure* (rev. ed.; Glencoe: The Free Press, 1957), pp. 368–386 on status-sets and related concepts.

Chamber of Commerce, property owner, tax payer, and the like. Focusing on the overlapping and interlocking networks of status-sets, rather than on concrete individuals, allows for a more complex and, for many purposes, more meaningful picture of the stratification system.

Vertical Differentiation

It is the differential ranking of units along a vertical hierarchy that constitutes perhaps the most central and widely recognized aspect of social stratification. Distinctive properties of vertical differentiation include: (1) the "height" of the hierarchy—the amount of differentiation between the highest and lowest units of the hierarchy; (2) the number of different levels that may be isolated by the researcher, by the actors in the system, or by both; and (3) the amount of "crystallization," or internal coherence of each stratum, which is closely related to the number of hierarchical levels.

It should be pointed out that differentiation into distinct levels is not at all synonymous with crystallization, although in some instances the two may occur together empirically. And crystallization does not necessarily imply difficulty of penetration from one level to the next; it is by no means synonymous with low social mobility. If in recent years there has been a similar rate of social mobility at certain levels in both the United States and selected European societies,[7] it in no way implies that there is no difference in crystallization of levels between the various societies.

The Shape of the Hierarchy

Distinct from the height and number of levels of a vertical hierarchy is its shape, its outline and contours. Stratification hierarchies may be classified as pyramidal, diamond-shaped, rectangular, trapezoidal, and the like. A particularly important property is the size and shape of the top: whether a system resembles a pyramid with a single individual at its pinnacle, or a truncated pyramid with numerous individuals on top, has profound consequences for the functioning of the entire system. A number of predictions can also be made about the relationships among different levels simply on the basis of the relative size of the top, middle, and bottom. Social systems with relatively large tops and bottoms and small numbers at the middle levels are likely to be more unstable; they are characterized by antagonistic and conflict-ridden interlevel relationships,

---

[7] See Seymour M. Lipset and Reinhard Bendix, *Social Mobility in Industrial Society* (Berkeley: University of California Press, 1959); S. M. Miller, "Comparative Social Mobility," *Current Sociology*, IX (1960), 1–89.

and harbor greater potentials for overthrow of the top than those with large numbers in the middle and smaller numbers at the top and bottom.

It should be kept firmly in mind that the varying shapes presented here refer only to the outlines of a *single* hierarchy. In a system with minimal horizontal differentiation, one diagram may suffice to describe the contours of the entire stratification system. But in a system where horizontal differentiation is relatively advanced, a schematic representation of the entire system would necessarily include as many diagrams as there are

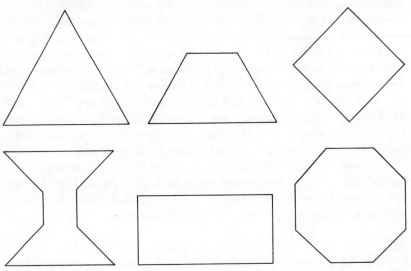

FIGURE 2. ALTERNATIVE POSSIBLE SHAPES OF STRATIFICATION HIERARCHIES

hierarchies. Implied, of course, is the possibility of a system composed of numerous hierarchies, each with a different shape. More likely, we may hypothesize, is a tendency toward isomorphism: the shapes of hierarchies in a stratification system tend to resemble one another.

Horizontal Differentiation

Horizontal differentiation refers to the degree to which separate and distinct vertical hierarchies coexist within a social system. The concepts of "situs," as developed in literature on prestige hierarchies,[8] and of "issue area," as utilized in studies of community decision-making,[9] both call attention to the horizontal differentiation of various hierarchies from one

---

[8] See Albert J. Reiss, *et al.*, *Occupations and Social Status* (New York: The Free Press, 1961).

[9] See Chapter 3.

another. The incorporation of the idea of horizontal differentiation into the literature on social stratification was a slow and sometimes painful process. From it, however, emerged the multi-dimensional conception of social stratification which will be discussed shortly.

Horizontal differentiation seems to advance with increasing industrialization. It is frequently accompanied by the breakdown of traditional, highly crystallized social sectors, such as castes or feudal estates, which tend to restrict horizontal differentiation. Horizontal differentiation also advances as new functions are performed by a social system, giving rise to new structures alongside existent ones.

The progressive differentiation of structures and functions with advancing complexities of social organization and increasing industrialization is a basic theme developed later at several points. It will be used to interpret changing relationships in such distinct but interpenetrating areas as hierarchies of stratification, community organization, distribution of power resources, and influence across issue areas.

Values for Ranking

To evaluate the relationships among hierarchies, and to make possible the ranking of levels within hierarchies, it is necessary to introduce values into an analysis of stratification. Power, status, material possessions, personal qualities, and lineage are utilized most frequently for the ranking of social units. Status and power probably have been the two values most often confused in community studies. Such is the case where two, three, or seven "classes" are reported in a community. While it is clear from the research procedures that it was primarily prestige or status that was investigated, such results have occasionally been interpreted as implying that power is differentially stratified among two, three, or x "classes" in the community.

Confusion on this particular point is due partially to the differing uses of the term "class." Marx and Weber generally used the term to refer to stratification in terms of power, primarily in an economic sense.[10] In

---

[10] Recognized ambiguities in Marx's use of the concept of class are not ignored, but they are not crucial for the present discussion. On Marx's concept of class, see Theodor Geiger, *Die Klassengesellschaft im Schmelztiegel* (Cologne and Hagen: G. Kiepenheuer, 1949); Reinhard Bendix and Seymour M. Lipset, "Karl Marx' Theory of Social Classes," in Bendix and Lipset, eds., *Class, Status, and Power* (Glencoe: The Free Press, 1953), pp. 26–35; and Ralf Dahrendorf, *Class and Class Conflict in Industrial Society* (Stanford: Stanford University Press, 1959), pp. 3–35.

For Weber's concept of class see Gerth and Mills, *From Max Weber: Essays in Sociology*, pp. 180–195, and "Social Stratification and Class Structure," Max Weber, *The Theory of Social and Economic Organization*, translated by A. M. Henderson and Talcott Parsons (Glencoe: Free Press, 1947), pp. 424–439.

contrast, most contemporary American sociologists use class to refer to stratification in terms of prestige or honor.

An additional aspect of the value dimension is the degree to which similar values are institutionalized throughout the system. A highly consensual system is one in which units will be ranked according to relatively similar criteria by all of its members; in a dissensual system, a single unit may be ranked very differently by different members. Seen from another point of view, a system where each unit pursues different values will be characterized by different sorts of influence relationships between units than another system where the majority of units is oriented toward the same general values.

Interrelationships among Hierarchies

The degree to which various stratification hierarchies are autonomous or, conversely, are interrelated, is a major point of division among various stratification theories. With advancing horizontal differentiation, the possibilities increase for a single unit to rank differently on separate hierarchies. The implication is that an individual, or even large aggregates of persons, may rank relatively high on one hierarchy, at a middle level on a second, and low on a third. It is this possibility, of course, which provides the essential foundation for studies of "status crystallization." The bulk of the status crystallization literature, however, considers such hierarchies as occupational prestige, education, income, and ethnic status, and does not deal with power or influence.[11] But some of the most interesting types of situations from the standpoint of community decision-making are the varying patterns of interrelationships among separate hierarchies of power resources and one or more issue areas, leading to the complex problem of the "rate" of exchange between various resource hierarchies and influence in different issue areas, which will be explored in the next chapter.

Autonomy of the System

Directly analogous to the phenomenon of the autonomy of individual stratification hierarchies, but on a higher level, is the degree to which the particular stratification system is autonomous. Generally, the autonomy of stratification subsystems decreases with advancing industrialization in a society. This relationship implies that the distinctive stratification systems of individual communities disclosed by earlier studies are likely to become increasingly similar with continuing industrialization. Within a single

---

[11] See for example, Gary B. Rush, "Status Consistency and Right-Wing Extremism," *American Sociological Review*, XXXII, No. 1 (February, 1967), 86–92, and the works cited there.

society at any given time, however, there remain strong differences in autonomy among communities. It appears, other things being equal, that the larger the community, the more autonomous its stratification system. To qualify this proposition, however, it may be hypothesized that the more autonomous the community is in terms of its many functions,[12] the more autonomous is the stratification system.

Social Mobility

The rate at which social units (generally individuals) move either up or down in a system, between higher and lower levels, may be referred to as the rate of vertical social mobility. While charting the paths followed by various individuals is not inordinately difficult in a system with a great deal of overlap among hierarchies, increasing horizontal differentiation of hierarchies makes mapping mobility paths a far more complex exercise. Most empircal studies of social mobility have operated on the assumption—more often implicit than explicit—that an individual's successive positions on a hierarchy of occupations ranked by income or prestige are a sufficient characterization of his social mobility. While this assumption may be warranted in more simple stratification systems, it appears to be increasingly untenable as the systems gain in complexity.

It is also important to distinguish between first, general structural changes that serve to force up or down whole sectors of the system and second, the movement of individuals up or down within a relatively unchanging structure. Only the latter type of movement will here be considered social mobility.

Further, in a system relatively differentiated both horizontally and vertically, the precise levels at which upward and downward mobility are most frequent should be specified for each vertical hierarchy considered important by system members. Only by following this procedure can individuals who have maintained a high degree of status crystallization as they have moved up or down be distinguished from those who have not. The consequences for the system of these two different types of mobility have far-reaching implications. Although even the most sophisticated present empirical studies fall short of these desiderata, we may hope for more in the future.

Having discussed very briefly eight basic dimensions of social stratification, it may be useful to present in schematic form some examples of the

---

[12] The problems of defining and measuring relative functional autonomy of local communities is taken up in Chapter 4.

range of types and polar extremes on each of these dimensions for two fundamental hierarchies of social stratification: status, or prestige, and power.

TABLE 1. RANGE OF TYPES AND POLAR EXTREMES OF EIGHT DIMENSIONS OF STRATIFICATION FOR STATUS AND POWER HIERARCHIES

Dimension	Status	Power
1. The Unit Ranked	status-role; individual; community; national society	status-role; individual; community; national society
2. Vertical Differentiation	egalitarian system—low number of levels-low crystallization; caste system—high number of levels-high crystallization	mass democracy; elite rule
3. Shape of the Hierarchy	pyramidal; trapezoidal; rectangular	pyramidal; trapezoidal; rectangular
4. Horizontal Differentiation	one dimensional; multidimensional	monolithic; pluralistic (or centralized, decentralized)
5. Values for Ranking	highly similar throughout the system; highly differentiated throughout the system	one value pursued by all units in the system; many values pursued by different units in the system
6. Interrelationships among Hierarchies	low status crystallization; high status crystallization	"inexpensive" exchanges between resource hierarchies and issue areas; "expensive" exchanges between resource hierarchies and issue areas
7. Autonomy of the System	highly distinctive prestige system; highly integrated into larger system	dominant system; autonomous system; dependent system
8. Social Mobility	status increases in proportion with advances in other hierarchies; status does not increase in proportion with advances in other hierarchies	power increases in proportion with advances in other hierarchies; power does not increase in proportion with advances in other hierarchies

While it is analytically useful to distinguish these eight basic dimensions of social stratification, it is also important to consider some of their combinations in different system types.

TYPES OF STRATIFICATION SYSTEMS

In elaborating a typology of stratification systems—or of any other kinds of system—a basic conflict arises between maximizing conceptual and typological elegance on the one hand, and maximizing the "fit" of types to concrete empirical materials on the other. A number of typologies have been advanced that follow this second path, attempting to match as closely as possible some of the best known systems of stratification, such as caste systems, aristocratic systems, class systems, and the like.[13]

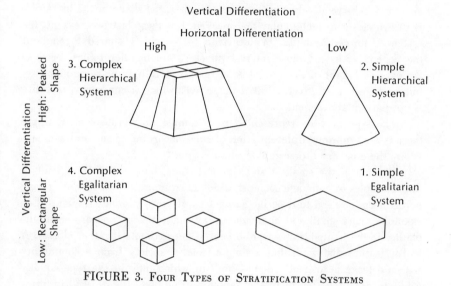

FIGURE 3. FOUR TYPES OF STRATIFICATION SYSTEMS

For present purposes, it is useful to move to a slightly more abstract level and work with a typology based on three fundamental dimensions of stratification: vertical differentiation, horizontal differentiation, and the shape of the hierarchy. If vertical and horizontal differentiation are simply dichotomized into high and low and then cross-classified with one another, and if a more peaked shape is then associated with high vertical differentiation, and a more rectangular shape with low vertical differentiation, four types of stratification systems are generated. (See Figure 3)

A rough line of historical evolution can be discerned which corresponds to the numbering of the system-types, from (1) the simple egalitarian, to

---

[13] These are some of the types of systems stratification analyzed in Terry N. Clark, "A Respecification of the Concept of Social Stratification," dittoed, Columbia University, 1965.

(2) the simple hierarchical, to (3) the complex hierarchical, to (4) the complex egalitarian.

The Simple Egalitarian Stratification System

In this first type of system, there is very little vertical differentiation between the "highest" and "lowest" members. Crystallization is minimal. Correspondingly, the system is designated "egalitarian." At the same time, there is only minimal horizontal differentiation into separate and distinct hierarchies; virtually all members are ranked along the same hierarchical dimensions. And since, empirically, members of social systems of this type also tend to be relatively similar to one another, the shape of the hierarchy is drawn closer to rectangular than peaked. For these last two reasons, the system is termed "simple." Values tend to be widely shared throughout the system, with very close interrelationships among hierarchies. Because the over-all height of the system is not great, there may be some mobility, but as there is a relatively limited range over which it can occur, mobility is not particularly salient.

The type may be represented by a simple preliterate society where there is only minimal differentiation of roles according to sex and age, and where there is very little established authority.[14]

Outside of the smallest and simplest cases, however, it is difficult to find examples of complete societies which correspond to this model. It may nevertheless be used to describe subsectors of more complex societies. For example, many small and homogeneous communities of farmers or suburbanites in the United States would seem to approximate it rather closely. A major feature distinguishing a simple isolated society from a community within a large industrial society—both of which may fit the type equally well—is, of course, the relative autonomy of the two systems. And in terms of the impact on the system of extra-system forces—for changes in system membership, decision-making patterns, and many other central matters—the difference in autonomy has far-reaching consequences.

The Simple Hierarchical Stratification System

This second model is similar to the first in that there is very little horizontal differentiation, but it differs from the first in being much greater in height and more vertically differentiated. The values still seem to be widely shared throughout the system although less than in the first case.

---

[14] See Ralf Dahrendorf, "Amba und Amerikaner: Bemerkung zur These des Universalität von Herrschaft," *European Journal of Sociology*, Vol. V, No. 1 (1964), 83–98.

Where there are value differences, it can be hypothesized that they are vertical—those on the bottom being least ready to accept the values of those higher in the system. Values do not tend to be differentially institutionalized horizontally because of the low amount of horizontal differentiation. Social mobility, when it does occur, is more visible than in the first case, since the over-all height of the system is so much greater.

Distinctiveness of levels and rate of mobility distinguish the three major empirical examples of this type of system: the caste, aristocratic, and class variations. In ideal caste systems, the various castes are far more rigidly separated than the strata of aristocratic or class systems. The styles of life, occupations, and to some extent the values, differ more among castes than among strata of an aristocratic system; there are even fewer distinctions within a class system. Blood descent (in principle) determines status in a caste system at virtually all levels, whereas this is true only at the uppermost levels in an aristocratic system, and only to a very limited degree, and generally indirectly, in a class system. Consequently, possibilities for social mobility increase as one moves from a caste, to an aristocratic, to a class system.

The closest empirical example of a caste system was Hindu India of earlier years. Variations of aristocratic systems have been far more common, the best known examples being most European societies during the late Middle Ages. Class-system models—perhaps the best known is that of Marx—are applicable to capitalistic societies in their early stages of development. On the local community level, New Haven in the early and mid-nineteenth century as described by Dahl [15]—embodying elements of the aristocratic and class variations—seems to have been a reasonably close approximation of the simple hierarchical system.

The Complex Hierarchical Stratification System

A number of separate vertical hierarchies distinguishes the third system type from the last. Differentiation is likely as a system begins to perform new functions, for the sectors performing these functions, over time, develop distinctive norms and values for evaluating their members. Correspondingly, new and differentiated prestige hierarchies, or situses, develop alongside older ones. Through specialization in the activities related to a particular new function, individuals or groups can achieve social mobility by advancing with the new hierarchy. Then, once having established a new hierarchy within the system, they may compete with the older hierarchies for status and power. Examples of new hierarchies emerg-

[15] Robert A. Dahl, *Who Governs?* (New Haven: Yale University Press, 1961).

ing with new functions and establishing their own values and prestige systems are war and the military; large-scale commerce and industry, and the bourgeoisie; and technology and science, and technical experts.

These changes leading to a multidimensional system often took place more rapidly than the stratification models developed by observers within the system to explain what was going on around them. Ever since the end of the nineteenth century, most Western industrial societies have developed many significantly differentiated vertical hierarchies, although many writers on stratification have analyzed these societies using variations of the simple hierarchical system.

Other writers have been more perceptive. Weber, in his "Class, Status, Party," [16] pointed out three separate hierarchies: one centering primarily around the performance of economic functions; a second, partially a carryover from earlier periods, centering on agricultural and military pursuits; and a third, relating to the organization of various social groups for the pursuit of power. Sorokin distinguished economic, political, and occupational dimensions of stratification.[17] Parsons has applied his framework for functional analysis to stratification systems, distinguishing separate hierarchies related to the performance of each of the four general system functions: adaptation, goal-attainment, integration, and latent pattern-maintenance and tension-management.[18]

The Complex Egalitarian Stratification System

This fourth type differs from the last only in the extent to which separate hierarchies are tall or short: the extent to which differences between units on a vertical hierarchy are great or small. In the last century, perhaps the most salient change in stratification in most Western societies has been the general movement toward egalitarianism. Given the strong ideological commitments to egalitarianism in most Western societies, this tendency may well continue in future years.

It should be emphasized at this point that neither of these last two "complex" or "multi-dimensional" models in any way implies that separate dimensions are equivalent in their importance or influence. Indeed, an essential factor differentiating stratification systems is the relative importance of each dimension, and the ease with which an actor may alter his rank on one hierarchy following a change on a second.

[16] Gerth and Mills, eds., *From Max Weber: Essays in Sociology*, pp. 180–195.

[17] Pitirim A. Sorokin, *Social Mobility* (New York: Harper, 1927), esp. chap. ii.

[18] Talcott Parsons, "A Revised Analytical Approach to the Theory of Social Stratification," in *Essays in Sociological Theory* (Glencoe: The Free Press, 1954), pp. 386–439.

TYPES OF DECISION-MAKING STRUCTURES

Four types of decision-making structures generally correspond to the four types of social stratification systems (see Figure 4).

The Mass Participation Model

Type 1, the "mass participation" model, is characterized by highly active members who tend to participate in all types of decisions in the system. Unlike actors in the pluralistic (#4) type, actors here do not specialize in particular areas; but like the pluralistic type, and in contrast to the other two, there is little vertical differentiation between "leaders" and other system members. It is also relatively easy to replace leaders. Like the simple egalitarian stratification system which it resembles, there are few empirical examples of this type, and they tend to be rather small. The small community where the entire population must vote on every significant decision—partially realized in parts of New England—is probably one of the closest approximations of this type on the community level, although smaller organizations or families may come still closer.

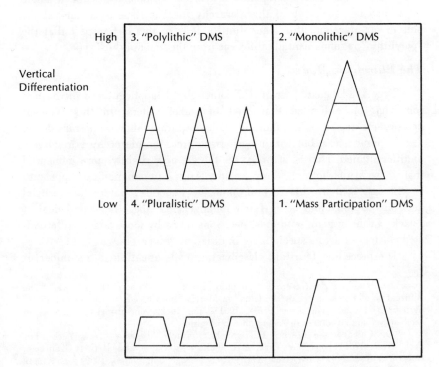

FIGURE 4. FOUR TYPES OF DECISION-MAKING STRUCTURES

The Monolithic Model

Type 2 is the traditional "monolithic" decision-making structure. Here a small number of actors at the top of the hierarchy have greater influence than those at middle or lower levels. In contrast to the "polylithic" type, however, the same actors are influential in virtually all issue areas. The monolithic type is represented by most formal organizations today and many American communities in the nineteenth and early twentieth centuries.[19]

The Polylithic Model

Type 3 is designated "polylithic" as there is a plurality of differentiated issue areas, but each issue area is characterized by a monolithic decision-making structure. Many large American cities may be characterized as "polylithic" in that there exists no single "power elite" with dominant influence in all issue areas, but within many separate issue areas (housing, education, hospital construction, and the like) there are certain well-defined and firmly established structures of influence.[20] Still, a single actor may be at the top of the hierarchy for one issue area, and at the bottom for a second, third, and fourth. It is in this last respect that the "polylithic" is fundamentally different from the "monolithic" type.

The Pluralistic Model

Type 4 is labeled "pluralistic," although this application of the term is somewhat more limited than that of some writers. In this type of decision-making structure, there are many separate influence hierarchies in distinct issue areas, but within each issue area, the hierarchy is relatively undifferentiated. That is, actors at the top are only slightly more influential than those at the bottom. Many wealthy American communities appear to be characterized by this sort of influence structure: having few crucial decisions to make and being fairly homogeneous, there is a good deal of "slack" in the system, with most decisions taken by loose and undifferentiated clusters of actors specializing in different issue areas.

The preceding four-fold classification calls attention to a number of

---

[19] See Dahl, *Who Governs?*, Chapters i–vii; and Robert O. Schulze, "The Bifurcation of Power in a Satellite City," in Morris Janowitz, ed., *Community Political Systems* (Glencoe: The Free Press, 1961), pp. 19–80, on historical changes in decision-making structures in American communities.

[20] On Chicago, see Edward C. Banfield, *Political Influence* (New York: The Free Press, 1961); on New York, esp. Wallace S. Sayre and Herbert Kaufman, *Governing New York City* (New York: Russell Sage Foundation, 1960); and more generally, Edward C. Banfield, *Big City Politics* (New York: Random House, 1965).

distinctive situations which have been confused frequently in discussions of community power, in part, it appears, for ideological reasons. Some of the so-called "pluralists" have on occasion presented a "polylithic" situation as "pluralistic," overlooking the fact that while no single actor or group of actors dominates a given community, the total number of persons making important decisions is nevertheless very limited, and, as a result, it is virtually impossible for discontented actors to make themselves heard. However, if this confusion has occasionally marred the work of pluralists, it has also led to misdirected attacks by their critics, who, pointing to polylithic situations, argue that since they are not pluralistic, they are closer to the traditional monolithic type.[21] This confusion arises from a failure to distinguish horizontal from vertical differentiation.

Critics of the reputational method have argued that the method, as traditionally used, does not distinguish between horizontally differentiated and undifferentiated decision-making structures. But a criticism of both the reputational and decisional methods is that neither sufficiently distinguishes vertically differentiated from undifferentiated communities. That is, they do not gauge the difficulty or ease with which members low on a hierarchy can exercise influence on those higher up. And perhaps as a partial consequence of these methodological limitations, the conceptual distinctions between polylithic and pluralistic types, and between monolithic and mass participation types, have become blurred.

If nothing else, this brief presentation of various social stratification models has demonstrated that the diversity of stratification systems is sufficiently great to make it possible for a student of decision-making—whether his persuasion be monolithic or pluralistic—to articulate his analyses with one or more general models for social stratification. Sociologists who in the past turned to the study of community power, guided more often by an aristocratic or class model than by a multi-dimensional model, represented a deviant trend in the general sociological community, which in the past few decades has been increasingly adopting multi-dimensional models for analyzing social stratification and decision-making.[22]

---

[21] See Floyd Hunter, Review of *Who Governs?* by Robert A. Dahl, in *Administrative Science Quarterly* (March, 1962), 517–519.

[22] This fact seems to have been largely ignored by several of the commentators on the differences in orientation toward community decision-making of sociologists and political scientists. See Polsby, *Community Power and Political Theory*; John Walton, "Substance and Artifact: The Current Status of Research on Community Power Structure," *American Journal of Sociology*, LXXI (January, 1966), 430–438; Claire W. Gilbert, "Community Power Structure: A Study in the Sociology of Knowledge."

MECHANISMS FOR INTEGRATION

The four models of stratification and decision-making delineated above are based largely on the amount of differentiation among various structures.

Integration is a general functional problem which all social systems beginning to differentiate—vertically or horizontally—must eventually deal with unless they are to disintegrate. In most systems, integrative functions are performed by more than one type of mechanism. Several mechanisms may be present, but some are only minimally important, while others are highly important. Systems similar in their extent and type of differentiation may also adopt differing integrative mechanisms. The mechanisms that are adopted have important consequences for subsequent change within the over-all system, including changes in decision-making patterns. Five alternative mechanisms for integration warrant a brief examination. (See Figure 5 for a schematic representation of the types.)

The Institutionalized General Value System

A first mechanism usually present before a system differentiates into subsystems is an institutionalized general value system. This mechanism provides the basis for the classical form of mechanical solidarity discussed by Durkheim.[23] General values inculcated by the elementary socialization structures of a society are reiterated and reinforced by religious organizations, politicians, and general cultural leaders—and in industrial societies, often through the intermediary of the mass media. These same structures may also transmit in the form of norms certain applied patterns for guiding social behavior, but in this instance these norms apply equally to all members of the social system, not merely to occupants of specific roles. The more a social system relies on integration through the enforcement of system-wide values and norms, the more it is likely to be characterized by a greater homogeneity of values, and a more monolithic decision-making structure. The level of outputs is also likely to be higher than in a situation where there are greater differences in values between sub-systems.

(unpublished Ph.D. dissertation, Northwestern University, Evanston, Ill. 1966). See also, Terry N. Clark, et al., "Discipline, Method, Community Structure, and Decision-Making: The Role and Limitations of the Sociology of Knowledge."

[23] Emile Durkheim, The Division of Labor in Society (New York: The Macmillan Company, 1933). In much of the present discussion, differentiated systems are seen as growing out of less differentiated systems, as if differentiation were a temporal process. While it is often useful for heuristic purposes to consider differentiation as advancing over time, this assumption is by no means necessary.

Norms Relating to the Performance of Specific Roles

A second mode of integration is the inculcation and reinforcement of norms relating to the performance of specific roles in a social system.[24] Formal and informal organizations of individuals occupying similar statuses are the principal mechanisms for such integration. Training in professional schools, organizations, journals, and codes of ethics are classical examples of these mechanisms for norms relating to professional roles.[25] Both newspapers and neighborhood ethnic and leisure-activity organizations perform the same types of functions for other roles. Decision-making in social systems which rely heavily on this sort of integrative mechanism is likely to be more pluralistic than in systems relying more on integrative mechanisms of the first type.

Bureaucracy

A third type of mechanism, the bureaucracy, may grow out of the first or second, but nevertheless represents a distinctive type in itself. Bureaucracies which have at least partial claim to authority over two (or more) subsectors of a social system can integrate these subsectors with one another. This same type of mechanism is also frequently used within a single larger bureaucracy, particularly when it is differentiating. When two or more new specialized departments are formed, a supervisory position, or supervisory department, is also frequently created to coordinate and integrate the two departments.

A cohesive bureaucratic structure capable of enforcing decisions on sub-units moves a system toward a centralized structure of decision-making, which, in turn, promotes at least formal rationality and facilitates implementation of the values of those at the head of the bureaucracy. A highly bureaucratic structure of decision-making tends, however, to impair the upward flow of communications and lead to decisions taken with insufficient consideration of the values and interests of those lower in the hierarchy. This, in turn, may provoke creation of counter-structures by the lower sectors to oppose decisions from above.[26]

---

[24] While Durkheim did not precisely conceive of what he called organic solidarity as resting on shared norms relating to the performance of specific roles, it is only a short step from his analysis to this position. See Talcott Parsons, "Durkheim's Contribution to the Theory of Integration of Social Systems," in Kurt H. Wolff, ed., *Emile Durkheim, 1858–1917* (Columbus: Ohio State University Press, 1960), pp. 118–153.

[25] See Terry N. Clark, "Institutionalization of Innovations in Higher Education: Four Models," *Administrative Science Quarterly* (forthcoming June 1968).

[26] See Michel Crozier, *The Bureaucratic Phenomenon* (Chicago: University of Chicago Press, 1964) for a discussion of related problems.

1. Institutionalized Value System

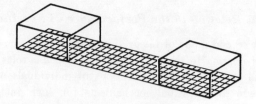

2. Norms Relating to the Performance of Specific Roles

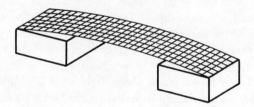

3. Bureaucracy

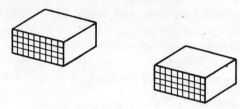

4. The Juridical System

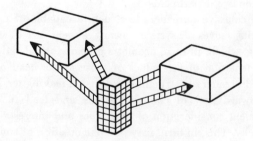

5. Interchange between Subsystems

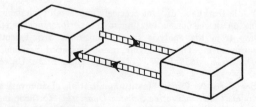

FIGURE 5. FIVE MECHANISMS OF INTEGRATION

The Juridical System

A fourth mechanism that partially overlaps with other integrative mechanisms is the juridical system. A juridical system may enforce general values and norms of the society, thus complementing the first mechanism. Or, it may enforce norms specific to individual roles within a social system. It is, moreover, likely to operate through a bureaucratic structure, although crucial ancillary roles are performed by a corps of legal experts without any necessary formal relationship to the juridical bureaucracy. Much of the impact of a juridical system is also indirect: few individuals are ever directly involved in legal action. The mere knowledge that behind a general structure of values and norms, institutionalized in law, there lies a legal system to sanction deviants, generally suffices to control most persons in most societies. When juridical systems are restricted to enforcing laws already accepted by members of a social system, and do not have the complete support of law enforcement agencies, their impact on decision-making processes of subsystems will be limited. But where the "rule of law" is highly respected within a social system and supported by strong law enforcement agencies, then the juridical system may have a significant impact on any subsystem that attempts to deviate from the rest of the system. The example of the Supreme Court in such matters as school desegregation and the establishment of equal representation from all geographical areas demonstrates the enormous power of the juridical system in the United States.

Interchange between Subsystems

The fifth mechanism for integration is interchange between subsystems. The interchange may be entirely symbolic; it may consist solely of the exchange of communications between two subsystems. Even if initially there are no institutionalized structures joining two systems, over time, with continued contact, norms are likely to develop at the systems' borders to help regulate future interchanges. Many types of institutionalized structures are possible. A first, and very common type, is overlapping memberships of one or more individuals in the two subsystems. The market is another type of structure which recurrently brings members of two or more systems into contact.

Interchanges between subsystems obviously can lead to the development of role-related norms, and merge into the second mechanism mentioned. And the roles may in turn be formalized in bureaucratic structures—the third type of mechanism. Over longer periods of time norms emerging from subsystem interchanges can grow into laws and even become institutionalized as general system values. This fifth mechanism is a fundamental and powerful mode of integration deserving intensive scrutiny; this will be undertaken in the next chapter.

3

THE CONCEPT OF POWER

☯

To say that much has been written on the concept of power would border on egregious understatement. The problem, however, is that many of the innumerable writers on the subject have frequently chosen to investigate facets of the concept which overlap only slightly, if at all. Given such a division of labor, it has generally been true that any single author deals only with those aspects of power which are especially important for clarifying a particular theoretical or empirical problem. This section will reexamine some of the traditional aspects of the concept of power, suggest some new perspectives on traditionally recognized problems, and begin to elaborate certain basic ideas concerning social organization and decision-making that will be related to more specific structures of communities in the next chapter.

CONTRASTING CONCEPTIONS OF POWER

Some of the general orientations toward power reflected in earlier theoretical writings and empirical research bear reviewing.

A first orientation, that can be termed "individualistic," focuses on the degree to which a single actor achieves his desired goals. This orientation was represented in Weber's well-known definition of power: " 'Power' (*Macht*) is the probability that one actor within a social relationship will be in a position to carry out his own will despite resistance, regardless of the basis on which this probability rests." [1] The basic elements in this orientation are the individual actor and his goals; neglected are other actors, as well as the structure of the system within which action occurs. Although Weber himself was quite careful to analyze the importance of structural factors involved in power relationships, his general formulation does not include these factors, and others adopting the same perspective have not always been so careful as he was.

---

[1] Max Weber, *The Theory of Social and Economic Organization* (New York: Oxford University Press, 1947), p. 152.

Second is the "dyadic" orientation. Here, power is conceived primarily as a relationship between two actors, where one is able to effect a change (in activity, belief, or something else) in the second. Dahl's general discussions of power represent this orientation,[2] as do those of many students of small groups, for example Cartwright.[3]

These dyadic formulations, unlike the first, tend to omit any reference to goals or to the broader structure, emphasized by the third, within which power is exercised.

The third orientation for adoption can be referred to as a "systemic" orientation toward power. *"Power" is the potential ability of an actor or actors to select, to change, and to attain the goals of a social system.* This formulation emphasizes that power is a system-relevant property not readily transferable to another arena. Power is not a characteristic of an individual actor, as in the case of "individualistic" orientation. An individual actor is considered powerful only in relation to a given social system because it is often extremely difficult for an actor powerful in one system (such as, a legislature) to transfer his resources to a second system (such as, another legislature).

Second, power is not conceived as a property relating two actors, as in the "dyadic" orientation, for even though a given actor may be capable of exercising a great deal of influence over a second actor in one system (for example, a football game), the relationship between the same two actors in different roles may be the exact opposite in a second system (for example, a formal debate).

This systemic orientation thus emphasizes as basic units not individual persons or groups, but actors operating in one or more status positions within a specific social system. It focuses on the abilities of different actors to restrict the inputs to the system, to convert the inputs into specific demands, to redirect the flows of decisions within the system, and to regulate the outputs of the system. It calls immediate attention to the distribution of resources within a social system that may serve to provide the actors controlling them with influence over others.

But power is restricted to the "potential ability" of actors to bring

---

[2] "My intuitive idea of power, then, is something like this: A has power over B to the extent that he can get B to do something that B would not otherwise do." Robert A. Dahl, "The Concept of Power," *Behavioral Science*, II (July, 1957), 202–203.

[3] "When an agent, O, performs an act resulting in some change in another agent, P, we say that O *influences* P. If O has the capability of influencing P, we say that O *has power* over P." Dorwin Cartwright, "Influence, Leadership, Control," in James G. March, ed., *Handbook of Organizations* (Chicago: Rand McNally & Co., 1965), p. 4. See also Cartwright, ed., *Studies in Social Power* (Ann Arbor: Institute for Social Research, University of Michigan, 1959).

about changes in the system. Power, conceived as a distribution of resources, may be converted into influence. *"Influence" is the exercise of power that brings about change in a social system.*

Power, through influence, may be brought to bear in concrete *"decisions,"* which *are conceived as choices among alternative goals.*

From these distinctions among power, influence, and decisions logically follow the distinctions between power structures and decision-making structures. *A power structure is a patterned distribution of power in a social system.* The concept of power structure therefore refers only to the potential ability of actors to bring about change within a given social system, and is distinguished from a *"decision-making structure," which is the patterned distribution of influence in a social system.* To study a power structure, it is necessary to measure the distribution of resources and the potential ability of actors to bring about change in the system. Implied is a strategy for analyzing the system at one point in time. A decision-making structure, on the other hand, is best analyzed by studying actual processes of influence as exercised over time. (Methods for studying power and decision-making structures will be discussed further at the end of the chapter.)

A DIGRESSION ON ALTERNATIVE STRATEGIES OF STUDYING DECISION-MAKING: POWER AND COMMUNICATIONS APPROACHES

Over the last few decades, two relatively distinct approaches to the study of decision-making have developed which recur in such substantive areas as formal organizations, small groups, and local communities.

The first, which can be called the power or authority approach, focuses on hierarchical authority patterns, asymmetrical relationships between actors, subordination and superordination of roles—essentially vertical types of relationships. Hierarchical authority patterns underlie Max Weber's formulations on bureaucratic organization, which have engendered an enormous literature on organizations elaborating this same basic model.

Most of the discussions of "power structures" in local communities, as well as in other substantive areas, are based on a power model.

And, while not necessarily involving vertical relationships, a model of conflicting forces of varying strength has been used frequently, particularly by Kurt Lewin and his intellectual heirs, in the study of small groups.[4]

---

[4] See especially Cartwright, ed., *Studies in Social Power.*

Graph theory is an appropriate device for use with power relationships and it has been applied to represent the vectors of field force, to quantify their varying strengths, and to solve problems of balance and outcome by methods which recall those of classical mechanics.

The second general approach is the communications approach. Here, power is neglected—or at least it is not a central variable—and it is the flow of communications and their feedback through various circuits that provide the central focus of theoretical attention. Much of the work on organizations by Chester Barnard [5] and Herbert Simon [6] involved developing communication models, and a relatively separate and distinct tradition in organizational analysis—heavily influenced by their contributions—has grown up centering more on communications than power.

A communications perspective has been central to many studies of small groups as well. One example among many is the work of Robert F. Bales—based largely on a communication model.[7]

On a slightly more general level, the work of Norbert Wiener and others on cybernetics has been influential in a number of substantive areas. Karl Deutsch has been one of the leaders in adapting cybernetic thinking to the social sciences in such diverse areas as international relations, communities, and political parties.[8]

Work based on a communications model employs, rather than diagrams plotting field forces against one another, flow charts, communication nets, and similar types of graphic representation to symbolize the basic relationships among units.

Researchers adopting each of these two general approaches, working in relative isolation, have achieved important and significant results—results sufficiently important that it is strategically incorrect to abandon one approach in favor of the other, or to attempt to reduce one approach to the other, as some commentators have intimated doing.[9] A more rigorous

[5] Chester Barnard, *The Functions of the Executive* (Cambridge: Harvard University Press, 1938).

[6] Herbert A. Simon, *Administrative Behavior* (2d ed.; New York: The Free Press, 1957).

[7] See Robert F. Bales, *Interaction Process Analysis* (Cambridge: Addison-Wesley, 1950) as well as his later works.

[8] See especially his general programmatic statement, Karl W. Deutsch, *The Nerves of Government* (New York: The Free Press, 1963). Many of these general ideas are applied to communities in Philip E. Jacob and James V. Toscano, eds., *The Integration of Political Communities* (Philadelphia and New York: J. B. Lippincott Co., 1964).

[9] While no major writer seems to have fully embraced the position that the *exclusive* adoption of one or the other approach is the solution to our many sins, a good deal of discontent has been expressed from time to time with one approach or the other. See, for example, David Easton, *The Political System* (New York: Alfred A.

theory of decision-making than exists at present in any of the three fields mentioned will have to integrate, on theoretical and empirical levels, both the power and communications approaches to decision-making. Any contribution toward such a synthesis would be strategic for research in all three fields.

In many ways, this problem of contrasting orientations is similar to the earlier dichotomy—particularly apparent in studies of organizations and community decision-making—between formal and informal types of organization and decision-making. To achieve a coherent and enduring synthesis is by no means a simple task, as indicated by the unintegrated presentation of materials based on all four approaches—power, communication, formal, and informal organization—often juxtaposed in separate chapters of textbooks on organizations.

While more than one type of synthesis is no doubt possible, a particularly useful framework for integrating these varying perspectives is to be found in an adaptation of exchange theory.

INTERCHANGE, EXCHANGE, COMMUNICATION, AND POWER

Recalling the discussion of interchanges as a mechanism of integration, system interchange can be considered a special type of relationship involving both communication and, potentially, exchange. By analyzing exchange patterns among actors or subsystems, it is possible to predict the changes likely to occur both in communication channels and in power relationships.

More precisely, changes in communication and power relationships will be analyzed by elaborating certain ideas which derive in part from the body of thought habitually termed exchange theory.[10]

Knopf, 1953), pp. 115 ff.; James G. March, "The Power of Power," in David Easton, ed., *Varieties of Political Theory* (Englewood Cliffs: Prentice-Hall, 1966), pp. 39–70; William H. Riker, "Some Ambiguities in the Notion of Power," *American Political Science Review*, LVII (June, 1964), 341–349; Amitai Etzioni, *A Comparative Analysis of Complex Organizations* (New York: The Free Press, 1961); Deutsch, *The Nerves of Government*.

[10] The first serious work on exchange theory was the study by Marcel Mauss, "Essai sur le don," originally published in the 1923 *Année sociologique*, reprinted in *Sociologie et anthropologie* (Paris: Presses Universitaires de France, 1950), and in translation as *The Gift* (Glencoe: The Free Press, 1954). Peter Blau presented several ideas relating to exchange in organizations in *The Dynamics of Bureaucracy* (Chicago: University of Chicago Press, 1955). George C. Homans was more systematic in *Social Behavior* (New York: Harcourt, Brace, & World, 1961), as was Alvin Gouldner,

Consider the situation where two actors (individuals or subsystems) come into contact for the first time. They begin to interact with one another. Interaction (verbal or non-verbal) in itself may be considered a process of exchange, as each actor gives to the other time and attention, and usually communicates some of his thoughts. A number of possible interaction patterns may then develop.

If two actors continue to interact, with each doing about half of the communicating and exchanging roughly equal amounts of such a limited commodity as information, the situation remains balanced.

However, if one actor begins to do more communicating than the other, offering more information and desirable commodities than the first, an imbalance will result. If this situation continues over time, it is likely, other things being equal, that the actor who is, continually talking and offering information will grow tired of doing so. This situation—in which there is a discrepancy of inputs and outputs between actors in the system—leads to an imbalance which may be corrected in a number of different ways.

The first, and most simple, is that the actor who has been "receiving" most will begin to reciprocate by returning information or some other desirable commodity through normal interaction. This can move the situation toward a new equilibrium.

Or the communication may be terminated; the two actors may decide that further interaction is not "interesting" to either of them, and each may go his separate way.

But third, it is possible that although the receiving or "silent" partner may find the interaction situation rewarding and therefore wish to continue it, he may be incapable of reciprocating with commodities or information sufficiently attractive for the other actor to desire its maintenance. At this point, the actor wishing to continue the interaction may do one of three things. He can attempt to modify the situation within which interaction takes place; for example, he may utilize brute force, threatening physical punishment if the other actor does not continue interaction. Second, he may introduce into the relationship some commodity not initially involved. He may utilize money, or some other desirable commodity such as flattery or status deference, and offer (explicitly or implicitly,

---

in "The Norm of Reciprocity," *American Sociological Review*, XXV (1960), 161–178. But the most comprehensive statement to date is Peter M. Blau, *Exchange and Power in Social Life* (New York: John Wiley & Sons, 1964). Norman W. Storer, in *The Social System of Science* (New York: Holt, Rinehart & Winston, 1966) also has several insightful observations.

consciously or unconsciously) to grant to the second actor some amount of this commodity in return for continuing the relationship. The third alternative is essentially a special case of the second: the actor may offer himself, in one way or another, as a commodity in exchange. In offering himself as a commodity, however, there is a striking change in the relationship: an imbalance in *power* between the two actors has now been established.

Consider the possibility of one actor gaining power over a second (or a third or a fourth, the logic is easily extended to more than a dyadic relationship) and some of the alternative strategies that he might pursue. The essential step is taken when one actor is able to offer to others some kind of commodity which places them in his debt. Ideas or suggestions defined as valuable by the other actors constitute one useful type of commodity that can provoke a situation of indebtedness.

A variation of this case—and a highly important one—is the situation where an actor is able to offer efficient means to the attainment of goals that are recognized as important by a number of other actors in a social system. The actor with good ideas places in his debt simultaneously all other actors in the system. He can then expect in return deference, or power, or both. If an actor is able to offer suggestions that once or twice lead to the attainment of system goals, or ends rewarding to most actors in the system, he can, if skillful, exercise some of the power gained to better organize the system to attain further system goals. Then, with more power at his disposal, he may continually move back and forth between exercising small amounts of it (but never all of it, or he will then become equal, once again, to the others) and guiding the group toward generally desired goals. In time, a skillful actor will become increasingly powerful and eminent. Power and status, in this instance, become assets analogous to capital— they may be invested, and a certain return expected if invested intelligently. But if not continually reinvested—but instead, simply hoarded—their value will soon decline.

Thus far the analysis has not considered norms or values except as certain "givens" in the system—such as the goals of the various actors, and, implicitly, the norms defining the operating procedures of the system, or the "rules of the game." The "rules of the game" will now be examined; later, more general norms and values and the role they play.

Mauss, and later, Gouldner, argued that certain norms relating to exchanges are widespread, and practically universal. First is that an actor is obliged to accept a gift offered him; it is a rule of the game not to refuse gifts, at least gifts offered with no immediate reciprocal action implied when they are given—and after all this condition is part of the definition of the term "gift." The second norm is that every actor must offer gifts to other members in the system. The third norm relates the first to the second. It is the norm of reciprocity: although gifts are, strictly speaking, given freely, and not in exchange for any specific commodity, it is expected nonetheless that, over a period of time, an actor receiving a certain number of gifts will reciprocate in one way or another. Each actor's over-all balance of inputs and outputs tends to be approximately equal.

There are, however, a number of different procedures by which reciprocation may be accomplished.[11] First, and most simple, is reciprocation in kind: one gift is reciprocated for another.

Second, one type of gift may be reciprocated by another of an entirely different sort. For example, in certain societies, women and money are exchanged throughout the system through the institution of bride price. This alternative raises the issue of "exchange rates" of various desirable commodities to be dealt with shortly.

Third, certain institutionalized norms such as altruism, or "*noblesse oblige,*" may sanction occasional, but recurrent, exceptions from the norm of reciprocity. Still, the norm of altruism seems almost inevitably destined to imperfect achievement in actual social situations, as "receivers" usually reciprocate with some form of deference, thanks, or offer of themselves as a commodity to the "giver." That if they did not, they would often be held as "ungrateful" demonstrates how loosely the norm of altruism is actually followed. But, however imperfectly applied, the norm of altruism must be introduced to explain certain structured deviations from the pure exchange model.

Fourth, and overlapping with the third, there may be sufficiently large differences in power among actors in a system that altruistic norms may be institutionalized as a sort of escape valve for pressures that build within the system. The augmentation of power by one member of a system through the exchange of other commodities for power does not constitute a violation of the norm of reciprocity, but rather confirms it, as in the case where different types of commodities are exchanged in order to achieve reciprocity.

Fifth, although not really an exception to the norm of reciprocity, it should be pointed out that many exchanges are highly indirect. A may give to B, B to C, C to D, and D to A; that is, the path followed by exchanges may be circular.

---

[11] Although the argument at this point is phrased in terms of reciprocation of gifts, it generally applies to exchanges of commodities not so defined.

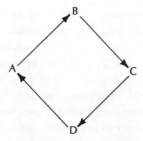

In this case, all four actors are systematically interrelated through exchange, but none gives to the person from whom he receives. Nevertheless, the indirect structure of relationships assures an equal balance of exchanges.[12]

Three major factors limit the range and complexity of exchange systems. First is the generality of the resources involved: the more general the resource—as reflected by utility in many diverse situations—the greater the potential for extension of the exchange system. Generality as a characteristic of resources will be discussed further.

Second is the absolute quantity of resources present in a system: the larger the number of resources available for circulation, the more indirect, complex, and extensive exchanges in the system may become. Consider, for example, economic situations in which the very poor are unable to enter into extensive and complex relationships with other actors in what poten-

---

[12] Examples of this sort of exchange may be found in certain elementary economic systems. This case should, however, be sharply distinguished from the economic relationships found in modern money-based economies with a high division of labor where physical commodities flow in a circular pattern analogous to that in the first diagram, but concurrently money flows in the opposite direction, as shown in the following diagram:

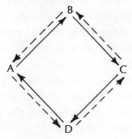

———— = physical commodities

– – – – = money

tially could become extensive exchange systems. They cannot become involved because they do not have the necessary quantity of resources either to maintain themselves over a certain minimal period of time before they are reimbursed, or to support the infra-structure devoted to the mechanics of organizing and coordinating exchange among distant members of a system. And, with insufficient resources, it is difficult to develop a reserve of credit—a fundamental basis for complex and indirect exchanges.

The third general factor limiting the range of the system is the extent of institutionalized value consensus. The greater the consensus among members of a social system on basic values, as well as on their application in system-related norms, the more extensive, complex, and indirect may be the exchange relationships among members of the system. Both widespread value consensus and increased resources make possible greater expansion of credit, which in turn favors the extension of the system.

Having thus emphasized the importance of institutionalization of norms and values in a system for setting the rules of the game, restricting the types of reciprocity, and regulating the more complex and indirect exchanges that may develop, the process by which norms and values become institutionalized can be discussed.

NORMS, VALUES, INSTITUTIONALIZATION, AND DECISION-MAKING

All social action is to some degree regulated by norms and values. And most social action takes place within a structure of norms and values without changing them. It is this type of action—a "balanced" type of communication and exchange—that will be examined first; subsequently imbalanced action which engenders normative change will be considered.

As stated earlier, power is the potential ability of actors to select, to change, and to attain the goals of a social system. Power thus refers to an institutionalized set of arrangements among actors—in other terms to a system of norms and values. The term power structure refers to a patterned distribution of power in a social system, or the set of norms and values regulating the distribution of power resources in the system. (This patterning does not imply, however, that all system actors necessarily regard this patterning as legitimate.) In this sense, the power structure must be more than simply continuing influence.

Influence, on the other hand, is social action within the general normative framework of a power structure. The power structure may be seen as placing certain very general constraints on the processes of influence and decision-making that take place within the system. Influence may take place within a structure that consists of little more than the distribution of power bases throughout the system. Particularly in the United States, where ideological commitments are weak and social classes fluid, the exercise of influence in local communities is very loosely structured. What almost always is institutionalized, however, in addition to the bases of power, are the "rules of the game"—the set of norms regulating social exchange and the exercise of influence within the system. As a fundamental structural constraint on all social action taking place within a system, these rules demand more attention than they have received in studies of decision-making, particularly community decision-making.

The behavior taking place within a system which consists principally of actors, resources, and a set of basic rules can be analyzed to a large extent using non-normative models, such as those developed in the body of studies referred to as game theory, or that part of exchange theory in which norms and values are largely neglected.[13] But if there were no more normative structure in most situations than the elements just described, it would be unnecessary to study empirical cases of decision-making. The writing and reading of decisional case studies would have no intrinsic meaning if they offered no more than a random portrayal of strategies used by actors in non-normative situations.

But people write and read case studies for more than this reason alone. Through case studies one can learn something of the ways in which normative systems structure decisions—particularly when the normative system is so loosely structured that it is difficult to portray clearly and explicitly. The set of norms specifically relating to the processes of influence and decision-making—in contrast to power—is what has been referred to as the decision-making structure. It is less easily portrayed than a power structure, but it exists nevertheless in most social systems.

The emergence of the norms constituting the decision-making structure can be explained theoretically by an extension of the theory used to explain the emergence of power. A skillful individual, it was pointed out, could contribute desired commodities, first, individually to individuals, or second, collectively to members of a group. In the second situation, it was emphasized, the relative gain in "debts" accruing to the coordinator-leader is far greater for each unit of investment that he himself must make than in the first.

These debts, in turn, may be regarded as a resource that can be converted into influence. Exerting influence on members of the system by expending small amounts of the resources available to him, a leader can

---

[13] Especially the work of Homans.

organize further collective activity, and through attaining collectively desired goals, lead the other actors to incur further debts to him, thereby further augmenting his resources.

After this process has been repeated a number of times, however, a skillful leader who has amassed a sizable reserve of debts will "spend" some of these resources by meeting the individual and collective desires of the system members more liberally than in the past. A leader, in effect, accomplishes the same thing simply by allowing his reserve capital of debts to grow beyond the level of demands that he makes of his followers.[14] It is by this general process of increasing system members' indebtedness to him that a leader may insure good will and continuing support. Then, through recurrent interaction with one another and with the leader, system members gradually evolve a set of norms which institutionalize and legitimate the dependency relationship. Once established, the norms serve as an independent mechanism of social control, since each system member will be constrained in his interaction with other members to conform to the norms which have now become generally accepted.

Norms spread downward from those who are closest to a leader to others in less direct and less frequent contact with him. Much of the exchange process has been viewed as taking place within a single system. But as systems become integrated and institutionalize intra-system exchanges, there will also be a tendency to integrate with actors in adjoining systems (toward *Gleichschaltung*). The system in question will not become submerged into some broader system, but norms in adjoining systems will tend to converge. These matters are similar to the problem of emerging institutions and professions obtaining legitimation from the broader society,[15] and are to some extent resolved through the mechanisms for integration presented earlier.

Subsystems are never fully integrated into larger systems; some remain quite autonomous from outset, while others tend to integrate into larger systems. The degree of integration into various larger systems is then a useful continuum for classification of systems. To consider an example from community decision-making: it is useful to classify various subsystems in the community—business, labor, ethnic and neighborhood

---

[14] There are unquestionably differences among various types of "debts," since some commodities may be exchanged "more profitably" than others. While the consequences of exchanging different types of commodities are ignored for the moment, they will be taken up shortly.

[15] These questions are taken up in some detail in Terry N. Clark, *Institutionalization of Innovations in Higher Education: Social Research in France, 1850–1914*, forthcoming.

groups, and the like—in terms of the degree to which they are integrated with the larger community. To what degree do they share the norms of other community groups? To what degree are they in continual and intimate contact with one another and with other community subsystems? Are the leaders of one subsystem powerful only within their own subsystem, or are their relationships with other subsystems sufficiently strong that they may be considered general community leaders? These basic questions can be answered only through careful empirical study of the norms relating to decision-making in individual communities.

RESOURCES FOR POWER, PRESTIGE, AND NORM FORMATION

Thus far no distinction has been made among 1) the various types of commodities that are exchanged for one another, or 2) the many types of "debts" that may be incurred from an imbalance of exchange, or 3) the several types of resources that may be converted into influence or institutionalized in norms. These questions will be examined by considering some of the major resources of social exchange and their basic characteristics.[16]

There is necessarily a certain arbitrariness involved in the establishment of any inventory of resources,[17] but the following list is useful nonetheless:

(1) Money and credit
(2) Control over jobs
(3) Control of mass media
(4) High social status
(5) Knowledge and specialized technical skills
(6) Popularity and esteemed personal qualities

---

[16] This examination is founded on the belief that exchange theory and related theories of power and influence have suffered by not analyzing with sufficient precision the specific types of commodities that are exchanged and circulated. One line of analysis is to consider various commodities that seem more "legitimate" than others for circulation in different systems; this line has been followed by Storer, in *The Social System of Science*. A second alternative is to analyze not specific commodities, but general characteristics of commodities, or resources. This second alternative is more promising for development of a more general theory, and consequently has been followed in the present section.

[17] For discussions that contain some of the same items, see Peter H. Rossi, "Theory, Research, and Practice in Community Organization," in Charles R. Adrian, ed., *Social Science and Community Action* (East Lansing: Institute for Community Development and Services, 1960); Floyd Hunter, *et al., Community Organization* (Chapel Hill: University of North Carolina Press, 1956), pp. 37–39; and especially Robert A. Dahl, *Who Governs?* (New Haven: Yale University Press, 1961), pp. 266 ff.

(7) Legality
(8) Subsystem solidarity
(9) The right to vote
(10) Social access to community leaders
(11) Commitments of followers
(12) Manpower and control of organizations
(13) Control over the interpretation of values

A first and basic characteristic of resources is their *generality*. Resources that are highly specific to a particular situation, or valuable to only a narrow range of persons, or which may be exchanged only in restricted markets, are less valuable for many purposes than more general resources. The more general the resources, the more extensive, complex, and indirect may be the structure of exchange relationships. The archetypical example of this pattern is, of course, the transition from a barter-type economy to one based on more general media of circulation, whether these media be salt, sheep, gold, or bank credit. The adoption of more general media permits more complex relationships and extensive exchanges.

Generality of resources is a characteristic central to analysis of power and decision-making.[18] Given a set of actors in a system, each with limited resources at his disposal, what are some of the ways in which decisions may be effected? To answer this sort of question, one must be able to characterize the types of resources available to the various actors. Then, knowing how much of each type of resource is available to each actor, the range of situations in which each resource is valuable must be characterized. It may be that no single actor commands the range and quantity of resources necessary to effect a given community decision. In this case, two basic strategies may be followed. First, community actors may attempt to form coalitions that can bring about the decision. This situation is typically analyzed in game theory,[19] which constitutes, perhaps, the most

---

[18] Despite the enormous theoretical importance of this characteristic, it has been examined by almost no writer on power with the notable exception of Talcott Parsons. His major discussions of power and closely related phenomena are "On the Concept of Influence," *Public Opinion Quarterly*, XXVII (Spring, 1963), pp. 87–92; "On the Concept of Political Power," *Proceedings of the American Philosophical Society*, CVII, No. 3 (June, 1963), 232–263; and "Some Reflections on the Place of Force in Social Process," in Harry Eckstein, ed., *Internal War* (New York: The Free Press, 1964), pp. 33–70.

[19] See for example, J. von Neumann and Oskar Morgenstern, *Theory of Games and Economic Behavior* (Princeton: Princeton University Press, 1944); Martin Shubik, ed., *Readings in Game Theory and Political Theory* (New York: Random House, 1954); R. Duncan Luce and Howard Raiffa, *Games and Decisions* (New York: John Wiley & Sons, 1957).

appropriate method of analysis for legislative-type situations where the consent or votes of a minimal number of actors is essential for a decision.

A second strategy for decision-making, and a second line of analysis, is necessary in a situation where coalitions are not formed, but resources are exchanged. Here, actors may exchange resources so as to transfer to one or more actors at the appropriate times the necessary resources to effect the decision. This second type of strategy often appears in situations more complex than those of the legislative type. Situations of this sort are far less structured: there is no single procedure (such as a vote of members) by which all decisions must be taken. A wide array of combinations and strategies is possible, but essential to each is the manipulation and exchange of resources among actors in the system. This second type of decision-making strategy is frequently observed in small groups, organizations, and communities, although sometimes in combination with the first as well.

Let us imagine a hypothetical situation in which there are thirteen actors, each possessing a fixed quantity of each of our thirteen resources, but possessing virtually none of the others (even though this may be empirically impossible). Assuming that the actors are unsuccessful in creating coalitions, a decision may still be effected if a single actor is able to exchange his one resource for the necessary quantity of other resources essential for the decision. In this situation, which actor possessing which one of the 13 resources is in the most advantageous position? This question can be answered only by evaluating the generality of each resource and the rates at which they may be exchanged.

These examples demonstrate the theoretical importance of generality, and particularly exchangeability, of resources. But what specific criteria may be applied for measurement? No theoretical discussion has thus far come to grips with this particular problem. Generality, like several other characteristics of resources, is a theoretical concept that would take on greater analytical utility if it were quantifiable. Because of the precision which may be added to such a characteristic as generality through quantification, an admittedly crude procedure will be presented which may at least set an example for subsequent studies to improve upon.

This procedure was to consider how easily any of the 13 resources could be converted into any of the other 12, and to classify each resource simply as high, medium, or low in its ease of convertibility into the 12 others.[20] The result was the 13 by 13 matrix of the resources shown in

---

[20] There are, of course, variations in generality of resources with different situations. In some cases, a single resource may be so important that virtually all

Table 2. Reading from left to right across a row, one finds the ease with which the row resource (for example, 1. Money) may be converted into each of the other 12 resources, which are listed in the vertical columns.

To quantify the concept, "high" entries were scored 3, "medium" entries 2, and "low" entries 1. The row and column marginals were then computed. The row marginal scores represent the ease with which a given resource may be converted into other resources, and may be taken as one crude measure of its generality, more specifically of what can be called its *buying power*.

The column marginals represent the ease with which each resource may be acquired, or its *selling price*. .

The difference between the buying power and the selling price for a resource can be considered its *exchange value,* which can be interpreted as a third, more sophisticated measure of generality. The exchange value score for each resource is presented in Table 3.

It is interesting to note that money has the highest buying power of any of the resources, scoring 32, while the next highest score was 25—achieved by knowledge, popularity, and social access to leaders.

However, the selling price of money was lower than that of several other resources. (Note that a numerically high score indicates a low selling price as it implies that many other resources may be easily converted into the resource in question.) Knowledge and expertness, and control of mass media, for example, scored 16 and 17, respectively, in contrast to 25 for money and credit.

Consequently, the exchange value for knowledge is slightly higher than that of money, although both of these, along with control of mass media, would seem to be particularly valuable as *general* resources.

These results call into question the dichotomy often developed in discussions of social power between the cluster of characteristics associated with wealth and high status on the one hand, and low status and mass support on the other. Each resource is viewed in this study—following a

others may be neglected, and in this case questions of generality are immaterial. Some of the resources listed are characteristics of individuals and others of relationships between individuals or groups; in every case, individuals were considered members of separate competing groups within a larger system. All of the resources have meaning only with respect to a given social system, and generality no doubt varies to some degree with the characteristics of the particular system. Our basic reference has been the local community and community-wide decisions in Western societies, although an attempt at reclassification for decisions in national societies and in organizations led to relatively similar results—which would seem to offer further evidence for the general tendencies of our conclusions. Nevertheless these classifications are to some extent arbitrary; the efforts of others to improve upon the results presented here are welcomed.

TABLE 2. CONVERTIBILITY MATRIX OF RESOURCES

	Money and credit	Control over jobs	Control of mass media	High social status	Knowledge and technical skills	Popularity and personal qualities	Legality	Subsystem solidarity	The right to vote	Social access to community leaders	Commitments of followers	Manpower and control of organizations	Control over interpretation of values	"Buying power"
Money and credit	—	H	M	H	H	M	M	M	M	H	H	H	M	32
Control over jobs	H	—	L	L	M	L	L	M	L	L	H	H	L	21
Control of mass media	M	L	—	L	M	H	M	H	M	M	H	L	H	23
High social status	H	L	L	—	L	M	M	M	M	H	M	L	M	22
Knowledge and technical skills	H	M	M	M	—	M	H	M	M	M	M	L	M	25
Popularity and personal qualities	M	L	L	H	L	—	M	H	M	H	H	M	M	25
Legality	L	L	L	M	L	M	—	L	H	M	M	L	M	19
Subsystem solidarity	M	L	L	M	L	H	M	—	M	L	L	M	M	23
The right to vote	L	L	L	L	L	L	H	L	—	L	L	L	M	15
Social access to community leaders	M	M	M	M	M	M	H	L	H	—	M	M	M	25
Commitments of followers	M	L	L	M	L	H	M	H	M	M	—	M	L	22
Manpower and control of organizations	H	L	L	M	L	M	M	M	M	M	M	—	L	21
Control over interpretation of values	L	M	L	H	L	H	H	M	H	M	M	L	—	24
"Selling price"	25	17	16	26	16	28	27	24	26	25	28	20	21	

Legend:

Symbol	Meaning	Score
H	high	3
M	medium	2
L	low	1

TABLE 3. "Exchange Value" Scores
for Each Resource

Knowledge and specialized technical skills	+9
Money and credit	+7
Control of mass media	+7
Control over jobs	+6
Control over the interpretation of values	+3
Manpower and control of organizations	+1
Social access to community leaders	0
Subsystem solidarity	−1
Popularity and esteemed personal qualities	−3
High social status	−4
Commitments of followers	−4
Legality	−8
The right to vote	−9

hackneyed expression—as having its "price." And given the very high exchange value of our three leading resources—knowledge, money, and control of mass media—an actor commanding large quantities of any of these resources stands in an excellent position to convert them into other resources as well as such desirables as social status, influence, and the institutionalization of norms and values.

These last considerations are a reminder that the exchange of one resource for another is seldom the final result desired by an actor, nor is generality the single important characteristic of a resource. A second basic characteristic is the *prestige value* of a resource, the contribution—direct or indirect—which possession of the particular resource makes to the prestige of an actor. Once again, it should be noted that the value of a resource varies with the social system, but in most industrial societies there is enough similarity to permit an approximate classification.[21] As with generality, the resources are grouped into one of three broad categories with respect to the importance of the resource for its contribution to prestige: directly important, indirectly important, and very indirectly important. (See Table 4.)

A third characteristic of resources is importance for the institutionalization of norms and values, or *institutionalization importance*. Here again, the same general procedure was followed for categorization as for

---

[21] On the great similarity of prestige hierarchies in industrial, as well as many nonindustrial, societies, see Robert W. Hodge, Donald J. Treiman, and Peter H. Rossi, "A Comparative Study of Occupational Prestige," in Reinhard Bendix and Seymour Martin Lipset, eds., *Class, Status, and Power* (2d ed.; New York: The Free Press, 1966), pp. 309–321.

TABLE 4. "Prestige Value" of Resources

Directly Important	Indirectly Important	Very Indirectly Important
Knowledge	Control of mass media	Manpower
Money	Control over jobs	Commitments of followers
[High social status]	Legality	Subsystem solidarity
[Popularity]	Social access to leaders	The right to vote
	Control over values	

[ ] = essentially tautological.

prestige value: each resource was classified into directly important, indirectly important, and very indirectly important. (See Table 5.)

A fourth characteristic of resources is importance for conversion into influence, or what may be called *power value*. Virtually all of the resources seem to be either directly or indirectly important. They were classified as shown in Table 6.

TABLE 5. "Institutionalization Importance" of Resources

Directly Important	Indirectly Important	Very Indirectly Important
Control over interpretation of values	Knowledge	Manpower
Legality	Subsystem solidarity	Control over jobs
Control of mass media	Commitments of followers	
	Money	
	Access to leaders	
	The right to vote	
	High social status	
	Popularity	

TABLE 6. "Power Value" of Resources

Directly Important	Indirectly Important
Money	Control over jobs
Control of mass media	High social status
Knowledge	Popularity
Legality	Subsystem solidarity
Social access to leaders	The right to vote
Control over interpretation of values	Commitments of followers
	Manpower

Having classified the 13 resources in terms of their *prestige value, institutionalization importance,* and *power value,* it is only a short step to quantifying the rank of each resource on these three dimensions, and compiling an aggregate score. This aggregate score may be interpreted as an index of *general applicability* for each resource, representing its general value for these three types of applications. The aggregate result, or index of general applicability, is presented in Table 7 for each resource.

TABLE 7. INDEXES OF "GENERAL APPLICABILITY" FOR EACH RESOURCE

	"Prestige Value"	"Institutionali- zation Importance"	"Power Value"	"Index of General Applicability"
1. Money and credit	3	2	3	8
2. Control over jobs	2	1	2	5
3. Control of mass media	2	3	3	8
4. High social status	3	2	2	7
5. Knowledge and specialized skills	3	2	3	8
6. Popularity and esteemed personal characteristics	3	2	2	7
7. Legality	2	3	3	8
8. Subsystem solidarity	1	2	2	5
9. The right to vote	1	2	2	5
10. Social access to community leaders	2	2	3	7
11. Commitments to followers	1	2	2	5
12. Manpower and control of organiza- tions	1	1	2	4
13. Control over the interpretation of values	2	3	3	8

Comparing the exchange values for conversion of resources into one another with the general applicability index, three resources are found to be very high on both: money and credit, knowledge, and control of mass media. These three resources appear extremely valuable not only for conversion into other resources, but also directly for application in three central areas. Scoring just as high on general applicability, however, also are control over the interpretation of values and legality. Control over the interpretation of values was still in the upper half of the exchange value scores, but legality ranked next to lowest in exchange value. It thus emerges as a resource which may be acquired relatively easily, but which nevertheless is quite important for ranking high in prestige, effecting decisions, or institutionalizing norms and values.

A sixth characteristic of resources may be termed *resource expendability*, referring to the degree to which a resource is expended through application. Some resources are highly expendable; money, for example, once spent, is gone.

Other resources, however, are low in expendability; that is, they remain relatively unchanged after having been drawn upon for such purposes as exercising influence or institutionalizing norms. High social status, for example, would seem to be relatively unchanged after having been applied to these ends—except for extreme cases, such as those leading to a change in the criteria for evaluation of status itself.

A third type of resource is difficult to classify as either expendable or non-expendable, as it may be augmented, remain the same, or decrease through application. Consider, for example, popularity or commitments of followers. If a leader is skillful, he will be able to augment both his popularity and the commitments of his followers by exercising influence—for example, by passing legislation of which they approve. But it is almost inevitable that on occasion a leader—either through ignorance, error, or because of outside forces that he cannot control—will be forced to take an action that will decrease his popularity and lower the commitments of his followers. But on other occasions, he will either change his popularity and commitments only minimally through his actions, or increase them with some followers and lower them with others.

Expendability, and the closely related dimension of *durability*—how long the resource will last without continual replenishment—are important additional criteria for evaluating the costs and gains involved in exchanging resources for one another. For example, money, which ranked so high in exchange value and general applicability, appears far less desirable a resource when considered in terms of its expendability.

Importance at different stages in the development of a decision is a seventh characteristic of resources. Decisions generally consist of six stages:

(1) Issue Recognition
(2) Information Collection
(3) Formulation of Policies
(4) Evaluation of Policies
(5) Policy Selection
(6) Policy Enactment

The first stage consists of the application of pressures (planned or unplanned, human or non-human) on those who can regulate the labeling of matters as "issues" or "non-issues." [22] The general problem is for a small number of actors within a social system, the initiators, to convince others that the particular matter is of importance not only to them, but also to others throughout the system. In a community, access to leaders is an essential resource at this stage, as is control of the mass media. Less directly important, but helpful, are popularity, and, in most cases, high social status, in order both to attract followers and to gain access to leaders. If these factors are not sufficient in themselves, because the "attention threshold" which must be surpassed before issue recognition may be achieved is high in some communities, then it may be necessary to mobilize money, manpower, and control of organizations. In some instances, however, this whole process may be completed very rapidly if certain persons controlling the interpretation of values in a particular area (for example, a judge, a lawyer, a public health official, a fire inspector, and the like) bring to light a matter that demands immediate attention by the very nature of the case (for instance, declaring the water in a popular recreation area polluted). In all types of issues, commitments of followers to a spokesman will certainly help amplify his voice in raising a particular question to issue status, as can the knowledge that he has behind him the support of a subsystem in the community that is relatively solid.

The second stage is information collection. Assuming that this task falls primarily to a relatively small group within the community, but that it may be influenced by "outsiders," the resources that are particularly important for outsiders in order to bring information to the attention of the small group are similar to those central to issue recognition: control of mass media, popularity, high social status, money, and manpower.

If the third and fourth stages—formulation of policies and evaluation of policies—are held entirely separate from the other stages, then knowledge and specialized technical skills are the resources of prime importance.

It is, however, with the fifth stage—policy selection—that a whole range of resources comes into play. Virtually every one of the 13 resources can serve as a potentially important base of influence if actors having these resources at their disposal choose to mobilize them. Their relative importance, however, would seem to vary almost entirely with the nature of the situation, and correspondingly almost defy generalization.

For the final stage, policy enactment, resource importance varies

---

[22] See David Easton, *A Systems Analysis of Political Life* (New York: John Wiley & Sons, 1965) for a penetrating analysis of problems relating to issue recognition.

largely with the type of enactment procedure. At least three generic types may be distinguished.

First are purely administrative policies that pose relatively few problems for enactment. Here, virtually no resources are necessary beyond the basic essentials of most governments: legality, manpower, control of organizations, and minimal commitments of followers.

Second are quasi-administrative policies which involve enactment of a program by a central agency, but which are potentially open to influence by interested parties outside the agency, for example, building a road through a town. In policy areas of this sort, extra-governmental groups and organizations may be able to divert enactment, or even to force action to a halt if they control sufficient quantities of almost any of the 13 resources, although particularly important are control of mass media, high social status, knowledge, subsystem solidarity, social access to leaders, and commitments of followers. Common examples of this sort of influence include smaller modifications made to conform to the interests of subgroups, such as the sparing of a manufacturing plant or an exclusive neighborhood in building a new expressway. More impressive have been such matters as fluoridation of water or urban renewal programs in the United States, which in many cases have passed through the first five decision stages with no visible opposition whatsoever, but have then been halted by the mobilization of groups opposed to the plan.

Third are policy enactments that rely principally on extra-governmental forces for their success, for instance, a community fund drive. This procedure necessitates more active mobilization of resources before action is possible, since the established administrative agencies of government are not available. In such instances, control of mass media, manpower, and subsystem solidarity are the most directly important resources, with money, high social status, knowledge, and popularity only slightly less so.

ISSUE AREAS AND OUTCOMES OF DECISIONS

The themes of stratification, exchange, resources, and decision processes all combine in the analysis of issue areas and decisional outcomes. The neglect of distinct issue areas was a fundamental weakness of some of the early studies in the power structure tradition, particularly those completed or inspired by Floyd Hunter and C. Wright Mills.[23] But if this

---

[23] Hunter, *Community Power Structure*; C. Wright Mills, *The Power Elite* (New York: Oxford University Press, 1956) ; Floyd Hunter, *Top Leadership U.S.A.* (Chapel Hill: University of North Carolina Press, 1959).

first weakness was pointed out by some of the critics of these earlier works,[24] and corrected in many subsequent studies,[25] most studies in the community power tradition have nevertheless remained more concerned with the identity of actors in different issue areas, and their overlap across issue areas than with the actual outcomes of decisions. Only quite recently are community outputs coming to be systematically considered—most often in studies comparing several communities.[26] But due to the difficulties of collecting data on decision-making as well as on outputs in large numbers of communities, community outputs have generally not been systematically related to issue areas and decision-making structures.

This problem of failing to relate issue areas to outputs systematically is not, however, simply empirical—insoluble at some earlier point due to the inherent difficulties of data collection. There are certain fundamental theoretical problems involved as well.

It is possible to distinguish analytically among three different characteristics of decisions:

(1) The *identity of the actors* involved in various coalitions formed to implement their respective goals.

(2) The *functional areas* in which decisions are taken regarding a particular type of community function: for example, education, public health, and the like.

(3) The *outcome* of a decision, considered in terms of a change in the relationship between inputs and outputs of various actors within and outside of the community.

In analyzing issues and classifying issue areas, many empirical studies as well as theoretical discussions have considered uniquely the relationship between the identity of actors and the functional areas. But it is also

---

[24] Robert A. Dahl, "A Critique of the Ruling Elite Model," *American Political Science Review*, LII (1958), 463–469; Daniel Bell, "Is There a Ruling Class in America? *The Power Elite* Reconsidered," Chapter iii of *The End of Ideology* (Glencoe: The Free Press, 1960); Talcott Parsons, "The Distribution of Power in American Society," Chapter vi of *Structure and Process in Modern Societies* (New York: The Free Press, 1960).

[25] Most especially in Dahl, *Who Governs?*

[26] See Robert C. Wood, *1400 Governments* (Garden City: Doubleday Anchor Books, 1964); Oliver P. Williams, Harold Herman, Charles S. Liebman, and Thomas R. Dye, *Suburban Differences and Metropolitan Policies* (Philadelphia: University of Pennsylvania Press, 1965); Jack Fisher, *Yugoslavia—A Multinational State* (San Francisco: Chandler Publishing Co., 1966); and the articles by William A. Gamson, Robert L. Crain and Donald B. Rosenthal, and Bryan T. Downes in this volume.

essential in any meaningful discussion of issue areas to take into account the outcome or potential outcome of a decision.

To elaborate this point, it is useful to consider four types of actors generally involved in decisions:

(1) "Producers"—those who supply the commodity whose distribution is decided upon.

(2) "Consumers"—those who receive the commodity allocated through the decision.

(3) "Entrepreneurs"—those who initiate, mediate, bargain, and compromise in decisions between various sets of producers, consumers, and other system actors.

(4) "Enactors"—those whose duty it is to supervise the enactment and implementation of a decision.

When considering an issue area from a strictly functional standpoint, attention will turn first to the analysis of those actors who are involved, or likely to be involved, in the particular functional area. For example, in considering public education in most American communities, one expects to find involved producers—teachers; consumers—children and their parents; enactors—school administrators; and entrepreneurs—the mayor or other leading executive officials, the board of education, and citizens' groups with a particular interest in education. Here is a generally adequate classification of the actors involved in this particular issue area, so long as there is no question of altering the basic relationship between inputs and outputs. If the possibility of raising the quantity of inputs (probably though an increase in the budget for education) comes to be explicitly considered, however, then it is likely that another category of actors will become involved: taxpayers and their representatives. With the entrance of this new category of actors, the substance of the discussion—and the classification of the issue area in terms of personnel overlapping with other areas—may be altered significantly.

For this reason, it is essential when classifying decisions as belonging to one or another issue area to bear in mind these three characteristics of a decision, since actors, strategies, resources, and decision processes are likely to change whenever a fundamental reallocation of community resources is at stake.

Another central characteristic of decisions and issue areas [27] is issue

---

[27] A list of characteristics of issue areas and decisional outcomes is found at the end of this section.

importance. Studies based on the "decisional method" generally examine a restricted number of issue areas in some detail, and in most cases the researcher seeks to study the "most important" issues in the community. A number of different criteria may be applied to evaluate importance. One measure is the total number of persons directly involved in the decision. Elections and referenda are the most important issues according to this criterion. Whether issues ranking high on this measure also rank high on others varies with the electoral system, the extent of governmental control of important decisions (since elections or referenda are usually held only for government-related decisions), and the degree to which the citizenry can influence the government through elections and referenda.

A second empirical measure is the importance accorded issues, ascertained either by a sample of the general population, or by knowledgeable community informants. Their opinions may be sounded through interviews. But unless one is willing to rely upon each respondent's definition of importance—yielding responses which are essentially subjective, probably unclear, and very likely to be based on criteria that vary from one respondent to the next—it is necessary to specify criteria for each respondent to apply. As a general axiom it is certainly important to adopt criteria that are also viewed as significant by members of the system, but interviewing may not be the most appropriate procedure for applying their criteria. However, if one does not accept their criteria, interviewing community members does not constitute a separate measure of issue importance.

A third measure is the total quantity of monetary resources involved in a particular issue area. However, because some decisions in which there is virtually no local initiative or community participation may involve very large sums of money (for example, decisions by a private corporation or the federal government to construct a large installation in a local community), this measure must be interpreted with caution. This is particularly true for communities in countries where there is less local autonomy than in the United States.

A fourth measure is the quantity and extent of reallocation of community resources brought about by a particular decision or a series of decisions in a particular issue area. This criterion is appealing from many standpoints; its major disadvantage, at this point at least, is difficulty in operationalization.

A fifth measure is the number of persons in the community affected by the outcome of decisions. The difficulty with this measure is that it does not indicate *how much* each person is affected—another variable difficult to operationalize.

A sixth measure is the degree to which separate institutions within the community are affected. This measure, however, poses the same problems as the last, in that although they may be large in number, the institutions may not be affected very profoundly.

None of these six criteria is without significant disadvantages, but, taken in combination, they constitute workable criteria for measuring issue importance. And explicit, systematic application of a set of some of these criteria for issue selection is certainly preferable to haphazard choice, which seems to have been used more than once in past studies.[28]

The following is a list of some basic characteristics of issue areas and decisional outcomes. Propositions relating certain of these characteristics to other variables are presented in Chapter 5.

TABLE 8. CHARACTERISTICS OF ISSUE AREAS AND DECISIONAL OUTCOMES

I. *Inputs and Outputs of Resources*
   Total amounts of different resources involved
   Source of inputs (producers)
      Outside the community
         Foreign source
         Federal government
         State government
         National private source
         Regional private source
      Inside the community
         Ethnicity of producers
         Religion of producers
         Education of producers
         Sex of producers
         Age of producers
         Economically advanced sectors
         Economically retarded sectors
         All economic sectors equally
         Specific geographical area
         Homeowners
         Market consumers (sales tax)
         Other classification by subsector
   Receivers of outputs (consumers)
   [Classification corresponds to that for Source of inputs]
   Extent of reallocation of resources

II. *Actors Involved (Separate Classification for Each Faction—Opponents, Supporters, and the like)*
   Identity of initiators, supporters, opponents
   [Classification corresponds to that for Source of inputs in I above]

---

[28] See Terry N. Clark, "The Concept of Power: Some Overemphasized and Underrecognized Dimensions," *Southwestern Social Science Quarterly* (December, 1967), Vol. 48, No. 3, 271–286, for further discussion of issue importance and bibliographical references.

TABLE 8—*Continued*

Identity of producers, consumers, entrepreneurs, enactors
   [Classification corresponds to that for Source inputs in I above]
Homogeneity or heterogeneity on basic characteristics
Cohesive or fragmented organization
Overlap with different functional areas
Values and immediate goals
Relationships to inputs and outputs
Number of actors
Psychic intensity of involvement

III. *Decisional Goals*

Change community functions
   Classified by functional area
Change community structures
   Decision-making structure (norms)
   Legal structure
   Basic value structure
Move toward more complete attainment of general values (for example, honesty,
   efficiency, free enterprise, socialism, social harmony, and the like)
Change physical environment (for instance, housing, hospitals)
Change social composition of community (for example, exclude the poor, attract
   the rich)
Change leadership personnel

IV. *Criteria for Evaluation of Outcomes*

Benefits to subgroups or to entire community—self or collectivity orientation
   (Parsons); private-or public-regarding (Banfield)
Effects on future of community as perceived by various actors involved
Specific values maximized

METHODS FOR MEASURING POWER AND
DECISION-MAKING STRUCTURES

In the field of community power, debate over theoretical issues has overlapped with problems of a methodological nature; "elitists" incline toward one sort of technique and "pluralists" another. It has been asserted that employing one type of technique or another biases subsequent findings. Although a systematic review of these criticisms and debates—many of which have been intellectually sparse if rhetorically colorful [29]—will not be attempted, the principal techniques used will be outlined briefly and some of the advantages and disadvantages of each quickly sketched.

---

[29] A reinterpretation of this controversy is offered in Clark, *et al.*, "Discipline, Method, Community Structure, and Decision-Making: The Role and Limitations of the Sociology of Knowledge."

As many as ten different techniques have been used to identify leaders, but only three are commonly employed: the Positional Method, the Reputational Method, and the Decisional Method.[30]

The Positional Method

One technique for designating the "leaders" in a community is to compile a list of the occupants of important positions in major community organizations. One problem with this method concerns the criteria for selection of top organizations and positions. The discussion on issue importance is relevant here, and most of the alternatives outlined are applicable to this analogous problem.

Once the positions have been selected and the list of occupants compiled, the next major problem is to infer the amount of influence wielded in the community by the occupants listed. If it is found, for example, that most members of the school board in a community are recruited from the upper classes, is it legitimate to infer that the schools are run by the upper classes and in their own interests? The first obstacle to so facile a conclusion is that one must pose the question of whether the interests of the upper classes are significantly different from those of other groups in the community with regard to school affairs. Second, even if a possible conflict of interest can be shown to exist, there is no proof that the social background of office holders determines their behavior. Each person at any one time occupies a complement of statuses that Merton has called the status-set,[31] and a recurrent problem to which one becomes sharply alerted in status-set analysis is that the various role obligations associated with the array of statuses comprising an individual's status-set frequently result in status-conflict and cross-pressures for the status-set occupant concerning the role appropriate to a given status.[32] Such findings underline the degree of

---

[30] In addition to these three methods, Bell, Hill, and Wright cite studies utilizing the "social participation approach" which measures the individual's rate of participation (primarily) in voluntary associations, "the personal influence approach," "studies of social class related behavior," "participation of business leaders in government affairs," "analysis of newspaper stories," "participant observation," and analysis of published listings such as *Who's Who*. See Wendell Bell, Richard J. Hill, and Charles R. Wright, *Public Leadership* (San Francisco: Chandler Publishing Co., 1961), pp. 5–33.

[31] See Robert K. Merton, "The Role Set: Problems in Sociological Theory," *British Journal of Sociology*, VIII (1957), 106–120; and Merton, *Social Theory and Social Structure*, pp. 368–386.

[32] See, for example, Bernard C. Rosen, "Conflicting Group Membership: A Study of Parent-Peer Group Cross-Pressures," *American Sociological Review*, XX (1955), 155–161; J. W. Getzels and E. G. Guba, "Role, Role Conflict and Effectiveness: An Empirical Study," *American Sociological Review*, XIX (1954), 164–175; Neal Gross, Ward S. Mason, and Alexander W. McEacher, *Exploration in Role Analysis* (New York: John Wiley & Sons, 1958), esp. pp. 244–328.

naiveté involved in predicting the behavior in one status, for example, school board member, through the assumption of direct congruence with another status, for instance, occupation, assumed to be dominant.

The third problem arises from the fact that as an actor in his daily activities moves from one status to another, the "structural context" impinging on each status constrains the status-occupant to behave in a certain fashion.[33] Thus, even if a school board member desires to act solely as a taxpayer, for instance, the social pressures exerted on him by virtue of his being a member of the school board are bound to constrain his behavior. For example, an active PTA may exert pressure on a school board member to allocate more funds than he otherwise would for construction of a new school.

The very definite research limitations presented by the positional method are obvious. In many instances, however, it is the only technique feasible, as is often the case in studies of the past, and for this reason the method is frequently used in historical analyses of community decision-making. In the study of contemporary communities, the next two methods are more frequently employed.

The Reputational Method

This procedure for investigating the leadership structure of a community derives its name from the fact that a panel of community members is queried about the leaders of the community, and, on the basis of the "reputation" of certain individuals in the opinion of panel members, a list of leaders is compiled. Complexities associated with the reputational method involve the number of leaders to be chosen, the method for selecting the panel, and the wording of questions asked panel members. Such matters will be passed over here,[34] in favor of a few of the more general advantages and disadvantages associated with this widely debated method.[35]

---

[33] See Merton, *Social Theory and Social Structure*, esp. pp. 52–55, 248–250, for a theoretical statement of the problems involved in analyzing the structural context of social phenomena.

[34] For a more detailed discussion of technical complexities involved in the reputational method, see Bell, Hill, and Wright, *Public Leadership*, pp. 13 ff.; Hunter, *Community Power Structure*, "Appendix: Methods of Study"; and William H. Form and Delbert C. Miller, *Industry, Labor, and Community* (New York: Harper, 1960), pp. 516–551, as well as the works cited in the following footnote.

[35] For criticism of the reputational method by pluralists, see Herbert Kaufman and Victor Jones, "The Mystery of Power," *Public Administration Review*, XIV (1954), 205–212; Dahl, "A Critique of the Ruling Elite Model," *American Political Science Review*, pp. 463–469; Robert A. Dahl, "Hierarchy, Democracy, and Bargaining in Politics and Economics," in Stephen K. Bailey, ed., *Research Frontiers in Politics and Economics* (Washington, D.C.: The Brookings Institution, 1955), pp. 45–69;

A practical advantage of the reputational technique is its relative simplicity of design and ease of application. And although in this respect the reputational method has been compared by Wolfinger to "frozen dinners that may not taste like much, but are marvelously easy to prepare," his plea to "bury the reputational method" [36] does not seem to be taking hold.

What do critics find objectionable in the reputational technique? At least six recurrent criticisms can be identified. First, the reputational researcher biases his results from the outset by assuming the existence of a pyramidal decision-making structure when he poses a question such as "Who are the 'top leaders' in the community?" The first question should not be "Who rules?," but, "Does anybody rule?"

Next, in collecting names of "top leaders," the reputationalists report a list of 20, 40, or 200 individuals reputed to be key influentials in their community, although there is no intrinsic method for arriving at an appropriate cut-off point for this precise number of persons. "Why not 21, or 45, or 208?" critics ask.

Third, and closely related, is the criticism that the separation of the so-called "top leaders" from "second stringers" is based on an arbitrary decision by the researcher. These criticisms of the reputational technique might be partially avoided if the researcher were to develop a deep enough

Polsby, "Three Problems in the Analysis of Community Power," *loc. cit.;* Polsby, "The Sociology of Community Power: A Reassessment," *Social Forces,* XXXVII (1959), 232–236; Raymond E. Wolfinger, "Reputation and Reality in the Study of Community Power," *American Sociological Review,* XXV (October, 1960), 636–644; Polsby, "Community Power: Some Reflections on the Recent Literature," and Wolfinger, "A Plea for a Decent Burial," both in *American Sociological Review,* XXVII (1962), 838–847; Polsby, *Community Power and Political Theory,* pp. 47–53, 63–65, 116.

For further discussions of the reputational technique, see Form and Miller, *Industry, Labor, and Community,* pp. 516–551; Howard J. Ehrlich, "The Reputational Approach to the Study of Community Power," *American Sociological Review,* XXVI (1961), 926–927; William V. D'Antonio and Eugene C. Erickson, "The Reputational Technique as a Measure of Community Power: An Evaluation Based on Comparative and Longitudinal Studies," *American Sociological Review,* XXVII (1962), 362–372; Lawrence J. Herson, "In the Footsteps of Community Power," *American Political Science Review,* LV (1961), 817–830; D'Antonio, Ehrlich, and Erickson, "Further Notes on the Study of Community Power," *American Sociological Review,* XXVII (1962), 848–854; Peter H. Rossi, "Community Decision Making," *Administrative Science Quarterly,* I (June, 1956), 415–443; T. J. Anton, "Power, Pluralism, and Local Politics," *Administrative Science Quarterly,* VII (1963), 425–457; and the subsequent exchange printed in Dahl, "Letter to the Editor," and Anton, "Rejoinder," *Administrative Science Quarterly,* VIII (1963), 250–268; Presthus, *Men at the Top,* especially pp. 33–61, 405–433; Agger, Goldrich, and Swanson, *The Rulers and the Ruled,* "Appendix A: Operational Definitions," pp. 688–759.

[36] Wolfinger, "A Plea for a Decent Burial," *American Sociological Review,* pp. 843, 847.

knowledge of the specific community he was studying. He could then at least specify what "top" meant through empirical examples.

A fourth problem concerns the empirical referent both of the panelists and of the researcher. To speak of "general influentials" without specifying areas of competence is to misrepresent most American communities, pluralists claim, where practically no true "general influentials" exist. Most persons, they argue, are only influential over a relatively narrow range of issues.

Fifth, even if the concept of "influential" is clear to the researcher, many community members are prone to confuse influentials with social notables or widely publicized persons who may not wield any actual influence in community decisions. The validity of this criticism can best be determined by empirical investigation. At present, the results are still somewhat contradictory.[37]

Sixth, the method only gives a "reputation" for power or *potential* influence which, even if the "influential" actually does have available to him, he may not choose to exert, or he may only exert infrequently or over a narrow range of issues. This last criticism indicates the principal strength and weakness of the reputational method.

In the face of hard and persistent attack, however, the technique continues to be widely used (although increasingly in conjunction with other methods) and criticism against it is vigorously contested by its supporters. The method has many important advantages. First, as was already mentioned, the cost and effort involved in applying the technique to the study of a community are markedly less than those of the decision method, the pluralists' methodological choice. This advantage, although mocked, is recognized in Wolfinger's frozen dinner analogy. The crucial question, to follow the metaphor, concerns the "taste" of the dinner. And in this respect there are a number of advantages to the reputational technique not to be found in its major rivals.

Second, there is the conceptual parsimony of the reputational technique. It isolates the power aspect of a community and allows the researcher to analyze this aspect without becoming involved in often rich but frequently irrelevant details of local community life. It was only after Hunter that communities were studied solely for purposes of testing or refuting hypotheses about community power and decision-making, and, if only for this achievement, all subsequent community power studies are indebted to him.

---

[37] See footnote 41.

Third, the reputational method is highly reproducible. Its operations are sufficiently simple and clearly defined to allow numerous researchers to investigate several different communities with a relatively high degree of assurance that the operations for measuring the dispersal of community influence can be closely duplicated in other communities, and thereby reduce the coefficient of human error.

Whereas statistical reliability is a recognized strength of the reputational technique, critics have singled out validity as its principal weakness. Does the reputational method *really* yield a description of the decision-making structure?

A highly important point frequently overlooked in much of the criticism and debate concerns the distinction between the *technical procedures* of a given method and subsequent *interpretation* of the results produced by the use of these procedures. The researcher asking a panel who the influential persons in a given community are need not deduce that the list of influentials reported actually constitutes an omnipotent "power elite." Hunter never really did so.

Once a list of influentials has been established, a minimal interpretation—all that the most extreme critics will accept—is that the individuals listed are those *perceived* as powerful by the panel of informants. A second interpretation is that the reputational method yields results about the distribution of potential influence, or power, in contrast to the decisional method which yields actual *exerted* influence. Thus, according to this interpretation, the results produced by the reputational method would be analytically similar to those yielded by an analysis of the distribution of the resources for power within a community.

And, of course, if one accepts the interpretation that the reputational method yields only results concerning the distribution of power, or potential influence, all of the problems raised earlier apropos of the distinction between power and influence become relevant once again.

A third interpretation, that the results of the reputational method reflect the *actual* distribution of *influence* within the community, raises once more the question of validity. How is one to find an outside measure of the *actual* decision-making structure by which to validate the results obtained through use of the reputational method? Two possibilities are the issue-specific reputational method and the decisional method.

The "Issue-Specific Reputational Method"

One particularly interesting variation of the classical reputational approach was used in a study of decision-making in 51 American communities conducted by the International Studies of Values in Politics and the National Opinion Research Center. Designated the "issue-specific reputational method," it consists of asking informants to rank or score individual community actors in terms of their power in specific issue areas (hence the name). Its variations, use, and interpretations are discussed in the concluding article of this volume.

The Decisional Method

This third general approach involves tracing the history of a specific decision or decisions relating to one or more community issue areas. By identifying the persons who actually participate in concrete decisions and whose suggestions are actually followed, this approach escapes the charges of vagueness and imprecision ascribed to the reputational method by its critics.

In principle, the decisional method has numerous advantages. First, in contrast to the positional method, no questionable inferences need be drawn concerning the relationship between organizational position-holders and actual decision-makers; the problem can be subjected to empirical investigation. Second, in contrast to the reputational method, "top leaders" can be identified and distinguished from second-level leaders who carry out the work once the initial high-level decisions have been made. The actual number of persons involved in a decision at its several levels can be determined empirically. Third, the overlap of an individual's influence from one decision area to other decision areas can also be spelled out empirically. Fourth, the overlap, if any, between social and economic notables and influential decision-makers can likewise be established empirically.

What are some of the limitations of the decisional method? As it is generally used, at least, the decisional method does not cope adequately with the problem of indirect influence. Nor does it face squarely the problems of non-decisions, patterns of value distribution, and the "mobilization of bias." [38] Both the knotty problem of selecting the issues for investigation and the possible significant differences in findings depending on the issues selected were alluded to earlier.

The most general methodological problem of the decisional method is

---

[38] These dimensions of power are discussed in more detail in Terry N. Clark, "The Concept of Power: Some Overemphasized and Underrecognized Dimensions," *Southwestern Social Science Quarterly* (December, 1967), Vol. 48, No. 3, 271–286.

that while it yields concrete, empirical data in the hands of a competent researcher, the data are often *too* concrete. That is, since it is impossible to study every important community decision in its full complexity, even over a relatively short period of time, the researcher is forced to generalize from a restricted sample of decisions that he can examine in detail. If his results are to be accepted as representative of important community decisions, the researcher must demonstrate that he has successfully avoided the theoretical pitfall of the fallacy of misplaced concreteness. Just as surely as the reputational method yields perceived power, the decisional method yields information on a sample of cases of exercised influence. Both confront similar problems, however, when the time comes for inferences to be drawn with regard to *how far* it is legitimate to extrapolate from the actual data collected.

The last point is similar to several already mentioned. Past decisions are of utmost importance in determining the power structures at later periods; the structure of a community at any point in time may be conceived of as the cumulative result of innumerable past decisions. On a national level, the electorate's mandate of Franklin D. Roosevelt in 1932, and subsequent decisions made as part of the New Deal and the mobilization for the war effort, were of crucial importance in readjusting the balance of government-private industry relations from that of the pre-New Deal period. To understand contemporary American governmental-industrial relations and the forces that were involved in effecting these far-reaching changes, it would be more meaningful to examine the influence patterns behind the decisions of the 1930's and 40's than to focus on the decision-making structure of small government anti-trust suits and other day-to-day decisions at the present time, where only a handful of lawyers is involved. Similarly, on the community level, the change in structure of the New Haven political parties in the first decade of the twentieth century determined the course of politics for almost a half a century. At that time, the Republican political leaders mobilized the support of the Italian community and, as a result, were able to take power away from the Democrats. Subsequent activities in the New Haven political arena should be viewed within this general framework, for it was this structuring of party affiliation that determined the rules of the game for years afterward.[39]

These examples suggest that a situation at one point in time can be analyzed as constituting the structural context of subsequent periods within

---

[39] See Dahl, *Who Governs?*, pp. 32–51.

which the more restricted process of decision-making takes place. From this point of view, when the historical dimension is introduced, it is possible for the researcher to consider important past events as crucial *decisions* in evaluating the power structure of a community.[40] This is one of the many ways in which the decisional method can be refined and extended.

Before concluding, it should be noted that a growing number of studies have employed several, as opposed to a single, measurement technique for studying community power and decision-making structures. Many of these explicitly compare the results obtained by one method with those obtained using another.[41]

If any trend can be distinguished, it is probably an increasing reliance of community researchers on a number of different methods to study power and decision-making structures. In addition, the different methods are often "mixed" to some degree so that there are increasingly fewer studies whose results are based solely on one unrefined method. At least to this

---

[40] See Raymond Aron, "Macht, Power, Puissance: prose démocratique ou poésie démoniaque?" *European Journal of Sociology*, V, No. 1 (1964), 27–57; and Ralf Dahrendorf, "Amba und Amerikaner: Bemerkung zur These des Universalität von Herrschaft," *European Journal of Sociology*, I, No. 1 (1964), esp. 95–98, on the impact of crucial decisions in structuring subsequent power relationships.

[41] See, for example, Robert O. Schulze and Leonard U. Blumberg, "The Determination of Local Power Elites," *American Journal of Sociology*, LXIII (1957), 290–296, where almost no overlap between the reputational elite and occupants of major economic positions in a 20,000 inhabitant Midwestern satellite industrial city was found.

An investigation of one community comparing the reputational elite with occupants of the fourteen objectively defined public statuses used by Stouffer in *Communism, Conformity and Civil Liberties* (New York: Doubleday & Company, 1955) found only 4 of the 18 nominated leaders to overlap with the fourteen status occupants. See Frank A. Stewart, "A Sociometric Study of Influence in Southtown," *Sociometry*, X (February, 1947 and August, 1947), 11–31 and 273–286, respectively.

In Seattle, Washington, only 17 of 44 nominated leaders overlapped with 44 official position holders. See Form and Miller, *Industry, Labor and Community*, pp. 523 ff.

More recent studies comparing results from positional, reputational, and decisional methods include the Syracuse study, partially reported in Linton C. Freeman *et al.*, "Locating Leaders in Local Communities," *American Sociological Review*, XXVIII (October, 1963), 791–798; Presthus, *Men at the Top*, D'Antonio and Erickson, in *American Sociological Review*; and Aaron Wildavsky, *Leadership in a Small Town* (Totawa: Bedminster Press, 1964). Wildavsky summarizes the results of his comparison of the reputational and decision methods as follows: "the reputational method appears to have about a 50/50 probability of naming leaders who actually are leaders." (Leaders, for Wildavsky, are actually identified with the decision method.)

The most systematic report on the findings from different methods will be available from the ISVP-NORC study, where some of each of these methods were used.

limited degree, the polemical debates and acrimonious discussions of earlier years seem to have resulted in a greater understanding of the implications of various methods for studying community power.

4

COMMUNITY
OR COMMUNITIES?

ℰ

One observation to be made with reference to studies dealing with the problem of community power concerns the concept of community: by far the majority of such studies employ the concept with no regard for possible differentiation among the entities designated by the single generic term "community." Isolated rural hamlets, small college towns, major industrial centers, state capitals, exclusive suburbs, and resort towns—all are lumped together in the same category. It is perhaps such undifferentiated usage that has given methodological legitimation to so many isolated studies of power and decision-making in a single community, wherein the author concludes that the configuration of power found to exist in his particular community (regardless of the specific techniques utilized) is generalizable to, and therefore representative of, if not all, at least most other communities. (Some qualifications may be offered—contemporary America, modern industrial society—but they are still too broad to be considered true differentiation.) Doesn't this procedure flaunt the principles both of logic and scientific methodology?

Before the study of community decision-making can progress further, the undifferentiated concept of "the community" must be broken down into a number of *types* of communi*ties*. Study of the power and decision-making structures in these typologically differentiated communities can then lead to the development of a series of propositions relating the different types of communities to different types of power and decision-making structures and different types of community outputs.

After a brief review of some of the previous approaches to analysis of the community (generally not by students of community power), a relatively abstract typology for use in the classification of communities will be presented. A number of possible empirical indicators for each general type (for which it is fairly easy to gather data) will be discussed next. These types will be used to specify various dimensions of decision-making in the next chapter.

83

THE CONCEPT OF COMMUNITY

Despite diversity of approaches, a number of common elements tend to recur in most analyses of the community. In his 1948 review of community literature, Hollingshead classified studies according to their central focus as "ecological, structural, and typological." [1] A 1955 review of the literature concluded that most students were "in basic agreement that community consists of persons in social interaction within a geographic area and having one or more additional common ties." [2] Parsons has recently advanced a similar conception of the community, emphasizing territorial location and social interaction among community residents.[3]

A slightly different approach was taken by MacIver when he used as his basic criterion the fact that a person could spend his entire life in the community.[4] This emphasizes that the community is a *functional* entity, but, curiously enough, uses the individual as its reference point.

A concept of the community slightly broader than most of those currently in use is that of a *functionally autonomous social unit.* The majority of community studies focus primarily on the functional autonomy of the *political* system with its particular geographical limits as the criterion for setting community boundaries.

From the present point of view, however, it is useful to employ a two-fold conception of the community: first, following the more traditional usage, as a relatively autonomous *political* system, but second, and generally encompassing a larger geographical social unit, as a relatively autonomous *social* system. Here the additional criteria for autonomy are the economic, educational, religious, and other basic social systems that together with the political system can be viewed analytically as comprising a single autonomous social system. For present purposes, this larger social unit will be termed a "community complex." To be considered functionally autonomous in this broader sense, the social system would have to perform on the community level [5] the four analytically exhaustive categories of

---

[1] August B. Hollingshead, "Community Research: Development and Present Conditions," *American Sociological Review,* XIII (April, 1948), 135–156.

[2] George A. Hillery, Jr., "Definitions of Community Areas of Agreement," *Rural Sociology,* XX (June, 1955), 111.

[3] Talcott Parsons, "The Principal Structures of Community: A Sociological View," in Carl J. Friedrich, ed., *Community* (New York: The Liberal Arts Press, 1959).

[4] Robert M. MacIver, *Society: its Structure and Changes* (New York: Ray Lang and Richard R. Smith, 1933), p. 10; Robert M. MacIver and Charles H. Page, *Society: An Introductory Analysis* (New York: Reinhart & Co., 1949), p. 9.

[5] The interpretation of this essential phrase, "on the community level," is developed in the following paragraphs.

functions designated by Parsons as adaptation, goal-attainment, integration, and latent pattern-maintenance and tension management,[6] or in abbreviated form, AGIL. Since 1953 Parsons and others have applied these functional categories to total societies, bureaucratic organizations, families, and even individual personalities. Thus, the functional categories have a broad range of applicability. However, the consequential looseness of fit emphasizes the necessity of specifying as precisely as possible the exact level of analysis to which the concepts are applied. Practically no social unit in industrial societies is *entirely* autonomous, but for analytical purposes, various units may be conceived as distinct from others and therefore analyzed as separate, if not totally isolated systems.

Local community autonomy decreases as both national and regional governments and national and regional private corporations take over many of the functions previously performed at the community level. International ties with other countries are also much more important than in the past. Still, the modern nation state, for many purposes, is a relatively autonomous unit. Likewise, in larger communities a high proportion of functions are still performed for the inhabitants by other persons within the boundaries of the same social unit. However, many smaller communities, of which extreme examples would be the dormitory suburb and the resort town—are almost entirely dependent on extra-community systems for vital input and output functions. Using the concept of community-complex, an industrial center together with its functionally specialized satellite suburbs can be conceived of as a single autonomous social unit. The "greater" New York or New Haven area exemplifies this concept to some degree. The rationale for this designation in such instances, however, is generally based on the territorial proximity of several units. Territorial and functional autonomy generally overlap to a large degree.[7] Still, from the present standpoint, it is the relative *functional* as opposed to *territorial* autonomy that will serve as the criterion for establishing units of analysis.

Nevertheless a basic question remains: precisely *how great* a degree of autonomy must exist before a community or community-complex can be

---

[6] These four concepts are to be found in most of Parson's theoretical writings following the appearance of Talcott Parsons, Robert F. Bales, and Edward A. Shils, *Working Papers in the Theory of Action* (Glencoe: The Free Press, 1953). See especially Chapter V. For a recent general but concise formulation, see Talcott Parsons, "An Outline of the Social System," in Talcott Parsons *et al.*, *Theories of Society* (Glencoe: The Free Press, 1961), esp. pp. 33–40.

[7] See Talcott Parsons, *The Social System* (Glencoe: The Free Press, 1951), pp. 90 ff. and Parsons, "The Principle Structures of Community: A Sociological View," in Friedrich, ed., *Community*, on the interrelations between territoriality and the performance of social functions.

classified autonomous? An arbitrary quantitative criterion of 75 per cent or 90 per cent could be set, for example, but any theoretical meaning that such a criterion might have practically disappears when the enormous difficulties involved in the empirical application of such a criterion are confronted.[8] However great such difficulties are, they are not especially relevant in the present context where the germane point is that the concept of community, for certain purposes, can be used in the second sense of community-complex. This broader concept calls attention to the functional integration of several smaller communities which, when joined, comprise the community-complex; it suggests as well that possible consequences for the distribution of power result from variations in patterns of interdependence.

Introducing the AGIL categories adds further analytical insight principally because social units similarly classified as "communities" from the political standpoint are extremely diverse entities in many other respects.[9] Some of these units fulfill primarily economic or adaptive functions, such as an industrial community. Others, such as the dormitory suburb, primarily fulfill the latent pattern-maintenance and tension-management functions.

A FUNCTIONAL CLASSIFICATION OF COMMUNITIES

A problem that should be dealt with at this point concerns the identification of the four broad AGIL categories with structures in the community that perform each of the four functions. It should be strongly emphasized that, as most frequently elaborated by Parsons, the four functions are specified in purely analytical terms and do not perfectly "fit" any empirical phenomena; consequently, there is a certain amount of inevitable overlap. Still, when the scheme is applied at the community level, there is a general correspondence between goal-attainment and the polity; adaptation and the economy; integration and the juridical system, political parties

---

[8] For a consideration of some examples of criteria that have been used in urban research for specifying boundaries, see Jack P. Gibbs, "Methods and Problems in the Delimitation of Urban Cities," and the other articles in chapter ii of Jack P. Gibbs, ed., *Urban Research Methods* (Princeton: D. Van Nostrand Co., 1961).

[9] A number of functional classifications of communities based on census data are reported in Howard J. Nelson, "A Service Classification of American Cities," L. L. Pownall, "The Functions of New Zealand Towns," both in Gibbs, ed., *Urban Research Methods*; Chauncy D. Harris, "A Functional Classification of Cities in the United States," *Geographical Review*, XXXIII (1943), 86–99; Victor Jones, "Economic Classification of Cities and Metropolitan Areas," *The Municipal Year Book*, 1953, pp. 49–54; Grace M. Kneedler, "Functional Types of Cities," *Public Management*, XXVII (July, 1945), 197–203.

and interest groups; and pattern-maintenance and tension management, and the family, education, and cultural organizations.[10]

The amount of structural differentiation among the various units performing these several functions is a variable that is vitally important to the analysis of community power. An extreme case, and yet one not uncommon in modern industrial societies, is the situation where a single family unit resides in one community, the children go to school in a second, the father works in a third, and the parents vote in a fourth. Using the family unit as a reference point, some of the four AGIL functions are dispersed among four different communities. Of course, the four communities may very well perform different functions for a second family unit; that is, the same community may perform different functions depending on the observer's frame of reference. Nevertheless, if one aggregates the various types of functions performed by a single community in one way or another for all individuals associated with it, varying patterns will emerge for different communities. To simplify the situation for the moment, it could be assumed that a community performs or does not perform one or more of the four AGIL functions. Table 9 is a typology of communities in terms of the primary functions served.

Only a limited number of the logically possible combinations are presented, namely those that appear to be empirically most frequent and analytically most useful. The typology could be further elaborated along a number of dimensions, although they will not be considered at this point.

These different configurations of community functions are related to differing types of decision-making processes. The next chapter will develop a series of propositions relating certain of these functional variables to power and decision-making.

OPERATIONAL INDICATORS OF COMMUNITY TYPES

To measure the extent to which a community fulfills the adaptation function, one could use the ratio of the number of occupational positions in the community to the total number of residents in the community.

---

[10] See Parsons, Bales, and Shils, *Working Papers in the Theory of Action*, pp. 163–269; Talcott Parsons, and Neil J. Smelser, *Economy and Society* (Glencoe: The Free Press, 1956), pp. 39–100; Talcott Parsons, "Voting and the Equilibrium of the American Political System," in Eugene Burdick and Arthur J. Brodbeck, *American Voting Behavior* (Glencoe: The Free Press, 1959), pp. 80–120; Parsons, *Structure and Process in Modern Society*, esp. Chapters i, iv, v; Parsons, "An Outline of the Social System," *loc. cit.*; and Parsons, *Societies* (Englewood Cliffs: Prentice-Hall, 1966), pp. 1–29, for discussion of empirical correlates of the theoretical categories.

TABLE 9. PARTIAL TYPOLOGY OF COMMUNITIES
CLASSIFIED ACCORDING TO FUNCTIONS

Community Type	Function and Approximate Empirical Correlate			
	(Economy) A	(Polity) G	(Legal Profession, Political Parties, Interest Groups) I	(Family, Education System) L
Functionally Autonomous Community	+	+	+	+
Residential Community, POLITICALLY AUTONOMOUS, ECONOMICALLY DEPENDENT	−	+	+	+
Residential Community, ECONOMICALLY AND POLITICALLY DEPENDENT	−	−	−	+
Residential Community, POLITICALLY DEPENDENT, ECONOMICALLY AUTONOMOUS	+	−	−	+
Non-residential Community, ECONOMICALLY AUTONOMOUS, POLITICALLY DEPENDENT	+	−	−	−
Non-residential Community, ECONOMICALLY AND POLITICALLY AUTONOMOUS	+	+	+	−

A measurement of the goal-attainment function could be the degree to which the political institutions within a community's boundaries make important political decisions. The term "important" is of course relative, given the decreasing amount of autonomy for the individual community in most modern industrial societies. This problem can probably be dealt with most effectively by examining the legal documents establishing the jurisdiction of the local community, or interviewing informed community residents for the same type of information.[11] A general index of community autonomy can then be constructed, based on a list of such functions as taxing property, maintaining a police force, regulating commercial activities, zoning land, and so forth. Once an index is devised, communities can be ranked according to the amount of legal and political autonomy they possess. It is not necessary to investigate *all* perogatives of the local community, but only a sample of those types of decisions which are

---

[11] See the section on issue areas and decisional outcomes in Chapter 3 for a discussion of related problems.

approximately on the same level of importance. To construct a scale for ranking the importance of all functions performed in a community would be a Herculean task, but to establish the *comparative* amount of autonomy of two or more communities is well within the capacities of mortal men. In a comparative situation one need only establish the limited range of decisions that one community performs and another does not. For example, one community will have its own police force, while another will not; one will maintain its own roads and another will not, and so forth. By searching out such borderline cases, it would be possible to develop a detailed index of functions, ordered from most to least important, by which communities could be ranked according to their degree of autonomy. In studying only a limited number of communities, however, the researcher need only determine the *differences* between the communities, and on this basis rank them according to their relative amount of autonomy with respect to goal-attainment.

The degree to which a community performs an important integrative function could be roughly measured by the number of voluntary organizations per resident in the community and the range of activities and number of the local political parties.

If the latent pattern-maintenance and tension-management function is identified largely with the family and its primary territorial nexus as the place of residence, the ratio of the number of community residents to the number of non-residents who hold occupational positions in community institutions would provide a crude index of the intensiveness of the L function. The existence and number of community newspapers and radio and television stations could be used as another indicator. In addition, the density of educational facilities, which could be measured by the ratio of students enrolled in community educational institutions to the number of community residents of school age, could serve as a third measure. Fourth, religious, ethnic, and cultural institutions, generally clustered near residential areas, may be considered an additional type of indicator of the L function. Their density may be measured by the ratio of the number of members .(and/or estimated attendance) in religious, ethnic, and cultural institutions to the size of the community population.

5

COMMUNITY STRUCTURE
AND DECISION-MAKING

☯

This final chapter brings together a number of the ideas already presented and develops a series of propositions relating community structural characteristics, leadership characteristics, decision-making structures, and community outputs. These propositions provide more specific content for the framework of ten sets of variables presented in the introductory chapter.

Chapter 2 emphasized the importance of vertical and horizontal differentiation as general dimensions for classifying stratification systems, and distinguished several types of systems of stratification and corresponding types of decision-making structures. Several possible mechanisms of integration were also presented. Discussing the concept of power, Chapter 3 focused on, among other topics, the distinction between power and decision-making and the importance of various characteristics of resources for exchange and decision-making. Chapter 4 examined the different types of functions that may be performed by communities, and emphasized that while some communities perform all of these functions, others perform a limited number of them. Community decision-making processes, it was suggested, differ according to the degree to which communities perform various functions. Some of the ways in which these various distinctions, typologies, and propositions may be more closely integrated will now be examined.

To this end, a series of statements will be developed, which, although worded as propositions, should be viewed as a set of partially verified hypotheses: empirical investigation has supported some quite consistently; for others there is little such support. To the degree that the statements form an *interrelated* set of propositions, their aggregate plausibility is greater than if each of them is considered in isolation.[1]

---

[1] See Carl G. Hempel, *Fundamentals of Concept Formation in Empirical Science* (Chicago: University of Chicago Press, 1952); Hans L. Zetterberg, *On Theory and Verification in Sociology*, revised edition (Totawa: Bedminster Press, 1963).

Frequently an empirical study will be cited in support of one or more propositions, but the purpose of such citation is in some cases only illustrative; a good deal more comparative empirical work must be completed before it will be possible to substantiate many of the propositions.

The propositions are of several different types. Most state a relationship between two or among three variables. All are *stochastic* (if x, then probably y); none are *deterministic* (if x, then always y); most are *sequential* (if x, then later y), and may be considered causal statements as opposed to simply reported associations; most are *irreversible* (if x, then y; but if y, no conclusion about x); most are *substitutable* (if x, then y; but if z, then also y) as well as *contingent* (if x, then y, but only if z).[2] Several have as their dependent variable the type of community decision-making structure; others may be viewed as intermediate links in a chain that eventually terminates in a statement about the type of community outputs. Most propositions concerning decision-making structures are stated in terms of a centralized-decentralized continuum. This continuum may be conceived of as a series of structural types, such as the four presented in Chapter 2 that range from monolithic to polylithic to pluralistic to mass participation.

FIVE GENERAL FORMULATIONS

Five general formulations of relationships will first be presented from which many subsequent propositions will follow.

Structural Differentiation

Our first general formulation is as follows:

I. *The greater the horizontal and vertical differentiation in a social system, the greater the differentiation between potential elites, the more decentralized the decision-making structure, which without the establishment of integrative mechanisms leads to less coordination between sectors and a lower level of outputs.*

This formulation can be broken down into its various components. The degree of structural differentiation in a community (as well as

---

[2] See Zetterberg, *On Theory and Verification in Sociology*, pp. 11–34 for a discussion of types of propositions and patterns of their interrelationships. On the importance of causal statements in propositional theories, see R. H. Costner and R. K. Leik, "Deductions from Axiomatic Theory," *American Sociological Review*, XXIX (December, 1964), 819–835; and comments by Allen Barton, Patricia R. Ferman, and Jerald Hage in *Administrative Science Quarterly*, XI, No. 1 (June, 1966), 134–156.

other types of social systems) is one of the major variables influencing patterns of decision-making. As horizontal differentiation advances, increasing numbers of separate structures develop in various sectors of a community. These various sectors, each with some quantity of potentially mobilizable resources, serve as alternative bases of power within the community. Through these separate structures, potential elites may be socialized and recruited; these sectoral elites, in turn, may mobilize each of their sectors for participation in decision-making. Of course, the potentialities of the situation may not be realized: separate structures may never develop any elites, or the elites may never be able to effectively mobilize their sectors for community decision-making. Additional variables will be introduced to explain some of the differences among various community sectors that do or do not tend to become mobilized for decision-making. In general, however, greater structural differentiation along horizontal lines will predispose a community toward more decentralized and pluralistic decision-making patterns.

Vertical differentiation also leads to the creation of separate structures which serve as distinct power bases that potentially may be mobilized for decision-making. For a number of reasons, however, the lower sectors of a community are less likely than the upper sectors to become mobilized for decision-making. Correspondingly, vertical differentiation is likely to contribute less toward decentralization of decision-making than is horizontal differentiation, particularly in cases where lower sectors possess severely limited resources.

This decentralization of decision-making may, however, lead to a fragmentation of power as well as to difficulties in coordinating the various subsectors for concerted action. Those mechanisms for integration discussed in Chapter 2 represent the major possibilities for integrating subsectors of a system. Especially important mechanisms in local communities are the governmental bureaucracy, the political party, and community-wide voluntary organizations. If it is argued, other things being equal, that the greater the degree of structural differentiation, the greater the decentralization of decision-making, and the lower the level of community outputs, the qualification is added that the stronger the mechanisms for integration of various community subsectors, the higher the level of outputs.

Leadership Characteristics

To say that the level of outputs will be higher with greater centralization and integration assumes that the values of the leadership favor at least some type of outputs, which it will be impossible to achieve fully in a less centralized and less well integrated system. But it is important to specify the exact nature of the leadership values and characteristics, as in the second general formulation which relates leadership characteristics of communities to types of outputs:

II. *The more centralized the decision-making structure, the more predictable the outputs, and the more the outputs reflect the values and interests of the dominant sectors of the system.*

When a decision-making system is highly decentralized, it is possible to have a large number of different coalitions which may lead to eventual decisions. Correspondingly, it is more difficult to predict the types of outputs likely to emerge from such a system than if it were more centralized, with a relatively small number of actors determining most of the important decisions. A more centralized system tends to reflect more directly the values and desires, beliefs and interests of the dominant actors within the system, and the sector or sectors from which they are drawn.

Functional Orientation

Over time, the relative size of various sectors in a community changes, as does the functional orientation of the community. But at any one time, it is possible to classify a community according to the degree to which it performs various functions—as seen in the last chapter. Knowing the functional orientation of a particular community, certain propositions about its decision-making processes may be deduced. It would appear that

III. *The more important any single function in a community, the more community members from the sector performing that particular function will be active in community decision-making, and the more community decisions will be oriented toward the values and interests of that sector of the community.*

Distribution and Generality of Resources

The more important any particular function in a community, the larger the number of resources that actors within the sector who are oriented toward that function will tend to have at their disposal. While resource availability and functional orientation tend to overlap empirically, it is useful to point out the independent importance of resource availability:

IV. *The larger the number of resources available to a particular sector of a community, the more actors from that sector are likely to become involved in decision-making, and the more decisional outcomes are likely to reflect their values and interests.*

Following the distinction developed in the chapter on power between quantity and generality of resources, it may be further specified:

V. *The higher the exchange value of resources available to a particular sector in a community, the more actors from that sector are likely to become involved in decision-making, and the more decisional outcomes are likely to reflect their values and interests.*

Sectoral Variations

The last three formulations focused more on characteristics of individual sectors of a community than on characteristics of the community as a whole. When focusing on individual sectors, it is useful to consider the amount of structural differentiation within each sector. The first two general formulations may be applied to individual sectors of communities (hence the subscript "s") as well as to the community at large:

I_s. *The greater the horizontal and vertical differentiation within a sector of a community, the greater the differentiation between potential elites within that sector, the more decentralized the decision-making structure, which without the establishment of integrative mechanisms leads to less coordination between elements within the sector and a lower level of outputs.*

II_s. *The more centralized the decision-making structure within a sector of a community, the more predictable and the more reflective the community outputs of the values and interests of that sector of the community.*

Following a few remarks on inputs, these general formulations will be applied to entire communities, focusing first on general demographic variables. Then various sectors of communities will be considered. Following the classification of community functions developed in the last chapter, the structural characteristics of community sectors associated with the functions of adaptation, goal-attainment, integration, and latent pattern-maintenance and tension-management will be examined in turn.

COMMUNITY INPUTS

A relatively simple, but nonetheless important, proposition is:

1. *The higher the level of community inputs, the higher the level of outputs.*

Particularly in societies where local communities have very limited autonomy, and where there is little possibility at the local level of changing the levels of inputs or outputs, the level of community inputs may constitute the most determinative factor of the level of outputs.

But in almost every society there is some possibility for local organization to alter the level of outputs, whether by influencing the level of inputs, or by other means. Federal programs in the United States such as urban renewal and the anti-poverty program are perhaps extreme cases where the level of inputs from outside the community are almost entirely determined by the initiative and organization of local community members. The factors determining the ability of a community to organize itself effectively for increasing inputs are similar to the factors determining the level of outputs. Following Formulation II, for example, it would seem that

2. *The more centralized the decision-making structure, the more predictable the inputs, and the more the inputs and outputs reflect the values and interests of the dominant sector of the community.*

BASIC DEMOGRAPHIC VARIABLES

A fundamental demographic characteristic—closely interrelated with many others—is the size of the population, the number of inhabitants in the community. As size increases, structural differentiation—both horizontal and vertical—is likely to advance,[3] thus precipitating the whole series of changes analyzed in Formulation I.

Specifically,

---

[3] The dynamics of this general process, so basic to many sociological theories, have been analyzed from Durkheim in *The Division of Labor in Society* (New York: The Macmillan Company, 1933; First ed., 1893) to the present. A review of more recent work on this same process is Leo F. Schnore, "Social Morphology and Human Ecology," *The Urban Scene* (New York: The Free Press, 1965), pp. 3–28.

3. *The larger the number of inhabitants in a community, the greater the structural differentiation, the greater the differentiation between potential elites, the more decentralized the decision-making structure, which without the establishment of integrative mechanisms leads to less coordination between sectors and a lower level of outputs.*

Support for the relationship between increasing size and decentralization of decision-making was found by Gilbert, although not by others using smaller numbers of communities.[4] Some evidence for the relationship between size and outputs comes from studies of fluoridation which indicate that larger communities have more difficulties than smaller communities in effecting the decision to fluoridate their water.[5]

For many purposes, however, it is not the absolute size of the population that reinforces the tendencies toward greater structural differentiation and decentralized decision-making, but rather the size of the population that is integrated into local community organizations and active in community affairs. New arrivals in a community, or people planning to leave shortly, are less likely to become involved in community activities than persons who have resided in the community for some time, and, planning to remain there, have an enduring interest in the community. Migration, therefore, is a factor, in addition to size of the population, that may trigger the series of effects itemized in Proposition 3.

The same argument also holds true for other characteristics of the population leading to greater involvement in community affairs. Two such characteristics appear to be income and education, particularly the absolute size of the population that is college educated and enjoys a relatively high income—say over $10,000 per year in the United States. This highly educated and wealthy sector is particularly important for community decision-making, as it tends to be composed of individuals who are much more active in community affairs than somewhat less privileged persons.

Thus, these three factors may be substituted for size in Proposition 3, so that it reads,

4. *The lower the rate of migration, the more wealthy, and the more highly educated the inhabitants of a community, the greater the structural differentiation, the greater the differentiation between potential*

---

[4] See Claire W. Gilbert, "Community Power and Decision-Making: A Quantitative Examination of Previous Research," this volume.

[5] William Gamson and Peter H. Irons, "Community Characteristics and Fluoridation Outcome," *The Journal of Social Issues*, XVII, No. 4, 66–74.

elites, the more decentralized the decision-making structure, which without the establishment of integrative mechanisms leads to less coordination between sectors and a lower level of outputs.

Some support is offered for wealth and education as factors leading to more decentralized decision-making structures and lower levels of outputs by an NORC study of school desegregation [6] as well as by preliminary analysis of the ISVP-NORC joint study of 51 American communities.[7]

An increase in size almost inevitably leads to an increase in structural differentiation. With growth, pressures are also exerted toward the development of certain integrative mechanisms—even though integrative mechanisms do not tend to increase in number and importance at such a rate that over-all coordination can remain constant with increases in size. But what are the pressures which operate toward the development and strengthening of various integrative mechanisms?

First of all, as the number of inhabitants in a community increases, there are certain almost inevitable demands placed on the government for expansion of some of its basic facilities. New migrants demand housing, which leads to increased housing construction; associated with housing are demands for more streets, sidewalks, street lights, sewage and electrical facilities, fire and police protection, and the like. Demands for educational, cultural, and health facilities also increase—schools being the single item of most immediate importance in most cases; pressures for more libraries, museums, other civic services, and hospitals generally develop less rapidly.[8]

In addition to expanding facilities associated with established functions, increasing size tends to lead to proliferation of new functions that local governments must begin to perform. The demand for many of these functions increases by a multiplier effect as larger cities generally become centers for coordination of activities of many smaller surrounding cities and towns. For example, more complex types of transportation systems—

---

[6] Robert L. Crain *et al., School Desegregation in the North* (Chicago: National Opinion Research Center, University of Chicago, 1966). See also Charles R. Adrian, *Governing Urban America* (New York: McGraw-Hill Book Company, 1961), esp. Chapters i and v.

[7] See the concluding article of this volume for a discussion of the ISVP-NORC study.

[8] These assertions are generally supported by the findings of Robert C. Wood, *1400 Governments* (Garden City: Doubleday & Company, 1964); and Oliver P. Williams *et al., Surburban Differences and Metropolitan Policies* (Philadelphia: University of Pennsylvania Press, 1965).

airports, expressways, harbor facilities, subways, bus lines, and the like—must be constructed and administered. Related to the increased transportation of goods is the necessity for the continuing inspection and regulation of certain commodities—especially food products—and the supervision and protection of commodities as they are transferred to warehouses and to distribution channels. More extensive contacts are generally needed with higher level governmental offices, and permanent staffs must be established for maintenance of these relationships. This list of examples could be greatly extended but the essential point is that increasing population implies increasing governmental activities, which in turn bring about an increase in staff of government bureaucracies. With increasing governmental activity and size, autonomy from surrounding institutional structures also tends to increase, and governmental officials become progressively more capable of taking decisions with less dependence on surrounding institutions.

Political parties also tend to expand with population increases as new voters are recruited. Often in the past, particularly in the larger American cities, one of the major functions of political parties was to mediate between the population—particularly the new population—and governmental bureaucracies.[9] This function seems to have been less important for political parties in other countries, and has apparently declined in importance in American cities in more recent years.[10] Nevertheless, particularly in the United States, the larger cities have been the centers for the development of massive political party machines. While it is possible for these machine parties to remain decentralized, in many cases where the governmental structures have remained relatively fragmented—Chicago is the archetypical example [11]—the political party has served as the basic integrative structure for decision-making within the community. The highest elected political official often is a central actor in the coordination of both governmental and party activities, and in some medium-size cities, he

---

[9] The classical discussions, of course, are James Bryce, *The American Commonwealth* (New York: The Macmillan Company, 1912) ; and M. Ostrogorski, *Democracy and the Organization of Political Parties* (Garden City: Doubleday & Company, 1964).

[10] See the article in this volume by Donald B. Rosenthal; Aristide R. Zolberg, *Creating Political Order* (Chicago: Rand McNally & Co., 1966) ; the volume of articles edited by Joseph La Palombara and Myron Weiner, *Political Parties and Political Development* (Princeton: Princeton University Press, 1966) ; and Wallace S. Sayre and Nelson W. Polsby, "American Political Science and the Study of Urbanization," in Philip M. Hauser and Leo F. Schnore, eds., *The Study of Urbanization* (New York: John Wiley & Sons, 1965), pp. 115–156.

[11] Edward C. Banfield, *Political Influence* (Glencoe: The Free Press, 1961).

may play the crucial role in binding together the entire party organization.[12,13]

Overlapping memberships between higher governmental and political party positions facilitate coordination of government and party in decision-making. It has been stressed that the activities of the government and political parties undergo an absolute increase with community size, but it also appears that their decision-making importance increases relative to other community sectors—particularly the commercial-industrial sector.

In this regard it should be noted that commercial and industrial organizations—like governments and political parties—almost always increase in size and number along with the population. But as cities grow beyond two or three hundred thousand, the commercial-industrial sector begins to specialize and diversify to such a degree that integrating the individual firms into a cohesive group for even occasional unified action becomes a far more difficult task than in smaller communities.[14]

On the other hand, the structural constraints against integrating governmental bureaucracies and political parties seem to be far less strong. While governmental bureaucracies may tend to become isolated from one another—a tendency often exaggerated by the constitutions of many American cities [15]—the various local governmental bureaucracies must nevertheless remain at least formally responsible to the local political officials; there is no corresponding integrative structure for the commercial-industrial bureaucracies.

Thus, even though political parties may develop factions, parties are almost universally organized—at least formally—as bureaucracies, and tend to develop a cadre of officials devoted largely to maintenance of the party structure. Community-wide integration therefore becomes far more important for parties, both as an ideological and strategic goal, than it is for commercial or industrial bureaucracies, for without unity a party is unable to perform its primary function: mobilizing electoral support.

Following the analysis of Formulations I_s and II_s, with increased integration any sector of a community is better able to implement its values and interests than if it remains fragmented. As integration of the political

---

[12] See Donald McDonald, *The City* (Santa Barbara: Center for the Study of Democratic Institutions, 1962).

[13] Robert A. Dahl, *Who Governs?* (New Haven: Yale University Press, 1961).

[14] See the article by Claire W. Gilbert, this volume. This tendency would seem to be increasingly marked as the economy of a community is proportionately less socialized.

[15] Donald McDonald, *The City*; Edward C. Banfield, *Big City Politics* (New York: Random House, 1966).

sector tends to increase disproportionately with increases in community population, so does its relative dominance in community decision-making.

Our essential argument regarding population size, integration, and institutional dominance may be summarized as follows:

5. *The larger the number of inhabitants in a community, the more demands for governmental activities, the larger the governmental bureaucracies, the larger the political parties, the more numerous the full-time political roles, and the faster and more direct the implementation of the values and interests of political leaders on community outputs.*

While these last ideas are useful in explaining some of the differences in decisional structure and outputs between larger and smaller communities, it is also interesting to consider the changing relationships between sectors in a community during the actual processes of growth. Without reviewing here the many and diverse factors behind migration, it can be suggested nevertheless that one major factor leading to migration into a community is the expansion of the local employment market.

It would generally seem that sectors most involved in expansion of a community's employment markets (for example, the military in a community with a growing military base, university officials in a community with an expanding university, and the like) will tend to become involved in community decision-making. And, participating more actively in decisions, actors from the expanding sector tend to influence outcomes toward their particular goals.

Thus,

6. *The more rapid the expansion of a particular sector within a community, the greater the involvement of members of that sector in community decision-making, and the more community decisions are oriented toward the values and interests of that sector.*

Since, however, in at least the last decades in most American communities, expansion of industry has provided the primary impetus for job expansion, it is likely that communities with rapidly increasing employment markets will have an especially active industrial sector—more so than in communities with stable employment markets. And if industrial leaders have been particularly active in expanding their activities within the industry, they are likely also to have expanded their activities outside. They are practically forced to cultivate closer contacts with leading com-

munity (particularly political) decision-makers—to obtain building permits, zoning variances, water and electrical facilities, and the like—than
industrial leaders in more static and stable communities. Correspondingly,
during periods of rapid growth in industry, employment markets, and
population, even in communities performing all four basic functions, community decisions are likely to reflect disproportionately the values and
interests of industrialists and others associated with them who favor rapid
community growth.

ADAPTATION: ECONOMIC VARIABLES

Regarding the community sector associated with the adaptation function, Formulation I_s can be applied as follows:

7. *The more diverse the economic structures within a community, the
more decentralized the decision-making structure.*

While variations of this proposition have frequently been advanced in
the literature,[16] there is very little empirical support for it, at least thus
far.[17] However, as economic diversification is generally accompanied by
many other structural changes, it is often difficult to untangle its effects
from those of other factors, for instance, population size.

A second facet of community economic structures of no little importance is the extent of local ownership and local management. Executives of
enterprises owned and managed largely from outside a community are
usually less involved in local decision-making processes than those of
locally owned and managed enterprises. Or if executives from absentee-
owned enterprises do become involved in local public life, they tend to
select activities with minimal possibilities for antagonism and conflict:

8. *The more absentee-owned and managed an enterprise, the more its
executives tend to withdraw from instrumental community activities
and apply their talents to more consummatory activities.*

Local charity, educational, and cultural activities are the archetypical
leisure-time pursuits of executives of large, absentee-owned corporations.[18]

---

[16] See Peter H. Rossi, "Theory, Research and Practice in Community Organiza-
tion," in Charles R. Adrian, ed., *Social Science and Community Action* (East Lansing:
Michigan State University, 1960), pp. 20–21; Morris R. Stein, *The Eclipse of
Community* (Princeton: Princeton University Press, 1960), pp. 94 ff.

[17] No support for this proposition was found by Gilbert (article in this volume);
or by John Walton (article in this volume).

[18] See Peter H. Rossi, "The Organizational Structure of an American Community," in Amitai Etzioni, ed., *Complex Organizations* (New York: Holt, Rinehart &

In many communities—particularly the smaller, functionally unspecialized ones—if a single sector dominates community decision-making, it tends to be the economic sector. Within the economic sector it is the owners or managers of the largest locally owned and managed enterprises who tend to dominate.[19] Consequently, factors leading to a decrease in the (instrumental) community-wide activities of executives of local enterprises tend to lead to a more decentralized decision-making structure. Absentee-ownership is one important factor in the non-involvement of executives from large enterprises, which in turn influences the community decision-making structure:

9. *The greater the number of absentee-owned and managed enterprises in a community, the more decentralized the decision-making structure.*

A number of studies provide various kinds of empirical support for this proposition.[20]

There are many exceptions to the absentee-ownership-executive-withdrawal syndrome, however, and it is useful to consider some possible factors in addition to local ownership predisposing executives toward involvement in (particularly instrumental) activities.[21] One such factor is the ability of the enterprise to leave the community. It seems that

10. *The more immobile an enterprise, the more likely is its management to participate actively in instrumental as well as consummatory community activities.*

Immobility, in turn, may result from two types of factors: inputs and outputs of the enterprise.

11. *The more geographically stationary its inputs, the more immobile the enterprise.*

A stationary input derives from a specific geographical region, and has no readily available alternative—for example, inexpensive labor as in

---

Winston, 1961), pp. 301–312 which discusses the pattern for the United States. How similar the situation is in other countries is a practically unresearched question at this time.

[19] See Gilbert, article in this volume.

[20] Robert O. Schulze, "The Bifurcation in a Satellite City," in Morris Janowitz, ed., *Community Political Systems* (Glencoe: The Free Press, 1961); Robert E. Agger, Daniel Goldrich, and Bert E. Swanson, *The Rulers and the Ruled* (New York: John Wiley & Sons, 1964), pp. 680–682; Walton (this volume).

[21] See Robert E. Lane, *Political Life* (Glencoe: The Free Press, 1959), esp. Chapter XXI; and Lester W. Milbrath, *Political Participation* (Chicago: Rand McNally & Co., 1965), esp. Chapter V for more general discussions.

the American South, or the crucial raw materials of all extraction industries.[22]

An analogous proposition follows for outputs:

12. *The more the outputs from an enterprise are directed toward a fixed and limited geographical region, the lower the mobility of the enterprise.*

One important class of enterprises with very fixed regional outputs is intermediary industries, such as dress designers or specialized law firms, or producers of coke or alfalfa.

If the mobility of an enterprise is low, its managerial representatives will be more concerned with the outcome of basic community decisions, and their possible impacts on the enterprise, than if the location of the enterprise could be changed without undue difficulty. Of course, it is expensive for any sizable enterprise to change its base of operations, regardless of dependence on the local community for inputs or outputs. However, threatening to leave a community (or to curtail local operations) will be taken much more seriously—and serve as a much stronger point for bargaining—when there are few essential inputs or outputs binding an enterprise to the local community. On the other hand, in enterprises which are both relatively mobile and uninfluenced by most local *political* decisions, the policy followed by the management will incline to engagement in local community activities of a more consummatory nature, designed to help develop good will and create a favorable public image for the enterprise in the eyes of the community. Since active involvement of its management in political affairs could lead to possible antagonism toward the enterprise, it is likely that engagement in local political activities will be discouraged.

Labor organizations will be examined now while considering the impact of vertical as well as horizontal differentiation within the economic sector. Labor union organization has been rather neglected in studies of community power and decision-making. Still, the few studies that have examined the community impact of labor organizations offer evidence to suggest that such organizations can perform an important role in balancing

---

[22] However, the character of an industry is often difficult to isolate from its community context. For example, in the United States, extraction and processing industries are more frequently found in smaller communities than manufacturing industries, which more often locate in larger communities. See. O. D. Duncan *et al., Metropolis and Region* (Baltimore: Johns Hopkins University Press, 1960).

the influence of other community groups.[23] Such findings, taken in conjunction with Formulations IV and V, imply an additional proposition:

13. *The better organized and more active the labor movement in the community, the more decentralized the decision-making structure—up to the point where the labor organizations exert such extensive influence that other groups withdraw from community activities.*

Presthus described a community, Riverview, where labor organizations in alliance with other groups had become so dominant in community affairs that the economic and social leaders withdrew altogether from community politics as well as many other local activities. The resulting decision-making structure was decidedly less pluralistic than the one found in Edgewood, a similar community in many ways, but one in which both labor and management groups competed with one another in community affairs.[24] Such a situation suggests that

14. *The lower the involvement of business elites in community activities beyond a certain minimal point, the smaller the number of competing elites and the less decentralized the decision-making structure.*

This proposition may well hold true other things being equal, but it has seldom been reported that the business elite withdraws *completely* from community activities, and other factors accompanying a withdrawal of business elites from politics are likely to minimize the effect of this situation. It appears more probable that business leaders, especially the more cosmopolitan, tend to withdraw from local community *governmental* activities, but still continue to engage in relatively non-political voluntary organizations, social activities, and the like. Moreover, the withdrawal of the business elite from local government generally takes place in association with an over-all decline of crucial decision-making at the community level. There is a change in the type of functions performed at the

---

[23] See C. W. M. Hart, "Industrial Relations Research and Social Theory," *Canadian Journal of Economics and Political Science*, XV (1949), 53–73; James B. McKee, "Organized Labor and Community Decision-Making," (unpublished Ph.D. dissertation, University of Wisconsin, 1953); William H. Form, "Organized Labor's Place in Community Power Structure," *Industrial and Labor Relations Review*, XII (1959), 526–539; Warren L. Sauer and William H. Form, "Organized Labor's Image of Community Power Structure," *Social Forces* (May 1960), Vol. 38, No. 4, pp. 332–341; Form and Miller, *op. cit.*, pp. 572–586; Charles R. Walker, *Steeltown* (New York: Harper, 1950).

[24] See Robert Presthus, *Men at the Top* (New York: Oxford University Press, 1964), esp. Chapters iii and viii.

community level. As more and more decisions—within private and public enterprises, trade unions, and government—are made on non-local levels, instrumental involvement at the local level of actors from all institutional sectors tends to decline.

15. *The smaller the proportion of instrumental decisions made at the local level within private and public enterprises, labor organizations and government, the more consummatory and pacific the general nature of community relations.*

The difficulties involved in operationalizing the variables involved in this proposition may be formidable, but it nevertheless isolates important theoretical elements. One step toward operationalizing the instrumental-consummatory distinction is to consider it in terms of the number of *subsequent* decisions affected by a single decision. An instrumental decision would affect a large number of subsequent decisions; a consummatory decision, a smaller number.[25] A second possibility would be to compare the relative proportion of A and G (generally instrumental) and I and L (generally consummatory) functions using the measures suggested in the last chapter.

The same proposition may be broken down for the various community institutions as well.

16. *The smaller the proportion of instrumental decisions made on the local level within any one institution in the community—public or private enterprises, labor organizations or government—the more consummatory the behavior of the members of that institution with respect to community life.*

Consider, for example, a community where the employees of a large national corporation or members of one of the armed forces residing in the community rely upon the national organization for educational facilities, health insurance, medical care, and recreation facilities, while a second group of other community residents not employed by the national corporation or the armed forces relies on the local community to provide these same facilities.[26] In such a community, those persons not employed by a

---

[25] See the last section of Chapter 3 on other characteristics of decisional outcomes.

[26] For a discussion of a ship-building community dominated by the U.S. Navy during World War II, see Robert J. Havighurst and H. Gerthou Morgan, *The Social History of a War Boom Community* (London: Longmans, Green, 1951).

national organization will tend to participate more actively than the others in instrumental local community affairs.

A crucial variable often related to the extent of economic diversification, the percentage of absentee-ownership, the non-local character of inputs and outputs, the development of labor organizations, and the nationalization of many economic decisions is the degree of industrialization.[27] On a more general level, industrialization, and the accompanying bureaucratization and rationalization of economic life, may be viewed as the central independent economic variable behind these other changes.

It can thus be generalized that

17. *The higher the degree of industrialization in a community, the more decentralized the decision-making structure.*

Because the changes accompanying industrialization do not occur in the same order in all situations, however, it is useful to break down the general process of industrialization into the various components which impinge most directly on community power relationships. In this way it is possible to specify the differential impact of the various individual factors—as in Propositions 7–13—on the changes in community decision-making.

Industrialization leads to increased horizontal differentiation and decreased vertical differentiation—bringing about changes in stratification in the directions indicated in Chapter 2. These general social structural changes in turn bring about a more decentralized decision-making structure—as pointed to in Proposition 17. Industrialization also makes possible an increase in community outputs, but it is necessary to introduce many other variables to determine the actual changes in their rates and types.

GOAL-ATTAINMENT: LEGAL AND POLITICAL STRUCTURAL VARIABLES

Another class of community structures important for balancing the distribution of community power are those related to the performance of the goal-attainment function: they are primarily the legal and political arrangements of the community. (Although political parties and voluntary organizations are involved to some degree in the goal-attainment function,

---

[27] See Stein, *op. cit.*; Schulze, "The Bifurcation in a Satellite City," *op. cit.*; Rogers, "Community Political Systems," in Bert E. Swanson, ed., *Current Trends in Comparative Community Studies* (Kansas City: Community Studies, Inc., 1962), pp. 31–48.

they are more directly related to the problem of integration and are therefore relegated to the next section.)

One legal arrangement of particular importance in structuring the distribution of power within American communities is the non-partisan election. Sixty-one per cent of American communities with more than 5,000 inhabitants presently have non-partisan elections.[28] Although non-partisan electoral procedures to date have been largely neglected by students of community power, there is evidence suggesting that non-partisanship tends to favor the better organized (and wealthier) segments of the community population over the amorphous (and less well-to-do) segments.[29] At least three factors seem to offer support for this assertion.

First, in partisan elections the issues and candidates will tend to be more clearly distinguished from one another because of candidates' ties with political parties, which, in turn, are characterized by relatively enduring ideological differences and repose on fairly distinct social bases. Voting turnout will be higher than if the issues at stake and the candidates' positions on these issues remain vague and imprecise to the majority of the electorate. Since lower over-all rates of voter turnout characterize non-partisan elections, and since, moreover, the privileged social strata need less inducement than the poorer strata to bring them to the polls, the candidates supported by the active and better organized middle-classes will tend to fare proportionately better in non-partisan elections. Turnout may be further curtailed by scheduling local elections at different times from regional or national elections. The result is still greater autonomy of the local community from regional and national ideologies and lines of cleavage.

Second, candidates for office under non-partisan elections are more likely to depend on business organizations and wealthy private individuals

---

[28] See Edward C. Banfield and James Q. Wilson, *City Politics* (Cambridge: Harvard University Press and M.I.T. Press, 1963), p. 51.

[29] See Banfield and Wilson, *City Politics,* Chapter xii, and Seymour Martin Lipset, "Introduction: Ostrogorski and the Analytic Approach to the Comparative Study of Political Parties," in M. Ostrogorski, *Democracy and the Organization of Political Parties* (Garden City: Doubleday & Company, 1964), pp. ix-xvii, for discussions of the effects of non-partisanship. Frank M. Steward offers a history of the National Municipal League, a group that was important in bringing about the acceptance of non-partisan elections in American communities in the past half-century, in *A Half Century of Municipal Reform* (Berkeley and Los Angeles: University of California Press, 1950). See also Richard Hofstadter, *The Age of Reform* (New York: Alfred A. Knopf, 1955), esp. Chapter iv.

Schattschneider's discussion of the "socialization" of political issues is also directly relevant to non-partisanship. See E. E. Schattschneider, *The Semi-Sovereign People* (New York: Holt, Rinehart & Winston, 1960).

for campaign contributions than if it were possible to derive financial support from a political party.

Third, in the absence of a party label distinguishing candidates from one another when the voter actually enters the voting booth, pre-election day information about the individual candidates assumes a more important role than in partisan elections. And since the means of communication are most often disproportionately controlled by the wealthier segments of the population, the poorer strata are disadvantaged.

For these reasons and others, one would expect conservative candidates to fare better in non-partisan elections than in partisan elections, an assertion supported by the available empirical evidence. For example, in twenty-six California communities of over 50,000 inhabitants, it was found that 80 per cent of the mayors and 68 per cent of the city councilmen were registered Republicans although the great majority of the registered voters in these same communities were Democrats.[30]

This brief review of the effects of non-partisanship suggests the following proposition:

18. *The larger the number of governmental statuses in a community filled according to non-partisan procedures, the more dominant are the wealthy in decision-making.*

Another proposition relating governmental structure to the distribution of community power that can be derived from the general Formulations about structural differentiation (I) and resources (IV), is

19. *The larger the number of full-time non-elected officials in the community government, the more pluralistic the community (up to a certain point).*

Several examples of (generally small) communities have been reported where the political institutions are dominated by individuals whose primary occupation is non-political, for example, business or one of the professions.[31] Such persons fill the vacuum created by the absence of any

---

[30] Eugene Lee, *The Politics of Nonpartisanship* (Berkeley: University of California Press, 1960), pp. 56–57.

[31] See, for example, Arthur J. Vidich and Joseph Benseman, *Small Town in Mass Society* (Princeton: Princeton University Press, 1958) and Oliver P. Williams and Charles R. Adrian, *Four Cities* (Philadelphia: University of Pennsylvania Press, 1963). Both works offer perceptive analyses of the ideological support for weak governmental institutions found in American political mythology.

autonomous political institutions and the full-time occupational roles associated with them in larger communities where structural differentiation is further advanced. If, for the performance of many central tasks, a community government must rely upon an elite group of citizens acting solely in a voluntary capacity, it will be more susceptible to outside domination than if it had an autonomous core of full-time officials whose principal function was to serve the entire community. Demands from unrepresented groups are more likely to be heard by a community official whose specific job it is to listen to such grievances than by "leading citizens" who must be approached directly.

Because the communities whose decision-making structures have been studied to date have been in Western non-socialist countries,[32] it has frequently been a latent assumption that communities tend to be dominated by economic elites. A strong and autonomous set of governmental institutions has consequently been perceived as a means of forestalling economic domination of local communities. Consideration of a hypothetical socialist community, however, where the political institutions could dominate community affairs (unless there were some sort of countervailing power) should serve as a warning to the limitations of Proposition 19. The next section will take up a general model of the interrelationships of diverse community institutions that should lead to an optimally democratic situation.

INTEGRATION: POLITICAL PARTIES AND VOLUNTARY ORGANIZATIONS

Community integrative mechanisms are heavily influenced by the types of segmented elements within a community that must be integrated. In addition to the differentiation of economic and governmental structures, one important factor leading to segmentation is the social diversity of the general population—diversity being understood as variation among community residents in terms of such fundamental characteristics as ethnicity,

See also Floyd Hunter, Ruth C. Schaffer, and Cecil G. Sheps, *Community Organization: Action and Inaction* (Chapel Hill: University of North Carolina Press, 1956), esp. Chapters iii, iv, vii, and xiii; and Harry Scoble, "Leadership Hierarchies and Political Issues in a New England Town," in Janowitz, ed., *Community Political Systems,* pp. 117–145.

[32] This deficiency is being corrected by work undertaken in the framework of the International Studies of Values in Politics. An early report is Krzysztof Ostrowski and Adam Przeworski, eds., *Local Political System in Poland* (Warsaw: Institute of Philosophy and Sociology, May 1965). The writer and William Kornblum are also presently undertaking work on Yugoslav community decision-making with some of the Yugoslav participants in ISVP.

national background of immigrants, religion, occupation, income, education, and the like. A first crude generalization is

20. *The larger the number of inhabitants in a community, the more socially heterogeneous is its population.*

But then,

21. *The more heterogeneous a community's population, the greater the possibilities for interlocking memberships and cross-cutting status-sets.*[33]

And

22. *The greater the density of cross-cutting status-sets, the more controlled are community conflicts.*

Coleman, among others, has developed this last idea at some length.[34] Further relationships between conflict and decision-making processes will be taken up shortly.

While it is true that in larger and more heterogeneous communities there are more possibilities for cross-cutting status-sets (Proposition 21), nevertheless it appears, paradoxically, that

23. *The larger the number of inhabitants in a community, the less dense the cross-cutting status-sets.*

---

[33] A cross-cutting status-set refers to a social structural situation where two or more persons occupy one or more *common* statuses, but they include a number of *differing* statuses in their status-sets as well. The cross-cutting status-set is thus a specifically *sociological* concept that is not to be confused with the closely related social psychological concept of cross pressure.

The cross-cutting status-set must also be distinguished from the narrower concept of interlocking membership. An interlocking membership refers only to common *organizational* statuses and neglects *non-organizational* statuses that may be even more important than many organizational ones—for example, age, sex, ethnic and religious statuses.

The concept of cross-cutting status-set has been developed by Professor Robert K. Merton in lectures at Columbia University. It grows out of his analysis of status-sets that may be found in *Social Theory and Social Structure* (Glencoe: The Free Press, 1957), pp. 368–386. See Paul F. Lazarsfeld, Bernard Berelson, and Hazel Gaudet, *The People's Choice* (New York: Columbia University Press, 1944), pp. 52–64 for a classic analysis of cross pressures on voting behavior, and James S. Coleman, *Community Conflict* (Glencoe: The Free Press, 1957), for a discussion of the effect of cross pressures on community conflict.

[34] Coleman, *Community Conflict.*

This decline in cross-cutting status-sets appears to derive from the greater social homogeneity of smaller, closer-knit communities, where, far more than in larger communities, persons are forced into contact with a larger number of persons having social backgrounds different from their own. In larger communities, where there are more persons of any given social background, it is easier for people of like tastes and orientation to interact more exclusively with one another.[35] As a result of interaction, such persons may form an equal or a proportionately larger number of voluntary organizations than will be formed in a smaller community, but the organizations in the larger community will less frequently overlap the basic lines of social cleavage. The density of cross-cutting status-sets thus tends to be lower than in smaller communities.

The density and extensiveness of cross-cutting status-sets are structured by two factors in addition to the size of the community (although both seem to be frequently associated with size):

24. *The fewer the fundamental lines of cleavage within the community (for example, ethnic, national, economic, and the like) the more extensive the cross-cutting status-sets.*

And,

25. *The stronger the intra-community ties of community residents, the more extensive the cross-cutting status-sets.*

These ideas can be related to more general aspects of decision-making. An idea basic to the general argument—a central element of Formulation I—is that the greater the structural support for a plurality of competing elites in a community, the more decentralized the decision-making structure. But structural support may derive from many possible sources. One is social heterogeneity of the population, which can lead to horizontal and vertical differentiation of community organizations, and to the subsequent effects implied by advanced differentiation.

But, although social heterogeneity can serve as *one type* of structural support for competing elites, two qualifications should be emphasized. The first is that there are a large number of latent issues and areas of potential conflict ready to be mobilized at almost any time in almost any community; social heterogeneity of the population is far from being the only basis for political differences. In other words, political cleavages need not reflect

---

[35] This general process was analyzed with no little perspicacity by Gabriel Tarde. See Terry N. Clark, ed., *Gabriel Tarde* (Chicago: University of Chicago Press, forthcoming, 1968).

only social cleavages. The political career of Mayor Lee as documented by Dahl demonstrates this qualification rather well. From the turn of the century into the 1950's, New Haven politics were largely ethnic politics. Candidates were assessed by political machines and the electorate alike largely in terms of being Irish, Jewish, Italian, Old Yankee, or Negro. Slates were balanced to a large degree so as to reflect the nationality distribution of the New Haven population.

By 1950, however, the previously cohesive and distinct ethnic groups had become relatively assimilated—economically, socially, and politically. Richard C. Lee took advantage of this situation in his campaigns during the 1950's by emphasizing the collective benefits that would accrue to all citizens of New Haven if the extensive urban renewal program he supported were implemented. Lee's victory marked a deep shift in New Haven political alignments.[36]

A second point not to be neglected is that the minimal *amount* of structural support necessary for an individual or group of citizens to challenge effectively the policies of the community leadership in many cases need not be very large, especially in smaller communities. In a homogeneous middle-class suburb, for example, a single group of active citizens and a single party may dominate community politics and general community affairs year after year. It is possible, however, that a dynamic housewife could mobilize enough support in a relatively short amount of time to alter significantly the policy of the community leadership in a given area, or even to displace several established leaders from office.

In one case we studied in Waukegan, Illinois, a single housewife who was dissatisfied with the racial imbalances resulting from the community school district boundaries undertook to change the situation singlehandedly. She could gain no sympathetic attention from any school board officers or elected political officials, and only two or three other citizens, none of them wealthy or generally influential, offered her support in the matter. But after continual rebuffs for three years from community citizens and officials, she secured the support of the American Civil Liberties Union. The case was taken to the courts, and is pending action in the Illinois Supreme Court at the present time; it could have profound consequences for school districting throughout the state of Illinois.[37]

---

[36] See Dahl, *Who Governs?*, esp. pp. 32–61. A somewhat different interpretation is offered by Raymond E. Wolfinger, in "The Development and Persistence of Ethnic Voting," *American Political Science Review*, LIX (1965), 896–908.

[37] This case is analyzed in Terry N. Clark and James W. Wagner, Jr., "Community Values, Decision-Making, and Outputs: Configurations of Inactiveness," *International Studies of Values in Politics*, USA paper No. 83, April 1967.

In Alice H. Clark, "A Local School Board Election," a case is reported where a

If individual citizens can potentially exert such extensive influence on the community status quo, it seems inappropriate to term the situation monolithic or undemocratic, even if there is not active competition among candidates at every election.

The crucial variable for the maintenance of a pluralistic system, from this point of view, then, is some type of structural support for competing elites. The simple factor of size in a small enough community (in an industrial, democratic society) may lower what might be termed the "influence threshold" [38] to a point where almost any active and interested citizen could exert a substantial amount of influence and perhaps even become entrenched in the community decision-making structure.[39]

In larger communities, however, a pluralistic decision-making structure is likely to emerge only if there is more solid and permanent structural support for a plurality of competing elites. Such support can be provided, for example, by ethnic, national, linguistic, sub-regional, or economic solidarity. If within the community there are dividing lines in terms of the basic demographic characteristics of the population or their positions in the economic system, these lines of cleavage can be articulated with the political system through various integrative structures, such as voluntary organizations or political parties, performing what Almond has termed the functions of interest articulation and interest aggregation.[40]

Thus such factors as heterogeneity of the population along basic demographic lines or diversity of economic structures can provide a structural context favorable to a pluralistic community decision-making structure, but in themselves are by no means determinative. From this point of

---

single housewife was able to dislodge the party-supported candidate and secure a position on the Board of Education in a town of 60,000 simply by mobilizing the resources available to most other individual residents of the community.

[38] See Chapter 3 for a consideration of the importance of various resources at different stages of a decision that may help bridge the "influence threshold."

[39] For this reason it may be necessary to qualify Proposition 3. Size may be related to the influence threshold of a community in such a way that the relationship between the number of inhabitants and the power structure is in reality *curvilinear*. Thus, a monolithic power structure may be most characteristic of medium-small communities instead of very small communities. At either extreme of the size continuum—in relatively large and relatively small communities—the factor of size will exert a tendency in the opposite direction, that is, toward a pluralistic power structure. Precisely how small a "medium-small" community must be before the factor of size exerts an influence in a pluralistic direction is a question that can only be answered after further investigation. Some first steps in this direction have been taken by Ruth Moser in an unpublished master's essay being completed with the writer at the University of Chicago.

[40] See Gabriel A. Almond, "A Functional Approach to Comparative Politics," in Gabriel A. Almond and James S. Coleman, *The Politics of Developing Areas* (Princeton: Princeton University Press, 1960), pp. 3–64.

view, integrative structures can be seen as intervening variables between the more fundamental community structures (demographic, economic, governmental) and the type of decision-making structure. Two propositions on this level which follow from these considerations are the following:

26. *The greater the density of voluntary organizations in the community, the more decentralized the decision-making structure.*

27. *The greater the number of effective competing political parties (or factions within a single party in a one-party community), the more decentralized the decision-making structure.*

At this point, it is appropriate to comment, especially apropos of Proposition 27, that pluralism, when carried to extremes, can lead to anarchy. If the dependent variable in these propositions were, for example, "responsible democratic government," Proposition 27 might be rephrased with just *two* parties or factions as the ideal number.[41]

The analysis relating to competing elites as developed thus far highlights one important aspect of the functional contributions of integrative institutions to the maintenance of a pluralistic decision-making structure. The aspect emphasized heretofore has been the necessity of the existence of *different* competing elite groups within the community. A second vital aspect of the problem, however, is that in order for effective competition to be maintained, there must be a certain minimal consensus among the competing groups concerning the "rules of the game"—tolerance of opposition groups, and the like. If this minimal consensus among various community groups does not exist, as soon as one group is able to seize control of certain community institutions, it may seek to dominate others by expanding its influence through illegitimate means. In such a situation, the community would become fragmented into warring groups so hostile to one another that application of the term pluralistic as commonly used would no longer be appropriate—no longer would there be fair competition, but instead, violent conflict.

It is this second general theme concerning the necessity of restraining

---

[41] See Seymour Martin Lipset, "Party Systems and the Representation of Social Groups," *European Journal of Sociology*, I, No. 1 (1960), 50–85 (reprinted with slight modification in Lipset, *The First New Nation* [New York: Basic Books, 1963], pp. 286–317), for an especially cogent and concise review of the classic discussions on the functional consequences of social structural cleavages, electoral arrangements, and party systems for the maintenance of democratic government.

conflict between integrative structures that underlies discussions on rates of citizen participation, cross-cutting status-sets, and the dampening of community conflicts.

Examining first citizen participation, it would appear that

28. *The greater the participation of community members in political parties and voluntary organizations, the greater their ego-involvement in community life.*

29. *The greater the ego-involvement in community life, the more complete the internalization of community values, norms, and traditions.*[42]

30. *The more complete the internalization by community members of community values, norms, and traditions, the less likely is violent community conflict to occur.*

Most previous discussions of the dampening of community conflict by such factors as high rates of citizen participation and the high density of cross-cutting status-sets have been phrased so as to apply to the *entire* population of the community.[43] Such analysis is based on an unrealistic view of most communities. It is more likely that only a small *minority* of the population (in most contemporary democratic societies) ever becomes sufficiently involved in any community issue to do more than vote or perhaps attend a few meetings a year.

Empirical studies of voting behavior have demonstrated the extensive apathy characterizing the vast majority of American voters.[44] According to the classical model of an ideal democracy, such widespread apathy is to be deplored. In actual practice, however, the apathetic citizen performs an

---

[42] Note that this refers to participation over *a certain minimal period of time.* Ego-involvement cannot be assumed to result from interaction until the relationships have become somewhat established. See George C. Homans, *The Human Group* (New York: Harcourt, Brace, 1951) for discussion of the development of social relationships through interaction.

Coleman (*Community Conflict*), among others, has emphasized the disintegrating effects of short-term and active participation of normally uninvolved individuals in community affairs.

[43] See Coleman, *Community Conflict*, and Rossi, "Power and Community Structure," this volume.

[44] See Lazarsfeld, Berelson, and Gaudet, *The People's Choice*; Bernard Berelson, Paul F. Lazarsfeld, and William N. McPhee, *Voting* (Chicago: University of Chicago Press, 1954) ; and Angus Campbell, Gerald Gurin, and Warren E. Miller, *The Voter Decides* (Evanston: Row, Peterson & Company, 1954).

important function for the maintenance of a democratic system: he changes his position and voting preference with greater facility than the actively involved citizen who is generally far more inflexible.[45]

These findings imply that a more realistic model of the ideal democratic system would consist of an elite of citizens whose rate of participation in community activities is relatively high, whose ego-involvement is great, and whose internalization of community-wide values, norms, and traditions is extensive. This elite ideally would be characterized by a network of cross-cutting status-sets sufficiently dense to transcend *to some degree* the potential lines of fundamental community cleavage: that is, ethnic, national, religious, and economic divisions. On the other hand, *only a minority* of citizens is deeply involved in community affairs; the majority of others is relatively uninvolved, has unfirm opinions on most community issues, and is capable of being persuaded in one direction or another without undue effort on the part of the more active citizens. Thus, according to this model of the ideal democratic community, the apathetic members are just as important as the active ones.

LATENT PATTERN-MAINTENANCE AND TENSION-MANAGEMENT: CULTURAL AND EDUCATIONAL VARIABLES

Using the term culture to refer to the transmitted patterns of values, norms, and ideas (as distinct from social structure which refers to the system of interaction),[46] two variables can be distinguished on a cultural level which have important consequences for the structuring of community decision-making.

Proposition 15, concerning the decline of instrumental decisions in communities, analyzed the consequences of the general process of structural-functional differentiation according to a widely utilized theoretical

---

[45] Almond and Verba's recent comparative study of the United States, Great Britain, Germany, Italy, and Mexico has pointed to the importance of participation for the maintenance of a democratic political system. Still, in their concentration on the differences in "political culture" *among* the five countries, the authors seem in general to have neglected the importance of the differences *within* single countries. In particular, the notion of the positive function of apathy for the maintenance of a flexible democratic system that has emerged from earlier empirical studies has been almost completely neglected. See Gabriel A. Almond and Sidney Verba, *The Civic Culture* (Princeton: Princeton University Press, 1963).

[46] See A. L. Kroeber and Talcott Parsons, "The Concept of Culture and of Social Systems," *American Sociological Review*, XXIII (1958), 582–583.

perspective.[47] In focusing on the process of structural differentiation, one may observe a remarkable similarity in the dynamics of change associated with industrialization for two social systems infrequently classified together: the family and the community.[48] Both institutions have been affected in such a way that they tend to perform certain functions only at a reduced level: specifically those of adaptation, goal-attainment, and integration, to use Parsons' categories. At the same time, their relative (and perhaps absolute) importance in performing the latent pattern-maintenance and tension-management function has greatly increased. Social structural as well as cultural modifications are closely interwoven and generally tend to develop together. Still, in certain cases changes develop more rapidly in one of these two areas, and a disjunction between the two results. This general situation has been identified by social scientists in a number of different substantive areas; [49] Ogburn has termed one manifestation of this general phenomenon "cultural lag." [50]

It is possible to consider the paternalistic value system of *noblesse oblige* characteristic of community elites in certain areas as a cultural value that is lagging behind the broad structural changes associated with the general processes of centralization and bureaucratization taking place in most modern industrial societies. This value system has had an influence on certain elite groups, especially in small, rural, isolated communities (as are frequently found in the American South). It helps explain the continual involvement of industrial managers of such communities in local politics and other community activities even when their enterprises have become absentee-owned and the majority of important decisions are no longer made on the community level.[51] Analyzing the paternalistic value system as an independent variable, it can be suggested that

---

[47] For two recent theoretical statements of the process of structural-functional differentiation, see Talcott Parsons and Neil J. Smelser, *Economy and Society* (Glencoe: The Free Press, 1956) ; and Talcott Parsons, "Some Considerations on the Theory of Social Change," *Rural Sociology*, XXVI (1961), 219–239, reprinted in Amitai Etzioni and Eva Etzioni, eds., *Social Change* (New York: Basic Books, 1964), pp. 83–97.

[48] The process of structural-functional differentiation as it affected the family under the impact of industrialization is analyzed in Neil J. Smelser, *Social Change in Industrial Revolution* (Chicago: University of Chicago Press, 1959), esp. pp. 180–312.

[49] Robert K. Merton in "Social Structure and Anomie," *Social Theory and Social Structure*, pp. 131–160, essentially analyzes the consequences of a disjunction between culture and social structure.

[50] William F. Ogburn, *Social Change* (New York: The Viking Press, 1922).

[51] Bert E. Swanson, Robert E. Agger, and Daniel Goldrich, "Political Influence Structure," in Bert E. Swanson, ed., *Current Trends in Comparative Studies*, pp. 81–88, for another discussion of the influence of paternalistic values.

31. *The more paternalistic the value system of elite groups in a community, the greater their involvement in community affairs.*

To a certain degree, the paternalistic value system is the antithesis of the pluralistic value system. Considering the pluralistic value system in relation to decision-making, one would expect that

32. *The more pluralistic the value system of members of the community, the more pluralistic the decision-making structure.*

In countries where general democratic values are inculcated in students through the educational system, the degree of internalization of the pluralistic value system will tend to be positively associated with the level of education of the members of the community, implying that

33. *The higher the educational level of community residents, the more pluralistic the decision-making structure.*

The isolation of the pluralistic value system from other values and skills generally associated with education doubtless poses a problem for the empirical testing of this proposition. Cross-national comparison of countries which differ in their degree of emphasis on the democratic value system in educational institutions can, however, provide a possible test.[52]

Another community institution that may play an important role in creating and reinforcing cultural patterns is the newspaper, particularly the local or neighborhood newspaper. Although the limits within which a newspaper can effectively exert influence are certainly restricted by the broader cultural values shared by community members, within these limits—and most community decisions fall inside these limits—the newspaper may indeed exercise a good deal of influence. Virtually no systematic comparative research has been done on newspapers as independent influences in community decision-making, but it can be suggested that—once again, of course, *ceteris paribus*:

34. *If the values represented by community newspapers fall within the general limits of community members' values, the more newspapers favor a particular goal, the more that goal will become supported by members of the community.*

---

[52] See Almond and Verba, *The Civic Culture*, for some data bearing on this matter.

One dimension of the "closeness" of a newspaper's values to those of community residents is the degree to which it focuses on community activities.

35. *The more a newspaper deals with issues of importance to its readers, the greater its potential influence.*

Correspondingly it would be expected that a large-circulation national newspaper, or a newspaper from a distant city, would exercise less influence in local community decision-making than a smaller, more locally oriented newspaper.

A newspaper's influence also seems to depend on the availability of alternative channels of organization and communication. In a community with a high concentration of voluntary organizations, and a good deal of face-to-face interaction and frequent informal communication among community members, a newspaper appears to be in a weaker position than where there are fewer competing alternatives. Thus,

36. *The smaller the number of communication channels outside a newspaper in a community (including other mass communication media),*[53] *the greater the influence of the newspaper.*

Particularly in small and medium-sized communities (under 200,000), the owner or editor of the newspaper is often a successful local businessman with very strong interests in community decision-making. He may well have purchased the newspaper to further his general interests in the community. And he is likely to be involved in extensive and numerous personal contacts with leading community decision-makers. In such cases, it may be difficult to disentangle the impact of the newspaper as an impersonal channel of communication from the personal role played by the owner or editor in a particular decision.[54]

In addition to considering how a newspaper may complement the

---

[53] Although these propositions refer only to newspapers, because in the past they represented the most important form of local mass media, in each case other mass media—radio or television—may be substituted for newspapers without changing the substance of the argument.

[54] The owner-editor of the newspaper was an extremely influential individual in two American communities that were the subject of intensive case studies by the present writer and his associates. See Clark and Wagner, "Community Values, Decision-Making, and Outputs: Configurations of Inactiveness"; and Terry N. Clark

other resources of powerful community actors, there is at least one way in which newspapers may lead to certain (generally) unanticipated consequences. If a newspaper is to attack its enemies, it generally must at least make them known to its readership, even if in a degrading presentation. But even degrading an individual or organization that deviates from the newspaper's values and norms makes known the existence of this "deviant" to others in the community. And making potential deviants aware that deviants are in fact to be found within the community leads to, if not the actual organization of deviant groups, at least the knowledge that there exist within the community others who are actively deviating from the newspaper's values and norms. Thus, newspapers may support the formation of numerous groups with varying orientations, so that it can be suggested that

37. *The larger the number of newspapers, and the greater their circulation, the more active are contrasting and competing sectors within the community, and the more decentralized the decision-making structure.*[55]

Another cultural variable that influences decision-making is the prestige hierarchy of social statuses within a given community. If, for example, a community judges its clergymen and teachers to be as important as its businessmen, it is likely that clergymen and teachers will play a more significant role in community affairs than if they are considered in the same category as skilled workers.[56]

and William Kornblum, "Community Values, Decision-Making, and Outputs: Configurations of Innovation and Activeness," *International Studies of Values in Politics*, USA paper No. 84, April 1967.

Preliminary results from the ISVP-NORC study of 51 American communities also show that newspapers, and owners and editors of newspapers, are among the most frequently named influential community actors in addition to (but often instead of) the mayor and his political party.

[55] Gabriel Tarde offered a number of propositions about newspapers and their publics that overlap to some extent with this one. See Clark, *Gabriel Tarde*.

[56] It is significant that it has been in cross-national (and cross-cultural) investigations of community power that the occupational prestige structure has been suggested as an important determinant of the distribution of community power. See Delbert C. Miller, "Industry and Community Power Structure: A Comparative Study of an American and an English City," *American Sociological Review*, XXIII (1958), 9–15.

In studies comparing the power structures of Mexican communities and communities in the United States, it has been found that more public officials are likely to be cited as key influentials in the former than in the latter. See William H. From and William V. D'Antonio, "Integration and Cleavage among Community Influentials in Two Border Cities," *American Sociological Review*, XXIV (1959), 804–814; and Orrin E. Klapp and L. Vincent Padgett, "Power Structure and Decision-Making in a Mexican Border City," *American Journal of Sociology*, LXV (1959), 400–406.

Thus, our last proposition,

38. *The higher the prestige of a social status, the more likely are its occupants to rank high in the community decision-making structure.*

CONCLUSION

As has been made clear at several points, the extent to which the above statements are based on firm empirical ground varies a great deal from one proposition to the next. More empirical research needs to be undertaken to elaborate some of the factors involved in the many propositions, and, particularly, to evaluate for different types of communities in different social systems, the relative importance of the many variables contained in the propositions.

As was pointed out in Chapter 1, much empirical work in the past focused on a somewhat limited range of variables, making it particularly difficult to generalize meaningfully about the importance of certain community characteristics. But this situation is changing rapidly. A large number of empirical studies of communities and community decision-making are presently being undertaken throughout the world, which, in the next five years should permit the systematic testing, verification, rejection, and reformulation of propositions such as these.

A major problem which emerges with regard to these larger, more ambitious comparative studies, is the matter of comparability. Can the comparative studies presently in progress be conducted in such a way that they, in turn, will be sufficiently comparable with each other that researchers will be able to test generalizations meaningfully by examining results from more than one study? These two related questions—what types of data can and should be collected in comparative studies? and, how can they be collected in such a way as to maximize comparability?—are the subject of the concluding article of this volume.

SUMMARY LIST OF FORMULATIONS
AND PROPOSITIONS

General Formulations

I. The greater the horizontal and vertical differentiation in a social system, the greater the differentiation between potential elites, the more decentralized the decision-making structure, which without the establishment of integrative mechanisms leads to less coordination between sectors and a lower level of outputs.

II. The more centralized the decision-making structure, the more predictable the outputs, and the more the outputs reflect the values and interests of the dominant sectors of the system.

III. The more important any single function in a community, the more community members from the sector performing that particular function will be active in community decision-making, and the more community decisions will be oriented toward the values and interests of that sector of the community.

IV. The larger the number of resources available to a particular sector of a community, the more actors from that sector are likely to become involved in decision-making, and the more decisional outcomes are likely to reflect their values and interests.

V. The higher the exchange value of resources available to a particular sector in a community, the more actors from that sector are likely to become involved in decision-making, and the more decisional outcomes are likely to reflect their values and interests.

I_s. The greater the horizontal and vertical differentiation within a sector of a community, the greater the differentiation between potential elites within that sector, the more decentralized the decision-making structure, which without the establishment of integrative mechanisms leads to less coordination between elements within the sector and a lower level of outputs.

II_s. The more centralized the decision-making structure within a sector of a community, the more predictable and the more reflective the community outputs of the values and interests of that sector of the community.

Propositions

1. The higher the level of community inputs, the higher the level of outputs.

2. The more centralized the decision-making structure, the more predictable the inputs, and the more the inputs and outputs reflect the values and interests of the dominant sector of the community.

3. The larger the number of inhabitants in a community, the greater the structural differentiation, the greater the differentiation between potential elites, the more decentralized the decision-making structure, which without the establishment of integrative mechanisms leads to less coordination between sectors and a lower level of outputs.

4. The lower the rate of migration, the more wealthy, and the more highly educated the inhabitants of a community, the greater the structural differentiation, the greater the differentiation between potential elites, the

more decentralized the decision-making structure, which without the establishment of integrative mechanisms leads to less coordination between sectors and a lower level of outputs.

5. The larger the number of inhabitants in a community, the more demands for governmental activities, the larger the governmental bureaucracies, the larger the political parties, the more numerous the full-time political roles, and the faster and more direct the implementation of the values and interests of political leaders on community outputs.

6. The more rapid the expansion of a particular sector within a community, the greater the involvement of members of that sector in community decision-making, and the more community decisions are oriented toward the values and interests of that sector.

7. The more diverse the economic structures within a community, the more decentralized the decision-making structure.

8. The more absentee-owned and managed an enterprise, the more its executives tend to withdraw from instrumental community activities and apply their talents to more consummatory activities.

9. The greater the number of absentee-owned and managed enterprises in a community, the more decentralized the decision-making structure.

10. The more immobile an enterprise, the more likely is its management to participate actively in instrumental as well as consummatory community activities.

11. The more geographically stationary its inputs, the more immobile the enterprise.

12. The more the outputs from an enterprise are directed toward a fixed and limited geographical region, the lower the mobility of the enterprise.

13. The better organized and more active the labor movement in the community, the more decentralized the decision-making structure—up to the point where the labor organizations exert such extensive influence that other groups withdraw from community activities.

14. The lower the involvement of business elites in community activities beyond a certain minimal point, the smaller the number of competing elites and the less decentralized the decision-making structure.

15. The smaller the proportion of instrumental decisions made at the local level within private and public enterprises, labor organizations and government, the more consummatory and pacific the general nature of community relations.

16. The smaller the proportion of instrumental decisions made on the local level within any one institution in the community—public or private

enterprises, labor organizations or government—the more consummatory the behavior of the members of that institution with respect to community life.

17. The higher the degree of industrialization in a community, the more decentralized the decision-making structure.

18. The larger the number of governmental statuses in a community filled according to non-partisan procedures, the more dominant are the wealthy in decision-making.

19. The larger the number of full-time non-elected officials in the community government, the more pluralistic the community (up to a certain point).

20. The larger the number of inhabitants in a community, the more socially heterogeneous is its population.

21. The more heterogeneous a community's population, the greater the possibilities for interlocking memberships and cross-cutting status-sets.

22. The greater the density of cross-cutting status-sets, the more controlled are community conflicts.

23. The larger the number of inhabitants in a community, the less dense the cross-cutting status-sets.

24. The fewer the fundamental lines of cleavage within the community (for example, ethnic, national, economic, and the like) the more extensive the cross-cutting status-sets.

25. The stronger the intra-community ties of community residents, the more extensive the cross-cutting status-sets.

26. The greater the density of voluntary organizations in the community, the more decentralized the decision-making structure.

27. The greater the number of effective competing political parties (or factions within a single party in a one-party community), the more decentralized the decision-making structure.

28. The greater the participation of community members in political parties and voluntary organizations, the greater their ego-involvement in community life.

29. The greater the ego-involvement in community life, the more complete the internalization of community values, norms, and traditions.

30. The more complete the internalization by community members of community values, norms and traditions, the less likely is violent community conflict to occur.

31. The more paternalistic the value system of elite groups in a community, the greater their involvement in community affairs.

32. The more pluralistic the value system of members of the community, the more pluralistic the decision-making structure.

33. The higher the educational level of community residents, the more pluralistic the decision-making structure.

34. If the values represented by community newspapers fall within the general limits of community members' values, the more newspapers favor a particular goal, the more that goal will become supported by members of the community.

35. The more a newspaper deals with issues of importance to its readers, the greater its potential influence.

36. The smaller the number of communication channels outside a newspaper in a community (including other mass communication media), the greater the influence of the newspaper.

37. The larger the number of newspapers, and the greater their circulation, the more active are contrasting and competing sectors within the community, and the more decentralized the decision-making structure.

38. The higher the prestige of a social status, the more likely are its occupants to rank high in the community decision-making structure.

III

COMMUNITY STRUCTURE
AND CENTRALIZATION
OF DECISION-MAKING

6

POWER AND
COMMUNITY STRUCTURE *

PETER H. ROSSI
National Opinion Research Center, The University of Chicago

This paper deals with some structural characteristics of local communities which are relevant to their power structures and decision making processes. The ideas presented constitute a theory both in the sense of a conceptual scheme and in the sense of a set of propositions, albeit only loosely interrelated. The theory has its origins both in the growing body of literature on the power structures of local communities and in the field experiences of the author.

The immediate impetus to the construction of this theory was a growing dissatisfaction with the non-cumulative character of the field to which it purports to apply. Case study after case study of communities has appeared within the past few years, each contributing its part to a body of knowledge best characterized by the statement, "It is different here than elsewhere." [1] The author often inserts a particular comparison somewhere

---

* A revised version of a paper delivered at the 1959 Annual Meeting of the American Sociological Association, Chicago, Illinois, September, 1959. Preparation of this paper and some of the author's research cited was supported by a grant from the Social Science Research Council, hereby gratefully acknowledged.

[1] An early bibliographic review was published by the author as "Community Decision Making" in *The Administrative Science Quarterly*, I (March, 1957), 415–43. An incomplete list of more recent studies follows:

Warner Bloomberg, *The Structure of Power in Stackton* (Unpublished Ph.D. dissertation, University of Chicago, 1960). James S. Coleman, *Community Conflict* (Glencoe, Illinois: Free Press, 1957). William H. Form, "Organized Labor's Place in the Community Power Structure," *Industrial and Labor Relations Review*, XII (July, 1959), 526–39. William H. Form and William V. D'Antonio, "Integration and Cleavage Among Community Influentials in Two Border Cities," *American Sociological Review*, XXIV (December, 1959), 804–14. Orrin E. Klapp and L. Vincent Padgett, "Power Structure and Decision Making in a Mexican Border City," *American Journal of Sociology*, LXV (January, 1960), 400–406. Delbert C. Miller, "Decision Making Cliques in Community Power Structure," *American Journal of Sociology*, LXIV (November, 1958), 299–310. Delbert C. Miller, "Industry and Community Power

into his paper: Hunter's Regional City, Schulze's Cibola, Rossi's Mediana, and so forth. Each author owns his own town, defending it from the erroneous and somewhat heretical conceptualizations of others much the way a feudal lord defends the integrity of the local patron saint against the false counterclaims of nearby realms.

One firm generalization emerges from the literature: the power structure of local communities and the decision making processes to be found therein show a significant range of variation. This range can be only partly dependent on the differences in research technology employed by each researcher, for the same researchers have found different patterns in different communities. No firm generalizations emerge, however, concerning the sources of these variations.

There are two main reasons for the failure of generalizations of this sort to emerge. First, with few exceptions, comparative studies are rare. Most studies are concerned with establishing a pattern within one particular community, setting it off at best against one other community. Studies in which a large number of communities are systematically contrasted with comparable communities are the sources from which desired generalizations will emerge. The empirical relationships between power structures and other community social structures will provide the data.

The second main reason lies in the inadequacy of social theory. Despite the many community studies which have been undertaken since the classic Booth study of London, we are still lacking a conceptual scheme specifying with some degree of clarity what are the important elements in community structure. Indeed, the operational form that Hunter gave to the conception of community power structure will probably remain as his

---

Structures," *American Sociological Review*, XXIII (February, 1958), 9–15. Roland J. Pellegrin and Charles H. Coates, "Absentee Owned Corporations and Community Power Structure," *American Journal of Sociology*, LXI (March, 1956), 413–19. Nelson W. Polsby, "Three Problems in the Analysis of Community Power," *American Sociological Review*, XXIV (December, 1959), 796–803. Nelson W. Polsby. "The Sociology of Community Power: A Reassessment," *Social Forces*, XXXVII (March, 1959), 232–36. Edwin H. Rhyne, "Political Parties and Decision Making in Three Southern Counties," *American Political Science Review*, LII (December, 1958), 1091–1107. Peter H. Rossi, "Industry and Community," National Opinion Research Center, Report No. 64, October, 1957 (mimeo.). Peter H. Rossi and Phillips Cutright, "The Political Organization of an Industrial Community," in Morris Janowitz and Heinz Eulau (eds.), *Community Political Systems* (Glencoe, Illinois: Free Press, 1960, forthcoming). Petter H. Rossi and Robert A. Dentler, *The Politics of Urban Renewal* (Glencoe, Illinois: Free Press, 1960, forthcoming). Robert O. Schulze, "The Role of Economic Dominants in Community Power Structure," *American Sociological Review*, XXIII (February, 1958), 3–9. Arthur J. Vidich and Joe Bensman, *Small Town in Mass Society* (Princeton, New Jersey: Princeton University Press, 1959).

greatest contribution.[2] Before Hunter only the Lynds [3] paid attention to this feature of social structure, and this interest of the Lynds did not start a tradition because they were unable to communicate the techniques by which they singled out the "X" family as the dominant center in Middletown. After Hunter laid out his quasi-sociometry, community studies experienced a revival, all centered around some modification of his device.

Of course without a conceptual scheme, comparative studies are difficult to plan and to achieve. What should the researcher and his team look for? He now knows that to define the powerful he can employ some modification of Hunter's balloting. The census and other published sources provide additional ways of classifying communities, but these provide at best only indirect indicators of social organization, and the researcher must still have a rationale for choosing among the possible indicators. Researchers are therefore forced to collect their own data. To do so obviously requires some *a priori* conceptions as to what is important. The vicious circle is closed: comparative community studies are one of the important sources of ideas concerning the structural concomitants of variations in power and decision making, but properly to conduct such studies requires some framework for the collection of such data.[4]

GAPS IN THE CONCEPTION OF COMMUNITY STRUCTURES

To characterize communities we need some sort of framework which can guide observations, alerting the researcher to the crucial elements in the structure of the community. What form should such a conceptual scheme take? Should we construct some grand scheme which would be the all around best way of characterizing communities or should we work piecemeal, building one scheme for one problem and another scheme for another? It is my conviction that the latter path will prove most fruitful: namely, the construction of schemes which are specific to the particular substantive problem at hand. Thus the best way of characterizing communities for the purpose of understanding fluoridation controversies in principle may be different from the best way for understanding some other community process.

---

[2] Floyd A. Hunter, *Community Power Structure* (Chapel Hill, North Carolina: University of North Carolina Press, 1952).

[3] Robert S. and Helen M. Lynd, *Middletown in Transition* (New York: Harcourt Brace and Company, 1937).

[4] An important exception to this characterization is the studies undertaken at Michigan State University by C. P. Loomis, W. Form and others.

Even if one were to grant the soundness of this notion of specific theories for specific purposes, there still remains a considerable problem in the construction of such theories. Although we have made much progress through the work of the human ecologists in classifying cities according to their economic functions and their relations to their environments, we have done little with the internal social organization of communities. In this last respect, perhaps the best known structural characteristic of communities is along stratification lines. A large enough body of research and thinking has gone into the definition of stratification both on the purely nominal level and on the operational level for the researcher to have a fairly clear idea of how to use this term, how to measure stratification systems, and how to locate the positions within such systems of particular individuals or groups. Similar amounts of thinking and effort have not been expended on invention of an appropriate methodology for studying other kinds of organized relationships among the members of a community. Although on the abstract level sociometric devices might seem useful tools in the study of large communities, on the empirical level they prove impractical.

The gap in the conception of community structure is most serious in the area of social organization. This paper is intended to fill in part of this conceptual hiatus by constructing a scheme for classifying the political structures of local communities. The scheme purports to be useful specifically for understanding variations in power structures. Hopefully it may also turn out to be of some utility in the study of closely related community characteristics.

A CONCEPTUAL SCHEME FOR THE POLITICAL STRUCTURE OF LOCAL COMMUNITIES

The purpose of the scheme to be described here is to account for the variations in power structures to be found among American local communities. It may also prove of some utility in other areas, for example, community conflicts. The general thesis underlying the scheme is a simple one: the pattern taken by the power structure of a community is a function of the kind of political life to be found therein. My reasons for postulating this relationship are also simple and somewhat obvious: the political institutions of a community are the ultimate locus of the decisions that are binding on the total community. Hence much of the power exercised is focused on the governmental institutions of the local community.

For our present purposes, it is useful to regard the political life of a community as occurring at two different levels, interrelated but to some degree independent. On the one hand, there is a set of governmental institutions manned by officials and employees with defined functions and spheres of authority and competence. On the other hand, there is the electorate, the body of citizens with voting rights, organized to some degree into political parties. We expect that phenomena appearing on each of these levels independently influence the forms taken by community power structures.

On the institutional level, there are several characteristics of local government that are of some consequence. First, communities vary according to the degree to which the roles of officials are *professionalized*. In many communities, mayors and city councilmen and often other officials are employed in their official capacities only part time and lack the opportunity to become fully engrossed in these roles. At the other extreme, some communities employ professionally trained officials—city managers, school superintendents, etc.—who are full time employees expecting to remain in their occupation—although not in any particular post—for long periods of time. In communities where local officials exercise their functions on a part time basis and where the qualifications for incumbency are not exacting, the incumbents are less likely to segregate their official roles from their other roles and hence extra-official considerations are more likely to play roles of some importance in their decisions. Thus the informal cabal which ran Springdale, as described by Vidich and Bensman,[5] hardly distinguish between their roles as city fathers and their roles as businessmen and professionals. At the other extreme are the professional politicians who run Chicago, whose independence is curbed very little.

A second important structural characteristic of local government refers to the rules by which officials are selected. Two aspects of electoral rules are significant. Electoral rules can either retard or facilitate the development of enduring political alignments in the community, and the latter are important determinants of the forms of decision making. In this respect, the crucial differences lie between communities which have non-partisan and communities which have partisan elections. Non-partisan electoral rules discourage the development of enduring political alignments by reducing the advantages to candidates of appearing on slates, whereas partisan elections facilitate cooperation among candidates and the drawing of clear lines between opposing slates of candidates. It should be noted in this connection that primaries are in effect non-partisan elections in communities which are predominantly Democratic or Republican.[6]

Another structural characteristic which tends to reduce the impor-

---

[5] Vidich and Bensman, *op. cit.*

[6] Non-partisan elections operate to the benefit of the highly organized political minority. Hence, usually, non-partisan elections operate to the benefit of the white collar groups in industrial communities and to the benefit of the Democratic Party in middle class suburbs.

tance of political organizations is the rule concerning the number of officials elected by popular vote. Short ballots on which only a few candidates compete for the major offices tend to reduce organizational importance by lowering the benefits to candidates of cooperation with each other.

These structural characteristics of the governmental institutions of the local community underlie the ability of these institutions to develop an independence of their own and also indicate the extent to which conflicts within the community are manifested in the political realm or in some other fashion.

Moving now to the level of the electorate and its organization, there are two important dimensions to be considered. First, we must consider the political homogeneity of the electorate, roughly defined as the extent to which the community is divided equally or unequally among the contending political factions of the community. The more unequally the community is divided, the less likely are open political struggles to be the major expressions of clashes of interest and the more likely is decision making to be a prerogative of a "cozy few."

Borrowing from Gerhard Lenski, a second characteristic of the electorate might be called "political crystallization": the extent to which the lines of political cleavage within the community coincide with major social structural differentiations. In this connection the crucial modes of social structural differentiation are along class and status lines. The more political lines coincide with class and status lines, the more likely are community clashes to take a political form. These are important lines of differentiation within communities because they are likely to endure over time.[7] Political differences which coincide with class and status differences are for these reasons likely to be reinforced by the double factors of differential association and connection with important interests.

If we now consider the entire set of community characteristics distinguished here, we see that they may be conceived of as indicators of two more abstract attributes of communities: first, the institutional indicators express the degree of segregation of political institutions from other community institutions; second, the indicators relating to the electorate reflect the extent to which partisan politics is a crucial arena for the important decision making within the community.

It is important to note that these characteristics of communities can be

---

[7] On a large space scale—i.e., for regions and nations—regional differences would also play important roles, but since the micro-regional differences in the American city tend to be wiped out quickly by residential mobility, they play only a minor role within communities.

easily translated into operational forms. The city charter can tell us how officials are elected and whether their jobs are full or part time. Election statistics and survey research can tell us the degree of political homogeneity and political crystallization.

Two broad hypotheses can be formulated at this point. (1) The more segregated are political roles from other roles played by incumbent officials, the more independent the governmental structure of a community from other institutional structures. (2) The more heterogeneous the electorate and the greater the degree of political crystallization, the more important the governmental institutions as loci for important decision making.

IMPLICATIONS FOR COMMUNITY POWER STRUCTURES

The studies of community power structures have universally found the upper levels of the occupational hierarchy to occupy prominent power positions. In no city—even heavily working class Stackton—have proprietors, managers, and professional men played insignificant parts. Often enough some members of these groups do not play as prominent a part as others, even though they are as wealthy and as important in the economic life of the city, but in all cities members of these groups were to be found in some kind of inner circle.

The disagreement among researchers concerns two important matters. First, there is disagreement over the pattern of power, with some researchers preferring the monolith as their model and others preferring polyliths or more complicated forms. Second, there is disagreement over the roles played by public officials and voluntary associations. Hardly anything could be written about Chicago, Stackton, or Philadelphia without reference to the mayor's office and other top level public officials. In contrast, in Regional City and some of the towns studied by C. P. Loomis and his research workers, public officials and often labor leaders appear as minor and insignificant personages. It should be noted that these two kinds of disagreements among researchers are related. A monolithic model for a power structure generally goes along with a very subordinate role for voluntary associations and public officials. Thus, in Hunter's Regional City public officials are explicitly viewed as the handmaidens of the elite group, and labor leaders are scarcely worth mentioning.

A polylithic power structure tends to mean a number of small monoliths each centering around a particular sort of activity. Thus in industrial Stackton, the civic associations and community service organizations were the preserves of the business community, whereas local government was safe in the hands of professional politicians resting on the mass base of the Democratic Party and its heavy support from among ethnic groups of relatively recent arrival from abroad. Indeed, respondents rarely reported that any one individual was powerful in all spheres of community life.

To some degree the disagreements among researchers on the forms taken by the power structures in communities and the place to be accorded public officials and associational leaders are functions of the different research techniques employed. Some approaches preclude the finding of polylithic power structures. However, in much larger part, the differences among researchers are functions of "reality," representing major ways in which communities *in fact* differ. My general thesis is that these differences are functions of the differences among communities in their political structures.

If we look carefully at the studies of community power structure we may discern the following types:

(1) *Pyramidal.* Lines of power tend to have their ultimate source in one man or a very small number of men. Decision making tends to be highly centralized, with lower echelons mainly carrying out major policy decisions made by the small group at the apex. — Examples: Middletown, Regional City

(2) *Caucus rule.* Lines of power tend to end in a relatively large group of men who make decisions through consensus. Decision making tends to be a matter of manufacturing consent among the "cozy few" who make up the caucus. Typical power structure in the small town or dormitory suburb. — Examples: Springdale, Mediana

(3) *Polylith.* Separate power structures definable for major spheres of community activity. Typically, local government in the hands of professional politicians backed by the solidary strength of voluntary associations, with the community service organizations in the hands of the business and professional subcommunity.

(4) *Amorphous.* No discernible enduring pattern of power. Logical residual category. No examples.

Note that the first two types of power structures are very similar, differing only in the number of decision makers who share power among themselves. The major differentiation is between the first two types wherein lines of power tend to converge and the last two types wherein lines of power tend to diverge.

The divergence of power lines has its source in the existence of the possibility for occupational groups other than business and professional to occupy positions of importance within major community institutions. This occurs typically when there is political crystallization in a community which is heterogeneous class wise or status wise. When the lower status or class levels have a political party representing them which has a chance to get into office, there is the possibility that public office can become one of the important sources of power.

The conditions under which the political parties have a vigorous life are defined by the structural features described earlier. Under partisan electoral laws, when officials are professionalized, when either the majority of the electorate favor the underdog party or when the parties are balanced in strength, then the political institutions and public officials assume a position of importance within the power structure of the community.

Another way of putting this thesis is to say that the leaders of the dominant economic institutions ordinarily wield power, but they are forced to take others into account when popular democratic rules allow the lower levels of the community an opportunity to place their representatives in public office. The elements of the community political structure we have distinguished here are those which facilitate the development of governmental independence from the business and professional community.

The general hypothesis may now be stated more precisely, as follows: *in communities with partisan electoral procedures, whose officials are full time functionaries, where party lines tend to coincide with class and status lines and where the party favored by the lower class and status groups has some good chance of getting elected to office, community power structures tend to be polylithic rather than monolithic.* Since these characteristics of community political structures are to some unknown degree independent of one another, different combinations of such characteristics can appear empirically. The patterns in such communities cannot be deduced from this hypothesis since we do not specify the weights to be assigned to each characteristic.

There are further expectations implied in the general hypothesis. Some examples follow:

(1) Homogeneous middle class communities, for example, dormitory suburbs and the like, will tend to have monolithic power structures, since the class basis for countervailing political power does not exist.

(2) In communities where the lower class party has a clear majority there will be moves on the part of the business and professional community

to introduce structural changes in city government to undermine this majority, as for example, nonpartisan elections, short ballot, and the like.

(3) In polylithic communities, city government and private community organizations try to limit the sphere of each other's operations by moving more and more functions into their own spheres of authority.

(4) In communities with monolithic power structures, conflicts tend to take on the character of mass revolts in which small incidents are magnified out of proportion because there are no regularized means for the expression of conflict.[8]

(5) Historically, the development of voluntary civic associations may be interpreted as a reaction to the loss of local political power by high status groups. Since these community organizations were not governed by the mass vote of the lower class groups, high status groups could keep control over them.

Additional similar propositions may be generated from the basic hypothesis set forth in this paper. Although I believe that such propositions will be upheld in general by empirical data, I am also sure that considerable modifications will be made in them.

CONCLUSIONS

To sum up, I have presented in this paper a conceptual scheme which provides a way of classifying the political structures of local communities. I have also tried to spell out how these political features may modify the power structures to be found in such communities. The utility of the scheme obviously requires for testing empirical data generated by comparative community studies. Though I have no doubt that the hypotheses presented here will at best suffer considerable modification when confronted with such data, I hope they will serve the purpose of providing some impetus for comparative community studies.

---

[8] See Coleman, *op. cit.*

7

COMMUNITY POWER
AND DECISION-MAKING:
A Quantitative Examination
of Previous Research*

CLAIRE W. GILBERT
Florida Atlantic University

This article reports some of the major results of a study of 166 American communities based on previously published materials. The major focus was on power and decision-making at the local community level, and there was an attempt made to review all published studies dealing with these topics. It has occasionally been remarked that studies in this general area provide an attractive topic for the sociology of knowledge. I agree, and in an earlier work examined results of these studies in terms of that perspective.[1] But the remark about the sociology of knowledge is only a half truth: for reasons which will be elaborated shortly, I am firmly convinced that these same studies provide a valuable basis for the testing of comparative propositions about decision-making patterns in local communities.

At outset it is imperative to deal with the problematic methodological questions inherent in an investigation of this nature, and demonstrate the procedures which promoted confidence in quantitative comparisons of the various studies. The next two sections take up this matter. The rest of the paper examines the results of the various studies, closely following the order of presentation of Table 1. The reader may wish to inspect Table

* This research was partially supported by the International City Managers' Association, The National Science Foundation (Grant GS-800), and The Center for Metropolitan Studies at Northwestern University.

[1] Claire W. Gilbert, "Community Power Structure: A Study in the Sociology of Knowledge" (Evanston, Ill.: Ph.D. dissertation, Northwestern University 1966), Appendixes A, B, and C.

139

1 on p. 143 before considering a more detailed analysis of it, and to refer to the Table while reading the text of the paper.

PROCEDURES

Data were analyzed for 166 American communities by coding the results of previously published studies. Supplementary information was added from United States Census reports.

Communities were not really sampled. I attempted to include all published works on power and decision-making in political units defined as cities, towns, or villages (rather than wards, countries, states, school districts, and the like). Studies of cities outside the United States were excluded because of cultural differences. Cities were included from 46 different states, and while those with larger populations were over-represented, they ranged from villages of fewer than 1,000 inhabitants to central cities of over 1,000,000. The population of studies, content analysis coding procedures, measures of concepts, interrelationships of measures, estimates of validity, reliability, and replicability are reported in more detail elsewhere.

DATA QUALITY CONTROL

The frequent conflicts in the field of community decision-making over theoretical orientation, methodology, and substantive results that developed in the late 1950's led many observers to despair of comparing separate studies. This problem of comparability is not, however, unique to the field of community decision-making. Anthropologists in particular have long been forced to evaluate conflicting results reported by different researchers. Perhaps the most powerful tool for dealing with this problem is "data quality control," a procedure adapted from industrial production control to social scientific studies by Raoul Naroll.[2]

Data quality control deals with groups of reports which have been compiled by a variety of inquirers under disparate observational conditions, rather than with single reports. It assumes that some reports are made under conditions of higher apparent trustworthiness than others. Data from reports made under "better" conditions are then compared with those made under "worse" conditions to see if they differ seriously. A difference is considered serious when the results of a group of reports made

---

[2] Raoul Naroll, *Data Quality Control—A New Research Technique* (Glencoe, The Free Press, 1962).

under one condition differ as much as three standard deviation units from a second group made under other conditions.

The effect of *one* erroneously measured variable in a correlation is almost always to *reduce* the strength of the relationship. However, if *two* variables in a correlation share an identical measurement error, the relationship may be spuriously *inflated*.[3] If it is found that two variables in a relationship share an identical measurement error, the control-factor can be held constant to see if the relationship continues to hold when sources of bias are controlled for in this fashion.

These procedures were utilized in the current research as follows. All community power studies examined were classified on a large number of factors which were hypothesized as possible sources of bias. Seventy-three such factors were considered, of the following sorts: (1) characteristics of the researcher, (2) conceptual characteristics, (3) conditions of observation, (4) breadth of the study, (5) methods of reporting, and (6) work process. All relationships in Table 1 have been cross-classified with *all* quality control factors. If any reported community attribute was correlated beyond three standard deviation units (P = .004) with any control factor, then the other variable was also examined for association with the same control factor. If the second variable was not correlated with the control-factor, the association was considered unbiased. For example, although the attribute of community conflict correlated with salience of issues studied, the presence of a city manager was not associated with the control-factor (salience of issues studied). Therefore, the correlation between city-manager cities and low levels of conflict was considered unbiased. Any correlation must be considered questionable, however, when both attributes are correlated beyond three standard deviations with an identical control-factor. Any such questionable correlation is indicated by attaching an asterisk to the probability value in Table 1. It should be emphasized, however, that where such a bias was found to exist the correlation was still found to hold in every case when the potential source of bias was controlled. For example, leadership by politicians or informals (people not holding political offices) was seriously associated with researcher's discipline in addition to being associated with population size: political scientists tended to study larger cities and to find leadership by politicians more often than sociologists. But when controlling for discipline, the relationship between leadership by politicians and large communities continued to hold. Similarly, in every case where biased results were examined by introducing control-factors, the original re-

---

[3] Naroll, *op. cit.*, Chapter 1.

lationships continued to hold. Thus, although some relationships in Table 1 are "biased"—as indicated by an asterisk—the relationships tend to persist even when the control-factor is held constant.

Most of the rest of this paper will be concerned with interpreting the results reported in Table 1.

PATTERNS OF COMMUNITY LEADERSHIP

I will first deal with patterns of interrelationships among five basic dependent variables—two measures of the power structure, the level of community conflict, the identity of the "upper level" leaders, and the type of governmental function (good government or mixed). Each variable is designated by an identification number that will be referred to in the following discussion. Our two measures of the power structure are 85 and 90. Measure 85 has been designated Shape of Power Structure; it ranges from *least pluralistic* (pyramidal, multi-pyramidal), to *most pluralistic* (fluid group alliance, structure varies with issue, or practically no structure). Measure 90, Elitist Power Structure, ranges from *most elitist* (a person or group controls all decision all of the time, or some decisions some of the time), to *least elitist* (there is no group or sector that regularly supplies leaders for decisions). As could be expected, the two power structure measures are highly correlated: most pluralistic and least elitist structures are found together.

The relationships between types of power structure and leadership have been analyzed by Miller, Polsby, Clark, Presthus, Truman, and others.[4] Tabulating measure 103 by 85 shows that in communities with more pluralistic structures, leadership is more likely by politicians and others than by informals. More extensive analysis of other measures of leadership type showed, however, that tightly concentrated power structures were found with many different types of leadership groups: informals, governmental officials, businessmen, union personnel and low income

---

[4] Delbert C. Miller, "Industry and Community Power Structure: A Comparative Study of an American and an English City, "*American Sociological Review*, Vol. 23 (Feb., 1958), 11; Nelson W. Polsby, *Community Power and Political Theory* (New Haven: Yale University Press, 1963), p. 10; Terry Clark, "Power and Community Structure: Who Governs, Where, and When?" *The Sociological Quarterly* (Summer, 1967), Hypothesis 19; Robert Presthus, *Men at the Top* (New York: Oxford University Press, 1964), p. 420; David B. Truman, "Theory and Research on Metropolitan Political Leadership: Report on a Conference," *Items*, Vol. 15 (New York: Social Science Research Council, March, 1961), 2–3.

TABLE 1. POWER STRUCTURE, CONFLICT, LEADERSHIP, AND GOVERNMENTAL FUNCTION, RELATED TO EACH OTHER AND TO TIME, REGION, CITY TYPE, POPULATION CHARACTERISTICS, AND GOVERNMENTAL STRUCTURE

There are four pieces of information in the table for each relationship. (1) Positive and negative or zero (blank cell) relationship between each of the attributes. (2) A probability value (for example, .027) based on Fisher's exact test of probability, calculated by summing both tails of the distribution according to definition D = 3 of P. Armsen. ["Tables for Significance Tests of 2 × 2 Contingency Tables," *Biometrika*, Vol. 42 (1955), 494–511]. (3) The number of cases is given in parentheses. (4) An asterisk is added if the relationship is biased according to data quality-control procedures (see text). No asterisk indicates an unbiased relationship.

The Dependent Variables

85. SHAPE OF POWER STRUCTURE
   Most pluralistic (+): Decision making structure is fluid group alliances or variable according to issues (N = 55).
   Least pluralistic (−): Decision-making structure is a pyramid, multipyramidal, permanent factions, or other (N = 101).
90. ELITIST POWER STRUCTURE
   Most elitist (+): A person or group controls all community decisions (N = 23).
   Least elitist (−): A weak elite (a group controls decisions some of the time), a quasi-elite (a definable list or aggregate of persons (not a group) from which some are involved in all decisions), a weak quasi-elite (an aggregate of persons who are involved some of the time in decisions), or an ecology of games (no definable aggregate who participate in at least some decisions some of the time) (N = 111).
99. COMMUNITY CONFLICT
   Highest conflict (+): High (not handled well by institutional channels) medium (handled better than high but not so well as medium low) conflict (N = 53).
   Lowest conflict (−): Medium low (handled well by institutional channels) or low (no overt) conflict (N = 90).
103. UPPER LEVEL LEADERS
   Informals (+)
   Politicians and others (−)
75. GOVERNMENTAL FUNCTION
   "Good" government (+): Local government is oriented toward good government (N = 68).
   Political or mixed (−): Local government is oriented toward mixed good government and machine politics, or toward machine politics.

	85.	90.	99.	103.	75.
85. Shape of Power Structure					
1. Most pluralistic		− .000		− .093	
2. Least pluralistic		+ (132)		+ (134)	

	85.	90.	99.	103.	75.
90. Elitist Power Structure 　　1. Most elitist 　　2. Least elitist					
99. Community Conflict 　　1. Highest 　　2. Lowest					− .000 + (124)
103. Upper Level Leaders 　　1. Informals 　　2. Politicians and others					
75. Governmental Function 　　1. Good government 　　2. Political or mixed					
TRENDS 　1. In the Year 　　1. 1945 or later 　　2. 1944 or earlier	+ .000 − (156)	− .000 * + (134)		+ .057 * − (140)	
2. In the Year 　　1. 1955 or later 　　2. 1954 or earlier	+ .068 − (156)	− .005 * + (134)			
REGION 　4. Located in the 　　1. South 　　2. Northeast, Northcentral, 　　　or West	− .015 + (153)				
CITY TYPE 　8. Present Character Is 　　1. Metropolitan central 　　2. Not metropolitan central	+ .001 − (150)			− .129 + (134)	− .026 + (123)
9. Present Character Is 　　1. Metropolitan suburban 　　2. Not metropolitan suburban					+ .127 − (123)
10. Present Character Is 　　1. Independent (not SMSA) 　　2. Not an independent city	− .023 + (150)				

144

	85.	90.	99.	103.	75.
21. Population per Sq. Mile Is					
1. Less than 5,000	− .034				
2. 5,000 or more	+ (57)				
POPULATION SIZE AND GROWTH					
23. Population Size Is					
1. Over 100,000	+ .018			− .007 *	
2. Under 100,000	− (155)			+ (140)	
28. Population Growth Rate Is					
1. High or moderately high	− .000	+ .132			+ .055
2. Moderate, low, or negative	+ (134)	− (119)			− (115)
ECONOMIC FUNCTION					
33. Per Cent of Population Earning $2,000 in 1950 or $3,000 in 1960 Is					
1. Lowest			+ .113		− .067
2. Highest			− (61)		+ (59)
36. Nelson Rating Is					
1. Diversified			− .023	+ .075	
2. Specialized			+ (61)	− (62)	
37. Nelson Rating Is					
1. Specialized in manufacture or finance		+ .097	+ .105		
2. Diversified or specialized in other than manufacture or finance		− (62)	− (61)		
40. Economic Base Judged					
1. Specialized				− .032	+ .087
2. Other than specialized				+ (111)	− (109)
SOCIAL CHARACTERISTICS					
45. Median Age Is					
1. Lowest	− .012				
2. Highest	+ (90)				
46. Proportion of Population under 5 Years Is					
1. Highest	− .045	+ .086		+ .010 *	
2. Lowest	+ (127)	− (114)		− (114)	

	85.	90.	99.	103.	75.
54. Nonwhite Increase Is					
1. Negative or low	− .034				
2. Medium or high	+ (57)				
59. Per Cent of Population with Less Than 5 Years Education Is					
1. Lowest					+ .001
2. Highest					− (75)
GOVERNMENTAL STRUCTURE					
62. Local Election Is					
1. National party ticket	− .103				− .000 *
2. Non-partisan	+ (102)				+ (100)
63. Electoral System Is					
1. Ward					− .028
2. At-large					+ (83)
66. Local Government Is					
1. City-manager			− .132		+ .001
2. Not city-manager			+ (117)		− (117)

groups.[5] The correlation of 103 with 85 is only indicative of the general relationship between pluralism and leaders from more than one sector of the community.

The functions performed by local governments are frequently classified into two types: *political* and *"good" government*.[6] The primary political function is mediating conflict between various interests in the community. Cities with governments performing the political' function tend to have partisan elections, representation from wards, and political machines. These characteristics are congenial to the culture of "self-serving" immigrant, ethnic, working-class groups. In contrast, "good governments" are those committed to businesslike efficiency and the elimination of graft and

---

[5] Four cities analyzed have either union personnel *or* low income sectors as the most important participants in local decision-making (Union personnel and low income sectors comprised one category for coding purposes.) These cities may *not* be characterized as having an elite so strong that it dominates all policy nor as being so pluralistic that no groups or individuals are consistently involved in policy-making.

[6] Edward C. Banfield and James Q. Wilson, *City Politics* (Cambridge: Harvard University Press, 1965), *passim*.

"corruption." They often assume that there are no conflicts of interest in the community and are likely to have non-partisan and at-large electoral procedures and a manager form of government. These characteristics facilitate the "public-serving" interests of the Protestant Anglo-Saxon upper and middle classes. One-fourth of the cities examined were classified as having a mixture of both functions, less than one-fourth a political function, and slightly more than one-half a good government function. Measure 75 dichotomizes cities into those with good government and those performing political functions or a mixture of functions.

Rogers suggests that governments performing a more extensive range of functions are associated with more pluralistic power structures. Table 1 shows no such relationship.[7]

Measure 99 compares cities characterized by absence of conflict or conflict well handled by institutional channels with those cities having more overt and extensive conflicts. Good government cities have significantly lower levels of conflict. There are two related explanations that may be offered for this finding. First, Protestant values of good government cities are conciliatory and facilitate the handling of conflict should it develop, and second, good government cities are more homogeneous in population and correspondingly have fewer internal differences to generate violent conflicts.

I will now turn to some of the factors that help explain differences between communities in terms of each of these five basic variables.

TRENDS IN LOCAL POLITICS

The scale of the United States is increasing—there is greater functional interdependence and differentiation between and among local communities than in earlier years.[8] Differentiation is developing along economic, social, educational, normative, and other lines. Communities are

---

[7] David Rogers, "Community Political Systems," in Bert Swanson, ed., *Current Trends in Comparative Community Studies*, (Kansas City: Community Studies, Inc., 1962), p. 47. Other data show that cities having only the political function of government tend to have concentrated power structures. An hypothesis is that politically oriented systems tend to be found among the most monolithic and pluralistic, whereas the middle of the continuum tend to be occupied with cities oriented toward "good government" or both good and political functions.

[8] For the concept of societal scale, see Eshref Shevky and Wendell Bell, *Social Area Analysis* (Stanford: Stanford University Press, 1954). See also C. Wright Mills, *White Collar* (New York: Oxford University Press, 1951); and Louis Wirth, "Urbanism as a Way of Life," *American Journal of Sociology*, Vol. 44 (July, 1938), reprinted in Paul K. Hatt and Albert J. Reiss, Jr., eds., *Cities and Society* (Glencoe: The Free Press, 1959), pp. 46–63. For a comparative national framework within which to conceptualize local communities, see Gilbert, *op. cit.* Chapter 2.

frequently highly specialized and diversified. But correspondingly, there is an increasing consolidation of business enterprises. Many functions of government are also increasingly carried out on federal levels. And communications are becoming increasingly concentrated and have wider spans of influence. Increasing scale seems to be one of the most fundamental changes in recent years, bringing about important modifications in patterns of community decision-making.

Measure 1 divides cities into two groups: those studied between 1900–1944, and those studied from 1945–1964.

The structure of political control is expected to change because the functional relationship of the community to the larger society has changed. Such studies as those of Booth and Adrian, and Schulze suggest that communities more extensively involved in larger economic, social, and ecological systems become more pluralistic.[9] Communities with few outside relationships are becoming increasingly rare, and therefore a decrease in concentrated power structures could be expected. Evidence in Table 1 supports these ideas.

There is no evidence, however, for a trend in levels of community conflict. Tendencies toward increased conflict (sharper social differentation and reduced ability of good governments to manage conflict) seem to be mitigated by other factors which tend to minimize conflict (increased living standards, assimilation of immigrant groups, and the like).

With increasing urbanization and fragmentation, it might be expected that economic leaders would withdraw from political activities.[10] Political bosses are also widely considered to be on the decline.[11] A long standing polemic concerns the role of informals—often economic elites—and their relative importance compared with that of governmental officials. Surprising, perhaps, is the slight rise in the importance of informal leaders since 1945—as shown in Table 1. Other data (not appearing here) show that a decreasing proportion of cities have governmental officials as their exclusive leaders, supporting the idea that political bosses are on the decline. Since the end of World War II, eight per cent of the cities have leadership composed of representation from *all* sectors within the city *or* from pres-

[9] David A. Booth and Charles R. Adrian, "Power Structure and Community Change: A Replication Study of Community A, *"Midwest Journal of Political Science,* Vol. 6 (Aug., 1962), 288 and 291; Robert O. Schulze, "The Role of Economic Dominants in Community Power Structure," *American Sociological Review,* Vol. 23 (Feb., 1958), 4. See also Walton's article, this volume.

[10] Schulze, *Ibid.*; Robert T. Daland, *Dixie City: A Portrait of Political Leadership* (Alabama: W. B. Drank and Son, 1956), p. 36.

[11] Harry M. Scoble, "Some Questions for Researchers," in Robert S. Cahill and Stephen P. Hencley, eds., *The Politics of Education in the Local Community* (Danville: The Interstate Printers and Publishers, Inc., 1964), p. 123.

sure groups and aldermanic blocs—a phenomenon not noted prior to 1945; seven of these cities (of eight) are metropolitan central cities. While politicians tend less to be the sole figures dominating politics, it is also rare today to find a city where politicians and their parties are of negligible importance, although in earlier decades towns were more frequently described as dominated by informal leaders, with political parties totally absent.

Banfield and Wilson predict a trend away from the machine-style ethos as a result of changes in the social class composition of the urban electorate. Protestant values are expected to prevail even in central cities, despite their immigrant populations, because state and federal government support take patronage away from the traditional machines.[12] No trend in Table 1 supports this hypothesized increase in cities with a purely good government orientation. However, cities formerly characterized by machine politics are increasingly performing good government functions as well.

REGIONS

It has more than once been suggested that local politics in the South differ from other regions of the United States.[13] Measure 4 compares northeast, northcentral, or western regions with the South, and shows southern cities to be less pluralistic in power structure. Scoble has emphasized the importance of regional economy as an underlying condition of local politics. The economy of the South is at a "take-off" stage in comparison to the economy of New England.[14]

In comparison with the rest of country, Southern population growth rates are higher, median incomes and ages of populations are lower, and unemployment rates are low or average. Southern cities also tend to be open to persons of high socio-economic status or to middle-class Anglo-Saxons, which is less true of the remainder of the nation. An explanation could be the greater traditionalism in the South, or the greater relative poverty.[15]

---

[12] Banfield and Wilson, *op. cit.*, pp. 329–330.

[13] Robert E. Agger, *et al., The Rulers and the Ruled* (N.Y.: John Wiley & Sons, 1964), p. 125; John Walton, "Substance and Artifact: The Current Status of Research on Community Power Structure," *American Journal of Sociology*, Vol. 71 (Jan., 1966), 435; and Walton article this volume.

[14] Scoble., *op. cit.*, pp. 119–120.

[15] Our data also show that government experts more often tend to suggest than to legitimate policy in the South. We may speculate that relatively rapidly growing places, such as the South, are more characterized by innovations from experts than more stable places such as New England.

CITY TYPE

Several previous studies have emphasized the importance of city type as a predictive variable for power structure.[16] Metropolitan areas, rather than smaller areas, offer greater opportunities for pluralistic patterns because of their high differentation of the polity from the kinship and economic systems,[17] and perhaps because of their having better organized social strata (class, ethnic, group, residential area) under their own leadership.[18]

Table 1 shows that metropolitan central cities strongly tend to be pluralistic in power structure. No differences appear in power structures when comparing metropolitan suburbs with other communities. It was also found, when using finer distinctions than are provided in Table 1, that

(1) In *residential suburbs*, factional structures and a ruling group of any kind are most frequent. In *industrial suburbs*, multipyramidal structures and aggregates of leaders who do not form a group are most often found.

(2) *Independent cities* (non-SMSA), as shown in Table 1, are less pluralistic than other cities. The greatest proportion of pyramidal structures are found in independent cities.

(3) *Rural villages* and *trade centers* are often in a state of flux. Rural trade centers frequently are characterized by an aggregate of leaders who do not form a cohesive group.

(4) *City type is a better predictor of power structure than is either population size or economic base* (attributes are discussed in the following sections).

Conflict is not correlated with city type in Table 1. However, it was found that while metropolitan central cities tend to have some conflict, conflict is more common in industrial (in comparison to residential) suburbs and rural farm (in comparison to rural trade) areas.

Metropolitan centers less often have informal leaders than do other cities. Central cities tend to have participation from all sectors.

---

[16] Lawrence D. Mann, "Studies in Community Decision-Making," *American Institute of Planners Journal*, Vol. 30 (Feb., 1964), 62; Delbert C. Miller, "Democracy and Decision Making in the Community Power Structure," in William D'Antonio and Howard J. Ehrlich, eds., *Power and Democracy in America* (Notre Dame: University of Notre Dame Press, 1961), p. 52; and Clark, *op. cit.*

[17] Rogers, *loc. cit.*

[18] Robert Lane, quoted in Presthus, *op. cit.*, p. 415. In metropolitan centers, decisions tend to be in the public realm (rather than private or both).

POPULATION SIZE AND GROWTH

Population size assumes a central role in theorizing about community power structures,[19] and is often used as a selection criterion in comparative studies. On the other hand the population growth rate is a less frequent subject of comment. I found, however, that growth rates correlate with political attributes more often and more strongly than does size.

Very large cities are more frequently pluralistic. But among smaller cities a variety of structures are found; concentrated power structures are not predicted by population size.

Pluralistic power structures tend to be found among cities with moderate, low, or negative growth rates; elitist structures tend to occur among cities with high growth rates.[20] Informals are also less likely to be important participants in large cities.

Despite Clelland's prediction that extremely rapid growth (coupled with economic fluctuations) generates abnegation of civic responsibility on the part of economic dominants,[21] there is no evidence in our data to support changes in participation by informals due to population growth.

Controlling for size of cities, structure, and participation are associated as follows:

(1) In all cities, *pyramidal* structures are most often headed by elected officials, but the tendency is greatest in cities of large population. Pyramids are headed by nonofficials about one-fourth of the time. In cities of more than 100,000, any combination of officials and nonofficials is rare, whereas combinations occur about one-fourth of the time in cities of fewer than 100,000.

(2) In large cities *multipyramidal* structures do *not* tend to have nonofficials as heads. Nonofficials are found in greater numbers as heads of pyramidal and multipyramidal structures in cities of fewer than 100,000.

(3) *Factions* are *never* headed by nonofficials. Although there are few

---

[19] Clark, *op. cit.*, Hypothesis 1; Presthus *op. cit.*, pp. 45–46; and ·Gladys M. Kammerer and John DeGrove, *Florida City Managers* (Gainesville: The University of Florida Press, 1961), p. 30.

[20] Neither Agger, *op. cit.*, nor Walton, *loc. cit.*, found any relationship between population growth rates and power structure. Ernest A. ·T. Barth reports other results in "Community Influence Systems: Structure and Change," *Social Forces,* Vol. 40 (Oct. 1961), 58–63.

[21] Donald A. Clelland, "Economic Dominance and Community Power Structure in a Middle-Sized City," paper delivered at the Ohio Valley Sociological Society meet-·ings, East Lansing, Michigan, 1962, p. 14.

cases from which to generalize, factions in large cities tend to be headed by officials and in smaller cities by a combination of officials and others.

(4) In cities of all sizes *fluid* structures are *not* likely to be headed *exclusively* by either officials or nonofficials.

Although no relationship appears in Table 1 between conflict and either size or growth, additional measures have been explored because of the theoretical importance of the relationships.[22] Very large cities (over 500,000) tend to have a higher level of conflict than do other cities; cities under 100,000 tend to have *no* overt conflict; 52 per cent of cities with negative growth rates have medium high or high levels of conflict, whereas 34 per cent of stable or growing cities are so characterized.

Good governments are more frequently found in cities with high population growth rates. Although no relationship appears in Table 1 between population size and function of government, it has been suggested that issues are suppressed in small towns in order to enable people to get along with each other while living together in close contact.[23] Following this reasoning, it would be expected that sizable cities handle issues politically and therefore perform the political function more than small town governments. Cities of over 500,000 less often have good governments, and cities under 25,000 more often have good governments, despite the fact that the cutting point of 100,000 shows no significant difference.

ECONOMIC FUNCTION

In view of the importance placed upon economic function by scholars such as Clark, Miller, Form, Walton, Presthus, and Mann,[24] it is surprising that several measures of economic attributes had to be omitted from Table 1 because they evidenced no correlation with the dependent variables. No support was found for the predicted association between economic diversification and a pluralistic power structure using four measures of economic diversification and nine measures of power structure.

Among nondiversified cities, however, cities whose economies are

---

[22] *Ibid.*, and from Clark's Hypotheses 8 and 9 can be deduced a relationship between conflict and size.

[23] Scoble, *op. cit.*, p. 25; and Clark, *op. cit.*

[24] Clark, *op. cit.*, Hypotheses 12 and 22; Delbert C. Miller, "Democracy and Decision-Making," p. 62; Miller, "Town and Gown: The Power Structure of a University Town," *American Journal of Sociology*, Vol. 68 (Jan., 1963), 432; Miller and William H. Form, *Industry, Labor and Community* (New York: Harper & Row, 1960); Walton, *op. cit.*, 435; Presthus, *op. cit.*, p. 46; and Mann, *loc. cit.*

dependent upon nearby areas for employment of their populations tend to have elite and group structures of power. There are 15 economically specialized cities included in the analysis (3 college, 3 resort, 2 government and education, 2 retirement and resort, 1 military, 1 retirement, and 3 unclassified specialized cities). Specialized cities have a disproportionate share of permanent factional structures—40 per cent contrasted to 4 per cent of other cities. Specialized cities tend *not* to have group structures of power.

Barth found that, especially in small communities, rapid expansion of the economic base is related to the development of influential cliques.[25] None of our measures of power structure correlated with growth of the economic base (relative to population growth), but where the employment base had not kept up with population growth, there was a tendency for factions to develop.

Table 1 shows that conflict is greater in cities with a large proportion of the population earning under $2,000 a year in 1950 or under $3,000 in 1960, and in cities judged diversified by the original researchers.

Economic function was found to be a good predictor of whether informals or politicians are the most important participants in the power structure if participation was from only one segment of the community. Economically diversified cities tend to be led by politicians and governmental officials. Specialized cities *never* have informals as the only important participants and *never* have only nonofficials as heads of the structure. Cities dominated by one or few industries tend *less* than other cities to have politicians as the most important figures in community decision-making.

SOCIAL CHARACTERISTICS

Pluralistic power structures are hypothetically associated with "socially integrated, heterogeneous populations," [26] "heterogeneity along ethnic, religious, and occupational lines," [27] and "high educational level of community residents." [28] Table 1 shows that pluralistic power structures tend to be found in communities having older populations, and elitist structures in those with younger populations. Cities with medium or high

[25] Barth, *loc. cit.*

[26] Walton, *op. cit.*, 435; Presthus predicts that integration and value consensus result in pluralism, and diversified populations have centralized control, *op. cit.*, p. 412.

[27] Miller, "Democracy and Decision Making," *op. cit.*, p. 52.

[28] Clark, *op. cit.*, Hypothesis 33.

rates of nonwhite increase in population (generally large cities) tend to be pluralistic. Educational level is *not* associated with any measures of power structure.

Presthus has suggested that more diversified populations are more disposed toward conflict.[29] None of the social attributes in Table 1 shows a correlation with conflict. Using other measures, however, I found medium or high levels of conflict more frequently among populations having a low proportion of persons earning over $10,000 and with an average educational level below the United States median.

Presthus has also suggested that communities with limited economic resources tend to be dominated by political leaders, whereas more affluent communities are more likely dominated by economic leaders.[30] Table 1 only shows the correlation between informals and population with a high proportion under five years of age. Other tabulations show that domination by nonofficials is positively associated with above average education (a high proportion completing high school) and wealth (a high proportion earning over $10,000 in 1960).

Communities with a low proportion of population having less than five years of education are more likely to have good government—those with a high proportion earning over $10,000 a year, where population growth is not over-represented by persons of low socio-economic status, where foreign born for any census year is 7.5 per cent or less, where population is educated above the United States median, or where the per cent of population completing high school is high.

GOVERNMENTAL STRUCTURE

The most striking findings in Table 1 with regard to governmental structure center around the function of local government. Good governments are associated with non-partisan and at-large electoral systems and with city-manager constitutions. Conversely, governments with the political functions have partisan and ward electoral systems and governmental forms without professional managers.

Crain and Rosenthal show that the handling of fluoridation issues is influenced by the ability of governmental leaders to innovate, which is related to governmental forms and electoral systems.[31] Clark predicts that

---

[29] Presthus, *loc. cit.*

[30] *Ibid.*, pp. 410–411.

[31] Robert L. Crain and Donald B. Rosenthal, "Structure and Values in Local Political Systems: The Case of Fluoridation Decisions," this volume.

the larger the number of governmental statuses in the community filled according to non-partisan procedures, the more monolithic the power structure will be.[32] Kammerer and DeGrove predict just the opposite: politics are more unstructured in non-partisan cities (because non-partisan elections are personality based and partisan elections are issue based).[33] Table 1 shows that towns with non-partisan electoral procedures are somewhat more pluralistic.

Although power structure measures 85 and 90 are uncorrelated with ward and at-large electoral systems, other power structure measures show that cities with ward systems and city managers are more pluralistic than those with at-large systems and other forms besides city managers.

CONCLUSIONS

Power Structure. Three things can be said about power structure. First, there is a trend in the United States away from centralized forms of power structures in local communities and toward more pluralistic structures. The increasing scale of our society, or what can be called *urbanization* in the most general sense of the term is the cause. Second, the degree of pluralism found in any community seems related to the history of the region. Communities in the West tend to be more pluralistic than those in the South and East. Third, type of city is a powerful predictor of power structure, but largely, it seems, because of the population characteristics associated with city type: population growth rates, density, age, and wealth.

Conflict. Although population size is an important factor in conflict—very large cities tend to be those with the most unmanageable conflicts—sheer numbers are not the "cause." Large cities have dispropor-

---

[32] Clark, *op. cit.*, Hypothesis 23.

[33] Kammerer, *op. cit.*, pp. 31–32; Charles R. Adrian ("Some General Characteristics of Nonpartisan Elections," *American Political Science Review*, Vol. 46 [Sept. 1952], 766–776) argues that non-partisanship weakens political parties. Scoble (*op. cit.*, pp. 121–122) claims correctly that non-partisan elections usually are at-large. The nonpartisan electoral scheme also normally depresses the effective role of political parties and of working-class interest groups. We found that 92% of non-partisan cities were dominated by neither political party, and politicians and parties were weaker than in partisan systems.

Robert C. Wood [*Suburbia: Its People and Their Politics* (Boston: Houghton Mifflin Co., 1958), p. 197] hypothesizes that the suburban man has grown apolitical because of his cloak of non-partisanship and the impossibility of keeping himself informed about every complex issue, while the expert is entrusted with the "touch" problems. I found no significant relationship between either suburbs or non-partisanship and the importance of experts.

tionately large numbers of persons who are poor and uneducated. These cities are also "over-diversified" economically in that they are national or regional centers of finance, manufacturing, communications, and the like. This differentiation verging on fragmentation seems to contribute to conflict.

Leaders. Population size is correlated with whether leaders will be governmental officials or not, although the relationship is not linear. But underlying the distribution of types of leaders by population size is the community economic function, and communities of various functional types tend to cluster around modal sizes. Recalling that pluralistic structures tend to have leadership from both officials and nonofficials, we conclude that economic function of a city is the best predictor of whether leaders will be officials or informals when the power structure is not overly diffuse.

Function of Local Government. Younger, wealthier, more educated, non-ethnic populations are likely to be found outside of central cities where politics is of the "good government" variety. Older, poorer, less educated, ethnic populations are likely to be found in central cities where conflict is more likely and governments must perform "political functions."

IV

COMMUNITY STRUCTURE AND DECISION-MAKING STYLES

8

POLITICAL ETHOS
AND THE STRUCTURE
OF CITY GOVERNMENTS*

☯

RAYMOND E. WOLFINGER AND JOHN OSGOOD FIELD
Stanford University

For years specialists in local politics have deplored the anecdotal quality of literature in the field and have called for theoretically-based comparative research. One of the most stimulating and ambitious attempts in this direction is Edward C. Banfield and James Q. Wilson's theory of "public-regardingness" and "private-regardingness," which states that much of what Americans think about the political world can be subsumed under one or the other of these conflicting orientations and that the prevalence of one ethos over the other influences the style, structure, and outcome of local politics.[1] Banfield and Wilson attribute these two ethics to different elements in the population and hypothesize that a number of political forms and policies are manifestations of each ethos. We intend to examine the associations between these hypothesized consequences and the demographic characteristics that are said to be the bases of the two ethics.

---

* We are grateful to Kuan Lee for writing programs and supervising computer runs for the data analysis, to Richard A. Brody, Jay Kadane, and Morris Zelditch, Jr. for advice on statistical matters, to James D. Barber, Martha Derthick, Heinz Eulau, Genevieve Knupfer, Sheilah R. Koeppen, Nelson W. Polsby, Alan Rosenthal, Gilbert Y. Steiner, Aaron B. Wildavsky, James Q. Wilson, and Barbara Kaye Wolfinger for their advice and comments at various stages of our research, and to the Graduate Division of Stanford University and the Stanford Computation Center for financial assistance.

[1] This is one of the major themes of their *City Politics* (Cambridge: Harvard University Press and the M.I.T. Press, 1963) ; see also James Q. Wilson and Edward C. Banfield, "Public-Regardingness as a Value Premise in Voting Behavior," this [*The American Political Science Review*] REVIEW, 58 (December, 1964), 876–887.

I. THE THEORY OF THE TWO ETHICS

Banfield and Wilson take their cue from a famous passage in Richard Hofstadter's *The Age of Reform* contrasting native and immigrant political values in the early twentieth century:

Out of the clash between the needs of the immigrants and the sentiments of the natives there emerged two thoroughly different systems of political ethics. . . . One, founded upon the indigenous Yankee-Protestant political traditions, and upon middle-class life, assumed and demanded the constant, disinterested activity of the citizen in public affairs, argued that political life ought to be run . . . in accordance with general principles and abstract laws apart from and superior to personal needs . . . The other system, founded upon the European backgrounds of the immigrants, upon their unfamiliarity with independent political action, their familiarity with hierarchy and authority, and upon the urgent needs that so often grew out of their migration, took for granted that the political life of the individual would arise out of family needs, interpreted political and civic relations chiefly in terms of personal obligations, and placed strong personal loyalties above allegiance to abstract codes of law or morals. It was chiefly upon this system of values that the political life of the immigrant, the boss, and the urban machine was based.[2]

Many specialists in local politics have referred to this passage in one context or another, but it remained for Banfield and Wilson to develop from it a comprehensive and persuasive theory to explain many aspects of American municipal politics. They introduce their argument as follows:

There is a tendency for [urban cleavages] to coalesce into two opposite patterns. These patterns reflect two conceptions of the public interest that are widely held. The first, which derives from the middle class ethos, favors what the municipal reform movement has always defined as "good government"— namely efficiency, impartiality, honesty, planning, strong executives, no favoritism, model legal codes . . . The other conception of the public interest (one never explicitly formulated as such, but one all the same) derives from the "immigrant ethos." This is the conception of those people who identify with the ward or neighborhood rather than the city "as a whole," who look to politicians for "help" and "favors," . . . and who are far less interested in the efficiency, impartiality, and honesty of local government than in its readiness to confer material benefits of one sort or another upon them.[3]

At first reading there are troublesome points in this passage, as in Hofstadter's. Is a strong executive part of the old American political ideal?

---

[2] (New York: Knopf, 1955), pp. 8–9.
[3] Banfield and Wilson, p. 46.

Are these "public-regarding" old settlers the same people who are usually considered devotees of Adam Smith's very private-regarding doctrine that the individual should pursue his own interests and that the public good would be achieved from the sum of individual interests? Did the peasants who came here from the monarchies of 19th century Europe introduce graft and the spoils system to America, or did they learn their bad habits from the Yankees? Did the Yankees withdraw from local politics because they could not stomach the newcomers' sordid political customs or because, outnumbered by the immigrants whom they had rebuffed and exploited, they wanted to avoid the consequences of the resulting hostility? Have Yankees led fights for municipal reform because they are more upstanding or because they find corruption a handy club with which to beat their opponents? [4]

It is well known, however, that many cities with large foreign-stock populations tend to have political orders in which good government is subordinated to favoritism and machine politics. Tammany Hall, the formidable Democratic organization in Chicago, and the confused, crooked Boston scene come immediately to mind. Furthermore, reform campaigns in these cities tend to be led by upper-middle-class Yankees and Jews whose life styles and political perspectives are a world apart from the outlook of ward heelers and clubhouse politicians.

But then one can easily think of an equal number of cases on the other side of the argument. Until its recent reformation, was Kansas City (11 per cent foreign stock) any less tainted than Boston (46 per cent)? [5] The South and the border states have notoriously corrupt politics and are just as notoriously Anglo-Saxon. Farther north, in Indiana, only 8 per cent of the residents are of foreign stock, but state employees are "maced" 2 per cent of their pay for the benefit of the ruling political party. In Pennsylvania, dominated until a dozen years ago by a Republican party based on small-town, native-born Americans, at least 40,000 state jobs are at the disposal of the party that wins control of the state government. [6]

---

[4] Here, with Banfield and Wilson, we refer not to the stylish young liberal club members of California and Manhattan, but to the more conservative "good government" forces in many cities.

[5] Throughout this article the "percent foreign stock" or "percent ethnic" refers to the proportion of a city's 1960 population that is foreign born or native born with at least one parent born abroad. Nineteen per cent of the total U.S. population is of foreign stock. Data on nativity and parentage are from U.S. Bureau of the Census, *County and City Data Book, 1962* (Washington: U.S. Government Printing Office, 1962).

[6] Perhaps because so much of the best scholarly research on local politics has been conducted close to the great universities of the Northeast and perhaps also because

The most obvious fact that emerges from this recital is that such comparisons are idle. Attempts to verify the existence of the two ethics and analyze their political consequences will have to proceed beyond discussion of simple honesty and dishonesty. Fortunately Banfield and Wilson have elaborated their basic hypothesis by drawing from the general theory of conflicting ethics a number of propositions about specific manifestations of one ethos or the other. "The logic of the middle class ideal implies also certain institutional arrangements" conducive to government by experts in the interests of the city as a whole: the city manager plan, nonpartisan ballots, election of the city council at large, or, if wards are used, from large districts.[7] On the other hand, the private-regarding ethos favors mayors, partisan ballots, and election of councilmen from wards, prefer-ably small ones. The differences between the two ethics are said to be reflected as well in various municipal policies. The public-regarding ethos favors complete civil service coverage of city employees in order to maxi-mize the professional and impartial conduct of public business. On the other hand, the private-regarding ethos emphasizes favoritism and patron-age and therefore opposes civil service. Because the public-regarding ethos is concerned with the city as a whole and with long-range attempts to manage and improve the local environment, it favors city planning and urban renewal. The private-regarding ethos opposes such policies because they interrupt neighborhood patterns and impose unwelcome restraints on the city's residents.

Other writers have seen much of this conflict as a clash between middle-class admiration of efficiency and the working-class' desires for representation of their interests.[8] Some critics of Banfield and Wilson say that the labels for the two ethics are much too value-laden and that preferences described as selfish or unselfish could more properly be inter-preted in terms of the different interests of different social classes.[9] For example, the fact that poor people protest urban renewal projects may be

---

most serious nonacademic writers live in a few northeastern cities, political organiza-tions in these cities have been described at great length, while very little is known about existing machines in other parts of the country.

[7] Banfield and Wilson, p. 330; see also *ibid.*, pp. 92, 95, 154, 170.

[8] See, e.g., Leo F. Schnore and Robert R. Alford, "Forms of Government and Socioeconomic Characteristics of Suburbs," *Administrative Science Quarterly*, 8 (June, 1963), 1–17.

[9] See especially Herbert Kaufman's review of *City Politics* in this REVIEW, 58 (June, 1964), 422–423. Kaufman asks, "are those measures designated 'public-regarding' by Banfield and Wilson *really* manifestations of selfless fellow feeling or are they the self-serving policies of a particular group in society that is trying to hold on to what it has?" (p. 423).

due not so much to private-regardingness as to the fact that the houses demolished in such projects usually are the homes of the poor.

These caveats are not germane to this study. We are not concerned for the moment with either the morality or the consequences of any particular governmental form or policy, nor are we concerned with how and where particular legal forms can be subverted by local political styles. We are examining the relationship between various forms and policies and the social properties of the relevant cities. It is sufficient for this purpose only to assume that the differences between the alternative forms are worth talking about.

A more important question remains: is the independent variable ethnicity or occupational status? Some parts of the country have scarcely any foreign-stock population, while the distribution of social classes is, of course, fairly even not only from one region to another, but also among most cities. Moreover, cities with large ethnic populations do not necessarily have small middle classes. The correlation coefficient between per cent ethnic and per cent in white collar occupations for all New England cities of over 50,000 population is −.04; it is faintly positive for other regions with appreciable ethnic populations: .29 in the Middle Atlantic states, .20 in the Midwest, and .24 in the West.[10]

Banfield and Wilson seem to consider the two dimensions interchangeable. Sometimes they attribute the two ethics to ethnicity, sometimes to social class, and sometimes they mingle both explanations. The weight of evidence suggests that ethnicity is meant to be the controlling independent variable. The theme of the two ethics is introduced in a discussion of cleavages between old settlers and immigrants.[11] In a more recent work they remark, "We do not think that income *per se* has this effect [making people private- or public-regarding]; rather it is the ethnic attributes, or culture, empirically associated with it." [12] But this interpretation is confounded by statements like this: "The assimilation of lower-class people into the middle class has, of course, entailed their assimilation to the political ethos of the Anglo-Saxon-Protestant elite . . ." [13]

Is a combination of ethnicity and working-class status the origin of the private-regarding ethos? If so, why would upward mobility produce a change? It might be argued that private-regardingness is a consequence of ethnic consciousness, which disappears when middle-class status is at-

---

[10] In these computations the Midwest includes Ohio, Indiana, Illinois, Iowa, Michigan, Minnesota, and Wisconsin.

[11] Banfield and Wilson, pp. 38–46.

[12] Wilson and Banfield, p. 885.

[13] Banfield and Wilson, p. 123; see also *ibid.*, p. 329.

tained. But the available data indicate that social mobility often has little effect on ethnic consciousness.[14] Nor is it plausible that upward-mobile ethnics will readily abandon their political perspectives in favor of views more characteristic of the middle class.[15]

Some of these difficulties may be resolved if "middle class" is interpreted, for present purposes, as "upper middle class." Indeed, in some passages Banfield and Wilson indicate that the important line of demarcation is between professional and business people on the one hand and lower status groups on the other. But the bulk of their treatment of the two ethics contradicts this. In particular, their discussion of the likelihood that "the middle class will in the very long run assimilate the lower class entirely" [16] suggests that they include everyone in a white collar occupation in the "middle class" as far as the two ethics are concerned.

Banfield and Wilson do not explain why immigrants should be private-regarding. Their silence on this point is a source of numerous complications. Did the immigrants bring the private-regarding ethos with them from their former countries or was it a product of interaction between their predispositions and the conditions of life they found in the United States? Hofstadter seems to favor the latter interpretation, but Banfield and Wilson speak of the ethos that "the new immigrants brought with them." [17] If the immigrants came with the private-regarding ethos, one would expect to find it distributed around the country in proportion to the number of persons of foreign stock. (This assumes, of course, that immigrants from different countries have similar inclinations to private-regardingness. Banfield and Wilson do not consider this point, except to single out Polish-Americans as particularly likely to be private-regarding, for reasons that are not explained.) [18]

On the other hand, if the ethos is a response to American life, one would expect that its distribution would be related not only to the proportion of immigrants in the population, but also to the character of their experience in America. Typical immigrant experiences differed considerably from one region to another. This was notably true of the West, where non-Anglo-Saxon immigrants arrived with or on the heels of the earliest

---

[14] Raymond E. Wolfinger, "The Development and Persistence of Ethnic Voting," this REVIEW, 59 (December, 1965), 896–908.

[15] In other areas of political behavior the upward mobile tend to have characteristics midway between their old and new classes; see James Barber, *Social Mobility and Political Behavior* (Chicago: Rand McNally, forthcoming).

[16] Banfield and Wilson, p. 123.

[17] *Ibid.*, p. 40.

[18] *Ibid.*, p. 235.

settlers. All shared the rigors of pioneering and the profits and instabilities of boom economies.[19] Compared to those in the settled Eastern cities, immigrants to the West were better off and better educated; labor was scarcer, wages were higher, and class distinctions were weaker and more unstable.[20] Status and income were neither so fixed nor so strongly stratified. If private-regardingness is an acquired characteristic, it seems likely that different regional immigrant histories might produce different levels of attachment to the ethos or perhaps different manifestations of it.

These observations do not invalidate the ethos theory, but they do suggest some necessary modifications. In particular, since the quality of the immigrant experience differed from region to region, it appears that a given level of foreign-stock population in, say, California and New York might produce very different levels of private-regardingness in the two places.[21] Our findings support this inference.

Several pieces of published research bear on the ethos theory. John H. Kessel found that the mayor form was more common in cities with large ethnic populations.[22] Schnore and Alford report the same finding in their study of 300 suburbs, but the difference here is slight: 9.3 per cent foreign-born population in mayor cities compared to 8 per cent in manager cities.[23] Both studies also found that manager cities had larger proportions of residents in white-color occupations.[24] Phillips Cutright suggests that partisan elections are more likely to be found where "community cleavages" are intense, because such divisions provide "political parties with the social basis necessary for effective organization and sufficient activity necessary for survival as a community force." [25] He used two measures of "high cleavage": more than 50 per cent of the population employed in manufacturing indicates economic cleavage; while more than 20 per cent

---

[19] See, e.g., Louis Berg, "Peddlers in Eldorado," *Commentary*, July, 1965, pp. 64–66.

[20] Earl Pomeroy, *The Pacific Slope* (New York: Alfred A. Knopf, 1965).

[21] Similarly, an analysis of local voting returns in the 1960 presidential election showed considerable regional variation in the responses of similar Protestant voting groups to President Kennedy's candidacy; see Lucy S. Davidowicz and Leon J. Goldstein, *Politics in a Pluralist Democracy* (New York: Institute of Human Relations Press, 1963).

[22] John H. Kessel, "Governmental Structure and Political Environment: A Statistical Note about American Cities," this REVIEW, 56 (September, 1962), 615–620.

[23] Schnore and Alford, *op. cit.*, p. 12.

[24] Edgar L. Sherbenou found that Chicago suburbs with higher priced homes are very likely to use the manager form, while more modest towns all have mayors; see his "Class, Participation, and the Council-Manager Plan," *Public Administration Review*, 21 (Summer, 1961), 131-135.

[25] Phillips Cutright, "Nonpartisan Electoral Systems in American Cities," *Comparative Studies in Society and History*, 5 (January, 1963), p. 218.

Catholics indicates religious cleavage. By either measure, high-cleavage cities were more likely to use the partisan ballot.[26]

These studies have severe limitations as sources of evidence for the ethos theory. They are concerned with only two of its dependent variables. More important, they do not include controls for third variables, particularly region. Since some parts of the country are almost devoid of foreign-stock residents (and Catholics), it is reasonable to try to separate the influence of region from that of local population characteristics. Furthermore, western and southwestern cities, whatever their economic bases, tend to have larger white-collar populations than cities in the Northeast and Midwest. Because of the historical development of land-use patterns, these cities usually have more extensive residential neighborhoods with suburban characteristics, and thus have suffered less from the postwar flight to the suburbs that has reduced middle class populations in core cities elsewhere.

II. RESEARCH DESIGN

The ethos theory states that the city manager form of government, the nonpartisan ballot, at-large election of city legislators, big wards, civil service coverage of municipal employees, city planning, and urban renewal are favored by the public-regarding ethos, which is a prominent aspect of the political perspectives of white Anglo-Saxon Protestants. The opposing private-regarding ethos, rooted in the immigrant experience, favors the mayor form, the partisan ballot, ward election of city legislators, and small wards; it is opposed to civil service, city planning, and urban renewal.[27] We have treated all these features as dependent variables and examined their relationship to the key independent variable, the proportion of a city's population that is of foreign stock. Other independent variables include social class (measured by the percentage of the labor force em-

---

[26] One proposition of the ethos theory states that public-regardingness is manifested in support for expansion of many government services that do not benefit the individual, but that will increase his tax payments. In their own work Banfield and Wilson have found that, among homeowners subject to property taxes, support for such measures to be financed by property taxation rises with the median income and home value of the voting unit. They also found that voting units with large foreign-stock populations were less likely to support such measures. They believe that the controlling element in these relationships is ethnicity, and attribute the findings to the prevalence of the private-regarding ethos among ethnic group members; see Banfield and Wilson, pp. 237–240; and Wilson and Banfield.

[27] A number of other political forms, styles, and policies are said to be favored by one or the other of the two ethics. Data permitting inter-city comparisons are not available on these other variables.

ployed in white collar occupations), median family income, and educational level (measured by the median school years completed by residents aged 25 or over). We examined the relationship between each independent and dependent variable within each major region of the United States. We also measured the degree of association between ethnicity and each dependent variable while controlling for social class, income, and education. The dependent variables and their hypothesized relationships to the two ethics are summarized in Figure 1.

FIGURE 1. The Dependent Variables

	Private-Regarding	Public-Regarding
Form of Government	Mayor	Manager
Type of Ballot	Partisan	Nonpartisan
Method of Electing Councilmen	Wards	At-Large
Size of Council Districts	Small	Large
Civil Service Coverage	Less	More
City Planning Expenditures	Low	High
Urban Renewal	Low	High

This study includes all 309 incorporated cities with 1960 populations in excess of 50,000 persons, excluding Washington, D.C. Data on all dependent variables except urban renewal were taken from *The Municipal Year Book 1963*.[28] The magnitude of urban renewal programs was measured by capital grants per capita for each city. Raw data on capital grants were obtained from the *Urban Renewal Directory* for December 31, 1963.[29] A variety of demographic data for each city was obtained from the *County and City Data Book, 1962*.

Cities are not always free to make their own decisions on what governmental forms they will adopt and what policies they will follow. State constitutions and legislatures often interfere with home rule by requiring cities to conform to particular forms or preventing them from adopting others. We have investigated this problem at some length and consulted scholars and officials of several professional organizations in the

---

[28] Orin F. Nolting and David S. Arnold (eds.), *The Municipal Year Book 1963* (Chicago: The International City Managers' Association, 1963).

[29] Urban Renewal Administration, *Urban Renewal Directory, December 31, 1963* (Washington: Urban Renewal Administration, 1964).

field of municipal government.[30] Whenever state law imposes constraints on cities' free choice with respect to any dependent variable we have omitted such cities from the relevant analyses.

It might be argued that our index of ethnicity is both too exclusive and too inclusive. Foreign-stock population percentages exclude Negroes, who might be considered inclined to the private-regarding ethos.[31] But 1960 levels of Negro population in northern cities reflect recent migration. In most such cities Negroes were scarce and politically unimportant until the postwar years; as with all newcomers, they still have not mobilized themselves so as to exert political strength commensurate with their numbers. In the South, of course, Negroes have been disfranchised until recently. Most southern cities have now gone a long way toward removing impediments to Negro voting, but the recency and unevenness of this development makes it difficult to use numbers as an index of Negro political influence.

The criterion might be considered too inclusive in that most Jews are first- or second-generation Americans, and Banfield and Wilson say that at least upper-middle-class Jews are public regarding.[32] Jews amount to three or four per cent of the total American population. Almost all of them live in northern cities; more than a quarter live in New York City, where they comprise almost 30 per cent of the population. Aside from New York and a few other places, Jews have not been sizable parts of most cities' populations. Since only some Jews are exempted from the charge of private-regardingness and since we exclude the very large cities where most of them live from many of our computations, this problem is not so great.

In recent years many Jews have moved to the cities of southern Florida, some of which now have foreign-stock populations as large as any

---

[30] For information on state restrictions on home rule we are grateful to, among others, David S. Arnold of the International City Managers' Association, William N. Cassella, Jr. of the National Municipal League, Eugene C. Lee of the Institute of Governmental Studies of the University of California (Berkeley), and Keith Ocheltree of the Public Personnel Association.

[31] Banfield and Wilson do not include Negroes in those groups they consider disposed to private-regardingness, although some political goals they attribute to Negroes, such as desires for representation and "recognition," might be thought to incline them in that direction (Banfield and Wilson, pp. 158–159, 293–294, 307–308). On the other hand, Negroes are described as disproportionately public-regarding in their voting on bond issues (ibid., pp. 237–239).

[32] See, e.g., ibid., pp. 42, 123, 330. While upper-middle-class Jews are often classified with Yankees as adherents of the public-regarding ethos, Banfield and Wilson do not say if they are any more likely to be public-regarding than Catholics of similar social status.

northern community. (In fact, Miami Beach, 53 per cent of whose population is ethnic, leads the nation in this category.) Since most Jewish Floridians have lived in the state only a few years, they are unlikely to have political influence in proportion to their numbers, and so one would not expect that the political practices of Florida cities would fully reflect their preferences. These cities are the exceptions to the general rule that 1960 levels of ethnic populations are a fairly reliable index of each city's relative ethnicity over the past fifty years.

The ethos theory does not refer to the actual incidence of its various dependent variables, but to attitudes toward the variables.[33] Therefore, propositions specifying relationships between cities' population characteristics and their political forms and policies are inferences from the ethos theory, not parts of the theory itself. These inferences are based on the assumptions that the strength of the public- and private-regarding ethics is related to the magnitude of the population groupings that supposedly give rise to one ethos or the other, *and* that the two ethics are important causal factors in city politics. Banfield and Wilson seem to have made the same assumption: "Obviously the social and ecological structure of a city largely determines which view as to the proper role of government will prevail in it."[34]

How valid are these inferences? Obviously it would be unwise to assert that there is a simple causal relationship between public attitudes toward a particular governmental feature and the likelihood that that feature will be adopted. Many other considerations affect the nature of local political institutions. Some of these other factors, such as state law, can be identified. Others, such as the interrelationship of other demo-

---

[33] We think it unlikely that most individuals' political knowledge has developed to the point of having opinions about, say, the relative merits of ward and at-large elections. Thus the ethics may exist at two levels: as general value systems for most people and as a set of specific political preferences for their leaders.

[34] Banfield and Wilson, p. 55. Our interpretation of this statement is based on its context, Banfield and Wilson's citation of the Sherbenou and Schnore—Alford correlational studies in support of their proposition about public-regardingness and the city manager plan (*ibid.*, p. 169 n), and passages like this:

"Many council-manager cities are upper-class or middle-class in character; few if any are predominantly lower-class. In the Chicago area, for example, . . . eighteen of the twenty cities with the highest home values had the [manager] plan, whereas none of the thirty-one cities with the lowest home values had it. Its popularity with people of the upper and middle classes explains its popularity in small communities, which are more likely to consist predominantly of those classes that are large ones" (*ibid.*, p. 169).

graphic variables, can be controlled by statistical manipulation. The effect of city size and region can also be controlled. Other factors, such as different national origins of immigrants, can be partially and indirectly isolated by analyzing the data by region.

When all these other variables have been taken into account, we do not think it untenable to assume that if the two ethics: a) exist, b) have the properties attributed to them, and c) are associated with the ethnic composition of urban populations, then this will be reflected in statistical associations between a specific hypothesized dependent variable and levels of ethnicity, when such associations are examined in large groups of cities. This assumption does not deny the existence of other independent variables, but it does require that the ethos be of sufficient importance so that, *in the aggregate*, its influence will be discernible. If the hypothesized relationship between ethnicity and a given political form is not found, three conclusions can be considered: a) a preference for that form is not part of the ethos; b) the ethos is not related to ethnicity; c) the two ethics are not translated into political reality.

We will explore three general questions in the following sections. First, to what extent do the structural dependent variables—form of government, type of ballot, and method of electing councilmen—go together? For example, do cities with mayors also use the partisan ballot and elect their councilmen from wards? Second, how do cities differ by size and region with respect both to ethnicity and to the structural dependent variables? Third, and most important, what are the relationships between ethnicity and the dependent variables?

III. THE CONSISTENCY OF POLITICAL FORMS

All the structural manifestations of public-regardingness were elements in the municipal reform movement that began with the 20th century. Civil service, nonpartisanship, at-large elections, and big districts were principal features of the National Municipal League's "municipal program," issued in 1900. Together with the manager plan and city planning, these measures were incorporated in the League's "Model City Charter," promulgated in 1916 and reissued several times subsequently.[35] Since these various features have all been part of a package, jointly promoted and presumably reflecting the same spirit, one might expect that they would be

---

[35] *Ibid.*, p. 141. The International City Managers' Association considers nonpartisanship and at-large election "main features" of the manager system (*ibid.*, p. 172).

found together in practice.[36] This conclusion follows both from the logic of Banfield and Wilson's argument and from their statement that "people who are decidedly public-regarding or decidedly private-regarding on one matter tend to be so on all matters." [37]

Of the 309 cities, 146 use the manager form, 126 have elected mayors, and 37 have commission government. We will omit the commission cities from consideration because this form does not figure in the ethos theory. Of the cities with mayors or managers, 85 use the partisan and 186 use the nonpartisan ballot (information on one city is missing) ; 153 cities elect their councilmen at large, 67 elect them from wards, and 49 cities use a combination of the two methods (data on two cities are missing).[38] How do these features go together? If a city follows one ethos in one structural feature, will it be consistent with the same ethos in the other two features? It is clear that there will be less than a perfect fit in this respect, since the number of cities with a particular private-regarding feature ranges from 126 (with mayors) to 67 (electing councilmen from wards).

Manager cities are fairly consistent in their adoption of the other two structural variables: 85 per cent of them use the nonpartisan ballot, 81 per cent elect their councilmen at large, and 70 per cent use both the nonpartisan ballot and at-large elections. Mayor cities are much less consistent: half of them have partisan elections, 41 per cent elect their councilmen from wards, and only 23 per cent follow both of these private-regarding practices. As Table 1 shows, cities with mayors seem to be very eclectic in their choice of governmental institutions. Less than a quarter of them are "pure" private-regarding types and almost as many cities have each of the five other possible combinations of type of ballot and method of electing councilmen.

Three out of four cities with partisan local elections have mayors, but less than half of these partisan mayor cities also elect councilmen from wards. Partisan manager cities overwhelmingly prefer at-large elections. Where local elections are nonpartisan, two out of three communities are on

---

[36] Cf. Banfield and Wilson, "The connection between the partisan and district systems, as between the nonpartisan and at-large systems, is of considerable significance, for, as we shall see later, the connected elements tend in both cases to produce the same style of politics and to reinforce one another" (p. 90).

[37] *Ibid.*, p. 235.

[38] Cities that elect at least three-quarters of their municipal legislators from wards are classified as using the ward system; the same criterion is used with the at-large system. Cities that elect more even proportions by the two methods are classified as "combination" cities. Since all cities using the commission form elect the commission at large, they are omitted from these tabulations.

TABLE 1. TYPE OF BALLOT AND METHOD OF ELECTING COUNCILMEN
IN MANAGER AND MAYOR CITIES

Form of Government and Type of Ballot	Method of Electing Councilmen			
	Ward	At-Large	Combination	Totals
Manager				
Partisan	3%(4)	11%(16)	1%(2)	15%(22)
Nonpartisan	9 (13)	70 (101)	6 (9)	85 (123)
	12%(17)	81%(117)	7%(11)	100%(145) [a]
Mayor				
Partisan	23%(28)	11%(14)	17%(21)	51%(63)
Nonpartisan	18 (22)	18 (22)	14 (17)	49 (61)
	41%(50)	29%(36)	31%(38)	100%(124) [b]

[a] Data on method of electing councilmen missing for one city.

[b] Data on method of electing councilmen or type of ballot missing for two cities.

the manager plan; and most of these cities also elect their councilmen at large. These data are presented in Table 2.

Cities electing councilmen from wards are very likely to have mayors as are cities with a combination of ward and at-large elections. Both of these groups of cities are rather evenly split between partisan and nonparti-

TABLE 2. FORM OF GOVERNMENT AND METHOD OF ELECTING COUNCILMEN IN
CITIES USING THE PARTISAN AND NONPARTISAN BALLOT [a]

Type of Ballot and Form of Government	Method of Electing Councilmen			
	Ward	At-Large	Combination	Totals
Partisan:				
Mayor	33% (28)	16% (14)	25% (21)	74% (63)
Manager	5 (4)	19 (16)	2 (2)	26 (22)
	38% (32)	35% (30)	27% (23)	100% (85)
Nonpartisan:				
Mayor	12% (22)	12% (22)	9% (17)	33% (61)
Manager	7 (13)	55 (101)	5 (9)	67 (123)
	19% (35)	67% (123)	14% (26)	100% (184)[b]

[a] Cities with the commission form of government have been excluded from this table.

[b] Data on method of electing councilmen are not reported for two cities.

san ballots. By a similar three-to-one ratio, at-large cities have managers, and most of these communities also have nonpartisan elections.

In short, there is a recognizable "public-regarding" structural syndrome in American cities. Most of the manager cities have followed the advice of the National Municipal League and adopted nonpartisan ballots and at-large elections. But the opposite is not true; there is no "private-regarding" syndrome. Instead, cities with mayors have, in fairly equal proportions, every conceivable combination of the other two structural

TABLE 3. TYPE OF BALLOT AND FORM OF GOVERNMENT IN CITIES ELECTING COUNCILMEN FROM WARDS, AT-LARGE, AND BY A COMBINATION OF METHODS [a]

Method of Election and Type of Ballot	Form of Government		
	Mayor	*Manager*	*Totals*
By Wards:			
Partisan	42% (28)	6% (4)	48% (32)
Nonpartisan	33 (22)	19 (13)	52 (35)
	75% (50)	25% (17)	100% (67)
At-Large:			
Partisan	9% (14)	10% (16)	20% [b] (30)
Nonpartisan	14 (22)	66 (101)	80 (123)
	23% (36)	76% (117)	100% (153)
By a Combination:			
Partisan	43% (21)	4% (2)	47% (23)
Nonpartisan	35 (17)	18 (9)	53 (26)
	78% (38)	22% (11)	100% (49)

[a] Cities with the commission form of government have been excluded from this table.

[b] Does not sum to 19% because of rounding.

variables. Forty-eight per cent of all cities with mayors or managers are "pure types"; the others are hybrids of one sort or another.

Civil service coverage of municipal employees is another element in the "good government" package and in the public-regarding ethos. *The Municipal Year Book* reports civil service coverage of various classes of municipal employees. These data refer only to the formal regulations. Undoubtedly the prevailing political style in many cities subverts the personnel laws. In Chicago, for example, all municipal workers except those in public utilities are "covered" by civil service. In fact, of course, a great many jobs in the Chicago government can be used for patronage purposes with little difficulty. Nevertheless we assume that in the aggregate the extent of official civil service coverage gives some indication of the reality of public personnel policies.[39] We have used *The Municipal Year Book* reports to develop four levels of civil service coverage that apply to almost all cities:

Level 1. All employees covered; 106 cities.

Level 2. All employees except manual workers covered; 13 cities.

Level 3. Only firemen and policemen covered; 57 cities.

Level 4. No civil service coverage; 33 cities.

Iowa, New York, and Ohio require their cities to use merit systems; in Massachusetts all local employees come under the jurisdiction of the state civil service commission. Since cities in these four states are not free to make their own personnel policies, we have excluded them from all tabulations involving civil service coverage.

We have compared the civil service coverage of municipal employees in mayor and manager cities.[40] Table 4 shows the proportion of each type of city that has each of the four levels of coverage. A slightly larger share of manager cities has complete coverage and somewhat more mayor cities are at level 2. These differences are small, however, and equal proportions of both groups are at levels 3 and 4. There is little more than a random chance that the two alleged manifestations of the public-regarding ethos, city manager government and civil service protection, will be found together.

The various hypothesized manifestations of the two ethics are often found in "inconsistent" combinations. This suggests that the two ethics may be somewhat less differentiated from each other than Banfield and Wilson say. The forces influencing a city's choice of any one of these variables probably differ considerably in strength and composition from

---

[39] "However important may be the evasions of the civil service system in particular cases, it is clear that in general the effect of the system everywhere has been to make it increasingly difficult for the parties to maintain effective discipline over their workers by giving and withholding jobs" (*ibid.*, p. 209).

[40] State law in Anglo-Saxon Indiana makes it almost impossible for cities there to deviate from the mayor form of government. Since form of municipal government is not subject to local choice, we have excluded the nine Indiana cities from the tabulation presented in Table 4. Several other states interfere with home rule in this respect, but their cities all use the commission form and on this ground are excluded from our tabulations.

TABLE 4. FORM OF GOVERNMENT AND LEVEL OF
CIVIL SERVICE COVERAGE [a]

Level of Civil Service Coverage	Mayor	Manager
1. All employees covered	49%	56%
2. All but manual workers covered	10	2
3. Only policemen and firemen covered	25	25
4. No civil service coverage	16	17
Total	100%	100%
N	(61)	(110)

[a] Excludes cities in Indiana, Iowa, Massachusetts, New York and Ohio.

the factors influencing choices of other variables. These data indicate the unevenness of the wave of structural reform that swept over American cities in the twentieth century. They also suggest that the pressures for and against different items in the catalogue of reform were not as similar as has been assumed.

IV. CITY SIZE AND REGION AS INDEPENDENT VARIABLES

The second general question is how cities of different size and in different regions vary in their formal governmental characteristics and in the ethnic level of their populations.

Size turns out to make surprisingly little difference with respect either to ethnicity or structural characteristics. Cities with more than half a million residents are much more likely to have mayors, but below this point there is only a slight trend toward use of the manager form as size declines further.[41] (Mayors become more popular again in cities below 50,000 population.) Only cities with more than a million inhabitants are much more likely to elect their council members from wards; below this level the trend is slightly and irregularly toward the at-large system. The pattern is more uneven with respect to type of ballot. Cities with populations of more than a million and those in the 100,000 to 250,000 category are most likely to have partisan elections (although the nonpartisan ballot

---

[41] Cf. Banfield and Wilson, "The larger the city, generally speaking, the more is at stake politically, and consequently the greater the effort that professional politicians will put forth to avoid being displaced. This is certainly a factor that generally tends to prevent adoption of the [city manager] plan in a large city" (pp. 182–183).

is still preferred by 60 per cent of the cities in each category), and cities in the quarter to half million group are least likely to hold partisan elections. But these differences are not, by and large, very great, and there is no consistent relationship between size and use of one ballot or the other. These data are presented in Table 5.

Similar findings hold with respect to the relationship between size and ethnicity. As Table 6 shows, small and medium-sized cities are just as

TABLE 5. GOVERNMENTAL FORMS AND CITY SIZE

Size	Form of Government [a]		Type of Ballot [b]	Method of Election [c]		Number in Each Size Category
	Mayor	Manager	Partisan	Ward	At-Large	
Over 1 million	100%	—	40%	60%	20	5
500,000 to 1 million	73%	27	33%	27%	53	15
250,000 to 500,000	43%	40	23%	17%	73	30
100,000 to 250,000	39%	48	40%	20%	67	79
50,000 to 100,000	37%	51	29%	22%	60	180
Mean for all cities over 50,000	41%	47	32%	22%	62	
N	(126)	(146)	(98)	(67)	(190)	(309)

[a] Cities with the commission form of government have been excluded from these columns but not from the base on which the percentages were computed.

[b] All other cities use the nonpartisan ballot, except for one city for which data on type of ballot are missing.

[c] Cities using a combination of the ward and at-large method have been excluded from these columns but not from the base on which the percentages were computed. Data on the method used in three cities are missing.

likely as the country's biggest cities to have large foreign stock populations. Whatever its importance in other areas, a city's size is an unimportant variable either for ethnicity or (with the exceptions noted) governmental structure.

The major operational conclusion to be drawn from these findings is that size need not be controlled in examining relationships between ethnicity and the structural dependent variables, except to exclude cities of over half a million population when form of government is a variable, and cities of over a million when analyzing the method of electing councilmen. Controlling for size turned out to be unnecessary for another reason: when we did it, there was no change in the results that are presented later in this paper.

Tables 7 and 8 show the distribution of alternative forms of govern-

TABLE 6. FOREIGN-STOCK POPULATION AND CITY SIZE

Proportion of Population of Foreign Stock	Population Size		
	Over 250,000	100,000 to 250,000	50,000 to 100,000
0% to 9.9%	30%	32%	26%
10% to 19.9%	16	15	21
20% to 29.9%	18	28	21
30% to 39.9%	28	10	14
40% to 49.9%	6	14	13
50% and over	2	1	6
	100%	100%	101% [a]
Per cent of cities with 20% or more foreign stock	54%	53%	53%

[a] Sums to more than 100% because of rounding.

ment, types of ballot, and methods of electing councilmen in different parts of the country. These tables demonstrate the striking regional variations in each of these characteristics. The mayor form is the predominant one in the Northeast, is somewhat favored in the Midwest, unpopular in the South, and even less popular in the West.[42] The distribution is similar for the type of ballot; partisan elections are preferred only in the Northeast. There are, however, two quite different patterns in the two sub-regions of the Northeast. Mid-Atlantic cities (in New York, New Jersey, and Pennsylvania) use the partisan ballot by a ratio of more than four to one, while almost two-thirds of the New England cities have nonpartisan local elections. Elsewhere in the country the nonpartisan system is heavily favored; in the West only three cities have partisan elections.[43] Regional variations in methods of electing councilmen are much milder, as Table 8 shows.

[42] The western cities are those in the conventionally defined eleven western states, plus Honolulu. The Northeast includes the six New England states plus New York, New Jersey, and Pennsylvania. The Midwest includes Ohio, Indiana, Illinois, Iowa, Michigan, Minnesota, Wisconsin, North Dakota, South Dakota, Nebraska, and Kansas. The South includes the eleven ex-Confederate states.

[43] Most western cities examined here are in California, where all cities use the nonpartisan ballot. California law does *not* require nonpartisan local elections, however. In 1913 the legislature required "general-law" cities (those without charters) to use the nonpartisan ballot. This did not apply to charter cities, of which there were 70 in 1960, including the communities in our sample. Any California municipality of more than 3500 persons may adopt its own charter. See Eugene C. Lee, *The Politics of Nonpartisanship* (Berkeley and Los Angeles: University of California Press, 1960), pp. 13–15, 23.

TABLE 7. FORM OF GOVERNMENT AND TYPE OF BALLOT—BY REGION

Region	Form of Government			Type of Ballot		Number of Cities in Region
	Mayor	Manager	Commis-sion	Partisan	Nonpar-tisan	
Northeast	65%	18	17	61%	39	76
Midwest	55%	37	8	33%	67	84
West	15%	81	3	5%	95	59
South	22%	59	19	19%	81	74
Border	38%	56	6	44%	56	16
All cities over 50,000	41%	47%	12%	32%	68%	
N	(126)	(146)	(37)	(98)	(210)	(309)

TABLE 8. METHOD OF ELECTING COUNCILMEN BY
REGION, EXCLUDING COMMISSION CITIES

Region	Ward	At-Large	Combi-nation	Total	
				%	N
Northeast	31%	38	31	100	61
Midwest	33%	46	21	100	76
West	18%	75	7	100	57
South	13%	73	13	99 [a]	60
Border	33%	53	13	99 [a]	15
(All cities) over 50,000	25%	57%	18%	100%	
N	(67)	(153)	(49)		(269)

[a] Does not sum to 100 because of rounding.

Midwestern and northeastern cities are most addicted to the "private-regarding" alternative; almost one third of each group elect legislators from wards. Three quarters of the cities in the West and South use the at-large system.

Just as regional variations in structure are immense, so are they in levels of ethnicity. As Table 9 demonstrates, the Northeast is the most ethnic part of the country, with 94 per cent of its cities having more than the national average (19 per cent) of first- and second-generation Americans, and more than half being over 40 per cent foreign stock. The New England sub-region has the heaviest concentration of immigrants and their children; 27 of the 33 New England cities in our sample are at least 40 per cent ethnic. The distribution is somewhat less skewed in the Midwest. Just under half of the cities there are less than 20 per cent ethnic, with almost all the rest in the 20 to 40 per cent range. The western cities show a different pattern; 84 per cent of them fall between 10 and 30 per cent foreign stock. Almost all the southern and border cities are homogeneously native, except for a few towns on the Mexican border and in the Florida

TABLE 9. FOREIGN-STOCK POPULATION OF CITIES—BY REGION

Proportion of Population of Foreign Stock	Northeast	Midwest	West	South	Border
0% to 9.9%	3%	16%	2%	80%	69%
10% to 19.9%	4	31	31	11	19
20% to 29.9%	17	24	53	4	6
30% to 39.9%	24	24	12	3	6
40% to 49.9%	40	6	3	—	—
50% and over	13	—	—	3 [a]	—
Totals	101% [b]	101% [b]	101% [b]	101% [b]	100%
Per cent of cities with 20% or more foreign stock	94%	54%	68%	10%	12%

[a] Miami Beach and Laredo.

[b] Does not sum to 100 because of rounding.

resort belt. The foreign-stock residents in the former cases are, of course, largely Mexicans who have not participated heavily in local politics.[44] In the latter case the ethnics are mostly Jews who have moved to Florida in recent years.

V. ETHNICITY AND POLITICAL STRUCTURES

We come now to the central question, the relationship between cities' ethnic populations and political forms. It might be assumed that the preceding section has already answered the question with a resounding affirmation of the ethos theory, for those regions with the largest foreign stock populations have the highest proportion of cities with elements of the

---

[44] For a description of Mexican-American political apathy in one Texas border city see Edward C. Banfield, *Big City Politics* (New York: Random House, 1965), pp. 76–78.

private-regarding ethic. There are some exceptions to this, notably in the popularity of nonpartisanship in New England and in the consistent deviation of the West, but by and large the pattern is as predicted by the ethos theory.

More precise measures produce the same result. Excluding cities with a commission form of government and comparing the mean foreign stock populations of cities with mayors and with managers, we find that mayor cities have a much higher mean ethnic population. All mayor cities have a mean foreign-stock population of 29 per cent; those with a manager form are 18 per cent foreign stock. This difference is significant at the .001 level of confidence.[45]

But since both ethnicity and types of governmental structure vary markedly from one part of the country to another, it is necessary to control for region when examining the relationships between these variables. The South, for example, has few foreign-stock residents and few institutional manifestations of the private-regarding ethos. Indeed, the relationship in the South is so strong that it probably accounts in large part for the nationwide findings described in the preceding paragraph. But it would be rash to attribute southern political patterns to the scarcity of immigrants there. (Southern and border cities are excluded from the following intra-region comparisons because there is so little variation in the level of their foreign-stock populations.)

When the relationship between ethnicity and form of government is examined *within* regions, this control eliminates most of the apparent relationship. (We have also controlled for size by eliminating all cities of more than 500,000 population.) Northeastern cities with mayors have a mean ethnic population of 39 per cent; those with managers are 40 per cent foreign stock. The predicted relationship is found in the Midwest,[46] where cities with mayors average 6 per cent more ethnic than cities with managers. This difference is significant at the .05 level. There is a similar finding in the West, although its importance is diminished by the fact that only six western cities have mayors.[47] It is noteworthy that the northeastern

---

[45] The significance of differences between means was measured with a two-tailed t test.

[46] In this and all other analyses of relationships between form of government and socioeconomic variables, the nine Indiana cities have been omitted.

[47] Controlling for social class by means of analysis of covariance did not produce greater differences in ethnicity between the two types of city. Whenever relationships between a dependent variable and a demographic independent variable are described in this paper, we have also controlled for the possible influence of other demographic variables by analysis of covariance. Except where noted, this procedure did not increase or diminish the explanatory power of the independent variable being examined.

manager cities are much more ethnic than cities in other parts of the country that use the mayor form.[48] This suggests that there is no nationally relevant, level of ethnicity above which one form of government is likely to predominate, i.e., there is no threshold level of ethnicity. These data are summarized in Table 10.

The only discernible variable distinguishing mayor and manager cities in the Northeast is the proportion of their populations in white-collar occupations, and even here the difference is neither large nor statistically

TABLE 10. FORM OF MUNICIPAL GOVERNMENT AND SELECTED POPULATION CHARACTERISTICS OF CITIES UNDER 500,000 POPULATION—BY REGION

Population Characteristic	Northeast			Midwest			West		
	Mayor	Man-ager	Sig. [a]	Mayor	Man-ager	Sig.	Mayor	Man-ager	Sig.
% foreign stock	39%	40%	n.s.	26%	20%	.05	26%	22%	n.s.
% white collar	42%	46%	n.s.	45%	49%	n.s.	51%	50%	n.s.
Median family income in 1959	$6200	$6395	n.s.	$6755	$6883	n.s.	$6481	$6975	n.s.
Median school years [b]	10.3	11.0	.05	11.2	11.4	n.s.	12.1	12.0	n.s.
Number of cities	(44)	(14)		(32)	(30)		(6)	(47)	

[a] The difference between mayor and manager cities for the relevant demographic variable, in a given region, is measured with a two-tailed t test.

[b] For adults 25 and older.

significant. The residents of northeastern mayor cities average 42 per cent in white-collar jobs, compared to 46 per cent in manager cities. The same difference is true in the Midwest. No such relationship is found in western cities. The levels of median income in manager cities are somewhat higher in all three regions. The differences range from $128 in the Midwest to $494 in the West. In the West this probably reflects nothing more than variations in the cost of labor, since there is no difference in the mean size of the working-class populations of the two types of cities there. Northeastern manager cities tend to have somewhat higher levels of education: 11.0 median school years completed as opposed to 10.3 in the mayor cities. There are no such differences in the Midwest and West.

---

[48] The same is true for the other structural dependent variables; the "public-regarding" northeastern cities are more ethnic than "private-regarding" cities in other parts of the country (see Tables 11 and 12).

The *nationwide* pattern of distribution of partisan and nonpartisan ballots is quite similar to that of form of government. All cities using the partisan ballot have a mean ethnic population of 25 per cent; those using nonpartisan ballots have a mean ethnic population of 21 per cent. While this difference is considerably smaller than that for forms of government, it is still significant at the .01 level.

This faint relationship breaks down or even reverses when examined within regions. As Table 11 shows, northeastern cities using a nonpartisan ballot have considerably *larger* ethnic populations than those which use the partisan ballot: 43 per cent v. 34 per cent; this difference is significant at

TABLE 11. TYPE OF BALLOT AND SELECTED POPULATION
CHARACTERISTICS—BY REGION

Population Characteristic	Northeast			Midwest			West		
	Partisan	Nonpartisan	Sig.[a]	Partisan	Nonpartisan	Sig.[a]	Partisan	Nonpartisan	Sig.[a]
% foreign stock	34%	43%	.001	23%	22%	n.s.	28%	23%	n.s.
% white collar	42%	41%	n.s.	45%	46%	n.s.	49%	50%	n.s.
Median family income in 1959	$6099	$6058	n.s.	$6689	$6607	n.s.	$6330	$6917	n.s.
Median school years[b]	10.3	10.4	n.s.	11.0	11.2	n.s.	12.1	12.0	n.s.
Number of cities	(46)	(29)		(28)	(56)		(3)	(56)	

[a] A two-tailed t test was used to measure the significance of the difference between partisan and nonpartisan cities with respect to the relevant demographic variable in a given region.

[b] For adults 25 years of age and older.

the .001 level. This striking negative finding is due largely to New England, which is the most ethnic part of the country and where 64 per cent of the cities use the nonpartisan ballot. There is no difference between those midwestern cities using the nonpartisan ballot and those that do not. There is a difference among western cities in the predicted direction. It is not statistically significant, perhaps because only three western cities have partisan elections.

Examination of other demographic indices reveals no consistent patterns. Neither class, income, nor education is related to use of one type of ballot or the other. Controlling for third variables such as occupation and income did not produce greater relationships between any demographic variable and the presence of party labels in municipal elections.

The method of electing city councilmen is also unrelated to the level of foreign-stock population. As Table 12 indicates, there are no differences in foreign-stock population between northeastern cities electing their legislators from wards and at large, nor are there differences with respect to any other demographic measure.[49] In the Midwest at-large cities are 4 per cent

TABLE 12. METHOD OF ELECTING CITY COUNCILMEN AND SELECTED POPULATION CHARACTERISTICS OF CITIES WITH LESS THAN ONE MILLION POPULATION—BY REGION

Population Characteristic	Northeast			Midwest			West		
	Ward	At-Large	Sig.[a]	Ward	At-Large	Sig.	Ward	At-Large	Sig.
% foreign stock	38%	38%	n.s.	25%	21%	n.s.	21%	23%	n.s.
% white collar	43%	43%	n.s.	45%	47%	n.s.	52%	50%	n.s.
Median family income in 1959	$6211	$6157	n.s.	$6643	$6758	n.s.	$6713	$6926	n.s.
Median school years [b]	10.4	10.5	n.s.	10.9	11.2	n.s.	12.3	12.0	n.s.
Number of cities	(18)	(25)		(24)	(35)		(9)	(43)	

[a] Significance measured with a two-tailed t test.
[b] For adults 25 and older.

less ethnic and also have slightly more middle class residents (2 per cent) and a higher median income ($115). While all these differences are in the predicted direction, none is statistically significant, much less of any substantive consequence. Western cities electing councilmen from wards have *fewer* ethnic residents and slightly larger middle-class populations, but these differences are even smaller than those in the Midwest.

The salient conclusion to be drawn from these data is that one can do a much better job of predicting a city's political forms by knowing what part of the country it is in than by knowing anything about the composition of its population. The reasons for this may lie in certain regional historical experiences related to the influx of immigrants and the responses to their needs reflected in municipal political systems. We will discuss the

---

[49] The five cities with populations of more than a million persons have been excluded from these tabulations involving methods of electing councilmen.

importance of regional differences in the concluding section of this paper. For the present, it is sufficient to note that only in the Midwest can we detect relationships in the direction predicted by the ethos theory with respect to two of the three dependent variables we have examined.

In addition to analyzing each of these dependent variables singly, we have combined them. There are eight possible combinations of form of government (we limit ourselves to mayor and manager), type of ballot, and method of electing councilmen (here limited to ward or at-large, omitting combinations), as shown in Table 13. Within each region we have

TABLE 13. MEAN FOREIGN STOCK POPULATION OF CITIES WITH EACH COMBINATION OF FORM OF GOVERNMENT, TYPE OF BALLOT, AND METHOD OF ELECTING COUNCILMEN—BY REGION [a]

	Northeast		Midwest		West	
Governmental Combination	per cent ethnic	N	per cent ethnic	N	per cent ethnic	N
Mayor-Partisan-Ward	40	16	26	7	23	1
Mayor-Partisan-At-Large	33	9	33	2	—	0
Mayor-Nonpartisan-Ward	37	2	27	12	25	5
Manager-Partisan-Ward	26	1	19	2	—	0
Manager-Nonpartisan-Ward	—	0	27	4	19	4
Manager-Partisan-At-Large	40	4	25	5	22	1
Mayor-Nonpartisan-At-Large	44	3	24	9	37	2
Manager-Nonpartisan-At-Large	43	7	18	18	22	40

[a] Cities using the commission form or a combination of ward and at-large election have been excluded from this table.

computed the mean foreign stock populations of those cities with each combination of characteristics. Conceivably the "pure type" cities would be more likely to display the ethnic characteristics said to be related to one ethos or the other. We can also evaluate Banfield and Wilson's suggestion that:

Among the modifications that might make the [city manager] plan more acceptable and more workable in cities (whether large or small) having a politically significant lower class are the following: partisan rather than nonpartisan elections, election of some councilmen on a ward rather than an at-large basis. . . .[50]

---

[50] Banfield and Wilson, pp. 183–184.

As Table 13 shows, there is no consequential difference in the ethnic populations of any of the groups of cities, in any region, except for "pure" public-regarding cities in the Midwest; these 18 cities have, on the average, fewer ethnic residents than do cities with any of the other seven combinations. In the Northeast the "pure" public-regarding cities have, in the aggregate, slightly larger foreign-stock populations than the "pure" private-regarding cities. Combining the manager form with partisan voting and ward-elected councilmen does not seem to have had the appeal suggested by Banfield and Wilson.

The difference between the two ethnics is also said to be reflected in the size of the districts represented by members of the municipal legislature where wards, in fact, exist. Small districts are thought to be a consequence of the dominance of the private-regarding ethos, while large districts, which force each councilman to respond to a more heterogeneous constituency, reflect the public-regarding ethic. This proposition can be tested by examining relationships between the size of cities' ethnic populations and the number of persons represented by their ward-elected councilmen. If the proposition were valid, one would find negative correlations—that is, the larger the districts, the fewer the ethnic residents in the city.

As usual, the proposition is confirmed on a nationwide basis. For all cities with at least some ward-elected councilmen, the correlation coefficient (Pearson's r) between the foreign-stock population and the number of persons represented by each ward-elected councilman is $-.23$. This is significant at the .05 level.[51] The coefficient remains at about the same level when a partial correlation is computed to control for social class; similar results are found when other variables are controlled.

The relationship persists when size is controlled. For cities with populations between 100,000 and 250,000 the coefficient is $-.30$; it falls only to $-.26$ when social class is partialled. Both of these values fall just short of the .05 level of confidence. In the smaller cities the coefficient is $-.28$ whether or not other variables are controlled; this is significant at the .05 level.

Once again, however, examining the data on a regional basis alters the picture drastically. In the Northeast the coefficient for all cities is .02; this vanishes entirely when class is controlled. In the Midwest the relationship is slightly in the predicted direction $(-.16)$, and persists when other variables are controlled, but falls short of statistical significance. In the West the 14 cities with some ward-elected councilmen present a strikingly different pattern; the relationship is opposite to that predicted by the ethos

---

[51] Significance of correlations is measured by the F value.

theory. The simple correlation coefficient is .30, which falls to .24 when class is controlled. Neither of these values is significant at the .05 level. It appears that the confirmation of the proposition obtained by examining cities on a nationwide basis is primarily an artifact of regional differences.

VI. ETHNICITY AND PUBLIC POLICY

The ethos theory states that the private-regarding ethic is hostile to civil service, city planning, and urban renewal. In this section we will test this proposition by examining the relationships between ethnicity and indices of these policies.

There is a strong relationship between a city's size and the likelihood that its municipal employees will be under civil service. As Table 14 shows, cities with more than 250,000 residents are very likely to have complete

TABLE 14. CIVIL SERVICE COVERAGE AND SIZE OF CITY [a]

Level of Civil Service Coverage	Over 250,000	100,000 to 250,000	50,000 to 100,000
1. All employees covered	75%	51%	45%
2. All but manual workers covered	14	6	5
3. Only policemen and firemen covered	7	25	32
4. No civil service coverage	4	18	18
Total	100%	100%	100%
N	(28)	(51)	(130)

[a] Cities in Indiana, Iowa, Massachusetts, New York, and Ohio are excluded from all tables concerning civil service coverage.

coverage; only one of the 28 cities in this group for which we have data does not have any coverage at all. A bare majority of cities with populations from 100,000 to 250,000 have total coverage, while more than 40 per cent either have none or protect only firemen and policemen. The trend continues for smaller cities.

Table 15 shows the foreign-stock populations of cities with different levels of civil service coverage, with size controlled. The data seem to contradict the ethos theory powerfully. Those cities with complete coverage have the highest foreign-stock populations in every size category except the

TABLE 15. Civil Service Coverage and Foreign-
Stock Population—by Size

Level of Civil Service Coverage	Mean per cent foreign-stock in population:		
	Over 250,000	*100,000 to 250,000*	*50,000 to 100,000*
1. All employees covered	21%	23%	24%
2. All but manual workers covered	24	15	16
3. Only policemen and firemen covered	6	10	18
4. No civil service coverage	4	16	14

largest, and even there the cities with minimal coverage are by far the least
ethnic.

As with all our other nationwide findings, these striking relationships
are an artifact of regional differences. Controlling for region makes it clear
that the very low ethnic population of the cities with scanty coverage is due
to the contribution of southern and border cities, which charasteristically
have neither extensive civil service coverage nor large foreign-stock populations. Unfortunately for the ethos theory, however, data for the rest of
the country do not support the hypothesis. The ethnic populations of
western and midwestern cities do not differ appreciably from one level of
coverage to the next. There are considerable differences among northeastern cities, but their impact is, if anything, contradictory to the theory. The
eleven northeastern cities in which only policemen and firemen are pro-

TABLE 16. Civil Service Coverage and Foreign-
Stock Population—by Region

Level of Civil Service Coverage	Mean per cent foreign-stock in population:							
	Northeast		*Midwest*		*West*		*South*	
	%	N	%	N	%	N	%	N
1. All employees covered	40	18	23	25	23	38	13	20
2. All but manual workers covered	38	3	22	3	—	—	7	6
3. Only policemen and firemen covered	23	11	23	16	21	4	7	23
4. No civil service coverage	45	2	21	6	21	8	4	13

tected have the fewest ethnic residents. The two cities with the least coverage have the highest mean ethnic populations, but this exceeds the mean for the 18 cities with complete coverage by only 5 per cent. In short, ethnicity does not make any difference in any region so far as civil service coverage is concerned. Relationships with other demographic variables are no more evident.

City planning supposedly comes close to being anathema to the private-regarding ethos. We have correlated per capita city planning expenditures with foreign-stock percentages for cities of different sizes and in different regions. These data are summarized in Table 17. If the ethos theory were correct in this respect, we would find negative correlations,

TABLE 17. CORRELATIONS BETWEEN PER CENT
FOREIGN-STOCK AND CITY PLANNING
EXPENDITURES PER CAPITA—BY
SIZE AND REGION [a]

Size of City	Northeast	Midwest	West
Over 250,000	−.11	.22	−.10
	(8) [b]	(15)	(10)
100,000 to	−.22	−.25	.21
250,000	(21)	(19)	(14)
50,000 to	−.04	.23	.09
100,000	(47)	(50)	(35)

[a] The value in each cell is the Pearsonian r of the relationship between per cent ethnic population and city planning expenditures per capita, for the given group of cities. A negative correlation is in the direction predicted by the ethos theory.

[b] Numbers in parentheses are the number of cases in each cell.

presumably at some level of statistical significance. No such pattern can be discerned in Table 17. Five of the nine cells show negative correlations, ranging from −.04 to −.25. Positive correlation coefficients range from .09 to .23. It is difficult to regard these results as due to anything but chance. These relationships do not change when partial correlations are computed to control for social class.

For somewhat the same reasons that they are believed to oppose city planning members of ethnic groups are said to be hostile to urban renewal. The amount of the federal capital grants reserved for a city is an accurate index of the extent of its commitment to urban renewal. We have used capital grants per capita as a comparative measure.[52]

While probably every city with more than 50,000 residents "needs" at least some urban renewal, it would be unsafe to assume that the need is equally important or recognized everywhere. The compact, aging cities of the industrial East and Midwest are losing residents and businesses to the suburbs, while most southern and western cities are growing more prosperous and populous. Quasi-ideological opposition to urban renewal is stronger in the latter areas.[53]

Renewal activity is also a function of a city's size. While 86 percent of cities with populations over 250,000 have at least one renewal project in the action phase, this is true of 71 per cent of cities with populations between 100,000 and 250,000, and only 47 per cent of cities in the 50,000 to 100,000 category.

For these reasons we have controlled for size and region when correlating ethnicity and urban renewal grants per capita. The findings, summarized in Table 18, resemble those for city planning. There is no consistent relationship, either in one region or in the country as a whole. Partial correlations to control for social class do not materially change this picture.[54]

The conventional wisdom holds that city governments headed by mayors are more responsive to the political preferences of ethnic groups. If this were the case and if ethnics were opposed to city planning and urban renewal, we would expect to find that while there was no relationship between ethnicity and the extent of these policies in all cities, such a relationship might appear in mayor cities. That is, in political systems

---

[52] We counted all projects classified in the execution stage, or where a loan and grant contract was approved but not yet formally executed, in the December 31, 1963 directory. A renewal project in the execution stage at the end of 1963 is the product of prior decisions extending at least two or three years into the past.

[53] Several western and southern states were very slow to pass enabling legislation to permit their cities to undertake urban renewal projects; one or two states still impose severe restraints in this regard. We excluded southern states from our analysis; the western states that followed this policy do not, with one exception, contain cities with populations over 50,000.

[54] Amos H. Hawley has found an inverse relationship between the proportion of businessmen and professionals in a city's population and the likelihood that it has begun to carry out a renewal project. See his "Community Power and Urban Renewal Success," *American Journal of Sociology*, 68 (January, 1963), 422–431. Hawley's study does not take account of the magnitude of a city's program. It has been criticized on other grounds by Bruce C. Straits, "Community Action and Implementation of Urban Renewal," *ibid.*, 71 (July, 1965), 77–82. See also Hawley's rejoinder, *ibid.*, pp. 82–84.

TABLE 18. CORRELATIONS BETWEEN PER CENT
FOREIGN-STOCK AND URBAN RENEWAL
CAPITAL GRANTS PER CAPITA—BY
SIZE AND REGION [a]

Size of City	Northeast	Midwest	West
Over 250,000	−.54	.12	.72 [b]
	(8)	(15)	(10)
100,000 to	.05	−.16	.34
250,000	(21)	(19)	(14)
50,000 to	−.10	.02	.17
100,000	(47)	(50)	(35)

[a] The value in each cell is the Pearsonian r of the relationship between per cent ethnic population and urban renewal capital grants per capita for all federally-aided urban renewal projects in the execution stage. A negative correlation is in the direction predicted by the ethos theory.

[b] Significant at the .05 level. This is the only value to attain this level of confidence.

where members of ethnic groups supposedly have more influence, this influence might be manifested in lower expenditures on city planning and urban renewal.[55] We can test this proposition by further subdividing the classes of cities in Tables 17 and 18 into mayor cities and manager cities (discarding those with the commission form). These tabulations are summarized in Tables 19 and 20.

This manipulation of the data does not yield any greater relationships between ethnicity and city planning, as Table 19 demonstrates. There are no consistent tendencies in any part of the country for the correlation coefficients in mayor cities to be in the negative direction. Table 20, on urban renewal, provides one ray of hope for the ethos theory in the cell for small midwestern cities. Those cities with mayors have a correlation coefficient of −.43 between foreign-stock population and urban renewal capital grants per capita. This value is just short of significance at the .05 level. The coefficient for small western cities is almost as high, but there are only four cities in this group with mayors. Interpretation of Table 20 is, by and

---

[55] An earlier study found no relationship between form of local government and magnitude of urban renewal. See George S. Duggar, "The Relation of Local Government Structure to Urban Renewal," *Law and Contemporary Problems*, 26 (1961), 49–69.

TABLE 19. Correlations between Per Cent Foreign-Stock and City Planning Expenditures per Capita in Mayor and Manager Cities— by Size and Region [a]

Size of City	Northeast		Midwest		West	
Over 250,000	mayor [b]	−.11	mayor	.21	mayor	.75
			manager	−.44	manager	−.16
100,000 to 250,000	mayor	−.39	mayor	−.37	[c]	
	manager	.08	manager	−.65	manager	.23
50,000 to 100,000	mayor	.11	mayor	.23	mayor	.32
	manager	−.12	manager	.12	manager	.13

[a] The value in each cell is the product moment correlation coefficient of the relationship between per cent ethnic population and city planning expenditures per capita, for those cities with the indicated form of government and size and region. A negative correlation is in the direction predicted by the ethos theory, which also predicts larger negative correlations for the mayor cities.

[b] One manager city in group.

[c] No mayor cities in group.

TABLE 20. Correlations between Per Cent Foreign-Stock and Urban Renewal Capital Grants per Capita in Mayor and Manager Cities— by Size and Region [a]

Size of City	Northeast		Midwest		West	
Over 250,000 population	mayor [b]	−.55	mayor	.15	mayor	.60
			manager	−.08	manager	.90
100,000 to 250,000	mayor	.06	mayor	.21	[c]	
	manager	.24	manager	.41	manager	.34
50,000 to 100,000	mayor	−.05	mayor	−.43 [d]	mayor	−.41 [e]
	manager	−.14	manager	−.14	manager	.21

[a] The value in each cell is the product moment correlation coefficient of the relationship between per cent ethnic population and urban renewal capital grants per capita, for those cities with the indicated form of government and size and region. The ethos theory predicts negative correlations, greater in mayor cities than in manager ones.

[b] One manager city in group.

[c] No mayor cities in group.

[d] Almost significant at the .05 level; the only value in either Table 19 or 20 that comes this close.

[e] Four cities in this sub-group.

192 • WOLFINGER AND FIELD

large, a matter of temperament. This one weak finding, in a mass of negative evidence, does not impress us as very important.

VII. CONCLUSIONS

Several conclusions can be drawn from the foregoing findings: (1) Contrary to specific propositions in the ethos theory, some of the political forms and policies are not manifestations of either ethos. (2) The two ethics are not as ethnically differentiated as has been suggested. (3) The ethics, as described, do not exist. (4) The propositions about manifestations of the ethics and their ethnic roots are all correct, but there are so many other factors bearing on political outcomes that the prevailing ethos in a city is not very important. The data at hand do not permit us to evaluate these conclusions, but we can be fairly confident of one other assertion: the propositions of the ethos theory need to be modified to account for special circumstances that limit their validity. Regional variations are the most obvious examples of such circumstances; they are a good starting point for this discussion.

The ethos theory is irrelevant to the South, where most municipal institutions seem to be corollaries of the region's traditional preoccupation with excluding Negroes from political power. A one-party system removes temptations to appeal to Negro voters, as does the city manager plan. With only one party, the partisan ballot is not meaningful. At-large elections minimize Negro voting strength. In view of these considerations, the scarcity of immigrants in the South appears to be a superfluous explanation for its local governmental practices.[56]

For other special reasons the theory is also inapplicable to the West, where cities do have a considerable range of foreign-stock populations. We suggested one cause earlier: the immigrant experience in the West was different, hence the conditions that allegedly produce private-regardingness

---

[56] This southern concern with unity may also explain why Mexican-Americans in Texas have been so apolitical, in contrast to the political involvement of immigrants in the North. Perhaps the political participation of newly arrived minority groups is enhanced when the political environment is competitive. European immigrants to northern cities typically arrived in political arenas where partisan competition motivated both sets of contenders to appeal for their votes. As the immigrants acquired political skill, their prices rose until they had attained political influence at least somewhat in proportion to their numbers. But if immigrants come to a political system where the elites shun conflict with each other, they are likely to find that the interest of those elites is to exclude them from politics rather than appeal for their support. The impact of immigrant political values obviously would be far greater in the former case.

did not develop there. This different history also probably accounts for the relatively low levels of ethnic consciousness in the West. Inhabitants of the West have never been as fascinated as Easterners with national origins (except where Orientals and Mexicans are concerned), and therefore the region has not displayed the ethnic politics characteristic of the East.[57] Some manifestations of the private-regarding ethos are conducive to ethnic politics. The election of councilmen from wards, for instance, makes it much easier to bestow "recognition" on nationality groups. In the absence of civil service regulations it is easier to give every ethnic group its "fair share" of public jobs without having to worry about qualifications. Where politics is viewed as conflict among nationality groups for jobs, nominations, and spoils, institutional forms consistent with these aspirations are likely to flourish, *quite apart from any other prevailing view of the political world.* Obviously, ethnic salience is a prerequisite of ethnic politics. A strategy of "recognizing" nationality groups is meaningless if most group members do not see politics in ethnic perspectives. To the extent that ethnic salience contributes to the strength of private-regardingness, one would expect that the ethos would be less evident in those places where ethnicity is not as prominent a feature of political life as it is in the Northeast.

Yet the theory also fares badly in the Northeast. It might be argued that this reflects a different kind of historical circumstance. Perhaps the Yankees there, anticipating their submergence in the rising tide of immigrants, took steps to minimize this trend by changing the political structure accordingly. This might, for instance, explain why northeastern cities that use the nonpartisan ballot are so much more ethnic than the region's cities that adhere to the partisan ballot. But this explanation presents several difficulties. Even those cities with, say, partisan elections, are highly ethnic. A generation ago ethnics must have been even more numerous in them. Why, then, did the Yankees in those cities not take steps to protect their interests? Why were the Yankees apparently most successful in those cities where the ethnics were most numerous? Why did the ethnics not change the system back when they took over?

When Yankees are as outnumbered as they are in the Northeast, they may prefer a system that gives them some minority representation. Perhaps any self-conscious minority prefers institutions that guarantee it representation and a chance to maximize its political resources, and there is no doubt that Yankees are a self-conscious minority in urban New England.

---

[57] Regional differences in ethnic politics and salience are discussed at greater length in Wolfinger, *op. cit.,* p. 898.

When Boston city councilmen were elected from wards some Yankees and Jews won seats. But when Boston adopted the public-regarding at-large system only Italians and Irishmen could get elected.[58]

Possibly the politics of the Northeast, with its virulent ethnic tensions, produces in the Yankees the same orientations that the ethnics are said to have. They develop the same interests in recognition, representation of their parochial interests, favors from city hall, and so on. When the choice is between doing business with a private-regarding regime and political isolation, perhaps all but the stiffest Brahmins adapt to the private-regarding style. This would explain why ethnicity appears to be worthless as an independent variable in the Northeast: everyone there except possibly the cosmopolitan upper-middle-class has succumbed to private-regardingness.[59] The triumph of the immigrants is complete. The outnumbered, affronted, overpowered Yankees go along with the immigrant political style both because they have to and because its values have replaced their own in the community.

The Midwest provides the best evidence for the ethos theory, but even there the differences between "public-regarding" and "private-regarding" cities are small and uneven.

Whatever the utility of these assorted speculations about the ethos theory, we still have not explained our striking positive finding, the great variations in each of the structural variables from one region to the next. Outside the South regional variations may reflect to some extent interaction between cities' natural histories and prevailing political enthusiasms at crucial periods in those histories. Most eastern and midwestern cities were important communities in the 19th century, before the National Municipal League's various structural reforms were seriously proposed. Their political institutions were well established and had seen hard service in the first

---

[58] Banfield and Wilson, p. 95.

[59] As we noted earlier, the scanty scholarly knowledge of nonmetropolitan political machines may be due to the fact that most of the best research on local politics has been done at schools like Harvard, Columbia, and Chicago. These universities are located in cities where politics is conducted almost entirely by members of ethnic groups. From the vantage point of Hyde Park or Harvard Square, almost everyone not connected with the university is an ethnic. Political practices in such cities typically are "private-regarding." Much of the opposition to these practices comes from people connected with or attracted to universities, that is, mostly from Jews and Protestants. College faculties and their social satellites are scarcely typical of the Protestant middle class. Banfield and Wilson may be overgenerous to the bulk of the Anglo-Saxon population. While professors and account executives are not particularly interested in patronage, ticket fixing, and the like, these and other elements of the private-regarding style may be quite congenial to people who have little in common with college faculties but nonmembership in the Catholic Church.

generation of industrialization. Politicians generally had vested interests in maintaining the existing forms and most political actors had at least developed means of dealing with those forms. These attachments and accommodations were weaker and less developed in newer cities or cities undergoing tremendous growth. They were even more irrelevant when it came to deciding on governmental institutions for brand new communities. In such cases there was no presumption in favor of the status quo, and the writers of municipal constitutions were responsive to contemporary political fashions.

Most southwestern and western cities were villages, at best, until the early twentieth century, when the new municipal governmental forms were all the rage. We think that regional differences in the age of cities may explain a good deal of the striking regional variations in form of government, type of ballot, and method of electing councilmen.

While sudden growth is the most common occasion on which constitutions are written *de novo*, other conditions may present similar opportunities. This seems most likely to happen after a major political upheaval. For example, California's wholesale conversion to local nonpartisanship was a result of the Progressives' great victory over the Southern Pacific Railroad in the election of 1910. Anxious to capitalize on their triumph, the Progressives were extraordinarily receptive to the prevailing nostrums of reform. Twenty years before, these measures were not yet plausible alternatives. Twenty years later, sophisticated reformers would have placed far less faith in such changes.

In short, the ethos theory clearly needs a good deal of modification. Whether a revised version will have much explanatory power remains to be seen.

9

RANCOROUS CONFLICT
IN COMMUNITY POLITICS

☯

WILLIAM A. GAMSON
University of Michigan

[Nine communities with high susceptibility to rancorous conflict are compared with nine others in which such episodes are rare. Those which experience such conflict differ, with certain exceptions, in the extent to which they are undergoing shifts in political control. They also differ with respect to several measures of structural integration and these differences explain some of the exceptions. Two measures of conduciveness to rancorous conflict—a participative political structure and the existence of clearly defined solidary groups—do not differentiate the two kinds of communities.]

Community issues differ in many repsects. Some involve vitriolic exchanges of threats and denunciations while others run their course through routine hearings and are resolved before unfilled council chambers. The same issue—for example, fluoridation—may run its course in undramatic fashion in one town, but prove to be the trigger for an explosive confrontation in another town with seemingly similar characteristics. This paper addresses itself to the structural differences between those communities in which such outbursts occur and those in which they do not.

In particular, two ways of carrying on conflict in the local community are contrasted. In *conventional conflicts,* established means of political expression are used to influence the outcome of issues. Opponents regard each other as mistaken or as pursuing different but legitimate goals, but not as the representatives of evil forces. Such tactics as threats of punishment, personal vilification, and deliberate, conscious deceptions are not involved. In contrast to conventional conflicts, *rancorous conflicts* are characterized by the belief that norms about the waging of political conflict in American communities have been violated. In such conflicts, actions occur which produce a shared belief that tactics used to influence the outcome are "dirty," "underhanded," "vicious" and so forth.

Some communities are much more prone than others to rancorous conflicts. The differences between rancorous and conventional communities can be organized under three general headings: structural conduciveness, structural strain, and structural integration.[1] *Conduciveness* refers to the extent to which structural characteristics in the community permit or encourage rancorous conflicts. *Strain* refers to the extent to which structural characteristics generate discontent or dissatisfaction among the community members. *Integration* refers to the extent to which structural characteristics prevent or inhibit rancorous conflict. Although integration is just the other side of conduciveness, each refers to different structural elements. In other words, we do not consider the absence of integration as an element of conduciveness or the presence of integration as the absence of conduciveness.

The three categories of determinant are highly related to each other. High conduciveness will not produce rancorous conflict if unaccompanied by strain nor if, although accompanied by strain, structural integration is great. High strain will not produce rancorous conflict unless the social structure is conducive to conflict and structural integration is inadequate. The absence of structural integration will not produce rancorous conflict if there is little strain or conduciveness. In other words, we shall expect rancorous conflicts *to occur most frequently in those communities characterized by high conduciveness, high strain, and low integration.*

Structural Conduciveness. Such highly general categories as conduciveness, strain, and integration need specification if they are to be measured. With respect to conduciveness, we will focus on two aspects of community social structure: the degree to which it encourages widespread citizen participation and the degree to which it offers highly visible targets for the expression of rancor.

Participative Political Structure. The more the political structure permits or encourages widespread citizen participation, the greater is the conduciveness to rancorous conflict. Since it is typically argued that such conflict is encouraged by the *closing* of channels of legitimate political expression, this hypothesis needs defense. The argument for the proposi-

---

[1] I draw here on Neil J. Smelser, *Theory of Collective Behavior*, New York: The Free Press of Glencoe, 1963. He organizes his discussion of the determinants of collective behavior under six categories. Three of them are covered here with slight differences in terminology and formulation. The other three—the growth and spread of a generalized belief, precipitating factors, and mobilization of participants for action—are not included because our objective is to understand the structural differences between communities rather than the outbreak of a given episode at a particular time in a community. The discussion which follows also draws heavily on James S. Coleman, *Community Conflict*, New York: The Free Press of Glencoe, 1957.

tion may take a weak or a strong form. In the weak form, a distinction is made between the intensity and the frequency of rancorous conflict. In high participation communities, it is argued, the political system offers not only an instrumental channel but an expressive one as well. Mild discontent which might otherwise find no outlet or a non-political one is encouraged to find political expression. In finding frequent release in this fashion, such discontent does not build up an explosive potential. Although rancorous conflicts may occur less frequently in communities with a non-participative political structure, they have more intensity when they do occur.

The stronger form of the argument is a denial of the counter-proposition that the blocking of channels of political expression encourages rancorous conflict. This argument challenges the assumption that there is a reservoir of discontent which will either find controlled outlet in legitimate political expression or will accumulate until the dam bursts. Instead, it is assumed that the relief or exacerbation of discontent depends on the nature of the resultant decisions made and not on the catharsis which comes from political expression. If the political system allows for high political participation but does not deal successfully with the sources of dissatisfaction, then rancorous conflicts are *more* likely to occur because strain is combined with high conduciveness. Only when political participation is combined with the influence which can alleviate the source of discontent do rancorous conflicts become less likely. This argument does not imply that high citizen participation is necessarily conducive to rancorous conflict (and hence is bad), but merely that participation does not automatically remove strain.

Given the truth of this proposition, then it is false that such actions as civil rights demonstrations must lessen the probability of other less orderly expressions. As long as the underlying sources of strain are not dealt with, such participation simply increases structural conduciveness and thus makes other expressions more likely. Of course, if the action also helps to remove the strain, for example, by aiding the passage of remedial legislation, then the *net* effect may be to reduce the probability of other less orderly expressions.

A study of fluoridation by Crain, Katz, and Rosenthal contains some suggestive results concerning this hypothesis.[2] They find that the participative nature of the political structure affects both the degree of controversy about fluoridation and the likelihood of its adoption. "Governments which do not place 'obstacles' such as political parties between the citizen and the

---

[2] Robert L. Crain, Elihu Katz, and Donald B. Rosenthal, *The Fluoridation Decision: Community Structure and Innovation*, forthcoming.

decision-makers experience the pattern of a large number of referenda and high controversy [as well as high rejection]." Fluoridation is at least more likely to provoke strong controversy where participative political structures provide conduciveness.[3]

Solidary Groups. The greater the clarity of solidary groups within a social structure, the greater is the conduciveness to rancorous conflict. Communities differ in the extent to which they contain sub-groups with: (1) feelings of membership or identification with a group or collectivity; (2) feelings of common interest with respect to political decisions; (3) a common style of life, norms, and values; (4) a high rate of interaction among themselves. The degree of solidarity of a sub-group is its magnitude on the above characteristics; the clarity of solidary group structure is the extent to which there exist community sub-groups of high solidarity.

Clearly identifiable solidary groups are conducive to rancorous conflict because they provide readily identifiable targets for hostility. Such subdivisions of the community do not in themselves signify cleavage. Nevertheless, any clear-cut basis of differentiation among the citizens of a town may provide a structural basis for the development of intergroup hostility if there also exist strains and low integration among solidary groups.

Structural Strain. Any part of the social structure may produce strains which are relevant for rancorous conflict in the community. Many strains originate outside of the community but have ramifications for the social and political life of the town. There are undoubtedly strains deriving from fear of nuclear war, increasing bureaucratization, depersonalization, commercialism, manipulation, and so forth. Such strains may make their own contributions to rancorous conflicts in the community,[4] but they are felt by all communities, rancorous as well as conventional. Therefore, we must turn to strains which can differentiate our communities in order to explain why some are prone to rancorous conflict and others are not.

There are many possibilities. Although the specification of such strains requires detailed knowledge of the particular communities in ques-

---

[3] The volatile nature of California politics may be due (among other things) to the structural conduciveness stemming from a long tradition of initiative and referendum.

[4] A good deal of recent work on such strains has used the rubric of "alienation." See, for example, John E. Horton and Wayne E. Thompson, "Powerlessness and Political Negativism: A Study of Defeated Local Referendums," *American Journal of Sociology*, 68 (March, 1962), pp. 485–493; Kenneth Keniston, "Alienation and the Decline of Utopia," *American Scholar*, 29 (Spring, 1960), pp. 161–200; and William A. Gamson, "The Fluoridation Dialogue: Is it an Ideological Conflict?" *Public Opinion Quarterly*, 25 (Winter, 1961), pp. 526–537.

tion, it seems likely that they are connected with change. The change might include, for example, rapid economic growth or decline, heavy in-migration or out-migration, or shifts in the distribution of power in the community. For two reasons I have chosen to focus on strains emanating from a shift in political control: (1) the existence or non-existence of a shift in control sharply differentiates the communities studied here: (2) a shift in political control is likely to be a reflection of other strains as well as a creator of strains in its own right.

Shifts in political control are a source of structural strain which contribute to rancorous conflict. I have in mind here something broader than the circulation of elites. In particular, two kinds of shift will be considered. They have in common the existence of a relatively homogeneous group whose leaders find that they face competition in areas of decision-making where they did not before, or that they are competing less successfully than before. In one type of community, there are clear solidary groups with one gaining or losing political power relative to others. In a second type of community, a homogeneous native population has been, or threatens to be, supplanted by a large, heterogeneous, and politically active group of newcomers.

Structural Integration. Strain and conduciveness deal with those characteristics of social structure that promote or encourage rancorous conflict. We now turn our attention to those features which tend to control or inhibit such expressions. Basically, we expect rancorous and conventional communities to differ in the extent to which potential antagonists are bound together. In particular, we examine the connections which exist between those with different opinions on community issues. Are proponents and opponents bound by associational ties, by friendship, or by shared backgrounds? If they are not, then we should expect a given amount of strain and conduciveness to be more likely to produce rancorous conflict. We will consider three kinds of tie here.

Organizational Ties. The greater the degree of common organizational membership among proponents and opponents, the greater the resistance to rancorous conflict. If the organizational life of a community puts potential antagonists together in a variety of meetings over a variety of issues, they are likely to find occasions for agreement, to develop bonds of friendship, a sense of joint accomplishment, and other integrative ties. When a disagreement occurs, it should be less likely to produce the kind of break in a relationship which rancorous conflict represents.

Interpersonal Ties. The greater the degree of friendship among proponents and opponents, the greater the resistance to rancorous conflict. If potential antagonists know each other well socially, such friendship bonds should help to provide that degree of trust and belief in good faith which inhibit rancorous conflicts.

Shared Background. The more proponents and opponents tend to be of different length of residence, nationality background, education, and religion, the less the resistance to rancorous conflict. These four bases of differentiation were chosen because they seemed particularly likely to be correlated with partisan divisions in the set of New England communities we studied. Since these are the bases of differentiation that presumably underlie solidary groups, this hypothesis might appear to be simply another statement of the earlier one on structural conduciveness. We argued above that the existence of clear sub-groups was conducive to rancorous conflict but that they did not, in themselves, signify cleavage. It is possible to have solidary groups which cross-cut issues, thus giving proponents and opponents an important common group membership. It is also possible to find the opposite—that proponents and opponents have different background characteristics but lack any feeling of membership or identification with distinct community sub-groups. Even where clear solidary groups are not present, the absence of these integrative bonds should make such communities more vulnerable to rancorous conflict. Finally, it is possible to have full fledged cleavages in which clearly defined solidary groups exist and do correspond to divisions on issues. This condition combines conduciveness with lack of integration; when strain is added, we should particularly expect rancorous conflict.

STUDY DESIGN

The data to be presented here are drawn from a study of fifty-four issues in eighteen New England communities. The towns ranged in size from 2,000 to 100,000, with a median of approximately 10,000. Seven of the communities were essentially suburbs of Boston, three were resort towns, and the remaining eight were more or less independent cities with some industrial base of their own. All but two of the communities were in Maine or Massachusetts.

Material on these communities was gathered through interviews with 426 informants, an average of twenty-four per town, supplemented by information from a variety of documents. Interviewing was done by teams of three or four individuals who stayed in each community for several days. Three issues were studied in each town, one of which, fluoridation, was common to all eighteen. The presence of a decision on fluoridation was, in fact, the basis of selection of these communities; the eighteen comprise all those New England communities which made a fluoridation decision during an eighteen-month period of data collection.

Before any interviewing began, each town was investigated through such sources as the local newspaper, formal statistical data from the state and federal censuses, city planning reports, annual town reports, and various state manuals. The persons interviewed fell into two categories: active partisans on both sides of each of the three issues; and people named by these "issue leaders" as influential in the community, i.e., as "reputational leaders."

Identifying Rancorous Conflicts. Respondents were not asked directly about the fairness or legitimacy of the tactics used to influence the outcome of the three issues studied in their town. They were asked what those in favor did and what those against did to promote their side, in addition to a number of more specific questions about activities designed to influence the outcome. To identify rancorous conflict, we must rely on charges made spontaneously about the illegitimacy of tactics used. Despite the absence of direct efforts to elicit such statements and the reluctance of some inform-ants to discuss such matters with outsiders, there were 161 different charges of illegitimate tactics made by the 426 people interviewed.

We coded various kinds of charge. They had in common the belief on the part of the informant that individuals or groups in the community deliberately and with full consciousness used improper means in an at-tempt to influence the outcome of a community decision. In a few cases, the objectionable tactics were not specified, but the campaign as a whole was described as dirty, vicious or underhanded. More specific charges con-cerned the use of threats, efforts to degrade or humiliate, attempts to punish people in ways like depriving them of their jobs, lying, and deliberate efforts to play on prejudice or irrational fears.[5]

In some communities, as many as half of the informants made such charges on at least one issue, while in others there was no more than a single charge. Even though some of the charges were doubtful, the exis-tence of charges by independent informants will be taken as sufficient evidence in itself of the collective phenomenon of rancorous conflict. In other words, we simply require assurance that the belief in illegitimate tactics is a *shared* and not an idiosyncratic one; the veracity of a charge of dirty politics is generally a matter of interpretation in any event.

---

[5] In coding charges of unfair tactics, five specific categories were used but no distinction is made in this paper among different types of charge. Intercoder agreement on the existence of charges was above 80%.

Those communities in which such charges are prevalent will be called *rancorous;* those in which they are rare will be called *conventional.* The following criterion divides the eighteen towns into two groups of nine: all towns in which at least two individuals make charges of illegitimate tactics on at least two different issues are rancorous; the remainder are conventional. In the nine rancorous towns so defined, an average of ten informants per town make such charges and in none of them do fewer than six different individuals make charges. In the nine conventional towns, an average of three informants per town make such charges and in only one of them [6] do more than four individuals make a charge.

Selection of Issues. Since we are classifying towns as a whole by what happens on as few as two issues, the question of how each issue was selected is important. The two issues studied in addition to fluoridation were chosen because of their local salience. To the extent that controversy, and especially hostile controversy, made issues salient to informants, it is highly unlikely that unchosen issues would produce as many charges of illegitimate tactics as chosen ones. Among the rancorous towns, there may have been other rancorous conflicts in addition to the ones studied, but this would not alter the classification of the town as rancorous or conventional.

Both "issue leaders" and "reputational leaders" were asked to name the most important issues that had arisen in their town in the previous five years and they named, on the average, between three and four issues. Clearly, there are many competing criteria of importance.[7] Degree of controversy, amount of money involved, and number of people affected are a few of those that might be invoked. Some issues may qualify on more than one criterion. Issues which involve a lot of money are likely to affect many people and in different ways, and thus provoke controversy.

Perhaps this latter fact accounts for the relatively high degree of consensus which one gets in answer to a question on important issues. Of the 54 issues studied, 26 were mentioned by a majority of the respondents

---

[6] The fluoridation issue, incidentally, produced two or more charges in 12 of 18 towns. All but one of the rancorous towns had a rancorous fluoridation issue. In one town, however, fluoridation was the only issue studied which did not produce charges. Charges over fluoridation, of course, were never sufficient to have a town classified as rancorous since at least two such issues were required; four of the conventional towns did have a single rancorous fluoridation issue.

[7] A number of authors have addressed themselves to the problems involved in selecting issues to study. See, for example, Nelson Polsby, *Community Power and Political Theory* (New Haven: Yale University Press), 1963, pp. 95–97; and Linton C. Freeman et al., *Local Community Leadership* (Syracuse: Syracuse University Press), 1960, pp. 7–8.

in the town.[8] Furthermore, there was a good deal of convergence on the issue mentioned first or singled out as most important. In eleven of the eighteen towns, a majority mentioned a particular issue first or as most important, and in all but one of these the issue was included in the 54 studied.[9] Eighteen of the issues concern fluoridation, eleven concern schools, eleven are issues over the development of some new community facility or service, eight are zoning issues, and the other six are an assortment which includes changes in the form of government and urban renewal.

Independent Variables. Participate Political Structure. This variable refers to the *formal* political structure of the community. Indices of a participative structure include formal provision for frequent referenda, direct primaries, and other occasions for direct citizen participation in decision-making.

New England communities are peculiar in political structure. An extremely large number of decisions are made by the electorate rather than by representative bodies. In some instances, state laws make referenda mandatory. For example, fluoridation can only be adopted through this form of decision in Maine and Massachusetts. Only 12 of the 54 issues studied were decided by representative decision-making bodies. However, since eleven of the communities studied had a town meeting form of government but seven did not, they can be differentiated on this basis. Nevertheless those designated here as "non-participative" would hardly warrant this description if we considered a national sample of communities.

Solidary Groups. The identification of solidary groups, when they

---

[8] Issues were selected for study through examination of community newspapers and some informal checking with newspaper editors and city clerks. It was possible to miss issues on whose importance there was considerable consensus since this could not be discovered until the interviews were completed. Thus, five issues named by a majority of respondents were *not* studied. Three of these were in rancorous towns and their inclusion would, thus, not affect the classification of the town. In one conventional town, none of the three issues studied produced as many as two charges; thus, the inclusion of the missed issue would not be sufficient to change the classification of the town even if it did produce charges. The other conventional town *could* have been shifted into the rancorous column by the inclusion of the missed issue, but there is no indication from examining the few sparse comments about this issue that it would have.

[9] What consensus exists is not an artifact of the use of active partisans as respondents. A comparison of self-rated actives and inactives shows almost no differences in their mention of issues or ratings of community concern about issues. On 23 of the 26 issues mentioned by a majority of all respondents, a majority of inactive informants named the issue as well. On seven of these issues, there is actually a higher proportion of mentions among inactive respondents.

play a prominent role in the political life of a town, is not difficult. They become such a salient part of the social landscape that their existence is explicitly or implicitly recognized in almost any detailed description of the town. Statements referring to any distinct sub-group in the community were identified in the interviews, and specifically those which attributed some common outlook to the groups mentioned. Questions on community changes, on the characteristics of newcomers, and on religious and ethnic groupings provided the major stimuli for such comments although they appeared spontaneously in many other parts of the interview. The following quotations from respondents in different towns are illustrative:

There is a terrific growth of population, an influx of largely Jewish Democratic voters, which is changing the complexion of the city.

[The newer group] tends to be younger, more liberal and not Protestant.

[One] thing is the influx of people from the larger towns who want to say that they live in a small town, but have big city ideas.

We have an extremely active Franco-American population. . . . never could see eye to eye with the rest of the town. . . . they are a very closely knit clannish group—church, political interests hold them together. They regard themselves as a minority group.

Communities were classified as having clearly defined solidary groups if 50% or more of the respondents in the town mentioned some specific group or set of groups. Nine of the eighteen towns have clearly defined solidary groups by this criterion. Seven of these nine have ethnic groupings while the other two have separate geographical enclaves which are not ethnically distinct. There is an element of arbitrariness in the ethnic label for those seven towns, since members of some of the solidary groups not only have the same ethnic origin but also live in a particular section of town, hold predominantly working class jobs, have the same religion, speak a common second language other than English, go to separate schools, and share a similar political ethos. The ethnic label is shorthand for a large number of similarities.

Shifts in Political Control. Respondents were asked a number of questions on political agreement and disagreement among groups and leaders in the town. At the end of this series, they were asked, "You've given me a description of the way the town is now. Has the town been like this throughout the last ten or fifteen years?" and, if they dissented, "What was it like before?" Only certain kinds of answer were coded as indicating shifts in political control. If the respondent said, "A younger, more vigorous group has taken over in the last few years," this was *not* coded as a shift unless some characteristic in addition to age was mentioned. Typical examples of the sort that *were* coded as representing a shift include:

Before the [X] plant opened this was pretty much a country town. Now the newcomers have pretty much taken over and introduced a lot of changes.

It used to be that the French were all concentrated in Ward 5 and they had one man on the Council. Now they have Ward 5 and 4 and a good part of 3. They could even elect a mayor now if they tried and that would have been simply inconceivable 15 years ago.

If at least five respondents *explicitly* mentioned such shifts, the community was characterized as undergoing shifts in political control. Four of the nine communities with solidary groups can be so characterized and three of those without solidary groups have recently undergone the radical transformation from a small, homogeneous, independent town to a much more heterogeneous, suburban town.

Organizational Ties. Respondents in each community were asked which "men's or women's clubs and organizations are most active in community affairs?" The eight most frequently mentioned organizations were coded and membership in these organizations was ascertained for all respondents. Our measure of organizational ties centers on the extent to which a single major organization provides a common focus for people active in political affairs. Here, we measure the ratio of the largest number of respondent-memberships in any single organization to the total number of respondents in the town.

Interpersonal Ties. Respondents were asked to name active partisans on each side of each of the issues. They were also asked to indicate how well they knew each of the individuals named, using a scale with four degrees of acquaintanceship—from "an intimate friend" at one end, to "someone I have no contact with" at the other end. To form an overall measure of proponent-opponent [10] friendship ties this information was used in the following way: only those friendship ratings for people named on the side which the particular respondent opposed were counted and those ratings were averaged for all respondents.

Shared Background. This measure focuses on four variables—length of residence, nationality background, education and religion. On each dimension, we ask to what extent the maximum possible correlation between issue position and the variable in question was achieved. The scores

---

[10] The terms proponent and opponent are used to include both active and inactive supporters of a position, i.e., we include those who have expressed an opinion about the issue even if they have not made any attempt at influencing the outcome.

on the four dimensions are summed to form a coefficient of cleavage which expresses the total amount of cleavage on a given issue.

More specifically, each of the four variables is dichotomized as follows: (1) length of residence is split at the median for a town; (2) nationality background is divided into the most frequent and all others; (3) education is divided into college and noncollege; (4) religion is divided into the most frequent and all others. Respondents' positions on each variable are compared, in turn, with positions on the issues, each separate combination of variable and issue forming a separate two-by-two table. The marginals of this table are used to calculate expected frequencies and maximum possible frequencies. The difference between the maximum possible and the expected frequency forms the denominator for the coefficient; the difference between the expected and the actual frequency constitutes the numerator.[11]

It is important to point out that whenever a town is homogeneous on a particular dimension, this dimension makes no contribution to the coefficient of cleavage. Thus, if every respondent in a particular town were Protestant, the denominator of the above coefficient would be zero for religion, and this dimension would simply be excluded. This means that the coefficient of cleavage tends, if anything, to overrate the degree of cleavage in homogeneous towns by giving them no credit for dimensions on which *all* proponents and opponents share a common characteristic. Put another way, a low coefficient of cleavage indicates not homogeneity, but high *cross-cutting* between these dimensions and issue position. Eight of the eighteen communities have at least one issue on which the coefficient of cleavage is 0.5 or higher.

RESULTS

As Table 1 indicates, shifts in political control are clearly related to rancorous conflict in this particular set of New England communities. Only one of the nine conventional towns is undergoing political change while two-thirds of the rancorous towns are undergoing such change. Are these

---

[11] For example, if there are 10 Protestants and 10 Catholics among 12 proponents and 8 opponents on fluoridation, we would expect by chance to get six Protestant proponents. However, we could get as many as 10 or as few as 2. Thus, the denominator of the coefficient of cleavage (CC) would be: 10 (Maximum frequency) — 6 (Expected frequency) = 4. If there were actually nine Protestant proponents, the numerator of the CC would be: 9 (Actual frequency) — 6 (Expected frequency) = 3, and the CC would be $\frac{3}{4} = 0.75$. The direction of relationship has no significance here. To avoid artificial results due to discontinuity and to simplify calculation, the expected frequencies were always rounded to the nearest integer.

TABLE 1. RANCOROUS CONFLICT AND
POLITICAL INSTABILITY

	Rancorous	Conven- tional
Undergoing political change	6	1
Politically stable	3	8
N	9	9

P < .05 (Fisher's Exact Test).

rancorous towns also higher on our measures of conduciveness and lower on integration than the conventional towns?

There is a limit to how far one can examine interrelationships among variables with only eighteen communities. Nevertheless, some attempt at this is necessary even at the risk of breaking these eighteen cases down into meaninglessly small cells. Eighteen may be a small number, but it is a great deal larger than the case study or comparison of two or three communities which is typical of the literature on community politics.

TABLE 2. RANCOROUS CONFLICT AND
STRUCTURAL CONDUCIVENESS

	Rancorous	Conven- tional
Has town meeting form of govern- ment	6	5
Does not have town meeting form of government	3	4
N	9	9
Solidary groups present	4	5
Solidary groups absent	5	4
N	9	9

There is little overall relationship between the measures of conduciveness used here—participative political structure and presence of clear solidary groups—and the presence of rancorous conflict. As Table 2 indicates, communities without town meetings are about as likely to have rancorous conflicts as those with them. Solidary groups are present about as often in rancorous as in conventional ones. These results are not, in themselves, negative evidence since we would not expect higher conduciveness alone (without evidence of strain) to produce differences between the two kinds of community. However, there is little suggestion in these data that, for those seven towns with political instability, the presence of town meetings or solidary groups increases the likelihood of rancorous conflict. It is true that four out of five politically unstable communities which have town meetings are rancorous, but then both of the unstable towns without town meetings are rancorous also. Three out of four of the unstable towns with solidary groups are rancorous but all three of the unstable towns without such groups are rancorous. Put another way, the one exception among the seven politically unstable communities is *not* lower on our measures of conduciveness; it has both solidary groups and town meetings to accompany its political strain but still it is not rancorous. For the measures used here the evidence on the conduciveness hypotheses must be considered inconclusive at best.

There is no overall relationship between rancorous conflict and the extent to which some organization provides a central focus for those involved in community affairs. However, if we focus specifically on the seven politically unstable towns, there is some indication that this variable does have an effect. Using as our measure the ratio of the largest number of respondent memberships in any single organization to the total number of respondents in a town, we find that the six politically unstable rancorous communities have an average ratio of 0.32 as against 0.41 for the eleven towns without political strain ($p < 0.05$) ; the one conventional town among the politically unstable has a ratio of 0.45, well above average on this measure of integration.

The average degree of acquaintance among opponents is substantially lower in rancorous than in conventional towns—2.89 vs. 2.39 ($p < 0.05$, using a one tailed text).[12] Among the politically unstable towns, the relationship is even stronger; the average is 2.97 for the six rancorous towns and the score is 1.50 for the conventional town, ranking it first among the set of 18 in friendship among opponents.

The Coefficient of Cleavage, our last measure of integration or lack of integration, shows similar results. As Table 3 indicates, six of eight towns which have at least one issue with a high degree of cleavage between proponents and opponents are rancorous. Five of the six politically unstable and rancorous towns have such sharp differences between proponents and opponents but only three of the other twelve.

Summary. In the towns studied here there were four exceptions to the relationship between political instability and the appearance of rancorous

---

[12] A lower score indicates closer friendship.

conflict. One of these, a town which is politically changing but is not rancorous, scores high on all our measures of integration. But there are also three towns without the kind of political strain measured here which are rancorous. One of these three is the only town among the eighteen which is experiencing severe economic strain. Seven years earlier, a major mill closed and the unemployment rate remained quite high. Numerous stores were empty on Main Street and many of those who were able to leave had already done so. The two other exceptions are not so easily explained. Not only are they not undergoing any political or other obvious

TABLE 3. Rancorous Conflict and Cleavage

	Rancorous	Conventional
All Towns		
CC of .5 or higher on at least one issue *	6	2
CC of less than .5 on all issues	3	7
N	9	9
Politically Unstable Towns		
CC of .5 or higher	5	0
CC of less than .5	1	1
Politically Stable Towns		
CC of .5 or higher	1	2
CC of less than .5	2	6
N	9	9

* (Or, 50% or less cross-cutting on at least one issue.) CC stands for Coefficient of Cleavage.

strain but they score high on our measures of integration as well. One can, of course, always find some sort of strain in any town but in the absence of special evidence to suggest such strains, rancorous conflict in these two communities must be regarded as unexplained by the hypotheses presented here.

There are two final variables which while they play no role in the hypotheses, might well be affecting the results. The first of these—the type of community—has no relationship to rancorous conflict for this set of towns; four of the nine rancorous communities and four of the nine conventional ones are independent towns rather than suburbs or resorts. Size of town, the second control variable, also has no overall relationship to rancorous conflict; five of the nine largest and four of the nine smallest

TABLE 4. RANCOROUS CONFLICT AND POLITICAL
INSTABILITY CONTROLLED FOR SIZE OF TOWN

	Rancorous	Conventional
Towns over 5000		
Undergoing political change	6	0
Politically stable	0	5
Towns under 5000		
Undergoing political change	0	1
Politically stable	3	3
(N)	9	9

towns are rancorous. Nevertheless it turns out that all of the exceptions fall among those with population under 5000. As Table 4 indicates, there is a perfect relationship between political instability and rancorous conflict for communities over 5000.

DISCUSSION

It is important to specify some content for such general classes of variable as structural strain, conduciveness, and integration. I have tried to do this here by explaining rancorous conflict in terms of the strain which political change provides or reflects, the conduciveness which a participative structure and solidary groups provide, and the integrative ties which a common organizational focus, friendships, and common bonds of nationality, religion, education and length of residence provide.

Rancorous conflict is similar in many respects to what Smelser has called "the hostile outburst."[13] But there are some differences worth noting. Connotatively, the term "hostile outburst" conjures up images of such dramatic and violent events as the Los Angeles riots. In the small communities studied here, even the most rancorous issue did not produce so much as a black eye. At best, we find a little public vilification and an occasional mild threat. However, even in a large community, it is easy to underrate the humiliation caused by apparently minor attacks. There was a day when men fought duels over insults no worse than many included here as manifestations of rancorous conflict.

A more important difference between the hostile outburst and the phenomenon described here resides in the relationship of rancorous con-

---

[13] Smelser, *op. cit.*

flict to collective behavior. Collective behavior is the mobilization of noninstitutionalized action on the basis of a generalized belief which redefines social action.[14] In Smelser's formulation, a critical element of the belief involved in collective behavior is its "short-circuiting" of the necessary steps between the highly generalized component of action on which the belief focuses and the specific operative solutions which are expected to follow from collective action. For example, the belief that the removal of encroachments of the federal government will ameliorate a variety of specific frustrations illustrates this sort of compression from generalized belief to operative solution. The hostile outburst in particular, involves "not only a redefinition of generalized forces in an ambiguous situation but also an identification and modification of persons thought to be agencies of these forces. The modification is to be effected by destroying, injuring, removing, or restricting a person or class of persons considered responsible for the evils at hand." [15]

By defining rancorous conflict in terms of beliefs about the means of influence used rather than the nature of the target of the generalized belief, we may include some episodes which would not be considered collective behavior as defined above. Specifically, it is not a criterion for inclusion that the target of the rancor be regarded as *symbolic* of some more generalized evil. Scapegoating need not be involved. In the issues studied here, it is frequently but not necessarily the case that the targets of rancor are regarded as symbolic of larger forces. Political opponents may be seen as agents or dupes of intricate conspiracies aimed at removing precious freedoms, or as tools of a giant "power grab." But they may also be seen as themselves, the ultimate perpetrators of some mischief. Nor is it assumed that these perceptions are inaccurate or oversimplified; the charges made may be true, the targets of hostility may be guilty.

This paper has a purpose more general than understanding modes of community conflict. Both the specific variables used and the general strategy of analysis are relevant to a wide variety of political expression. The politics of fluoridation is not so far removed from battles over open-occupancy housing or school Bible readings. The present explanation of rancorous conflict in small communities is not very different in kind from the explanation we would use in contrasting countries with or without revolutionary movements. Of course, the content of such general classes of variable as structural conduciveness, strain, and integration may vary in

---

[14] This is a paraphrase of Smelser, *op. cit.*, pp. 67–73. The brief discussion of relevant portions which is necessary here does not do full justice to Smelser's highly complex and interconnected discussion of collective behavior.

[15] *Ibid.*, p. 101.

different social-organizational settings. However, if one can establish that a participative political structure promotes conduciveness to rancorous conflict in one setting, it becomes a more plausible hypothesis for other settings. For example, this may explain why apparent improvements or efforts to remove strains may be accompanied by increases in rancorous conflict. Such changes may have their initial or most radical effects on conduciveness or on sources of structural integration or control and only secondary effects on the removal of sources of discontent. The study of such limited phenomena as rancorous conflicts in communities may teach us something more general about social movements and social change.

Because of the negative connotations of a term like "rancorous conflict," some final observations about the towns studied here are worth making. Many of the conventional communities are rather dull and stagnant, while some of the rancorous ones are among the most vital. Some of the conventional towns not only have an absence of rancorous conflict but a general absence of change; the rancorous towns have the strains that accompany change but some of them also have the advantages of stimulation and growth. The absence of rancorous conflict is no necessary sign of an "ideal" community.

10

STRUCTURE AND VALUES

IN LOCAL POLITICAL SYSTEMS:

The Case of

Fluoridation Decisions *

DONALD B. ROSENTHAL and ROBERT L. CRAIN
University of Chicago

Emulating developments in the study of national political systems, recent treatments of local politics have moved from an emphasis on the politics and government of specific cities to the development of concepts to permit comparative analysis of the structure and political style of American municipalities.

Williams and Adrian, for example, classify four middle-sized Michigan cities according to their differing "local political values." [1] Such values are manifested in the conceptions held by citizens and decision-makers of the purposes which their local government should serve. These may range from simply operating a "caretaker" government, maintaining certain traditional community services, to acting as an "arbiter" among competing groups and interests in the city.

Similarly, Banfield and Wilson distinguish among voters on the basis

---

* Reprinted with modifications from the *Journal of Politics*, 28 (February 1966) pp. 169–196. The research on which the present article is based was made possible by a grant from the United States Public Health Service to National Analysts, Inc., of Philadelphia. We wish to thank Aaron J. Spector of National Analysts for his cooperation through the many phases of the study. Our special thanks also go to Elihu Katz for the major part he played in the larger survey, and to him, John Crittenden, Morris Davis, and James Q. Wilson for comments on an earlier draft of the present paper.

[1] Oliver P. Williams and Charles R. Adrian, *Four Cities: A Study in Comparative Policy Making* (Philadelphia: University of Pennsylvania Press, 1963), esp. pp. 21–39.

of the "ethos" which they exhibit. Citizens adhering to a "Protestant ethos and middle-class political style" which they call "public regarding" are said to act differently from those having an ethos derived from immigrant and working-class values ("private regarding"). This point raises the possibility that communities with large middle-class and native populations will tend to pursue those ends which appear to benefit all citizens, and reject seemingly "self-interested" demands.[2]

On the basis of research in a number of Florida council-manager cities, Kammerer and her colleagues draw a distinction between communities which have monopolistic and competitive "styles" of politics. They relate these differences to such factors as demographic qualities in the municipalities themselves.[3]

In a related undertaking, Agger, Goldrich, and Swanson differentiate "power structures" and "regimes" at the local level. The former term points to the distribution of power in the community and the ideology of the political leadership; the latter to the "rules of the game" or values prevalent throughout the system. They have then proceeded to develop typologies for both of these dimensions.[4]

Whatever the specific shortcomings of each of these approaches, they have yielded suggestive answers to the question which *should be* central to any study of local decision-making: What are the factors which account for the observed differences among local political systems in handling demands made upon them? [5]

---

[2] James Q. Wilson and Edward C. Banfield, "Public Regardingness as a Value Premise in Voting Behavior," *American Political Science Review* 58 (December 1964), 876–887. The translation of these personal values into a community ethos raises some complex problems. See Raymond E. Wolfinger and John Osgood Field, "Political Ethos and the Structure of City Government," *American Political Science Review*, 50 (June 1966), 306–326, and an exchange between Wilson and Wolfinger in the December 1966 issue.

[3] For some of their ideas see Gladys M. Kammerer, Charles D. Farris, John M. DeGrove, and Alfred B. Clubock, *City Managers in Politics* (Gainesville: University of Florida Press, 1962) and Kammerer and DeGrove, "Urban Leadership During Change," *Annals of the American Academy*, CCCLIII (May, 1964), 95–106. Kammerer and her co-workers are talking only about one form of government—the council-manager system—in one state: Florida. The same limitation operates in another study where variations within one form of government in one state—the manager system in California—were investigated by Eugene C. Lee, *The Politics of Non-Partisanship* (Berkeley: University of California Press, 1960).

[4] Robert E. Agger, Daniel Goldrich, and Bert E. Swanson, *The Rulers and the Ruled* (New York: John Wiley & Sons, 1964), esp. pp. 40–51; pp. 69–124.

[5] By "local political systems" we mean throughout, the legally-described but community-influencing decision-making structures which exist in a given municipality. The social context of such structures is of considerable importance as our discussion

Obviously, all of these works point to the importance of *values* in accounting for variations in the decision-making process. In addition, we may find considerable support in the same literature for the suggestion that these values are expressed in different forms of government and in the acceptance of political practices like non-partisanship and at-large elections. However, this relationship is rarely spelled out. Williams and Adrian indicate that a connection exists between "local political values" and political structure, but they do not make a systematic linkage except in a brief discussion of the built-in conflict between the manager plan and minimal "caretaker" governments.[6] Agger, Goldrich, and Swanson, on the other hand, suggest that the structure of decision-making and the local value system may operate independently. For example, they argue, the "regime" may undergo considerable change over time, while the power structure remains the same.[7]

We will proceed on the assumption that political forms are an expression of community values. It is almost impossible to establish, however, once political practices have become legitimated, over time, what the direction of causality actually is. Rather, it must simply be recognized that once it is established, a particular political structure may permit certain kinds of demands to become more salient and more legitimate than another would. As Charles Adrian has put it:

> Structural arrangements do have an effect on government, but they neither guarantee good government nor prevent it. The forms are important because they affect the pattern of influence of various groups upon policy-making. The specific structure in any given case helps to establish behavior patterns and

---

indicates. Our usage follows the model developed by David Easton in his "An Approach to the Analysis of Political Systems," *World Politics*, IX (April, 1957), 383–400. Neither Easton nor any of those writers drawing upon his work have systematically attempted to apply his model to the local level, although Agger, Goldrich, and Swanson make some effort in this direction. Admittedly, there are many problems involved in such an application. Membership in a local political system in the United States involves very little commitment to a consensual system of values allegedly brought into play where the national political system is involved. For present purposes, however, it is sufficient to consider local decision-making as occurring within subordinate or truncated political systems where the values of the locality may only be significant for those who choose to be influenced by them.

[6] Williams and Adrian, pp. 282–287.

[7] Their discussion of "regime" resembles our consideration of the role of values. Their "power structures," however, bear little relationship to a traditional consideration of formal political structures. Indeed, the amount of attention given to forms of government is meager; where structural factors are brought in, the major concern is with parties, but even then the emphasis is not on distinguishing communities on the basis of the nature of their partisan structures.

attitudes toward power that definitely affect the process whereby decisions are made.[8]

Thus, we are suggesting that electoral practices and forms of government (the "political structure" of a community) express (or cause) varying political values. This assumption is exceedingly important in developing a method of studying local political decision-making which will permit large-scale comparison, rather than the small-scale study which is part of the current stage of comparative analysis.

FLUORIDATION AS A TEST VARIABLE

As a test of the importance of political structure for differentiating decisional results, we turned to one of the most controversial subjects in the experience of many American cities: fluoridation.[9]

Since shortly after World War II, the subject of fluoridation has received considerable attention from social scientists. Because of the "extremist" tone of much of the opposition which has formed to this proposal to reduce tooth decay by adding minute quantities of fluoride to municipal water supplies, a striking amount of space has been given to the subject both in popular magazines and in scholarly journals with particular emphasis being placed on the heated referenda battles which have taken place.

For the most part, however, these studies have stressed the social and psychological processes at work in American cities. This has been done through analyses of *public* reaction to fluoridation proposals (by sampling public opinion or by looking at the results of voting behavior on referenda) or through investigations of the attitudes and actions of the issue partisans (opponents and proponents). With the single exception of an unpublished case study by Ravenna Helson and Donald R. Matthews,[10]

---

[8] Charles R. Adrian, *Governing Urban America* (2nd edition, New York: McGraw-Hill Book Company, 1961), p. 197.

[9] It is problematic how much controversy arises on any given issue discussed in the power structure literature. One reason that non-political "influentials" may figure so prominently in decisions such as those discussed by Floyd Hunter and, more recently, by Robert Presthus in his *Men at the Top* (New York: Oxford University Press, 1964) may be due to the small number of issues on which there are meaningful differences in ideology between the non-governmental "elites" and the "politicians," on the one hand, and the "elites" and the "public" on the other. Even Robert Dahl, whose approach is considerably at variance with that of Hunter, does not choose for discussion "issues" which are essentially at controversy. For a more sophisticated treatment of local decision-making which does take controversy and ideology into consideration, see the Agger-Goldrich-Swanson volume.

[10] Ravenna Helson and Donald R. Matthews, "The Northampton Fluoridation Referendum: A Case Study of Local Politics and Voting Behavior," Unpublished paper, Smith College, 1959.

political scientists have given only passing attention to the fluoridation phenomenon and no one has tried to develop an understanding of the political systems within which these peculiarly volatile decisions have been made.[11]

In addition, studies of fluoridation controversies have been limited to analysis of only one city or at most a small number of cities. The research reported here was designed to complement these other studies with an analysis which was frankly political in approach and based on a large number of cases.

Questionnaires were mailed to the local public health officer, the city clerk, and the publisher of the largest newspaper in each of 1,186 cities; 1,051 of these were cities between 10,000 and 500,000 population which did not have fluoride naturally present and were the primary consumers of their water supply. (Many suburbs would be excluded.) The remaining seventy-five were cities between 5,000 and 10,000 population which had held referenda. These cities bias the sample of course, but their presence does not affect the direction or magnitude of any of the correlations reported here. Where they do have an effect, they are excluded. Other data were taken from the census and from the *Municipal Yearbook*.[12]

Response rates varied from 35 per cent to 57 per cent for the three questionnaires. (Since a small number of cities—less than a fifth of the cities in our sample—have never considered fluoridation at all, this deflates the response rates below their true figures.) In the analysis that follows, the numbers of cases vary sharply, depending upon which, if any, of the questionnaires are used in each table. (One table, which requires responses to all three questionnaires for each city, has a very small number of cases, and must be used gingerly for this reason.)

We realize, of course, a complete analysis of political values cannot depend upon an analysis of only one issue, and we hope that other writers will undertake similar studies of other types of decisions.

---

[11] Students of community power structure have been concerned about distinguishing among communities on the basis of the locus of decision-making; that is, whether a particular decision was made within the formal government structure or by some non-governmental elite either for subsequent private associational performance or for governmental ratification. In this connection, on any political continuum of decisions made at the local level, fluoridation must be treated as one issue handled through *public* mechanisms rather than *private* ones.

[12] A complete discussion of the methodology and findings of the study reported here may be found in Robert L. Crain, Elihu Katz, and Donald B. Rosenthal, "The Fluoridation Decision: Community Structure and Innovation," unpublished report to National Analysts, Inc., Philadelphia, 1964. A monograph covering this material is forthcoming, *The Politics of Community Conflict* (Indianapolis: The Bobbs-Merrill Co., 1967).

From the responses to our questionnaires, we conclude that fluoridation has the following political properties:

(1) It has almost unanimous support among the elite.

(2) Very few members of the elite have a strong interest in seeing it adopted.

(3) The opposition comes from an organized minority, usually including chiropractors, Christian Scientists, natural food faddists, and in a few cases, the radical right.

(4) The public at large is uniformed but is cautious because of the possible side-effects of any medical innovation.

(5) The medical profession is virtually unanimous in support of fluoridation.

While each of these statements requires a slight qualification, the general implications seem clear to us: fluoridation is an issue which can be adopted most easily by cities in which the political and civic elite's mild support is sufficient to offset the virulent opposition of a minority of ordinary citizens and only when it is possible to keep bounds on the level of public discussion so that the argument does not escalate into a confused debate involving large numbers of voters.

FORM OF GOVERNMENT AND THE FLUORIDATION DECISION

Since we are interested in governmental decision-making in this paper, our main variable is *not* whether or not the city adopted fluoridation, but how the city council decided the issue. The council has three options: to adopt fluoridation (*administrative adoption*); to hold a *referendum*, which occasionally may be required if citizens take advantage of provisions for local initiative); or to reject fluoridation without a public vote (*no action*). We are not here concerned with whether the referendum leads to adoption or rejection of fluoridation.

Table 1 considers sixteen cities which are too large to be included in this study. A single factor—whether the city is *legally* non-partisan in its council elections or not—tells us a good deal about the actions taken by that city in regard to fluoridation. By 1965 *all* of the partisan cities had adopted fluoridation; the non-partisan cities were divided among the various alternatives for action on fluoridation. If we had a more sensitive measure of true partisanship, we might be able to account for Chicago and Cleveland, where strong partisan organizations exist behind non-partisan facades. Similarly, late-adopting New York City probably has a weaker and more fluid party structure than the other partisan cities. Cincinnati, with

TABLE 1. PARTISANSHIP AND FLUORIDATION OUTCOME FOR
SIXTEEN LARGE CITIES: AS OF JANUARY 1965

Outcome	Partisan	Non-Partisan
Administrative adoption	Baltimore Buffalo Philadelphia Pittsburgh St. Louis New York	Chicago Cleveland Minneapolis
Held referenda		Cincinnati Milwaukee San Francisco
No action		Boston Detroit Los Angeles New Orleans

Note: Two cities are omitted. Houston has natural fluoridation
while Washington, D.C., has a Commission government appointed
by Congress. (Fluoridation was adopted by Congress for the District of Columbia.)

its traditions of non-partisan "good government" under influential managers has held three vicious referenda campaigns on fluoridation. That the
subject has come up several times is a tribute to the persistence of "good
government" forces.

The present analysis is concerned with reporting the relationship
between governmental structure and actions taken on fluoridation. It
should be recognized that fluoridation is in some ways a "hard case" to test
variations in community styles because it has had a rather lackluster
history under almost any conditions. In absolute terms, the differences we
are actually describing are rather small. Of all the cities which have acted
on fluoridation, only 35 per cent have adopted administratively. Similarly,
most referenda have lead to fluoridation's defeat.

Americans are continually experimenting with forms of local government. Lately they have turned from city government to metropolitan
government as an outlet for this propensity, but any examination of the
history of this century indicates the success of reformers in introducing
new ideas: the commission system; the council-manager plan; election of
councilmen on a city-wide basis; non-partisan elections. Old forms, like the
bicameral council, which once flourished, have either disappeared or been
severely modified.

The adoption of such changes, however, has followed a definite geographic trend so that at the present time certain parts of the country show a predilection for one form at the expense of the others. The N's in Table 2 indicate the number of cities using each type of government by region for the cities which are included in our study.

The Northeast and West provide the most contrast in terms of response to proposals for innovation in governmental forms. The older cities of the Northeast are primarily partisan, tend not to have city managers, and sometimes employ the now uncommon commission and town meeting

TABLE 2. OUTCOME ON FLUORIDATION BY FORM OF GOVERNMENT AND REGION

Regions	Mayor-Council			
	Manager	Partisan	Non-Partisan	Commission
Northeast				
Administrative adoption	24%	15%	9%	5%
Held referenda	15	5	25	11
No action	62	80	66	84
Total	101	100	100	100
N	(68)	(130)	(32)	(73)
South				
Administrative adoption	44%	35%	30%	30%
Held referenda	23	12	21	7
No action	33	52	48	63
Total	100	99	99	100
N	(127)	(40)	(33)	(43)
Midwest				
Administrative adoption	45%	36%	33%	33%
Held referenda	19	12	35	13
No action	35	52	32	54
Total	99	100	100	100
N	(110)	(94)	(72)	(39)
West				
Administrative adoption	9%	—	8%	—
Held referenda	26	—	24	—
No action	64	—	68	—
Total	99	—	100	—
N	(151)	(4)	(25)	(10)

Sources: *Municipal Yearbook;* Public Health Service Data.

forms. The West, in contrast, is heavily non-partisan and managerial. The difference can probably be traced in part to the greater enthusiasm with which the West greeted Progressivism, the relative youthfulness of its cities and the higher economic level of its population. The other two regions fall in between, both in extent of partisanship and in the percentage of cities utilizing the council-manager plan. Thus, the use of council-manager systems ranges from a high of 80 per cent in the West to 22 per cent in the Northeast, with the South closer to the West (52 per cent) and the Midwest closer to the Northeast (32 per cent).[13]

The fluoridation results illustrated in Table 2—whether a city made an administrative decision or decided to hold a referendum—are consistent with our hypothesis that forms of government relate to different styles in processing issues. Despite the small number of cases in some of the cells, the pattern is almost exactly the same in each region. In all regions, administrative adoptions are most frequent in council-manager cities, followed by partisan mayor-council cities. Referenda are more characteristic of non-partisan systems like the non-partisan mayor-council and manager cities. In general, partisan mayor-council cities and commission towns are more likely to fall in the "no action" category, and in all three test cases, the commission government is the higher of the two.

INTERPRETATION

The fluoridation literature gives us few clues as to why the relationship between governmental structure and decision-making appears in Tables 1 and 2. Only one writer—James Coleman, in his important monograph, *Community Conflict* [14]—develops a theory linking community structure to the presence of conflict. He is not, however, concerned with governmental structure. It seems to be possible to develop predictions about governmental structure from his paper, since he argues that conflict is more likely to occur when the government is remote from the public. As

---

[13] To the extent that the adoption of the council-manager system represents a consensual approach to local politics, it would seem proper to assume that the heavily white Protestant-governed South should be more like the West in its formal proclivities. Of course, the bases of political diversity exist in the South because of the presence of the Negroes, but for many years Southern politics at the local level proceeded *as if* the Negroes were not participants in the political process. It should be noted, however, that the South has never been peculiarly resistant to governmental innovation. The commission system originated in Galveston, the manager system in Staunton, Virginia.

[14] James S. Coleman, *Community Conflict* (Glencoe: The Free Press, 1957). For a consideration of the literature on fluoridation see Donald B. Rosenthal, "The Politics of Community Conflict," unpublished Ph.D. dissertation, Department of Political Science, University of Chicago, 1964, esp. pp. 89–179.

we shall see, our research indicates that this argument may be incorrect.

In order to develop an explanation for Tables 1 and 2, we consider it desirable to develop a typology using forms of government as *illustrative* of differing value systems and political structures. The implication is not that we assert a clear relationship between form of government and every other aspect of the political system, but rather, that if it is valid to treat a municipality as a political system, then one of the ways in which the values of that system are expressed is through the political structure (including form of government) which that system uses.

First, for the purposes of analysis, communities which place a high value on wide-spread public participation in decision-making will be called "participative." Such political systems are distinguished from others which restrict decision-making to formal political agencies. We will say that these cities have adopted a "non-participative" political value or style.

Along with this normative or stylistic dimension, we shall also be concerned with one particular structural aspect of the local political system: the extent to which there is executive centralization. Robert Dahl has written of New Haven as an "executive-centered coalition"; we suggest that the degree to which power is centralized in the hands of the administrative and political leadership of a city is an important index of the decision-making *control* exercised. In the literature discussing differences between the "strong mayor" and "weak mayor" systems we find some support for this point, but there has been little systematic effort to trace the relationship between degree of formal governmental centralization and policy decisions. "Strength," of course, is a summary of many factors, but we will mainly be concerned with this one aspect.

The material in Figure 1a traces the hypothesized connection between

		Participativeness of System	
		Participative (Many Referenda)	Non-Participative (Few Referenda)
Executive Centralization	Strong Structure (Many administrative actions)	I	II
	Weak Structure (Few administrative adoptions)	III	IV

FIGURE 1A. SYSTEM DIMENSIONS AND PREDICTIONS OF COMMUNITY ACTIONS ON FLUORIDATION

executive centralization and the "participativeness" of the system. The assumption is that the empirical manifestation of the latter value is the holding of many referenda in the municipality. On the other axis, a strongly centralized decision-making structure would favor actions at the administrative level. Furthermore, our proposition is that it would be *able* to act because there are fewer actors who must give their approval to the recommendations, and because the centralization of authority would insulate the decision-makers from the anti-fluoridationists, either through the use of an appointed executive or the use of strong political parties controlling recruitment to office and protecting the incumbent from defeat.[15]

A city of Type I would be one in which action on proposed innovations is high at both levels: government is centralized, but the public participates heavily. Whether the city prefers to adopt administratively or to hold a referenda, it would be highly disposed to action of some kind. Because of a disposition to encourage public participation, the referendum is a readily accepted device for attempting to reach a decision. The presence of a strong executive, however, would encourage a decision to be taken through established decisional structures. As we shall suggest shortly, the actual form of government most closely resembling this type exhibits a marked split-personality on the issue of fluoridation.

Cities of Type II, on the other hand, might be less readily activated in response to proposals for innovation, but having determined to act, would do so through established political channels, generally disdaining use of the referendum.

Cities of Type III, with a poorly articulated political center, and operating in a wide-open governmental milieu would have difficulty preventing the holding of referenda. The lack of a strong executive might mean an effort to shirk responsibility for action in an area of controversy—again a factor working for the holding of a referendum.

Finally, in Type IV cities there is neither an urge towards participation built into the system, nor a locus of executive responsibility. Such systems might be more readily inclined toward inaction.

While these types are "ideal," for present purposes they will be treated *as if* they were embodied in the four forms of government most common in the United States: the council-manager; partisan mayor-council ("strong mayor"); non-partisan mayor-council ("weak mayor"); and the commission. The most interesting empirical question is how closely these "fit" the typology we have outlined. Figure 1b indicates the hypothesized relationship between real forms and the typology. Because published materials do

---

[15] Given the general values of American society, we would further contend that the *ability* to act would lead to innovations under most contemporary conditions.

not offer standardized measures of the degree of executive centralization in American cities, we have built into our analysis the dimension of partisanship as a part of "political structure." [16]

Gabriel Almond has suggested that one of the major functions performed by political parties in most political systems is the aggregation of demands. This function reduces the pressures playing directly on the decision-making machinery. Such an "insulation" effect, we hypothesize, occurs at the local level by the presence of strong political parties. To the extent that decision-makers are secure in their positions, they are able to act on the basis of criteria which might not be immediately acceptable to

		Participativeness of System	
		Participative	Non-Participative
Executive Centralization	Strong Structure	I (Non-partisan council-manager)	II (Partisan mayor-council)
	Weak structure	III (Non-partisan mayor-council)	IV (Commission)

FIGURE 1B. System Dimensions and Related Forms of Government

certain vocal segments of the public.[17] For the purpose of argument, therefore, we assume that partisan mayor-council systems are more likely to have more powerful mayors than non-partisan mayor-council systems. Many of the former may appear to be formally weak mayor systems, but even where this is the case, the presence of a party system may help to

---

[16] There are other types of government, of course; the partisan council manager form, for example, is probably the strongest structure and is probably less open to participation than the non-partisan council-manager city. Thus these two forms could be added to cells II and III in Figure 1b. The town meeting is an even weaker, and more participative system than is the non-partisan mayor-council form. Our data do not permit us to discuss two other types, the partisan mayor-council system with a weak executive and the non-partisan mayor-council system with a strong mayor.

[17] Gabriel Almond, "Introduction," in Gabriel A. Almond and James S. Coleman, eds., *The Politics of the Developing Areas* (Princeton: Princeton University Press, 1960), pp. 38–45. This point is further developed throughout Myron Weiner, *The Politics of Scarcity* (Chicago: University of Chicago Press, 1962).

overcome the formal weaknesses of the local executive, as it has done in Chicago.[18]

The city manager form of government, on the other hand, is accompanied in its "classical" version by non-partisanship and a "political formula" which favors the referendum, thereby weakening formal political authority. However, the system is favorable to innovation (at least in theory) and the manager is vested with considerable administrative authority. Thus, the system would be expected to favor fluoridation and the manager to seek some action on the subject, but the participative bias of the system means that if any controversy is raised on fluoridation, the system will have considerable difficulty in resolving the issue. This characteristic derives from the "consensual" style which is built into manager systems; that is, they have a capacity for acting where issues can be defined as administrative or non-controversial, but situations of real political conflict strain the structure. When citizens are activated under these conditions, the lack of control over their participation may disrupt the system. It is partly for this reason that many matters may be referred to the public for decision or called from the hands of the government by public demands for a referendum.

The remainder of this paper will develop additional data to support the argument that these two variables—participativeness and executive centralization—are reasonable explanations of the correlation between the form of government and the fluoridation decision. We cannot, unfortunately, develop very pure measures, nor can we disprove all the possible alternative explanations. However, we can show in a variety of ways that our data are consistent with our interpretation, though we must leave some questions open.

EXECUTIVE LEADERSHIP AND STRUCTURAL "STRENGTH"

The central finding of the study of fluoridation decision-making is that the position taken on fluoridation by the mayor virtually determines the outcome.[19] We have data on 496 decisions made in 362 cities, and, as

---

[18] For a portrait of the ways in which party organization can overcome the forces of decentralization see Edward C. Banfield, *Political Influence* (New York: The Free Press, 1961).

[19] Our findings with respect to the influence of the system's executive are reported in Donald B. Rosenthal and Robert L. Crain, "Executive Leadership and Community Innovation: The Fluoridation Experience," *Urban Affairs Quarterly*, 1 (March 1966) pp. 39–57.

Table 3 indicates, if the mayor does not support fluoridation, there is very little chance for its adoption. Indeed, the mayor's neutrality on fluoridation is almost as unfortunate for the proponents as is outright opposition from the mayor. On the other hand, if the mayor does support it, fluoridation has a better-than-even chance of adoption without a referendum.

The close correlation between the mayor's position and the outcome may seem trivially obvious; after all, he is the most important figure in the government. The finding is interesting, however, not only because it runs counter to the argument of the purer of the power structure theorists, but also because the mayor is by no means the only decision-maker on the issue—in fact, it is usually the city council which has formal responsibility

TABLE 3. MAYOR'S POSITION AND GOVERNMENTAL
DECISION ON FLUORIDATION

Governmental Decision	Mayor's Public Position		
	Supported	Neutral	Opposed
Adoption	54%	5%	6%
Hold referendum	13	21	29
No action	33	74	65
Total	100%	100%	100%
N	(258)	(189)	(49)

Note: The cases are decisions, rather than cities; the 496 decisions come from 362 different cities.

for the decision. In many cities, furthermore, the mayor has little authority, holding a largely honorific post.

However one feels about the preceding table, there is no "obvious" reason why the mayor should have a great deal of influence upon the public vote in a referendum on fluoridation. Table 4, however, indicates that the mayor's public position has a great deal of effect, and in much the same way as it did on the governmental decision; fluoridation will rarely be approved unless the mayor publicly endorses it, but it has about an even chance of adoption if he does endorse it.

There is some justification, then, for treating the mayor's stand as a cause of adoption, rather than a mere spuriously associated correlate. One, therefore, could fruitfully analyze the factors which cause one mayor to support fluoridation while another opposed it. It is assumed that there is enough slippage in the system to permit an element of free choice to operate here; and it has been shown elsewhere that in the case of city managers, such factors as age, education, and professional mobility are associated with willingness to support fluoridation. However, this paper is concerned almost entirely with the way in which the political structure constrains the political leader, and will not touch upon the effect of personality.

The effect of partisanship will be considered more closely now, with a somewhat better measure than simply the presence of party names on the ballot. Two questions were addressed to publishers in the cities surveyed, "How important are political parties in the elections for city council and mayor?" and "Do these tend to be local or nationally affiliated parties?" We assume that the more "local" a party is, the less it will act like a strong

TABLE 4. Mayor's Position and Referendum
Decision on Fluoridation

Decision	Mayor's Public Position		
	Supported	Neutral	Opposed
Percentage of referenda leading to adoption *	46%	11%	7%
N	(34)	(37)	(14)

* In some cases, fluoridation was endorsed by the public vote but never installed.

Republican or Democratic Party is assumed to do, and that local candidates will be less able to depend upon coattail effects to guarantee their election. The local party is more likely to be fluid in its memberships, better able to enter coalitions with other groups and more amenable to reform and subversion. In all these respects, the local party is "weaker" than the sort of organization we hoped the publisher would identify as "national" in orientation.

In Tables 5 and 6 look, not at the decision itself, but at the health officer's report of whether the mayor publicly endorsed fluoridation, and look only at mayor-council cities. Tables 5 and 6 illustrate an anticipated pattern: the more local politics are influenced by political parties and the more national the identification of the parties, the more favorable the mayor will be to fluoridation. The mayor's freedom to follow the lead of the elites and his bureaucracy reflects the "strength" of the political order. The few mayors actually opposed to fluoridation tend to come from cities

TABLE 5. PARTY INFLUENCE AND MAYOR'S STAND, IN MAYOR-COUNCIL CITIES

Mayor's Stand	Very Influential	Moderately or Not Very In-fluential	Not at All
Favor	71%	55%	55%
Oppose	5	4	8
No stand	24	41	37
Total	100%	100%	100%
N	(41)	(56)	(62)

whose parties are locally based or non-partisan. These results, furthermore, are not merely the consequence of regional distribution of governmental forms. Indeed, controlling for region *increases* the correlation. For example, if the effects of region are removed (by the technique of standardization), in mayor-council cities where the publisher considers parties to be very influential in elections, 69 per cent of the mayors are found to be favorable towards fluoridation; in mayor-council cities where parties have no influence the percentage drops to 48 per cent. The difference is 21 per cent, compared to a difference of 16 per cent shown in Table 3. In a mayor-council system that demands leadership from the mayor, the chances appear greater that he will assume that policy-leadership on fluoridation under conditions of partisanship. In a non-partisan system, we suggest, the mayor is much less likely to feel responsibility for upholding the claims for support made by the local bureaucracy.

The finding that mayors in partisan towns are more favorable to fluoridation than in non-partisan towns is interesting not only in itself but

TABLE 6. NATIONAL AND LOCAL PARTIES AND MAYOR'S STAND, IN MAYOR-COUNCIL CITIES

Mayor's Stand	National Parties	Local or Mixed Systems
Favor	71%	51%
Oppose	2	8
No stand	28	41
Total	101%	100%
N	(51)	(39)

because it was the thesis of the early reformers of local government that non-partisanship would attract to office men likely to work for "good government" measures. While we are reluctant to classify mayors' attitudes towards good government by their stands on fluoridation alone, there does seem to be some support here for those who argue that non-partisanship has not lived up to the promises made for it. Furthermore, the weakness of the non-partisan mayor-council system in this respect cannot be compensated for. At least in the council-manager system, there is an alternate policy leader available.

Charles Adrian, drawing upon material from two city councils and two state legislatures, has proposed some general principles concerning the effects of non-partisanship. He argues, for example, that non-partisanship can attract the successful businessman into local government, as the system was intended to do, but at the same time it encourages the perennial office-seekers, or anyone who has had the opportunity to make his name familiar to the voters, even if it is merely because of a history of oppositionism.[20]

Following this reasoning, it could be hypothesized that the non-partisan office-holder would be more reluctant to support fluoridation than the partisan, since he must retain his office solely on the impression he has given the voters and without party support. It seems reasonable that he would want to avoid touching a sensitive nerve in even a small portion of the population by supporting fluoridation. On the other hand, a marginal candidate, a relatively unknown alderman in a large council, or a mayor whose powers are so limited that he is unable to get much attention from the newspapers—all might see opposing fluoridation as a possible way to gain attention. (Supporting fluoridation, on the other hand, does not seem to guarantee the electoral support of pro-fluoridationists, most of whom are not strongly interested in the issue the way the "antis" appear to be. In addition, supporting fluoridation is not an unconventional position and hence not as newsworthy.) In contrast, the partisan official might concern himself with the attitude of the party slating committee and the party's financial supporters toward him, for he might require such support to be renominated and re-elected.[21] The official who is more tightly structured

---

[20] Charles R. Adrian, "Some General Characteristics of Non-Partisan Elections," *American Political Science Review*, XLVI (September, 1952), 766–776.

[21] Given the large number of instances in which mayors do not support fluoridation, this consideration should not be overstated. It should be stressed that even in partisan towns the intra-party primary provides an opportunity for a candidate to use the support of the public to undermine the party organization. In broad terms, however, it remains a tautology that strong party organizations are able to exercise control over their members' actions, which is all we are saying here.

might be led into a political role to avoid "irresponsible" *opposition;* though this is no assurance he would *favor* fluoridation.

Throughout this discussion of the relationship between political structure and fluoridation decisions, we have emphasized both the types of people who are recruited by the several systems and the kinds of restraints placed upon their behavior by the contexts in which they find themselves. The manager is frequently a professional with a commitment to the application of scientific principles to administration. The partisan mayor is perhaps more "responsible"—not so much because of his personality or training—but because of the system in which he is functioning. He is, therefore, less likely than a "loner" non-partisan figure to take a radically negative stand on an issue like fluoridation. Indeed, he is more likely to take a positive position, because he has party support, and because he is

TABLE 7. TERM OF OFFICE OF THE MAYOR
AND HIS STAND

Term of Office	Per Cent of Mayors Favorable	N
1 year	36	11
2–3 years	59	75
4–5 years	70	54

more likely to feel central to the operation of the system and hence want to act as a spokesman for the city health department. On the other hand, even the commitment of the non-partisan mayor to "good government" may not give him enough strength to take a stand against the opinion of any sizable (or noisy) group.

If it is true that the differential allocation of power to the executive is a major variable in determining the actions taken by each city in dealing with fluoridation, we should be able to see it by comparing the positions of "weak" and "strong" mayors on fluoridation using other measures of "weak" and "strong" than simple partisanship. The former should be less favorable to fluoridation than the latter. This quality can be approached through two crude measures of mayoral power: his length of time in office (arguing that a mayor's term of office is an indirect correlate of his independence and power), and whether or not he has a veto over the council's decisions. Both indexes were applied to 140 cities for which both the health officer and publisher had returned questionnaires. We find in Table 7 that mayors with longer terms of office are noticeably more favorable, as predicted by the hypothesis. Short terms of office tend to occur in non-partisan cities, so the relationship is as expected. The nature of the mayor's veto power, however, does not appear to be an important influence on mayoral action.

Additional material, much of it anecdotal, suggests that systems in which policy-making is concentrated in a few hands are better able to cope with the controversy which surrounds fluoridation. In particular, cities which must deal with an independent water supply either privately owned or operated by a regional authority are less likely to adopt, because the water supplier is an additional actor with a partial or complete veto to override. The fight to eliminate decentralization of existing city governments has been going on for a long time, but many governments still have a collection of appointive and elective officials only vaguely responsive to each other.[22]

Fluoridation is the kind of issue which is peculiarly vulnerable in such a decentralized decision-making structure. It is an issue with an excellent ability to attract headlines; at the same time, it is not the typically "important" issue to which civic groups and leading businessmen will flock. In many cities, it is easy for officials to ignore fluoridation as not worth the noise and the opposition liable to arise, for fluoridation is the kind of unpleasant issue in which opposition can generate headlines about "encroaching socialism" or "putting the bureaucrats in control of men's minds."

The more decentralized the system, the greater the number of decision-makers who must make the difficult decision in favor of fluoridation. Given this situation, opposition by one official can often stop adoption; decentralization would thus appear to have particularly unfortunate consequences for fluoridation. We can even argue that doubling the number of decision-makers will more than double the chance for opposition. Each of these leaders is competing for the scarcest of resources in the political game: public attention and personal influence. If the rewards of conformity must be divided many ways (and divided unequally at that) then the unsuccessful politician may find that he can reap more benefit from opposition than from support. If the opponent has a veto, he can often set a

---

[22] For discussion of this problem see Banfield and Wilson, especially Chapters 6 and 8. The study by Helson and Matthews also gives an excellent example of how a system in which there are a great number of institutionalized participants complicates the decision-making process. This same sort of problem appears to be at work in the case of the Jacksonville, Florida, school system where so many governmental actors have their fingers in the making of school budgets and school policy that at one point the system reached near collapse and lost its national accreditation.

high price for his consent. Even if it is legally and institutionally possible to override the objections of the minority, to do so may require considerable expenditure in time, energy or political capital. It is part of our findings that fluoridation does not have many friends with this amount of power and the willingness to use it. The reader may recognize this argument as similar to the one made by Amos Hawley in his study of urban renewal adoptions: cities with many influentials will have power more widely distributed and thus be less able to act.[23]

Thus, if too many cooks spoil the fluoridated broth, cities which have the most difficulty with fluoridation should be those with the largest number of elected officials. In a quick test of this rather extreme hypothesis, four large states from the Midwest and South were selected at random

TABLE 8. Mean Number of Elective Officials for Cities Surveyed and Fluoridation Action in Four States *

Action	State			
	Michigan	Ohio	North Carolina	Minnesota
Held referenda	10.1 (11)	14.6 (8)	8.8 (8)	12.0 (6)
Administrative adoption	9.9 (19)	12.8 (11)	8.7 (12)	11.0 (4)
No action	8.7 (9)	12.0 (36)	7.8 (9)	10.1 (9)

* The number of cities in each category is indicated in parentheses.

and the mean number of elected officials, as given by the United States Census of Governments, was compared against fluoridation action where the data were available. The result is shown in Table 8 in all four states; the rank order was identical. (There is only one chance in 216 of this occurring by chance.) The cities which held referenda had the largest number of officials. After this surprisingly easy confirmation of that hypothesis, however, in every case it has been found that cities which have adopted administratively have more elected officials than cities which have not taken any positive action on fluoridation. The reasons for *not* acting,

---

[23] Amos Hawley, "Community Power and Urban Renewal Success," *American Journal of Sociology*, LXVIII (January, 1963), 422–431. Hawley implies that middle-class communities have more difficulty instituting urban renewal plans because they are likely to allow more scope for participation in the making of the decision under the style which we have described as "participative."

however, are so diverse that it is difficult to provide an explanation for this except to indicate that it runs contrary to our initial expectations.[24]

PARTICIPATIVENESS

Returning to the dimension of system values or style, we have suggested that "local political values" vary in the importance given to public participation and the attention paid to minority opinion. One measure, as previously indicated, is the number of referenda that the system holds. The commission system is a low user of fluoridation referenda, but it is also a poor adopter, so that the lack of referenda may also mean that this

TABLE 9. VARIATION BETWEEN COMMUNITY "TALK" OF REFERENDUM BEING HELD AND ACTUAL HOLDING BY FORM OF GOVERNMENT

	Form of Government			
	Manager	*Mayor-Council*		*Commission*
		Partisan	*Non-Partisan*	
Was there ever talk of holding a referendum? (per cent "yes")	46%	35%	54%	47%
N	(223)	(147)	(82)	(81)
Was one held? (per cent "yes")	48%	29%	52%	25%
N	(104)	(49)	(44)	(36)

particular form of government is incapable of any action on fluoridation. Of the remaining systems, it is the nonpartisan systems which hold the bulk of the referenda, and number of referenda held is a key factor in the failure of fluoridation.

Table 9 demonstrates the differences among the various political systems based on information provided by the health officer in each city. We asked him whether the possibility of holding a referendum was ever discussed in the city and whether one was actually held. The table demonstrates that partisan cities were less likely to discuss the possibility of

---

[24] While the data merits only a note, we should report that in three of the four states, the cities which *won* referenda tended to be cities which had few elected officials. Of course, the number of cases involved is very small.

holding a referendum and even if one was discussed, they were relatively unlikely to hold one. Non-partisan mayor-council cities, on the other hand, were most likely to consider holding a referendum and most likely to hold one, with the manager cities a close second in both cases.

The city with a participative style is likely to develop political practices over time which revolve around the public meeting, the citizen's committee, and the referendum. Fortified by non-partisanship, any group of citizens can agree to find a candidate for office and support him and his

TABLE 10. PERCENTAGE OF CITIES RECONSIDERING INITIAL ACTION ON FLUORIDATION, BY TYPE OF GOVERNMENT, WITH EFFECT OF TYPE OF INITIAL ACTION REMOVED

Initial Action on Fluoridation	Form of Government			
	Manager	Mayor-Council		Commission
		Partisan	Non-Partisan	
Percentage reconsidering	36.7%	29.6%	40.7%	41.1%
Expected percentage based on distribution of initial actions taken	34.2	36.0	35.6	41.1
Difference, between lines 1 and 2: the net effect of form regardless of type of initial action.	+2.5	−6.4	+5.1	0.0
N	(215)	(142)	(76)	(73)

chances for election will be meaningful. In such a system any vocal group must be recognized as part of the legitimate opposition.

Sometimes this participative style works in favor of fluoridation. The manager system, for example, is most likely to have the proposal for fluoridation introduced by a civic group, rather than by the public health professionals. Thus, the greater willingness or ability of citizens to participate means that fluoridation will have more supporters as well as more opponents. In addition, if the participative system rejects fluoridation, it is more likely to have the issue come up again, so that fluoridation gets more chances to be adopted. Unfortunately for fluoridation, the same is true once it is adopted; participative cities are more likely to cancel the program later. The top line of Table 10 demonstrates that the more participative systems are more likely to reconsider their decisions. The high percentage of commission governments reconsidering is a result of their tendency to take "no action," which is the easiest kind of decision to reconsider. Therefore in Table 10, we have controlled for the effect of the initial decision by standardization. In line two, we have presented the expected percentage of reconsideration if the forms did not vary in the probability of reconsidering a particular kind of action, but only varied in the type of initial action they took.[25] Then line three, which is the difference between line one and line two, shows the net effect of form of government on the chances for reconsideration, independent of the effect of initial type of action. As anticipated, the manager and non-partisan mayor-council cities are more likely to reconsider than would be expected, the partisan mayor-council cities less likely.

It is worth noting that citizen participation has a rather surprising effect on reconsideration. Not only are those cities which involve the citizens in decision-making least able to make a stable decision, but in addition, adoption by referendum is less likely to "stick" than adoption by administrative fiat (data not shown). One would think that resorting to a majority vote of all the eligible citizens would be a way to settle an issue once and for all. Such is not the case.

One would also except that if the conventional wisdom about democracy is valid, that the community which over the years encourages its citizens to participate in decision-making would educate its citizens to take more "rational" actions. In this case, it is known from the work of Gamson [26] and others that the voters reject fluoridation primarily because they are afraid of medical side effects and not because of any principled opposition to socialism. We know from our own work that they are more likely to vote "yes" if fluoridation is endorsed by the mayor and the local medical organizations. It is also known that Americans generally have high respect for medical science. Thus, it follows that the citizen's "rational" decision is to accept the advice of the near-unanimous medical profession. Cities which have a tradition of citizen participation in referenda will now be considered. Table 11 presents the referenda results in cities which have

---

[25] If the above explanation is unclear, we have simply computed for each form of government

$$\varepsilon_a = \sum_{x=1}^{x=4} \left(\begin{array}{c} \text{proportion of all cities} \\ \text{reconsidering action "x"} \end{array} \right) \left(\begin{array}{c} \text{percentage of type "a" cities} \\ \text{taking initial action "x"} \end{array} \right)$$

where ε_a is the expected percentage reconsidering for cities with type "a" form of government, and $x = 1, 2, 3, 4$ represents four types of initial action (adopt, win referenda, lose referenda, no action).

[26] William Gamson, "The Fluoridation Dialogue: Is It Ideological Politics?" *Public Opinion Quarterly*, 1962, 26, 526–537.

TABLE 11. BEHAVIOR OF HIGH AND LOW REFERENDA
SYSTEMS: REFERENDA CITIES ONLY

Referenda Systems	Cities Holding Five or More Referenda in Past Twelve Years	Cities Holding Less Than Five Referenda in Past Twelve Years
Per cent of referenda leading to adoption	26 (77)	27 (56)
Per cent of referenda actions "complex" *	39 (77)	21 (56)
Per cent of referenda hotly debated †	53 (34)	57 (30)
Per cent of mayors favorable	62 (26)	41 (22)

* "Complex" actions involve at least two actions: either two referenda, an administrative adoption preceding a referendum or some other combination.

† Derived from a question to publisher: "Compared to other issues with which you are familiar, would you say that fluoridation was: very calmly discussed; calmly discussed; warmly discussed; hotly discussed.

held over five referenda in the past twelve years compared to those which have held fewer.

At this point, the findings are no longer surprising. The cities with participative governments behave no more "rationally" than those which do not. In addition, they are less likely to be able to settle the issue with a single decision and they are just as likely to have controversy even though these cities do not need controversy as a pretext for holding a referendum. Finally, they are not more likely to vote for fluoridation despite the fact that their mayor is more likely to support it. We cannot present the cross-tabulation controlling for mayor's stand since the reports are from different cities. However, it is logical that if we could, we would find that "controlling" for mayor's position, the more experience a community had with referenda, the more likely it would be to reject fluoridation.

The reader may notice another rather complex interaction effect here.

Non-partisan cities have mayors who are less likely to support fluoridation. But in the table above, cities which hold many referenda are more likely to have mayors supporting fluoridation during a referendum. The answer to this puzzle is simple, but interesting. If a mayor in a partisan city supports fluoridation, it will be adopted administratively in most cases. The referendum is used when the administration wants to be neutral. In the non-partisan city, however, the referendum must often be used by a mayor who supports fluoridation, since he lacks the power or party discipline to get it adopted administratively. We must qualify this argument, however, since the difference in percentages of mayors favorable is only significant at the 10 per cent level.

When turning from the process of decision-making to the mechanics of the battle itself, some interesting differences are seen in the extent of public participation in partisan and non-partisan systems. Since non-partisan systems hold more referenda, they should be expected to display more of the preconditions of high controversy. However, even when comparing *only* cities which held referenda, the non-partisan mayor-council and manager systems are more likely to have held many public meetings. We asked health officers to indicate how many meetings were held on fluoridation. In non-partisan mayor-council systems 58 per cent of the cities reporting indicated that many meetings were held during a referenda campaign. In partisan mayor-council systems, however, 47 per cent of the campaigns were marked by many meetings.

Some of the difference in political action can also be traced to the interaction between the system and the opposition. In the course of the study, the characterisitics of persons who were regularly identified as leading proponents and opponents were analyzed. In general, we found that proponents were more likely to have a college education, a high status occupation (especially that of physician or dentist) and to be well-known in the community (on the basis of the judgment of the publisher of the leading newspaper) ; in two cases out of three, however, they had no past political experience.

The opponent leader, typically, was older, was not a college graduate and somewhat less high-status in occupation (though not as distinct from the proponent leaders as one might have presupposed).[27] He was less well-known than the proponent, and even less politically experienced. Out of 269 opponents who were characterized, only eighty-seven had some prior activity in political life.

---

[27] For a further discussion of the activities of the proponents and opponents of fluoridation, see Crain, Katz, and Rosenthal.

Table 12 compares the relative effectiveness of politically experienced and inexperienced leaders in cities with "weak" and "strong" parties. There is no difference in administrative adoptions, contrary to what might be expected, but there are striking differences in the number of referenda held. The partisan systems hold fewer referenda but when they do hold them the opponents are more likely to have political experience. In contrast, the non-partisan system seems to hold its referenda in response to the non-political opponent. Again the possibility is suggested that the referendum may serve different functions in the two systems: in the partisan system it may be used to relieve a stalemate within the government itself, whereas in the non-partisan system it may reflect a situation where the

TABLE 12. POLITICAL EXPERIENCE OF OPPONENT LEADER AND OUTCOME, BY PARTY INFLUENCE

Outcome	Parties Moderately or Very Influential		Parties Not Very or Not at All Influential	
	Opponent Experienced	Opponent Inexperienced	Opponent Experienced	Opponent Inexperienced
Administrative adoption	31%	29%	23%	22%
Held referendum	33	15	38	49
No action	36	55	40	29
Total	100	99	101	100
N	(36)	(65)	(48)	(96)

structure is more vulnerable to the politically "unsocialized" opponents, that is, the "radicals" of the community.

While we mentioned the partisan system as providing "insulation" from public participation, we have not specified any of the factors working towards this effect. One such element is the function performed by a minority party. When the minority party refuses to champion opposition to fluoridation, persons opposing fluoridation are left without any easy way to present their case. On most issues, the minority party may consider whether opposition will cost them support from their own party, from "good government" elements, or from financial supporters. These possibilities do not appear likely in the case of fluoridation. In addition, they may estimate that the anti-fluoridationists are not a lasting source of political backing. Table 13 supports this point by demonstrating the superiority of the two-party system as far as administrative action on fluoridation is

TABLE 13. PARTY STRUCTURE, FORM OF GOVERNMENT AND OUTCOME *

Outcome	Mayor-Council			
	Two-Party	*Local Parties*	*Non-Partisan*	*One-Party*
Administrative adoption	38%	28%	23%	20%
Held referenda	10	19	43	20
No action	52	53	34	60
Total	100	100	100	100
N	(63)	(32)	(33)	(30)
	Manager			
Administrative adoption	38%	32%	22%	18%
Held referenda	33	21	33	46
No action	29	47	44	36
Total	100	100	100	100
N	(21)	(34)	(90)	(11)

* The data are derived from the publisher's response to a question: How many of the present members of the city council are supported by the local Republican organization? . . The local Democratic organization? . . Other local parties? (Space for three . .) Independent?

concerned. For both mayor-council and manager forms of government, the two-party system is marked by the largest proportion of administrative adoptions (and, in the case of mayor-council cities, the smallest proportion of referenda held). Next best, in both cases, is the system of local parties where structural competition may still exist. The two non-partisan systems lag far behind.

CONCLUSIONS

What we have found, we think, indicates that ideally fluoridation has a better chance of consideration and possible adoption where the following conditions are met: there is a local political structure characterized by decision-making authority being centralized in a relatively strong executive like a manager or partisan mayor; the political structure provides the mechanisms through forms of government and strong parties which insulate mayors and managers from "irregular" pressures likely to arise on this issue; and, finally, that there is a low level of direct citizen participation both as a general rule and specifically on the fluoridation decision.

Broad popular participation, particularly in the absence of strong executive leadership and an institutionalized channel for confining the expression of opposition, spells defeat to fluoridation. We have elsewhere argued that it does so because fluoridation is a technical issue, the advantages of which are rather small from the citizen's point of view and equally minor from the viewpoint of the politicians as far as political capital is concerned.[28] On an issue of this sort the opposition can easily implant doubt. Doubt takes root and blossoms, the more the issue is discussed. For whatever reason the issue is raised for public discussion—whether it is because of a democratic debating tradition in the city's associations or a tradition of holding referenda—the opposition succeeds in arousing the citizenry to vote "no" and endless exhortations by proponents under the rubric of "educating" the public seem to fail, often rather badly.

Obviously we have not been able to produce "clean" measures for all the concepts we have put to use, but the very fact that some of the crude measures employed did show up relatively well indicates that there is considerable need for indexes of community decision-making which are able to take into account structural factors related to the local polity and which probe the political values of a community.

---

[28] *Ibid.*

11

SUBURBAN DIFFERENTIATION
AND MUNICIPAL POLICY CHOICES:
A Comparative Analysis
of Suburban Political Systems *

BRYAN T. DOWNES
Michigan State University

INTRODUCTION

Public policy, its formulation, promulgation, implementation, and effects, has long been one of the major questions to which students of politics have devoted their attention. However, it has been only in recent years that political scientists have begun to examine systematically how various environmental, structural, and process factors influence the adoption and implementation of such policies.[1] As a result, there are important gaps in knowledge about the variables which affect policy choices, especially policy choices at the local governmental level.

One of the purposes of the research discussed in this article has been to determine whether or not the existence of numerous municipalities in a single county in one metropolitan area has led to the development of distinct sets of local fiscal and land use policies reflecting the socioeconomic and political specialization of these subareas. Specifically, inquiry has been directed first toward understanding the effects of socioeconomic differentiation upon the policy choices, the operative commitment to spe-

---

* This article is drawn from several chapters of a doctoral dissertation prepared for the Department of Political Science, Washington University (St. Louis), submitted in August 1966. The author gratefully acknowledges the financial support of the National Science Foundation (Grant GS-803).

[1] For instance see: Oliver P. Williams, *et al.*, *Suburban Differences and Metropolitan Policies, A Philadelphia Story* (Philadelphia: University of Pennsylvania Press, 1965), and Oliver P. Williams and Charles R. Adrian, *Four Cities: A Study in Comparative Policy Making* (Philadelphia: University of Pennsylvania Press, 1963).

cific goals and objectives of individual governments within a metropolitan area; and second, to examining the effects of socioeconomic differentiation on political structure, recruitment of elected officials, and the council decision process in these same municipalities.[2] Moreover, these two research objectives are interrelated. If socioeconomic differentiation gives rise to separate and conflicting community interests, and these diverse interests are reflected in the political structure, elected leadership, and council decision process, it will certainly have an influence upon municipal policy choices.

THE THEORETICAL FRAMEWORK

The Community Political System Paradigm

Assuming an interest in increasing understanding of the factors affecting policy choices and that public policy is therefore the primary dependent variable to be explained, the next task becomes one of specifying the various independent and intervening variables which account for differences in municipal policy choices.[3] These factors and the possible relationships between them are set forth in the community political system paradigm in Table 1.[4]

Moving from left to right, in this paradigm it can be asssumed that various community socioeconomic characteristics influence the development of different types of political structures.[5] In addition, these same socioeconomic factors may directly affect various dimensions of the council decision process and the public policies undertaken by local governments. However, the influence of community socioeconomic characteristics upon policy choices may be mediated by a municipality's political structure

---

[2] For a discussion of a somewhat similar strategy see: Williams, *et al.*, *op. cit.*, pp. 19–21. Throughout the discussion in this article, the terms "community," "suburb," "city," and "municipality," have been used interchangeably and refer to a subsocietal political unit which consists of persons who share a common geographical area. For a more detailed discussion of these terms see: David Popenoe, "On the Meaning of 'Urban' in Urban Studies," *Urban Affairs Quarterly*, vol. 1, no. 1 (Sept. 1965), 17–33.

[3] For a discussion of this position see: James A. Robinson, "The Major Problems of Political Science," in L. K. Caldwell, ed., *Politics And Public Affairs* (Bloomington: Institute of Training for Public Service, 1962), pp. 161–188; and James Q. Wilson, "Problems in the Study of Urban Politics," in Edward H. Buehrig, ed., *Essays in Political Science* (Bloomington: Indiana University Press, 1966), pp. 131–150.

[4] For a discussion of a similar paradigm see: Richard E. Dawson and James A. Robinson, "Inter-Party Competition, Economic Variables and Welfare Policies in the American States," *The Journal of Politics*, vol. 25, no. 2 (May 1963), 265–289 and Robinson, *op. cit.*

[5] Dawson and Robinson, *op. cit.*, 265.

TABLE 1. Community Political System Paradigm

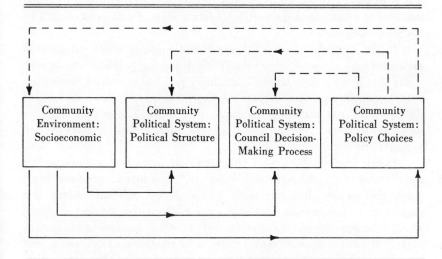

and/or its council's decision process. Public policy in this paradigm may be the outcome of the interaction among community socioeconomic characteristics, political structure, and the council decision process; or, as the outer solid lines indicate, community environmental characteristics may affect policy choices directly without being mediated by structure or process factors.

Some Related Concepts

The Political System. Several concepts have been used in discussing the paradigm in Table 1 which require further clarification. First of all, the term "system" refers to an integrated group of elements designed jointly to perform a given function.[6] The "community political system" is that set of interactions, abstracted from the totality of social behavior through which values are authoritatively allocated for a given community.[7]

The Council Decision Process. Second, "process" as used in the paradigm refers to decision-making activity within the political system and takes place in a municipality's city council. Political decision-making involves the actions of elected political leaders in the process of making

---

[6] Easton, David, *A Framework For Political Analysis* (Englewood Cliffs: Prentice-Hall, 1965), p. 57; and Talcott Parsons and Edward A. Shils, eds., *Toward A General Theory of Action* (New York: Harper 1951), pp. 190–233.

[7] Easton, *op. cit.*

choices. It is "a sequence of activities which results in the selection of one course of action from a set of socially defined alternative courses of action intended to bring about the particular future state of affairs envisaged by the decision-makers." [8]

In city councils, inputs of demands and supports which originate in the community are acted upon by individuals playing political roles in such a way that it is possible for the community political system to persist and for the council to produce outputs meeting the demands of at least some of the members and retaining the support of most. The council decision process is the way in which elected political leaders translate demands and supports into authoritative allocations.[9]

Policy Choices. Municipal policy can be defined as a community's commitment to specific goals and objectives.[10] In a formal sense municipal policy choices are ultimately made by the elected political leaders in a municipality and involve choosing among alternative modes of action about changes in or maintenance of existing services and institutions.[11] Municipal policies may be stated in resolutions, ordinances, and local laws or informally in reputation and understanding. They may affect the whole community, as is usually the case in tax matters, or a single family as would be true if a citizen requested that the street be repaired in front of his home. Policy changes may simply be routine or they may be adaptive or even innovative.[12] Furthermore, municipal policy choices may emphasize the maintenance of existing services only, provide and secure greater life amenities, promote economic growth, and/or arbitrate among

---

[8] Snyder, Richard C. and Glen D. Paige, "The United States Decision to Resist Aggression in Korea: The Application of an Analytical Scheme," *Administrative Science Quarterly*, vol. 3, no. 4 (Dec. 1958), 347. For a review of related literature see: Richard C. Snyder and James A. Robinson, *National and International Decision-Making* (New York: Institute for International Order, 1963).

[9] Easton, *op. cit.*, p. 131.

[10] Dawson and Robinson, *op. cit.*, 267.

[11] Rossi, Peter H., "Community Decision-Making," in Roland Young, ed., *Approaches to The Study of Politics* (Evanston: Northwestern University Press, 1958), p. 364. In this case, the particular type of issue defines the relevant decision-maker(s) according to rules laid down by custom and law.

[12] For a discussion of this typology see: Gladys Kammerer, "Role Diversity of City Managers," *Administrative Science Quarterly*, vol. 8, no. 4 (March 1964), 421–442. For a discussion of related issue typologies see: Ernest A. T. Barch and Stuart D. Johnson, "Community Power and a Typology of Social Issues," *Social Forces*, vol. 38, no. 4 (Oct. 1959), 29–32; Aaron B. Wildavsky, "The Analysis of Issue Contexts in the Study of Decision-Making," *The Journal of Politics*, vol. 24, no. 4 (Nov. 1962), 717–732; and Peter Bachrach and Morton S. Baratz, "Decisions and Non Decisions: An Analytic Framework," *The American Political Science Review*, vol. 57, no. 3 (Sept. 1963), 632–642.

conflicting interests.[13] They are the primary output of the political system and represent the allocation of scarce values in a community.[14]

Hypotheses and Variables

Our working hypothesis was that there is a clear and consistent relationship between the policy choices of local communities in a metropolitan area and the pattern of socioeconomic and political differentiation

TABLE 2. VARIABLE LISTING: COMMUNITY POLITICAL SYSTEM PARADIGM

Community Environment: Socioeconomic	Community Political System: Political Structure	Community Political System: Council Decision-Making Process	Community Political System: Policy Choices
SELECTED POPULATION CHARACTERISTICS: Total population Population increase Population density Age of adult population Ethnic and racial composition Social rank Community wealth	FORM OF GOVERNMENT: Council manager Mayor council Board of trustees Commission	COUNCILMEN BACKGROUND CHARACTERISTICS COUNCILMEN ROLE PERCEPTIONS COUNCILMEN POLICY ATTITUDES COUNCILMEN PERCEPTION OF ISSUE CONFLICT AND CONSENSUS COUNCIL DECISION PROCESS CHARACTERISTICS	FISCAL POLICIES: Total receipts Per capita receipts Total expenditures Per capita expenditures Per capita expenditures for various services Land use policy
SELECTED HOUSING CHARACTERISTICS: New housing units Population stability			PERCEPTION OF COUNCIL POLICY EMPHASIS: Encouraging economic growth Providing and securing greater life amenities Maintaining existing services only Arbitrating conflicting interests

which characterizes the urban environment. As communities strive to adapt to the forces in their environment, they will select policy alternatives designed to cope with these factors. More specifically, the impact of the

---

[13] This typology is developed in greater detail in: Oliver P. Williams, "A Typology For Comparative Local Government," *The Midwest Journal of Political Science*, vol. 5, no. 2 (May 1961), 150–164.

[14] Kammerer, Gladys, *et al.*, *The Urban Political Community: Profiles in Town Politics* (Boston: Houghton Mifflin Company, 1963). These authors employ a similar conception of politics.

socioeconomic character of a municipality on the following variables was investigated:

(1) The municipal political structure.
(2) Municipal policy choices.
(3) The characteristics of the individuals who are recruited to positions of formal leadership.
(4) The preferences and attitudes of elected political leaders.
(5) The extent of issue conflict in municipal councils.
(6) The characteristics of the council's decision process.

However, before examining these relationships, the specific variables for each general factor in the community political system paradigm had to be specified. Table 2 represents a preliminary specification of *some* of the more important dimensions of suburban political systems as discussed in the existing literature on community decision-making and small group behavior.[15] They were chosen not only for their ability to distinguish municipalities but also because of their possible relationship to differences in political structure, the council decision process, and municipal policy choices.

THE RESEARCH SETTING

The effects of socioeconomic differentiation upon the policy choices of individual governments and the effects of socioeconomic differentiation on the political structure, recruitment of elected political leaders, and the council decision process were examined in a number of suburban municipalities in St. Louis County. The County is in the St. Louis Metropolitan Statistical Area, an area which has over two million residents. The statistical area is composed of five counties, three in Missouri, two in Illinois, and the City of St. Louis (Table 3).[16] St. Louis County adjoins the City of St.

---

[15] For instance see: Williams, *et al., op. cit.*; Dorwin Cartwright and Alvin Zander, eds., *Group Dynamics, Research and Theory* (Evanston: Row, Peterson and Co., 1960), and Bernard Berelson and Gary A. Steiner, *Human Behavior: An Inventory of Scientific Findings* (New York: Harcourt, Brace, & World, 1964).

[16] For a discussion of the people and characteristics of this area see: John C. Bollens, ed., *Exploring the Metropolitan Community* (Berkeley: University of California Press, 1961); David B. Carpenter and Stuart A. Queen, *St. Louis: The Social Life of a Modern Metropolis*, St. Louis: Department of Sociology and Anthropology (Washington University), 1954, and Bryan T. Downes, "The Development of an Urban Community: The St. Louis Experience," Unpublished paper, Washington University, St. Louis (Fall 1964).

Louis and has a land area of 497 square miles. Although the central city has been steadily losing population over the last several decades, St. Louis County has tripled its population since 1930 until it now has over 700,000 residents.[17]

The governmental pattern in St. Louis County is highly fragmented. In addition to the County government, there are ninety-eight municipalities, twenty fire protection districts, twenty-seven individual school systems, and two county wide school districts—one for handicapped children and the other for vocational education. The County is also served by the Metropolitan Sewer District and the Bi-State Transit Authority.[18]

TABLE 3. POPULATION AND LAND AREA FOR SELECTED SUBAREAS IN THE ST. LOUIS METROPOLITAN STATISTICAL AREA

Area	Population, 1960	Population Increase, 1950–1960	Land Area in Square Miles
St. Louis Metropolitan Statistical Area	2,060,103	22.2	2,520
City of St. Louis	750,026	− 12.5	61
St. Louis County	703,532	73.1	497

Of the ninety-eight municipalities in St. Louis County, the majority have populations of less than 2,500. Because of the lack of adequate aggregate socioeconomic statistical data on cities with fewer than 2,500 inhabitants, all suburban municipalities which had less than 3,000 persons at the time of the 1960 census were excluded from the study.

On the basis of this consideration, forty municipalities (suburbs) were initially selected for inclusion in the study. They ranged in size from a high of 51,249 to a low of 3,089 persons. Fifteen were in the 10,000 to 50,000 range, an additional fifteen in the 5,000 to 9,999, and the final ten in the 3,000 to 4,999 range. Of these forty, thirty-seven communities agreed to participate. Table 4 lists these thirty-seven municipalities and also indicates a few of the dimensions which differentiate these communities from one another. They vary in total population, population increase over a ten year period, and total land area. Moreover, in the last ten to fifteen years differences among communities in the County have been

---

[17] See the discussion in: Henry J. Schmandt, *et al.*, *Metropolitan Reform in St. Louis: A Case Study* (New York: Holt, Rinehart & Winston, 1961).
[18] *Ibid.*

TABLE 4. MUNICIPALITIES INCLUDED IN THE STUDY

Municipalities	Population, 1960	Population Increase, 1950–1960	Date of Incorporation	Form of Government	Number in Legislative Body
Ballwin	5,710	*	1950	Board of Alderman	7
Bel Ridge	4,395	293.8	1947	Board of Trustees	9
Berkeley	18,676	254.5	1937	Council Manager	7
Breckenridge Hills	6,299	55.0	1950	Board of Trustees	9
Brentwood	12,250	63.2	1929	Board of Alderman	9
Bridgeton	· 7,820	3,771.3	1843	Board of Alderman	9
Clayton	15,245	− 4.9	1913	Council Manager	7
Crestwood	11,106	575.1	1949	Board of Alderman	9
Creve Coeur	5,122	151.1	1949	Board of Alderman	5
Dellwood	4,720	*	1950	Board of Alderman	9
Ferguson	22,149	91.4	1894	Council Manager	7
Florissant	38,166	921.3	1829	Mayor Council	10
Frontenac	3,089	181.1	1950	Board of Alderman	7
Glendale	7,048	43.0	1916	Board of Alderman	7
Hanley Hills	3,308	49.1	1950	Board of Trustees	9
Hazelwood	6,045	1,699.1	1949	Board of Trustees	5
Jennings	19,965	30.6	1946	Mayor Council	9
Kinloch	6,501	9.1	1948	Board of Alderman	11
Kirkwood	29,421	57.8	1865	Commission	5
Maplewood	12,522	− 6.4	1908	Commission	4
Normandy	4,452	93.1	1945	Board of Trustees	5
Northwoods	4,701	193.4	1940	Board of Alderman	7
Olivette	8,257	368.9	1930	Council Manager	5
Overland	22,763	96.8	1939	Board of Alderman	9
Pagedale	5,106	32.1	1950	Board of Alderman	7
Pine Lawn	5,943	− 7.5	1947	Board of Alderman	9
Richmond Heights	15,622	3.8	1913	Commission	4
Riverview	3,706	*	1950	Board of Trustees	5
Rock Hill	6,523	69.6	1929	Board of Alderman	7
St. Ann	12,155	166.7	1948	Board of Alderman	11
St. John	7,342	193.8	1946	Board of Trustees	9
Shrewsbury	4,730	39.9	1920	Board of Alderman	5
Sunset Hills	3,525	*	1957	Board of Alderman	7
University City	51,249	28.5	1906	Council Manager	7
Webster Groves	28,990	23.9	1896	Council Manager	7
Wellston	7,979	− 15.1	1949	Board of Alderman	12
Woodson Terrace	6,048	881.8	1946	Board of Alderman	9

* These cities were incorporated between 1950–1960.

accentuated, giving rise to greater socioeconomic heterogeneity among them.[19]

Table 4 also sets forth the form of government and number of elected political leaders in the legislative body of each of the thirty-seven municipalities as well as their date of incorporation.[20] Six have the council manager, twenty-one the weak mayor council, seven the trustee, and three the commission forms of government. Although the latter two forms of government are found in quite different suburbs, they are structurally very similar.[21]

In mayor council and council manager suburbs councilmen tend to be elected on a ward basis with the mayor being selected at-large. On the other hand, commissioners and trustees are elected at-large, with board members choosing their own chairman. The mayor in commission cities is elected at-large. The mayor has no council vote but he does have a veto in municipalities with the mayor council form of government. The reverse is true in municipalities with the other three forms. Table 4 also indicates that the legislative bodies under each of these plans vary in size.

As the foregoing data indicates, these suburban communities were by no means a universe of homogeneous municipalities. They varied in socioeconomic character, political structure, and also policy choices. But they do function within a single county and share a common legal framework imposed by the State of Missouri. They possess a similar cultural heritage and are enmeshed in a common political culture. As such, they provide the researcher with a number of accessible governmental units in which certain factors remain constant while others vary.

DATA COLLECTION

The information collected on these municipalities came from a variety of sources and required the use of a number of data collection techniques.[22] Data were gathered during the fall and winter of 1965–66. This information came from census materials, from questionnaires filled out by council-

---

[19] Bollens, *op. cit.*; and Stuart A. Queen and David B. Carpenter, *The American City* (New York: McGraw-Hill Book Company, 1953), pp. 95–131.

[20] There were a total of 279 elected political leaders in these thirty-seven municipalities.

[21] *Mo. Rev. Stat.*, vol. 1, ch. 80, arts. 80.010–80.670 and ch. 78, arts. 78.010–78.420 (1959). See also the discussion in: Bryan T. Downes, "Suburban Differentiation and Municipal Policy Choices: A Comparative Analysis of Suburban Political Systems," Unpublished doctoral dissertation, Washington University, St. Louis, 1966, pp. 42–52.

[22] On the strategy of combining research methods see: Eugene J. Webb, Donald T. Campbell, *et al.*, *Unobtrusive Measures, Nonreactive Research in the Social Sciences* (Chicago: Rand McNally & Co., 1966).

men and city clerks, from interviews with mayors and city councilmen, and through systematic observation of the decision process in suburban councils.

To examine the relationship between suburban socioeconomic differentiation and the policy choices of local governmental units the following data were considered. From the 1960 census came information on the socioeconomic characteristics of the municipalities studied—their total population, age, rate of population growth, age of adult population, ethnic and racial composition, social rank, and housing and influx. Ernst and Ernst, a St. Louis public accounting firm, provided data on municipal revenue and expenditure policies for the 1960–61 fiscal year.[23] Additional revenue and expenditure information was provided by the thirty-seven municipalities for the 1964–65 and 1965–66 fiscal years, but this has not been reported.[24] Municipal tax rates for 1960 and current land use emphasis were reported in a questionnaire filled out by the city clerk (or city manager) of each municipality.

In order to analyze the relationship between community socioeconomic differences and (1) the political structure, (2) leader characteristics, and (3) various dimensions of the decision process in city councils, it was necessary to collect the following information. Data on political structure or a municipality's form of government came from the city questionnaire. Information on the socioeconomic background characteristics, role perceptions, and policy attitudes of elected political leaders (councilmen) were taken from a questionnaire which each individual filled out and from the personal interview.[25] Finally, the interviews provided data on selected dimensions of the council decision process, issue conflict and council disagreements, and issue consensus and unanimity of decision-making. Questions were developed in an effort to increase understanding of how demands were initiated, processed, and how conflict over particular issues was handled by city councils. The systematic observations of suburban council meetings provided additional information on group conflict and cohesion, group structure and the problem solving process, and member

---

[23] Ernst and Ernst, *Financial and Statistical Information (Without Audit)*, *City of St. Louis, County of St. Louis, and Municipalities of St. Louis County* (St. Louis: Ernst and Ernst, September 1962).

[24] Although fiscal data were collected for the 1964–65 and 1965–66 fiscal years, comparison of that information with 1960 census material on community socioeconomic characteristics would not have been as valid a procedure as the one finally adopted. Instead, 1960 census information was correlated with 1960–61 fiscal data.

[25] Of the 279 individuals contacted, seventy-six per cent agreed to be interviewed. Prior to the interview each of the 279 councilmen and mayors was sent a questionnaire containing a series of background and attitudinal questions. Eighty-six per cent of those interviewed returned the questionnaire at the time of the interview.

satisfactions with various aspects of the council meeting. It has been assumed that if a council is able to cope with issue disagreements among its members and promote some degree of consensus then it will probably have a greater capacity to process demands made upon it.

THE MUNICIPALITIES:
SUBURBAN SOCIOECONOMIC DIFFERENTIATION

One of the variables which we found to be quite important in differentiating the communities studied was rate of population increase from 1950–60. Of the thirty-seven, thirteen had population increases of more than 100 per cent, another seven of 51 to 100 per cent, and the remaining thirteen of less than 51 per cent. It might be useful at this point to examine how this factor is related to some of the other socioeconomic characteristics which differentiate these municipalities. This examination will not only provide a useful initial characterization of these communities but also point out how these various socioeconomic variables are interrelated. Before summarizing the major findings of this study, then, attention will be focused briefly on the age of city from date of incorporation, total population, municipal social rank, per cent young adults, and per capita assessed valuation of suburbs with varying rates of population increase.

There was some tendency for those suburbs which had the most rapid rates of population increase from 1950–60 to be somewhat younger.[26] This tendency was particularly true of municipalities with population increases of 101 to 501 per cent. However, there were some younger suburbs—from one to twenty-five years old—which also had low growth rates. There were also several older communities—over sixty-five years old—which had fairly high growth rates. What seems to be taking place in this portion of the St. Louis metropolitan area is that the migration of people from the central city (St. Louis) is continuing, but that these people are not necessarily moving into the most recently incorporated suburbs.

---

[26] The primary measure of association relied upon in this analysis has been the contingency coefficient. However, this measure was supplemented by careful scrutiny of the distribution of data in contingency tables. For a more detailed discussion of this statistic see: Sidney Siegel, *Nonparametric Statistics For the Behavioral Sciences* (New York: McGraw-Hill Book Company, 1956), pp. 196–202.

Data on municipal socioeconomic characteristics were taken from the following primary sources: United States Department of Commerce, Bureau of the Census. *Eighteenth Census of Population: 1960* (Washington, D.C.: United States Government Printing Office), vol. 1, part 27, 1963; and United States Department of Commerce, Bureau of the Census. *County And City Data Book, 1962* (Washington, D.C.: United States Government Printing Office, 1962).

In general, higher growth rate municipalities, particularly those which more than doubled their populations from 1950–60, tended to be somewhat smaller in terms of their total populations. Moreover, there was a tendency for municipalities whose populations increased at a less rapid rate to be somewhat larger. It would appear that many smaller communities, particularly those with populations of less than 10,000 persons, are absorbing much of the influx of new residents from the central city and elsewhere.

A much stronger relationship was found between rate of population increase and the percentage of young adults in the total population of a community. There was a definite tendency for higher growth rate suburbs to have higher percentages of young adults in their populations—from twelve to twenty per cent. However, the relationship between population increase and municipal social rank was less clear and somewhat difficult to interpret.[27] There was a tendency for lower growth rate suburbs to have either high or low social ranking—very high, high, or very low. On the other hand, there was a tendency for municipalities whose populations increased by more than fifty per cent to be medium or low in social rank. It would seem that in this portion of the St. Louis metropolitan area people migrating to the suburbs tend to be young adults who move into communities which are somewhat older and lower in social rank. Thus the initial rush of upper and upper middle class families to the suburbs seems to have been replaced partially by the movement of middle and lower class families into communities which are either twenty-five years old or less or over sixty-five years in age. These municipalities are also generally lower in social rank.[28]

The relationship between population increase and per capita assessed valuation was equally difficult to interpret in these communities. First of all, very high growth rate suburbs tended to have higher per capita assessed valuations—more than $3,000,000. But with the exception of these very high growth rate communities there was a tendency for municipalities with lower growth rates to have somewhat higher per capita assessed valuations which ranged from $1,500,000 to $3,000,000. Thus there were

---

[27] The measure of municipal social rank is made up of various factors—median family income, median value of owner occupied dwellings, and per cent of professional workers. For a more detailed discussion of how this index was constructed see: Christen Jonassen and Sherwood H. Peres. *Interrelationships of Dimensions of Community Systems, A Factor Analysis of Eighty-Two Variables* (Columbus: Ohio State University Press, 1960), p. 37.

[28] See the discussion of recent developments in suburbia in: Robert C. Wood. *Suburbia, Its People And Their Politics* (Boston: Houghton Mifflin Company, 1958). It is also realized that people can only move into suburbs in which there is room for new families. They must either have adequate land upon which new homes can be built or an outflow of residents to other areas.

some higher growth rate suburbs which have very high per capita assessed valuations. But there were also a large number of rapidly growing communities which have low per capita assessed valuations. These are smaller, somewhat older, lower social ranking municipalities into which most young adults are moving.

Even though the findings were not always conclusive, there was a tendency for communities which had higher rates of population increase to be somewhat older, smaller, of medium to low social rank and medium to

TABLE 5. POPULATION INCREASE, 1950–1960 AND SELECTED COMMUNITY SOCIOECONOMIC CHARACTERISTICS: SUMMARY

Selected Community Socioeconomic Characteristics	Population Increase, 1950–1960:		
	Low (Lost Population to 50%)	Medium (51 to 100%)	High (101 to more than 500%)
Age of city	Older (over 45 years)	Mixed (1 to 45 years)	Younger (1 to 25 or over 65 years)
Total population	Larger (more than 10,000)	Medium (more than 5,000)	Smaller (3,000 to 10,000)
Per cent young adults	Low (7 to 12%)	Medium (10 to 15%)	Higher (15 to 18%)
Municipal social rank	High or Very Low	Medium to High	Medium to Low
Per capita assessed valuation	Higher (more than $2,000,000)	Medium ($1,500,-000 to $3,000,-000)	Medium to Low (less than $3,-000,000)

low per capita assessed valuation, with higher percentages of young adults. On the other hand, lower growth rate suburbs generally tended to be much older, larger, high or very low in social rank, somewhat higher per capita assessed valuation communities with low percentages of young adults (Table 5).

THE CLUSTERING EFFECT: COMMUNITY SOCIOECONOMIC ENVIRONMENT, POLITICAL STRUCTURE, LEADER CHARACTERISTICS, COUNCIL DECISION PROCESS, AND POLICY CHOICES

There are various ways in which the data analyzed thus far could be summarized. However, because of the theoretical interest in factors affecting municipal policy choices, this discussion will focus on a four-fold typology of fiscal and land use policies which has been developed. In so doing, various socioeconomic characteristics, form of government, leader characteristics, and aspects of the council decision process, will be examined in communities which have chosen to pursue one of four basic types of fiscal and land use policies. Not only will a more adequate characterization of these suburbs be provided but a summary of how various factors tend to cluster in communities which have very different fiscal and land use policies will also be achieved.

On the basis of previous analysis of the fiscal and land use policies followed by the thirty-seven suburban municipalities, a four-fold typology was developed.[29] First, high expenditure suburbs were identified. These communities had high tax rates and municipal receipts, and primarily residential land use. Second, and at the other end of our continuum of municipal policy choices, were low expenditure suburbs. These municipalities tended generally to have lower levels of expenditure and receipts, correspondingly low tax rates, and mixed land usage—mixed residential, commercial, industrial. Third, and somewhere in the middle of this continuum, were communities which also had low expenditures except for police and fire protection, low tax rates and correspondingly low total receipts, and primarily residential land use. However, it was found that because of their smaller size, in terms of total population, and their tendency to have very high per capita assessed valuations, per capita receipts in these suburbs were high. Finally, and again located somewhere in the middle of the continuum of municipal policy choices, were communities which had high expenditures for selected services, such as police and fire, parks and recreation, and public works. These suburbs tended also to have higher tax rates, medium receipts, and mixed land usage. Table 6 gives some indication of the range of variation in municipal expenditures and revenue in the thirty-seven communities. The data in Table 7 indicates the approximate level of expenditures and revenue in each of the four types of suburbs discussed above.

In this section, then, the socioeconomic characteristics; political structure; the socioeconomic status, role perceptions, and policy attitudes of city councilmen; and conflict, consensus, and the handling of issues in city councils—and the clustering of these factors—in suburban municipalities with varying fiscal and land use policies are examined. This is not an attempt to develop causal explanations but rather an effort to suggest relationships and associations of these basic characteristics of municipalities.[30]

---

[29] Downes, "Suburban Differentiation and Municipal Policy Choices," *op. cit.*, pp. 88–129.

[30] This summary is based solely on the analysis presented in: *Ibid.*, pp. 42–279.

TABLE 6. VARIATION IN COMMUNITY EXPENDITURES
AND REVENUE (SUMMARY)

| | Range of Variation | |
	Maximum	Minimum
Municipal Expenditure per Capita	$100.00	Less than $20.00
Police and Fire Expenditure per Capita	$ 29.00	Less than $ 5.00
Public Works Expenditure per Capita	$ 22.00	Less than $ 4.00
Park and Recreation Expenditure per Capita	$ 8.00	Less than $ .50
Municipal Receipts per Capita	$100.00	Less than $20.00
Municipal Tax Rate, per $100 of Assessed Valuation	$ 1.00	$ .20

TABLE 7. COMMUNITY EXPENDITURES AND REVENUE (SUMMARY)

Municipal Policy Choices	Per Capita Municipal Expenditure	Per Capita Municipal Receipts	Per Capita Municipal Tax Rate
Type I: High Expenditure	More than $40.00	More than $40.00	More than $.75
Type II: High Expenditure for Selected Services	More than $25.00 but less than $50.00	More than $30.00 but less than $40.00	More than $.55
Type III: Low Expenditure Except for Selected Services	Less than $25.00	More than $30.00 but less than $50.00	Less than $.55
Type IV: Low Expenditure	Less than $25.00	Less than $30.00	Less than $.55

TYPE I: High Expenditure Suburbs

Socioeconomic Characteristics and Form of Government. Type I suburbs tend to have high expenditures, receipts, tax rates, and primarily residential land use. In socioeconomic character they tend to be somewhat larger communities with medium to high growth rates. In addition they have higher per capita assessed valuations and social rank and lower percentages of young adults. The data in Table 8 give some indication of the relative size, increase in population, per capita assessed valuation, and percentage of young adults (persons aged 25 to 34) in Type I suburbs. The

TABLE 8. SELECTED SOCIOECONOMIC CHARACTERISTICS OF TYPE I SUBURBS

Municipal Policy Choice	Total Population, 1960	Population Increase, 1950–1960	Per Capita Assessed Valuation	Per Cent Young Adults
Type I: High Expenditure	More than 15,000	51 to 500%	$2,000,000 to $3,000,000	7.6 to 12.7%

range of variation in these characteristics in the thirty-seven municipalities is presented in Table 9. Type I suburbs also tend to have either the council manager or commission forms of government.[31]

Councilmen Characteristics. In these communities councilmen generally have higher levels of education, having completed college, and higher

TABLE 9. VARIATION IN SELECTED COMMUNITY SOCIOECONOMIC CHARACTERISTICS

Range of Variation	Total Population, 1960	Population Increase, 1950–1960	Per Capita Assessed Valuation	Per Cent Young Adults
Maximum	51,000	4,000%	$5,500,000	25%
Minimum	2,500	Lost population	Less than $1,000,000	7%

occupational status. Thus they tend to have somewhat higher socioeconomic status. There was a slight tendency for more of these councilmen to identify with the Republican Party and to vote for Republican candidates in presidential and gubernatorial elections. However, there were many of them—perhaps thirty per cent—who considered themselves Independents.

In high expenditure suburbs councilmen reported on the question-

---

[31] Although many of the relationships discussed in this section were not particularly strong, the general tendencies have been reported just the same.

naire which they filled out that the primary job or role of the council should be one of finding imaginative solutions to city problems, except those in high expenditure communities with the commission form of government. In these latter municipalities councilmen perceived hearing citizen's complaints and taking care of routine business as the most appropriate roles for the council. However, councilmen in Type I suburbs generally indicated that proposing programs to advance the city and hence providing community leadership was an important part of the job of being a councilman. Councilmen in these communities were somewhat more in favor of both increasing taxes to provide better city services and bringing new industry into the community, except those in commission cities. Nevertheless they did report the major policy emphasis of their councils as encouraging economic growth and providing for increased amenities (services).

The Council Decision Process. In these high expenditure suburbs, council meetings were characterized by high levels of overt issue conflict over such issues as zoning and planning, except in high expenditure suburbs with the commission form of government, which had very little issue conflict. In this instance, issue conflict refers to disagreements among councilmen which arise over issues before the council. However, councilmen reported during the interviews that there was little factionalism in their councils despite the high level of issue conflict among council members.

When councils in Type I suburbs were systematically observed, it was found that council meetings were somewhat less structured at least in terms of leader control and differentiation. Furthermore, issues were handled less openly, that is, councilmen emphasized that their councils attempted to work out issue disagreements in private or in committees before taking a final vote on the matter during a regular council meeting. Perhaps as a result, observers rated the problem solving process in these councils as being more thorough and efficient.[32]

Some Conclusions. High expenditure communities tend to be larger, medium growth rate, and higher social rank suburbs with high per capita assessed valuations. In addition councilmen in these suburbs tend to

---

[32] At least two meetings of each city council in the thirty-seven communities were systematically observed. The observer kept a running account of the substantive content of the meeting, the time spent on all agenda items, and the manner in which the council handled and disposed of the various issues before it. At the conclusion of the meeting the observer rated the council on over fifty variables. These variables were incorporated into a series of ten point scales. Some of the data presented in this section has been taken from this instrument.

have higher socioeconomic status and generally reported proposing programs which advance the city as an appropriate role for both their councils and for councilmen. Although councils in Type I suburbs had higher levels of overt issue conflict, they were not split by factions and generally had a more thorough and efficient problem solving process which may have resulted from their less open handling of issues.

TYPE II: High Expenditure for Selected Service Suburbs

Socioeconomic Characteristics and Form of Government. Type II suburbs tend to have high expenditures for police and fire protection, public works, and parks and recreation facilities; high tax rates; medium receipts; and mixed land usage. In socioeconomic character they tend to be small to medium sized, medium to high growth rate communities with higher percentages of young adults and medium social rank and per capita assessed valuations (Table 10). These municipalities generally tend to have the mayor council plan.

TABLE 10. SELECTED SOCIOECONOMIC CHARACTERISTICS OF TYPE II
SUBURBS

Municipal Policy Choice	Total Population, 1960	Population Increase, 1950–1960	Per Capita Assessed Valuation	Per Cent Young Adults
Type II: High Expenditure for Selected Services	5,000 to 15,000	Lost population to 50%	$1,500,000 to 2,000,000	12.8% to more than 18%

Councilmen Characteristics. Councilmen in these communities have about average socioeconomic status. In party identification and voting behavior they tend to be somewhat Democratic, but there were also substantial numbers of Republicans and Independents among these councilmen. In addition, they give equal emphasis in their councils to finding imaginative solutions to city problems, doing what the people want, and adjusting community conflicts. The role(s) they chose as councilmen also reflect this mixed emphasis. Councilmen in these suburbs reported that their councils tended to emphasize policies which both encouraged economic growth and secured greater life amenities.

The Council Decision Process. Issue disagreements were high in councils in Type II suburbs as was the extent of council factionalism. Moreover, council meetings tended to be more structured but the handling of issues more open. In this case councilmen reported they were more likely to try to talk their differences out at the public meeting before taking a vote on the matter before them. Thus both unanimity in making policy choices and the thoroughness and efficiency of the problem solving process were less than in Type I suburbs.

Some Conclusions. Type II suburbs tend to be about average in their socioeconomic characteristics and generally have the mayor council form of government. The same applies to the socioeconomic status of councilmen in these communities—it was neither high nor low but simply average. Councilmen tend to give equal emphasis to several roles for both their council and councilmen. However, councils in these communities were characterized by overt conflict, factionalism, more open handling of issues, and a less thorough and efficient problem solving process.

TYPE III: Low Expenditure Except for Selected Service Suburbs

Socioeconomic Characteristics and Form of Government. Type III suburbs generally have low expenditures, except for police and fire protection, low tax rates, correspondingly low total receipts, and primarily residential land use. However, they tend to have high per capita receipts because they are small or medium in size, and have very high assessed valuations. They also tend to have medium growth rates, very high social rank, few young adults, and the mayor council form of government (Table 11).

TABLE 11. SELECTED SOCIOECONOMIC CHARACTERISTICS OF TYPE III
SUBURBS

Municipal Policy Choice	Total Population, 1960	Population Increase, 1950–1960	Per Capita Assessed Valuation	Per Cent Young Adults
Type III: Low Expenditure Except for Selected Services	5,000 to 10,000	51 to 100%	More than $3,000,000	7.6 to 12.7%

Councilmen Characteristics. Councilmen in Type III suburbs have very high socioeconomic status and overwhelmingly identify with the Republican Party and vote for Republican candidates. They reported looking after existing services and finding imaginative solutions to city problems as appropriate roles for their councils. In addition, they indicated that councilmen should propose programs which advance their communities. Councils in these communities tended to emphasize the general policy of providing and securing greater life amenities.

The Council Decision Process. Although councils in these communities had a high degree of overt conflict—frequent issue disagreements between council members—particularly over zoning and planning questions, they were not split by factions. The handling of issues tended to be less open, the council meeting was less structured, and the thoroughness and efficiency of the council problem solving process was high.

Some Conclusions. Type III suburbs tend to be composed of upper middle and upper class families. They generally tend to be smaller communities with medium growth rates, few young adults, and very high social rank and per capita assessed valuations. Councilmen in these suburbs tend to have very high socioeconomic status and to emphasize policies which provide and secure greater life amenities. Although councils in these municipalities are characterized by frequent issue conflict they have less factionalism, less open handling of issues, and a very thorough and efficient problem solving process.

TYPE IV: Low Expenditure Suburbs

Socioeconomic Characteristics and Form of Government. Type IV suburbs generally have low expenditures and receipts, correspondingly low

TABLE 12. SELECTED SOCIOECONOMIC CHARACTERISTICS OF TYPE IV SUBURBS

Municipal Policy Choice	Total Population, 1960	Population Increase, 1950–1960	Per Capita Assessed Valuation	Per Cent Young Adults
Type IV: Low Expenditure	Less than 5,000	100 to more than 500%	$1,500,000 or less	12.8 to more than 18.0%

tax rates, and mixed land usage. In socioeconomic character they tend to be smaller, higher growth rate communities, which have low social rank and per capita assessed valuations, and higher percentages of young adults. Low expenditure suburbs correspond in both community characteristics and fiscal and land use policies to municipalities which have the trustee form of government (Table 12).

Councilmen Characteristics. Councilmen in these communities generally have the lowest socioeconomic status, in terms of their level of education and occupational status. They also tend to identify overwhelmingly with the Democratic Party and vote for Democratic candidates. They report that the primary role of the council should be that of adjusting community conflicts and doing what the people want, and generally being acquainted with business before the council. The general council policy emphasis tends to be one which encourages economic growth.

The Council Decision Process. Councils in these suburbs tend to be characterized by few issue disagreements and little factionalism. But because issues were handled more openly unanimity in making policy choices was low. The thoroughness and efficiency of the problem solving process in these councils was also quite low.

Some Conclusions. Type IV suburbs generally tend to be the natural habitat of lower social ranking families. They also were smaller, medium to high growth rate communities with high percentages of young adults and low per capita assessed valuations. Councilmen tend to have lower socioeconomic status and perceive rather limited roles both for the council and for councilmen. Finally, despite little overt council conflict and factionalism, councils in these communities have less unanimity and a less thorough and efficient problem solving process, which may have been the result of the more open handling of issues by these councils.

An Overview

The various characteristics of communities, councils, and councilmen in municipalities with varying fiscal and land use policies have been summarized in Tables 13, 14, and 15. However, because of the nature of the type of policy choices being examined it would be very difficult to argue that the council decision process had much effect on these aggregate measures of a community's operative commitment to particular goals and objectives. One might be able to make a somewhat better case for the effect of certain councilmen characteristics upon these four types of policy commitments. For example, it could be argued that because councilmen with higher socioeconomic status generally tend to emphasize as an important role for the council finding imaginative solutions and for a councilman proposing programs which advance the city, that suburbs with such councilmen would tend to have higher total and per capita expenditures, receipts, and correspondingly high rax rates. In effect they would be emphasizing or following a policy which provided and secured greater life amenities for community residents. However, this explanation for the fiscal policies pursued by communities whose councilmen have higher socioeconomic status is only partial and somewhat inadequate.

The position has therefore been taken, based on the analysis of data in this project and previous research, that community socioeconomic charac-

TABLE 13. COMMUNITY SOCIOECONOMIC CHARACTERISTICS, FORM OF
GOVERNMENT AND MUNICIPAL POLICY CHOICES (SUMMARY)

Municipal Policy Choices	Community Socioeconomic Characteristics					Political Structure: Form of Government
	Total Population	Population Increase	Assessed Valuation	Social Rank	Young Adults	
Type I: High Expenditure	High	High or medium	High	High	Low	Council Manager or Commission
Type II: High for Selected Services	Medium to low	Medium to low	Medium	Medium	Medium to high	Mayor Council
Type III: Low Except for Selected Services	Medium to low	Medium	Very high	Very high	Low	Mayor Council
Type IV: Low Expenditure	Low	Medium to high	Low	Low	Medium to high	Trustee

teristics are probably more important determinants of municipal fiscal
and land use policies (at least the particular ones examined in this
study).[33] More specifically, variations in community socioeconomic characteristics or municipal need generating factors, resources, and preferences
will have the greatest effect upon the fiscal and land use policies undertaken by local governments.[34]

By way of illustrating this point, I will examine briefly how various
community socioeconomic characteristics may affect municipal fiscal policy. First, in Type I or high expenditure suburbs, service needs are
generated by larger populations which can only be met through larger
outlays of municipal receipts. Because these communities also have more
adequate resources—high per capita assessed valuations and social

---

[33] See the discussion in: Williams, *et al.*, *op. cit.*

[34] See the discussion of these factors in: Downes, "Suburban Differentiation and
Municipal Policy Choices," *op. cit.*, pp. 86–88; and Williams, *et al.*, *op. cit.*, p. 78. In
this context, "municipal needs" refer to conditions within a municipality which by
themselves generate certain municipal policies. They are essentially objective conditions and set upper and lower limits on policy choices. Total population, population
density, and population increase were the primary need generating factors examined in
this analysis.

TABLE 14. COUNCILMEN CHARACTERISTICS AND MUNICIPAL POLICY
CHOICES (SUMMARY)

Municipal Policy Choices	Councilmen Characteristics: (Background and Role Perceptions)					Council Policy Emphasis
	Educational Level	Occupational Status	Party and Voting	Role of Council	Role of Councilman	
Type I: High Expenditure	High	High	Republican and Mixed	Finding Imaginative Solutions	Propose Programs or Hear Citizen Complaints	Encourage Economic Growth and Secure Amenities
Type II: High for Selected Services	Medium	Medium	Mixed and Democratic	Finding Imaginative Solutions, Doing What the People Want, Adjusting Conflicts	Multiple	Encourage Economic Growth and Secure Amenities
Type III: Low Except for Selected Services	High	High	Republican	Finding Imaginative Solutions, Looking after Services	Propose Programs	Secure Amenities
Type IV: Low Expenditure	Low	Low	Democratic	Adjusting Conflicts, Doing What the People Want	Find Out What the People Want, Be Acquainted with Business before Council	Encourage Economic Growth

265

TABLE 15. The Council Decision Process and Municipal Policy Choices (Summary)

Municipal Policy Choices	The Council Decision Process						Problem Solving Process
	Issue Dis-agree-ments	Fac-tion-alism	Overt Conflict	Handling of Issues	Meeting Struc-ture	Una-nimity	
Type I: High Ex-penditure	High	Low	High	Less Open	Less Struc-tured	Medium	Thorough
Type II: High for Selected Services	Medium to High	High	High	More Open	Struc-tured	Low	Not Thorough
Type III: Low Ex-cept for Selected Services	High	Low	High	Less Open	Less Struc-tured	Medium	Thorough
Type IV: Low Expenditure	Low	Low	Medium	More Open	Struc-tured	Low	Not Thorough

rank—they can afford to undertake higher levels of expenditure for all services.

Second, in Type II or high expenditure for selected services, higher tax rate municipalities, service needs are also generated but in this case by increases in population due to the influx of new inhabitants. However, because of the lower level of resources in these suburbs they are not able to undertake high expenditures for all services.

Third, in Type III or low expenditure except for selected services, low tax rate communities, another factor becomes relevant and that is munici-pal preferences. These factors may affect the structuring of values in a community. Citizens in these very high social rank suburbs, which also have very high per capita assessed valuations, prefer to limit local govern-ment expenditures, except in the case of police and fire protection, to services which are considered to be important. For example, expendi-tures for park and recreational facilities are deemed less necessary in an area with open spaces and low population density. Similarly, the existence of private streets which are maintained by exclusive subdivisions results in lower expenditures for public works projects.

In Type IV or low expenditure suburbs, service needs are generated by expanding populations, but these municipalities lack the necessary resources to undertake a higher level of governmental expenditure. The tax base in these communities is not very adequate due to the lower social rank of residents and lower per capita assessed valuations. These municipalities also have somewhat higher percentages of young adults who tend to eschew all services, probably not because they do not want greater municipal services but rather as a result of their inability to pay for expanding services given their other expenditure commitments. They are willing to forego services for the present, perhaps in the hope that in the future they may be in a better financial position to afford such an additional outlay in funds. However, in these low expenditure suburbs there probably are also a number of residents who are committed to keeping municipal expenditures low. They believe that local governmental authority should be severely circumscribed and municipal expenditures maintained at their lowest possible levels.

12

FUNCTIONS OF URBAN

POLITICAL SYSTEMS:

Comparative Analysis

and the Indian Case *

DONALD B. ROSENTHAL
State University of New York (Buffalo)

Interest in cross-national political analysis and the flowering of studies involving the comparative analysis of local political systems within the United States [1] have converged sufficiently to encourage thoughts about the study of urban political phenomena on a cross-national basis.[2] Little con-

* Field work for the present study was conducted in India during 1963–1964 under a grant from the American Institute of Indian Studies. Subsequent support was provided by the Research Foundation of the State University of New York. An earlier version of the present paper was prepared for the Comparative Urban Studies Group of the American Society for Public Administration. I wish to acknowledge the helpful comments on that draft by Francine F. Rabinowitz and James F. Guyot.

[1] Movement away from the "single-city" study has involved an increasing rejection of many of the traditional "institutional" categories of local government studies in favor of more "behavioral" concerns. Some early products of these inquiries of this nature are Kammerer, Farris, DeGrove, and Clubock (1962), Williams and Adrian (1963) and Agger, Goldrich, and Swanson (1964). A different kind of approach is involved in the use of American cities as units of decision-making for the study of policy questions; cities are so employed in Crain, Katz, and Rosenthal (1968), Wilson (1968), and, of course, in studies discussed elsewhere in the present volume.

[2] Indicative of this development is the formation of such organizations as the Comparative Urban Studies Group (mentioned in note 1) and the Committee for Comparability in Community Research (see Clark, 1966, and the Conclusion of the present volume). Another useful discussion of trends in the field is Robert T. Daland (1966). Among the more important studies of urban politics outside the United States are Frank Smallwood's study of metropolitan reorganization in London (1965) and Kurt Steiner's intensive review of Japanese local government (1965). The latter work, however, does not reflect a major concern with methodological and theoretical issues in comparative urban analysis. Closer to that kind of emphasis is the work being done as

sideration has yet been given, however, to the construction of a consistent rationale for organizing materials and identifying questions of significant cross-polity interest at the level of the municipality. Indeed, a central issue remains to be confronted: Are cities in different national political systems really comparable?

Local governmental structures differ considerably among nations, but I shall begin to respond to the challenge posed by advocates of comparative analysis [3] by examining local political systems in terms of some of the functions performed by participants in such systems.

The present article attempts to characterize government in two Indian cities in terms of several dimensions of political behavior observed during a year of field work in those two cities. To a greater or lesser extent, these dimensions are also present in American cities, but somewhat less attention has been given to them in American studies than they warrant.

At the time that the present study was undertaken, very little of a behavioral nature had been written about Indian city government. I proposed to do a study of decision-making in two Indian cities along the lines familiar to students of American politics. This effort followed closely upon my involvement in a study of fluoridation decisions, where we surveyed the actions of hundreds of American cities with respect to one particular decision.[4] It soon became apparent to me, however, that important concrete decisions constituted only a minor dimension of political activity in Agra and Poona; it was necessary to look beyond those aspects of the local political process concerned with collective decision-making, narrowly defined, and explore other dimensions of the local political arena.

For the most part, the literature on governing the American city in the last decade has emphasized the *decisional* dimension of the local political system. Studies in this mode have explored how such systems are structured for making decisions: who participates in achieving such results—the nature of *political representation;* and how local political actors interact in the process of formulating outcomes—the role of *personal influence* in political life. In the wake of work by Hunter (1953) and Dahl (1961), many questions have been raised about the correlates of centraliza-

part of the International Studies of Values in Politics (see the Conclusion of the present volume). See also, Werlin (1965), Greenstone (1965), Kesselman (1966), and Hoskin (1966).

[3] William A. Robson's compilation of discrete city studies (1954) is typical of the older, atheoretical, approach to "comparison." Contrast the contributions to that volume, for example, with the goal advanced by Fred W. Riggs (1962) for theory of a comparative nature at the local level.

[4] For a report of that study, see Crain, Katz, and Rosenthal (1968). An article by Rosenthal and Crain, based on that study, is reprinted in the present volume.

tion and decentralization of authority and influence in making community decisions; various writers have examined the types of relationships which exist among institutional and individual claimants to influence over decisions; [5] several attempts have been made to classify local political systems in terms of their decision-making processes. (See Gilbert, this volume.)

Studies of this kind appear to emphasize the "output" dimension of local political systems.[6] Less attention has been paid to other functions which do not directly manifest themselves in decisions. In considering Indian big-city government, I shall focus on four factors:

(1) The importance of bureaucratic interventions by political actors serving as intermediaries between the public and the local bureaucracy.

(2) The extent to which important symbolic values are involved in conflicts among status groups in public life, even where no decisional payoffs of a material nature are directly at issue.

(3) The role which local political actors play in integrating the local political system with higher levels of political organization.

(4) The degree to which the expenditure of resources by participants in local political life for the use of other participants (as a form of "side-payment") constitutes an integrative device at the local level, despite the limited implications it may have for the processing of particular decisions.[7]

It is obvious that these features of Indian urban life are not peculiar to the political system of that nation. Because of the great constraints exerted on decision-making by popularly elected personnel in the larger cities of India, however, the non-decisional aspects of local political systems in that country may be more apparent.

To better understand the connection between decisional and non-decisional dimensions of local government in Indian cities, I shall briefly describe the pattern of local government in India and then proceed to examine in some depth the four dimensions mentioned above in the context

---

[5] Comparative "power structure" studies have indicated some of the variations which exist cross-nationally. See, for example, Delbert Miller's work on an American and an English city (1958) ; also, the comparisons done among American and Mexican cities by Form and D'Antonio (1959) and Klapp and Padgett (1960). One overview of these studies is D'Antonio, Form, Loomis and Erickson (1961). An attempt at integrating these and other findings into a more systematic framework is Clark (1965).

[6] To borrow from the functional terminology of Almond (1960), there has been more emphasis in this literature on rule-making than on rule-application or rule-adjudication.

[7] For another approach to classifying the functions of local communities, including political as well as non-political functions, see Clark (1967a).

of two large Indian cities: Agra and Poona. After a consideration of political life in these two cities, I shall suggest, in a concluding section, some possibilities for further research in comparative urban government.

INDIAN LOCAL GOVERNMENT

While there is some disagreement at a theoretical level about the appropriate description of the Indian "federal" structure—the Indian states are constitutionally the creatures of the central government to an extent greater than is the case in the United States—there is no question that local governments in India are subordinate units deriving their powers from state legislation and many of their resources from state finances.

Local governments come in various shapes and sizes in India, but the over-all pattern is fairly uniform.[8] Each state is divided into districts; below the district level, one may distinguish between rural and urban governments. In many of the states, a system of rural government—*panchayati raj*—has been introduced in the last ten years. Drawing equally upon Gandhian notions of governmental decentralization and developmental ideas about the necessity of involving persons at the local level in decision-making in order to promote economic and social change, the *panchayati raj* system characteristically includes a three level structure with a legally-defined "village" as its base. A number of villages are then grouped together as a political unit and representatives are sent from each village to meetings which make decisions for the area and allocate resources. Above this second level, there is another indirectly elected body of district government. At each level, elected members have considerable autonomy in planning the work of their body, directing administrative

---

[8] Until quite recently, there had been very little behavioral study of local political systems in India. Aside from the chapter by Venkatarangaiya in Robson and a survey of the history of local self-government in India by Tinker (1954), the literature available in 1962 was mainly institutional. Since that date a number of studies which shed light on the urban political process have appeared. They include the following: Sharma and Jangam on Bombay municipal elections (1962); Sirsikar on state and national elections in Poona (1965); Srinavasan and Sharma's study of the corporations in Bombay, Delhi, Calcutta and Madras (1965); Congress Party factionalism in Kanpur as described by Brass (1965); and brief election studies of the 1962 general elections in urban areas in a volume edited by Weiner and Kothari (1965). See also, the contributions by Hart, Rudolph and Weiner to a symposium on urban politics (1961). Statistical data is available in various sources including the *Directory* published by the All-India Institute of Local Self-Government (1964) and a set of working papers for a conference on municipal corporations in the state of Uttar Pradesh (UP) published by the Institute of Public Administration at Lucknow University (1963).

activities and appointing some officials of their own. They work, however, in conjunction with officials designated by the state government.[9]

Most of the smaller municipalities in India have a form of government which resembles the commission system in the United States. These governments combine executive and legislative authority in a committee or board of popularly elected members. The board then selects a person to preside over the local bureaucracy as Executive Officer, but much of the effective decision-making authority in the system remains in the hands of the members of the board. The political power which flows from patronage in employment and from direct control over material resources in these cities, as well as in the rural governments, provides an important incentive to participation in political life.

In contrast, twenty-one of the *largest* cities in India have had imposed on them a form of government—the corporation—which restricts participation by elected members in decision-making. The corporation system follows an old American dictum of public administration by attempting to separate administration from politics. Thus, government is formally divided into two parts: a "deliberative wing" composed of the municipal councillors, numbering sixty in Agra and sixty-five in Poona; and, an "executive wing"—the municipal bureaucracy. The latter is headed by a state-appointed civil servant, the Chief Executive Officer or Municipal Commissioner, who is generally a member of the all-India elite civil service corps, the Indian Administrative Service (IAS).[10]

In addition to the limitations on formal powers, it should be recognized in the following discussion that city governments in India were severely handicapped by resource limitations. Both large and small cities in India were heavily dependent upon state and national governments for grants-in-aid and loans, particularly for the execution of capital projects. The ineffectiveness of the tax collection system in the cities meant that local taxes were barely able to maintain the already low standard of serv-

---

[9] The literature on rural government and administration in India is extensive. Some of the more useful materials include works by David Potter (1964; 1966), B. Maheshwari (1963), Reinhard Bendix (1964) and Taylor, Ensminger, *et al.* (1966). Most anthropological studies of villages devote some space to the contrast between traditional rural government and recent innovations. In this connection, see Bailey (1964), D. F. Miller (1965) and Beteille (1965). Politics in rural India has received attention from various political scientists including Retzlaff (1962), Shrader and Joshi (1963), Weiner (1959; 1967) and Brass (1965).

[10] The Municipal Commissioner is supposed to serve at least three years in a local position before being reassigned. Because the talents of this elite cadre are regularly in demand for service in state and national ministries and the post of Municipal Commissioner appears to rank rather low in IAS prestige, turnover at the local level is rather frequent.

ices.[11] At the same time, at least until very recently, the distribution of material resources at the local level was shared by popularly elected municipal corporation members with important figures in the local unit of the then (1964) ruling Congress Party. The influence of the latter was predicated, in part, upon the fact that some of the largest employers in the two cities were state and national enterprises like the railways, the transportation system and army depots. Special licenses and permits for the distribution of scarce goods were also handled through important Congress members.

The activities of local political leaders were explored through loosely structured interviews with all 125 members of the two municipal bodies. Interviews ranged in length from a half hour to six hours (over several days). Among other things, these interviews touched on questions of recruitment into politics, relevant activities in political and non-political arenas, the members' understanding of political and administrative relations in the two cities and their ideas about current and recent events. Similar interviews were done with about fifty members of the local bureaucracies and a like number of party leaders, state government officials, and political observers.

An effort was also made to study the lives of the municipal corporations through observation of general meetings, budget debates, committee work and public functions. One piece of analysis typical of this effort was a sociometric identification of friendship and deference patterns among elected members in terms of structured statuses like party membership and caste.[12]

In addition to studying political behavior within the arena itself, it was possible to investigate the elected members as representatives of particular political groups acting through the available political structure. As a result, the better represented a political group was in these local bodies, the more implicated I became in their local history and political performances. While both cities had political groups peculiar to the local scene, neither city council was non-partisan and contests for these councils were considered significant tests of strength and prestige by the major political parties.

Before exploring some of the ramifications of this political order, it is necessary to know something of the history and political character of Agra

---

[11] The major locally raised sources of funds are octroi and terminal toll duties (two kinds of levies on goods entering the city) and house and water taxes. The former are a regular source of administrative corruption involving as they do tax collectors posted at entrances into the city; the latter are indifferently collected and legal action in such matters is generally not pressed very hard.

[12] A report of some of that material is available in Rosenthal (1966a).

and Poona. I will then turn to a discussion of the four dimensions of political behavior mentioned earlier.

THE CITIES OF AGRA AND POONA

Agra is a city of 462,000 persons in the largest Indian state, Uttar Pradesh (UP). It is about 125 miles southeast of the national capital, New Delhi, in an area bordering on the deserts of Rajasthan. Located on the Jumna River, which flows to Agra from Delhi and the Punjab, it is a viable base for movements to the south and west. These physical advantages led the Delhi Sultan, Sikandar Lodi, to establish Agra as a major city in the sixteenth century. The Mughal Empire which followed made Agra the seat of government and the premier city of the Empire, which controlled much of the subcontinent. Agra held this position until the middle of the seventeenth century, when the capital was moved back to Delhi. The city remained important, but lost some of its former prominence.

After fifty years of wars among Indian Empires and against the British, Agra finally became British territory in 1803. For a brief period (1834–1836), the city was the capital of a separate provincial government, but its political importance in the last 150 years has been relatively limited. Within the state of Uttar Pradesh, it is industrially less significant than the city of Kanpur and politically inferior to the state capital, Lucknow.

Agra's major importance today is as a regional commercial and communications center. It lies on major highways and railway lines from Delhi to the east (Bengal) and to the southwest (Bombay). Under the British, such institutions as colleges and hospitals were founded and the city has some importance as a regional intellectual center, although cities like Mathura and Varanasi (Benares) are much more sacred to the Hindus.

Indeed, Agra was prominent historically as a center of Muslim political power in the sub-continent; partition of India with the attendant out-migration of Muslims, however, has reduced the Muslim component of the population. Today only about 12 per cent of the population belongs to the Muslim community. Rapid growth of the city based on in-migration from its hinterland and the arrival of refugee groups from areas now in Pakistan have enforced the Hindu qualities of the city.

Political life in Agra was dominated by upper-class and upper-caste groups under the British. The city then had a system of restricted franchise which limited participation in government to the commercial families and property-owners of the area. It was from the same group, however, that the first nationalists in the city appeared in the period after 1920.

Opposition to the Congress Party in Agra was not significant prior to Independence in 1947. That party was led by high-status leaders, principally Brahmans and Banias, the latter being the traditional merchant caste in the region. After Independence, conflicts within the national and state Congress Party organizations resulted in the resignation of the major figure in the Agra Congress from the party in 1952. There followed fifteen years of factional quarrels within the state and local Congress which increasingly debilitated that organization for effective political action in the city.[13]

The Banias constitute about 20 per cent of the population of Agra and if they were a politically united status group might easily continue to dominate Agra political life. In fact, not only is the Congress Party split into two factions, each led by a Bania, but the Banias also play a major part in the leadership of the major opposition party active among high-status Hindus, the Jan Sangh. The latter is an organization which has special appeal for orthodox Hindus. Its militant nationalism and anti-Muslim attitudes also appeal to the large refugee populations of the city. That the Jan Sangh has been less successful in Agra than it might have been is due to its own factionalism.

The Banias do not dominate all positions of authority in these political parties. Responsibilities are shared with the Brahman community, which is about 10 per cent of the local population, and with other high-status groups like Thakurs and Kayasthas.

Challenge to the Congress has come not only from the Jan Sangh, but from the political party of the Scheduled Castes (the "ex-untouchables"). Organized politically as the Scheduled Caste Federation in the 1940's, the Jatav community of leather-workers (a traditionally polluting occupation) comprise only 17 per cent of the city's population, as compared to the third of the population represented by the higher caste groups. But during the 1950's they were fairly well unified and were mobilized politically through their own political party—called the Republican Party after 1957—and, ideologically, through a massive conversion to Buddhism.[14]

No popularly elected municipal body functioned in Agra between 1943 and 1959. Instead, state-appointed officials directed administrative regimes for much of that time. In 1959, Uttar Pradesh introduced the corporation form of government for the five largest cities in the state: Agra, Varanasi (Benares), Allahabad, Lucknow, and Kanpur. The Act

---

[13] For a discussion of the factional struggles in Uttar Pradesh, see Brass (1965); the conflicts in Agra are considered in greater detail in Rosenthal (1966b).

[14] A major study of the Jatavs of Agra is available in Lynch (1966).

creating the corporations was drawn in large part from the Bombay Provincial Municipal Corporations Act of 1949, which established the corporation system in Poona.

Of the sixty seats in the Agra corporation, fifty-four were filled by direct election in 1959 from 27 two-man wards. Of the 228 candidates for these 54 seats, Congress supported 51, the Jan Sangh backed 34, the Republicans supported about 28. Most of the remaining 115 contestants ran as independents. The results of the election, by party and status groups, are indicated in Table 1. With the addition of six "aldermen" elected by the

TABLE 1. PARTY AND CASTE OF ELECTED MEMBERS,
AGRA CORPORATION, 1959

Primordial Group	Party				
	Congress	Jan Sangh	Republi-can	Inde-pendent	Total
Brahmans	2	1	—	4	7
Bania-Jain	7	4	1	4	16
Other High Hindu	6	—	—	3	9
Backward	1	—	—	1	2
Refugee [a]	—	2	—	—	2
Muslim	—	—	1	4 [b]	5
Jatavs	—	—	11	2	13
Total	16	7	13	18	54

[a] One is from the Punjab, the other from the Sind.

[b] One of these Muslims ran as a member of the Praja Socialist Party (PSP), but was the only representative of that party in the corporation. The PSP had little support in Agra.

members, there was the following membership in 1960: Congress—19; Jan Sangh—6; Republicans—15; Independents—20.[15]

Despite the challenge provided by the Jatavs and numerous internal cleavages, the higher strata of the city still tended to exercise economic, social, and political leadership.

In contrast, the city of Poona has undergone a political revolution in the last thirty years which has dissociated political dominance from more traditional economic and social bases of leadership.

Poona, located upland from the western coast of India, is 120 miles to

---

[15] Sixteen of the Independents formed their own political "group" in the corporation, the Swatantra Dal (Independent Group). Defections account for other shifts.

the south and east of the city of Bombay. It had a municipal population of 598,000 in 1961. Like Agra, Poona was the base for a major political power before the arrival of the British—the Maratha Empire. The latter was founded by Marathas, the major peasant caste of western India, but fell under the control of their Brahman officials, who ran the Empire from Poona. The Maratha Empire was the last major native kingdom in the Indian heartland to resist the British. It surrendered to the British in 1818. The Brahmans quickly adapted to the new political situation and managed to gain most of the important positions open to Indians in the British service; the Marathas constituted a body of substantial peasants and petty local rajas, but they were intellectually and politically inactive for the century following the British conquest. The non-Brahmans did not really become politically important in Poona until the 1930's. At that time, they worked with the Brahman-led local Congress.

Under the municipal board system, which preceded the corporations in Agra and Poona, the elected members ran their boards in a manner reminiscent of some commission governments in the United States.

A member of the Agra corporation, who had served on the pre-corporation municipal board, in an interview recalled the status and power attached to municipal membership in that earlier period of his services—1929 to 1943:

> Previously members were all respected people. They belonged to high families and were good speakers. They did not belong to parties. There was only Congress then and the people who were independents worked with Congress with no bad feelings. Back then we knew that the officials would not take money. Now that is not so. I used to like the job of being a member of the municipality. Previously I had the power to get jobs for people I liked; now, in order to get anything out of the corporation, it is necessary to give money. I have no use for the present corporation.

Others have offered a less kindly view of the earlier golden age:

> Unconstitutional acts, irregular appointments, withholding of the correct facts from the Board members and the public, and other unsavoury practices were some of the features of the Boards and techniques of their administration. Owing to the increase in nepotism and jobbery, the Boards became notorious for wasteful and extravagant expenditures.[16]

In the case of Poona, for instance, the provincial government of Bombay withdrew municipal authority over education after one of the members was

---

[16] Gupta (1961, p. 54).

kidnapped to prevent him from voting in an election for the committee responsible for overseeing the schools.

With Independence came universal franchise and the decline of Brahman political domination in Poona. The Congress Party, under Brahman control earlier, was gradually captured by the Marathas who became increasingly important in the local organization.

While the Marathas greatly outnumber Brahmans in the rural area around Poona, in the city of Poona the two groups are evenly balanced; each has about 20 per cent of the population. What has emerged in municipal politics resembles the conflict characteristic of many American cities earlier in this century: a working-class political machine competing against a fusion organization composed principally of middle-class citizens.

Against the non-ideological, materially based political power of the Marathas, the Brahmans and some middle class non-Brahmans have generated a variety of political organizations: on the left, the Socialists; on the right, the Jan Sangh; other parties and clusters of independents lie in between.

These rather disparate elements were drawn together for the first time in 1952, after the Congress swept the polls in the first general elections (for state and national representatives). In part, that Congress success in Poona was due to fragmentation of the opposition. Under the leadership of the editor of the leading newspaper in Poona, a man who regards himself as a crusading journalist, a municipal party was formed in 1952 called the Nagri Sanghatna (City Party). It won 30 seats in 1952 and control.

Despite the emphasis of its platform upon taking politics out of the corporation, many of the participants in the Sanghatna clearly aimed their attacks at the Congress. The party vied with the Congress, however, for non-Brahman support. It went out of its way to present a balanced slate of Brahman and Maratha candidates. This effort was aided by the candidacy of a highly respected Maratha public figure. In the process, conflicts between Marathas and Brahmans were muted and the Sanghatna's call was simply for "good government" without the taint of party politics. Table 2 shows the outcome of the 1962 elections, which led to another Nagri Sanghatna-dominated coalition within the corporation.

Electoral participation in both Poona and Agra exhibits features of what Almond and Verba would call a "participant" political culture. Not only do many candidates stand for office without prodding by formal organizations, but turnouts are quite respectable, particularly by American standards. They reached as high as 72 per cent in the 1957 general elections in Poona.

On the other hand, it would not be inaccurate to view Agra's political

TABLE 2. Caste and Party of Elected Members,
Poona Corporation, 1962

Primordial Group	Party			
	Congress	Sanghatna	Others	Total
Brahmans	2	7	6 [a]	15
Intermediate	2	6	—	8
Marathas	11	8	2	21
Low Hindus	1	3	2	6
Mahars	—	1	1 [b]	2
Other Scheduled Castes [c]	4	—	—	4
Muslims	1	—	—	1
Non-Maharashtrians	2	2	3	7
Others	—	1 [d]	—	1
Total	23	28	14	65

[a] Five of these constituted the entire group of Jan Sangh members elected to the corporation in 1962.

[b] Each of the Mahars is a member of one of the several fragments of the Republican Party in Poona. Though antagonistic to each other, they have both generally worked with the Nagri Sanghatna.

[c] In addition to the Mahars, there are several other sizable major ex-untouchable (Scheduled Caste) groups in Poona.

[d] There is one Christian in the corporation.

atmosphere as rather conservative and based upon personalistic factions. This contrasts with the relatively "modern" politics of Poona—if modernity is gauged by a greater concern with state and national issues, a somewhat greater ideological component to political arguments and a greater partisan consistency over time. As important as the figures on *total* candidacies are, it may be equally significant that at least 20 independents were elected to the Agra corporation as against only seven in Poona. The two cities are too similar, however, in too many respects for easy placement into distinct categories.

In particular, the systems are alike in the concern that members demonstrate for their roles as communicators of constituents' demands to the local bureaucracy, their emphasis on questions of personal and group status advancement and the degree to which they provide a forum for political training and orientation toward state and national affairs. If Agra is marked by more emphasis on the first two dimensions, Poona's municipal council members are inclined toward concern with all three.

FUNCTIONS OF URBAN POLITICAL SYSTEMS

I will now turn to an examination of the ways in which the four types of functions enumerated earlier—(1) intervention in the bureaucracy, (2) the enhancement of personal and group prestige, (3) advancement in the wider political arena, and (4) the distribution of legitimate and illegitimate side payments—are performed in Agra and Poona.

Again, the argument is that the presence of political structures like city governments in India does not necessarily indicate that such structures are employed with the same "mix" of ends in view as might be the case in the United States. Throughout, the non-material ends which political actors seek are considered *in addition to* their desire to influence the distribution of material benefits.

Clearly, many actors seek as much to *particularize bureaucratic performances* as to help in formulating uniform rules for application over a general body of citizens. In this process, locally elected politicians act as communicators of group or constituency attitudes and demands.

Participation by groups and individuals in local government, whatever the limitations on content, has important symbolic value and non-material benefits in terms of *status achievement* for groups which may not be as well-placed to affect the activity of larger, more substantive, arenas.

Similarly, while the formal material payoffs may not be great, municipal government provides an arena for the expression of *political ambition for participation in higher levels of political power* in the system. Only a small proportion of the membership of a municipal body can hope to use the municipality as a political stepping-stone, but from the perspective of the political system, some political recruitment does occur.

Finally, in Indian cities, low material benefits may be supplemented by *legitimate and illegitimate side-payments* which increase the inducement to participate for some persons, thereby tending to mute potential sources of social conflict.

Intervention in the Bureaucracy

Formal barriers do not mean that political relationships are completely distinct from administrative performance. As in most systems, politics does not end at the line of formal demarcation. Informal partisan pressures are exercised upon local administrators by local actors operating through the Congress party organization or through friendly members of the state government. More important, however, is the role of the elected

member of the corporation as spokesman for the public before the administration.

One can see in the responses of members of the corporations the
extent to which they see their major role as one of administrative intervention. When one member was asked to indicate the most important functions
of a member, he responded:

The foremost duty of a member is to serve the public which means he
should look after the well-being of the constituency which he represents including things like sanitation. He must visit the corporation and see that the
men of his locality are not harassed by the officials. He must try to help
people in their social functions like marriages and deaths by things like
helping them to get a proper amount of sugar in order to celebrate a marriage.[17]

Or, in a similar vein, another member replied:

My constituents ask me to help them get better water supply, improved
pipelines, help on house taxes and assessments, power connections and to make
recommendations for jobs or transfers.

To the outside observer cases of intervention may appear trivial, but
they are very important to the members themselves and to their constituents. In one typical instance, a tailor had put up two shops as part of his
own building, but they extended into a lane which was only three and a
half feet wide. Thirteen members of the corporation supported the petition
of the tailor who appealed against a decision of the administration. The
city administration was seeking to demolish the illegal construction and
even proceeded to the district civil court for action. Only a few high-status
members opposed the tailor's efforts. As one of these few described the situation:

The man had bought land by the roadside and then built without the sanction of the building department. The man claims he is the owner and that the
corporation has no right to order him around. The city's view is that it is an
unauthorized construction and must not be permitted. It is because of laxity of
this kind that Agra is planned badly and is so dirty. There is no civic feeling.

It is significant that very few members, particularly from among
low-status groups, shared these perceptions. Indeed, only a few high-status

---

[17] In the latter case, the intervention would be with a district official responsible
for food rationing, rather than with a municipal officer.

members expressed a general concern with the city as a whole as opposed to the welfare of their own constituencies.

Along with oversight of building plans in the city, the municipal administrators are responsible for house-keeping functions: water supply, maintenance of sewers and drains, construction and repair of roads and streets, regulation of bazaars and control of disease. Responsibility in these matters lies with the municipal bureaucrats. Elected members have only a feeble voice in how these agencies are run. Poona does run its own public bus system, which is a major local undertaking, but Agra does not.

Agra and Poona do not control their own police forces or courts— functions which are usually associated with autonomous units of local government. These major functions are performed for the cities by state-controlled district officials.

The initiative in most policy innovation rests with the administration. The budget is largely the product of the Chief Executive Officer, although budget items are gone over in great detail in committee and on the floor of the municipal body. Alterations, however, are generally minor. Formal budget debates are lengthy, but touch primarily upon complaints about the inadequate performance of existing functions or involve suggestions for bureaucratic improvement, to which almost no one (including members of the bureaucracy) objects in principle.

One of the few respects in which Agra members exercise direct control over administration is in the allocation of money to each ward for the specific improvement of pavements and drains. Under the system, as it was introduced in the first year of the corporation's existence, each corporation member is allowed to designate areas for corporation attention up to Rs. 4000 worth of work—something less than $850 by American rates in 1964. At the time it was introduced, the Congress and Jan Sangh opposed this approach as tending to undermine any effort to develop the city along planned lines, but neither party pressed its opposition and members within each group favored it.

In particular, most Republicans and many Independents saw definite advantages in this system which guaranteed their constituencies a certain amount of municipal attention. As one Swatantra Dal member expressed his attitude toward the practice, "I agree strongly with the policy. Otherwise, what use is there in being in the corporation? People come with so many problems. If we do not have funds in hand to get their work done, what good can we do?"

There were some dissenters from this view. A prominent member of the Congress party indicated their perspective:

I did not agree with the principle, but some things had to be done even here. I have been able to replace the bricks with cemented pavements. I favor the policy even though it may not be in the over-all interest of the city. Still, it is a way of seeing that at least a minimum number of things are done in each area.

For the Republicans these advantages were even clearer. As one suggested, "No other policy is really possible. Otherwise, there would be struggles in the corporation and only the group in power would be able to get work done."

Thus, in this situation of possible contention over a distributive decision, most participants were willing to compromise rather than drive the matter to an open debate. This attitude is very different from the contentiousness evident when electoral contests raising questions of personal and party prestige are involved.

Personal and Group Prestige

Conflicts over status take many forms in Agra and Poona. Not only are certain caste groups like the Jatavs and Marathas anxious to assert their claims to the symbols of political influence, but personal and party prestige is frequently at stake in corporation activities. Particularly in Agra, where every political group is marked by personal factions, these prestige questions have frequently given rise to bitter contests at the time of internal elections for the corporation—the choice of mayor and deputy mayor.

The chief mayoral function involves serving as presiding officer at corporation meetings, which allows the mayor to recognize certain speakers as opposed to others and to rule upon the making of motions, but these prerogatives are relatively narrow. The mayor also serves on some selection committees which make administrative appointments and he can make some minor expenditures on his own. On the whole, however, the role is honorific. In his capacity, the mayor is called upon by various organizations to attend meetings and he is expected to perform many of the ribbon-cutting and ceremonial functions associated with political office.

Since no single group commanded a majority in the Agra corporation, considerable time and energy went into the negotiation of agreements to elect officers. In both cities, mayors serve only one year terms and are virtually powerless; yet, it is difficult to convey the intensity of activity which surrounded these elections in Agra. Coalitions were made and unmade; members were enticed with various promises. In a few cases, members of political groups were guarded the night before an election to keep them from being contacted by opposition party candidates. It is alleged that some candidates for municipal office have spent considerable sums of money in trying to get themselves elected.

Because the balance of forces was somewhat clearer in Poona during the first three years of the body elected in 1962, contests for mayor and deputy mayor were more routine in that city. They did involve some annual bargaining among the Nagri Sanghatna, the Jan Sangh and the independents, but arrangements were fairly easily worked out. Since 1965, however, a fluidity resembling that in Agra has returned to the Poona scene—it was common enough in the corporation from 1959 until the election of 1962. Loyalties have shifted during the last three years as several former Congressmen quit the Sanghatna and gave their personal support to the Congress. By 1966, in fact, it was possible for the Congress to elect a mayor.

It is useful to examine the steps in the most recent disintegration of the Nagri Sanghatna, because it illustrates the extent to which substantive differences are subordinated to questions of personal status for some members.

Prior to the general elections of 1962, a long-time non-Brahman Congress member sought the nomination of that party to run for a seat in the state Assembly from the area where he lives. The party leadership refused to give him that seat; instead their nomination went to the President of the City Congress. The latter was a relative latecomer to the party, but was an important Maratha figure in the city. The Congress did offer the old Congressman a nomination for another district, but he was apparently offended by the loss of prestige that the offer implied. He then quit the Congress and ran against the Congress nominee; he lost by a rather wide margin, but did receive the support of a dissident element within the Congress.

When the new Nagri Sanghatna was activated after the general elections of 1962, the former Congressman joined it. Although he is not a Maratha, he is considered to be influential among them and among other non-Brahmans. Indeed, he took some Marathas out of the Congress with him. In the corporation elections, he and a few of his supporters were elected and they appeared to be stalwarts of the Sanghatna.

The Sanghatna determined to rotate the office of mayor among members of the various groups comprising it. In the first year, they nominated a man with enormous prestige both among the Marathas and the Brahmans—a well-known Maratha educator. Out of deference, he was supported by all of the members of the corporation. For the second year, the choice was left to the PSP; in the third year, the former Congressman was named.

As the end of his term approached, the Nagri Sanghatna decided to give its next nomination to a Maratha member belonging to an exclusively Maharashtrian party, the Peasants and Workers Party. The Congress, aware that its chances of electing its own nominee were slim, suggested that the incumbent be re-elected because of the state of emergency arising out of the Pakistani war of 1965. To most observers this represented merely an attempt to create divisions within the Sanghatna. If that was the intention, it succeeded. The incumbent stood, but was defeated by the candidate of the Sanghatna; in this case, a few of the Congressmen were not willing to support the opportunistic strategy of their own party.'

In the months that followed, the former Congressman was expelled with four others from the Sanghatna. A member of the Jan Sangh also left that party to join the swing to the Congress. The result was the election of a Congress mayor in 1966.

Similar personalistic cleavages have split the Congress Party in Agra. The two major factions within the Congress are both led by high-status Banias and it is difficult to identify any substantial matters dividing them in the city. Group self-assertion does carry with it potential reward of greater access to the material-distributing Congress organizations in the state and nation. Although the Congress was in a position to designate the mayoral candidate of a majority coalition in 1960, neither of that party's municipal factions was willing to give way to the other and it was necessary for them to resolve the matter by bringing in a candidate from a rural district who was not directly involved in these local disputes.

Personal conflicts within the City Congress became even more apparent in the 1962 general elections when supporters of the various party nominees for the state assembly and Parliament sometimes worked against each other. The result was defeat in two of the major races.

Personal rivalries may have some eufunctional aspects for the political system. It is significant that communal (Hindu-Muslim) and inter-caste conflicts are muted in the process of negotiations for the advancement of personal prestige. Explicit communal differences were rare in Agra. One of the few exceptions in that city involved a minor debate over the location of meat shops.

The Jan Sangh moved a resolution to centralize the Muslim-run meatshops. The Hindu-orthodox Jan Sangh argued not in terms of communal sentiments, however, but in terms of the unsanitary conditions alleged to be found in such shops, which one Jan Sangh interviewee described as "open to the dirt and dust of the city." On further questioning, however, he conceded that "all people in our country do not eat meat." Still, he argued, Muslims would benefit from a change of location of their shops and he attributed a cholera epidemic in the city in 1961 to the condition of these shops. Naturally, the Muslims in the corporation did not share this interpretation of a resolution which proposed to restrict their shops to a few designated areas, but they did not have the political influence to press the issue.

For most other participants in the system, the situation has not reached such extremes. Indeed, the Jatavs have pressed ahead with their efforts to establish their rightful place in political life. They were able to utilize their members in the corporation to form an expedient alliance with the Jan Sangh—an unlikely coalition partner if social likeness was the prime criterion—and the Swatantra Dal (which included four Muslims) in order to elect a mayor and deputy mayor. The result was a deputy mayor designated by the Republicans.

The Jatavs have been particularly concerned with protecting the position of Scheduled Caste employees in the corporation. They have attempted to hold the administration to governmental guarantees about better jobs for the ex-untouchables and they also keep pressure on to be sure that low-level employees like sweepers and door attendants are not abused. In terms of symbolic payoffs, they have succeeded in getting a picture of Dr. Ambedkar, culture hero of the Jatavs, hung in the corporation meeting-hall after some display of reluctance on the part of the other members. Typical of such decisions, the conflict was resolved by hanging a number of different portraits reflecting the attachments of each of the major groups to particular "personalities."

Their comparatively minor successes have given the Jatavs a new sense of self-confidence. It is significant that they are the group *most* satisfied with the operations of the corporation. High-status members frequently complain about the limited powers of council members or condemn the democratization of politics, but the Jatavs see their influence in terms of social justice and in distributive matters—no matter how small in absolute terms—as an important advance.

This sense of political efficacy is reflected in the following comments by a leader of the Republican Party (a non-Jatav):

I have been able to pave some of the areas where the Scheduled Castes live. Our party has a policy of upgrading these areas. To the outsider they may look terrible still, but there is an enormous improvement in some areas. We have been able to spend more money on these people in four years than was spent for fifteen years under the Administrator. Now our areas have drains, pavements and lights. This is because I and the party can shout and "cut some ice."

To a certain extent, it is those persons who were outside the mainstream of political life prior to the corporation who were most satisfied by the system. Some of these interviewees indicated specifically that the prior system had invested municipal funds in the development of new housing colonies and in beautification schemes for the central areas and better-off residential parts of the city, but paid no attention to the poorer sections. Table 3 indicates the extent to which groups in the corporation

TABLE 3. SATISFACTION OF CORPORATION MEMBERS,
AGRA CORPORATION, 1964 [a]

Party	Satisfied	Dissatisfied	No Opinion [b]
Congress	7	7	4
Jan Sangh	2	2	1
Republicans	13	1	—
Swatantra Dal	10	3	2
Independents	4	4	—
	36	17	7

[a] Question: Would you say that you are satisfied or dissatisfied with the working of the corporation?

[b] These were either members whose interviews were incomplete or who gave ambiguous responses. Party affiliations in 1964 in Agra differ from 1959 because of shifts between the two periods.

were satisfied with its activities. Not only were the Jatavs markedly favorable, but many of the members of the Swatantra Dal—who were also very constituency-oriented—looked favorably upon the system. One member of that group from a rural area indicated the feelings of some of these members when he remarked, "Only small things are in our hands, but in these things the corporation has been able to do something. Previously, there was nothing done in these village areas."

There is no allotment system in Poona, but the question of development does bear on both class and caste differences in the city. Many of the well-maintained and newer western wards of the city are inhabited by Brahmans, while the non-Brahmans (Marathas and others) live in the more congested eastern sections of the city. This feeling of deprivation was indicated by a non-Maharastrian Congress member's comment:

There is partiality for the West because the chairmen of the committees and the officials live in the West. In this part of the city [the East] there are more business people and minority groups. The officials do not pay attention to us even though we need road-widening very badly. It is only this year after many years that we got [some money] for road repairs but this is only for a few parts of the road. In the West they reconstruct roads all the time.

But as a leading Brahman member of the Nagri Sanghatna noted, the old caste character of the controversy was breaking down because of basic ecological changes in the city:

Formerly there was a communal aspect to the controversy between East and West particularly in the 1920's, but now there is little because Scheduled Caste people have settled in large numbers in the West. Very few differences remain. It is only like any city that there are new parts and old parts and better houses are in the West because of the later development of that area. In the corporation a majority is now from the East, so proper attention is being given.

Indeed, not only have population shifts altered the dispute, but it has taken on a slightly different shape because of the addition of several rural areas to the municipality when the corporation was created in 1950. These areas have different problems from the inner-city wards with the result that members who press for public investment in the old-city non-Brahman areas are not as eager to invest in developing the rural wards.

Thus a member from the ex-untouchable Bhangi (Sweeper) community argued, on the one hand, that the eastern areas required considerable municipal work, but reacted to a question about building up the rural constituencies with the following remarks:

The corporation gets no income from these rural areas. We spend three times as much as the income we receive from there. It is the responsibility of the corporation to help the rural areas, but the financial strain is great.

While the subject had never been directly raised in the Poona corporation, it was indicative of the kind of differences that existed in Poona that the Congress members were much more favorable to the idea of an allotment system than were members of the Nagri Sanghatna. One of the questions asked members was whether they would prefer a system where each ward was guaranteed a certain amount of maintenance work each year. Many members objected to this notion altogether and expressed their preference for an over-all plan of development for the city, but a narrow majority favored such a system. Table 4 indicates that members of the Congress, coming predominantly from the eastern part of the city, favored such a method while the Nagri Sanghatna split evenly on the issue.

TABLE 4. ATTITUDE TOWARD HYPOTHETICAL ALLOTMENT
SYSTEM, POONA CORPORATION, 1964 [a]

Party	Favored	Opposed	No Opinion
Congress [b]	15	8	2
Jan Sangh	1	3	2
Nagri Sanghatna	11	12	3
Others	3	4	1
	—	—	—
	30	27	8

[a] Question: Would you favor a system of allocating a specific
amount of money to each ward every year for members to appor-
tion among projects?
[b] Two members identified as Nagri Sanghatna in 1962 subsequently crossed over to the Congress on precisely this issue—they
wanted greater attention given to their rural wards.

Members of the corporation from rural areas were particularly in favor of
such a development scheme. One of the few exceptions was a man opposed
only because he felt that such a procedure would not go far enough since
"the rural areas would never develop while the advanced areas would go
further ahead."

There is only a slight class and caste aspect to these debates, but such
intergroup conflicts are more evident in cases of administrative appointments. The Marathas have succeeded in dominating the political life of the
state of Maharashtra, but their educational backwardness has only been
overcome recently. As a result, many of the administrative positions in
Maharashtra have remained in non-Maratha hands. One of the important
exceptions in Poona was the position of Transport Manager for the municipally owned bus system.

In 1954, when the position of Transport Manager fell vacant, a
Committee was appointed from among corporation members to look into
the selection of a new Manager. The corporation is the appointive authority in this case, but it is required to follow rather precise state guide-lines.
The nine members of the Committee worked with the Chief Executive
Officer and finally selected a Maratha who had worked in the corporation
for twelve years, five of them as Superintendent of Taxes. He was then
holding a subordinate position in the transport company, which was an
important qualification, since the state required some previous experience
in the area.

The nominee was actively supported by a Maratha leader, who subsequently became the leader of the Congress Party in Poona. Once in office, the Manager ran the company in a way that offended members of the Socialist party; in particular, he opposed the entry of a Socialist union into the company while looking favorably upon the Congress-affiliated union.

Opposition elements in the corporation were quite open about characterizing the Manager as anti-Brahman, anti-democratic and irresponsible to the corporation in his work. The Manager, himself, admitted that he tended to favor Marathas and other non-Brahmans in his hiring policy because they were in a "depressed condition," but he claimed no basis existed for the anti-Brahman issue. In an interview, he suggested that it was simply a matter of few Poona Brahmans wanting to drive a bus or serve in the repair shops. He thereby overlooked the question of positions in the company's administrative offices.

During the 1950's, there was a strong effort by his upper-status and anti-Congress opponents in the corporation to remove the Manager. At the height of this effort, the incumbent Maratha mayor (temporarily aligned with the non-Congress majority) threatened to withdraw his bloc of supporters if an enquiry was not dropped. Local opposition was closed off until an investigation in 1962 by the central government disclosed that the Manager was abusing import license regulations; he was suspended in 1964. In early 1965, the corporation voted 31 to 14—one of its rare votes —to put the Manager on half-pay while on suspension. All fourteen votes came from the Congress Party.

Many of these issues reflect a concern about material outcomes (although actual material gains may be minor). The prestige or status component, however, is equally important.

Orientation to Wider Arenas

The case of the dispute over the Transport Manager also points up the generalized concerns of certain politicians in Poona with the greater arenas of state and national politics. Jobs available to Congressmen for distribution may have provided an important political resource. It is significant that leadership against the Manager was provided by members of the Praja Socialist Party, who were particularly dissatisfied with the attitude the Manager had displayed in regard to their union's activities.

The Poona corporation also has become a major sounding-board for political controversy. These "political discussions" are usually brought in the form of adjournment motions and may touch on almost any subject from Indo-Pakistani relations to the price of grain. PSP and right-wing party members have been especially active in bringing such motions. Indeed, several of the non-affiliated members of the Sanghatna condemned the practice as out of character for a party supposedly interested only in municipal affairs, but others made free use of the method.

In these debates, the Congress members are usually forced to take the side of the state or national government, whichever is under attack, while the opposition party members mount heated attacks.

Typical of an issue which struck relatively close to home was the decision of the Maharashtra Government to take over electricity service from the city's private supplier. Opposition party members of the corporation roundly condemned the state's actions; they insisted that the city should have operated the service itself and benefited from the anticipated profits. Formal statements were drawn up, protest meetings were held, but these efforts were largely political shadow-boxing by the Opposition. The Congress members of the corporation were either quiet on the issue or supported the state position. In the end, the state government exercised its full jurisdiction in the matter.

Discussions of this kind are much less common in Agra. The Jan Sangh was too weak and ideologically too close to the conservative members of the Congress to make for important policy differences at the corporation level; the Republicans had neither the speakers nor the intellectual compulsions to engage in speech-making for its own sake.

Both corporations served, however, as political platforms for launching individual and group activities in state and national politics. In an important respect, these municipal bodies did contribute to the performance of the Almondian function of political recruitment.

In 1962, both of the victors from Agra's two state legislative seats were sitting members of the municipal corporation. In one contest, the winner was the chief organizer of the Swatantra Dal. He had used that group as a vehicle for advancing his own career; it provided him free publicity and a supporter of his served as Deputy Mayor during the period prior to the general elections. The Dal, as a whole, had been deferred to, because it held the balance of power in the corporation. The candidate gained considerably, however, from his past reputation as a leader of the Jan Sangh and from the factional battles within the Congress. His strategy of tacitly supporting the incumbent Congress MP, leader of one of the Congress factions, was useful to him against his Congress opponent for the state assembly seat. The Congress candidate was the leader of the other Congress faction.

Significantly, the leaders of the Jan Sangh and Republican groups in the corporation were two of the other contestants in this particular legislative contest. The Republican candidate, the only Bania in that party, came in second.

Building upon their successes in the 1959 municipal elections, the Jatavs constructed an electoral agreement with the Muslims in western UP in 1962. In Agra district, candidates put up by this coalition came in either first or second in most of the legislative races. In Agra City, the seat in the southern part of the city was won by a Republican member of the corporation; another Republican member won a rural seat for the state assembly.

The same pattern of the corporation acting as a channel for political recruitment to higher positions was apparent in Poona in 1962. Every one of the victorious Congress candidates for the state legislature—five in all—had worked in the corporation prior to his election. In one case, however, service consisted of administrative responsibilities; that candidate, S. G. Barve, was a high civil servant prior to his entry into politics and was acting as executive head of the Poona administration at the time that the corporation was created.

Again in 1967, many of the major candidates in both cities were involved in municipal government. In Agra, the incumbent representative of the Swatantra Dal faced two of his three major opponents from 1962. This time, he lost to the leader of the Jan Sangh; the Bania Republican was now the candidate of the Congress, having quit the Republican Party.

In the other contest, corporation ties were more remote. The Republican Party candidate was not a member of the corporation; he managed to win over the Congress candidate—the husband of the only woman member of the corporation.

It is significant, perhaps, that in 1967 no municipal corporation actually functioned in Agra. The term of the five corporations of UP had been due to expire in 1964. Rather than hold new elections, the Congress Government of UP extended the life of these bodies for two years. Some observers claimed that this refusal was based on a fear that such elections would simply exacerbate existent factionalism within the Congress. When extensions were no longer possible, the Government simply abolished the elective wings of these corporations in 1966 and turned full responsibility back to the administrators. This political maneuver failed not only in Agra, but in all of UP as Congress lost its majority in the state assembly.

The Poona corporation continued to function in 1967. Indeed, the seat for Parliament was won by a leader of the Socialists, S. M. Joshi, who was also a member of the corporation. State legislative seats were either retained by Congress incumbents or won by corporation members. All three of the new Congress candidates were councilmen. In one key contest, the last Sanghatna mayor (running as the candidate of an anti-Congress coalition) defeated a prominent Congress member, who had served as President of the City Congress for a term.

The Problem of Side-Payments

Members of the two corporations uniformly complained about the limited powers given to them and yet only a minority ruled out entirely the possibility that they would be willing to stand for the corporation in the next municipal elections. Given the additional fact that members were unpaid in Agra and that the corporation members in Poona received only rather small payments, their continued willingness 'to participate requires some explanation.

For the most part, individuals and groups entered corporation politics not so much for the personal benefits which they expected, but because the municipality constituted a public arena where they could symbolically express their importance in the order of things. In other words, the members placed a high value on the personal prestige which flowed from participating in the system, even if the *direct* payoffs from the system of government were not great.

Thus, all councillors were asked about their motives in standing for the corporation. Of the sixty members of the Agra corporation, only three participated as a continuation of family traditions. Many claimed that friends and neighbors had persuaded them to run because they had been involved in some group locally. Only five persons saw the corporation as a way of advancing in politics; only one mentioned any motive which had ideological overtones. Perhaps the following comment by a member of the Agra body sums up the prestige motive best: "Even though members do not have many powers, their desire for posts is 'an inborn thing.' Everyone wants to be in a superior position. . . . People enter simply for the importance it gives them."

In Poona, many of the same motives were at work. Some spoke of the service they could do for their constituencies; others commented on the personal satisfaction it gave them. Many, however, indicated they had no intention of standing again. As one Scheduled Caste member remarked,

I am satisfied with my work [in the corporation] because I have helped to give employment to men and women of my caste in the corporation, I have requested that the officials give them jobs and they have. I would not run again due to my financial condition. It is necessary that a man have money in his pocket.

The importance to a corporation member of the benefits he can distribute to his constituency is difficult to estimate. Certain members have gained irregular income from supporting candidates for mayoral or other internal offices, particularly in Agra. Indirect benefits like control over the placement of certain minor projects like drains or water taps may have motivated a few. Lower-caste members clearly sought to advance the collective interests of their communities. High-status individuals may have sought benefits for their wards, but personal benefits were exceptional. Indeed, there were several complaints against a former mayor who was said to have exercised influence to place a sewer near his home.

Of the three reasons mentioned for participation in municipal government—intervention in administration; personal or group status improvement; political training—only the first is likely to provide much beside psychic income. Some persons claim that constituents pay some members for these interventions. This claim, of course, is impossible to prove, as are most of the charges about corruption.

For the present, therefore, it must be concluded that most members participate in the operations of these corporations for the achievement of ends which are not essentially material (or, at least, not personally material) in nature. Of course, service in local bodies as a response to party requests or as an effort to express one's involvement in party work may indicate *ultimate* aims of a different sort. In this connection, a political career linked to party work seemed to be much more significant in Poona (at least in 1964) than in Agra.

CONCLUSION

To the extent that decisions reflect real conflicts within a political system, they may be important guides to understanding the nature of politics in a given arena. Arenas, however, are much more than simple decision-making instrumentalities. Indeed, it has been argued that both in terms of material rewards and actual decisions, the political actors in Agra and Poona get rather little concrete outcome for their expenditure of considerable effort. Nonetheless, in respect to status-registration functions, the symbolic and the group-related substantive rewards of the system are significant. Furthermore, for the larger system of political life these locally available arenas provide an important outlet for status claims; they also constitute a focus for individual and group socialization into democratic politics helping to mute social and economic conflicts which frequently promise to boil over in an underdeveloped economy and heterogeneous society of the kind that India possesses.

Such an evaluation of the role of local government in Indian cities does not mean that these features are peculiar to Indian politics. If one looks carefully at many of the studies done in the United States, it becomes immediately apparent that the aspects of politics we have stressed in regard to Agra and Poona are also, in greater or lesser degree, present there as well.

Thus, both of the Indian cities might well fall under the category provided in Williams and Adrian's typology of local government as being of the kind concerned with "arbitrating among conflicting interests." Of this type, Williams and Adrian write,

That the proper role of government is to serve as an arbiter is held most logically by interest groups that fall short of complete political control, including, especially, the more self-conscious minorities. The numerical or psychic majority does not have to settle for a process, but can act directly in terms of substantive conceptions of the community good. The minority can only hope for access [1963, p. 28].

Unfortunately, the distributive functions involved in such a system of government are reduced by the limited resources available to city government in India.

While one can get some idea of the kinds of demands which are advanced by members of the public through a study of the actions of their representatives, further research on the associational life of Indian cities is clearly the next step forward in determining the kinds of organized demands which exist in an Indian city. Such research might focus fruitfully upon the networks of voluntary and ascriptive associations which exist in such a city. Contrary to expectations which might be held about the development of secondary associations in an underdeveloped nation, Poona and Agra are alive with informal and quasi-formal social groups. The organization of annual festivals, for example, provides an important opportunity for the expression of ward and group rivalries in Poona; the athletic clubs, particularly wrestling associations, are an important base for political action in Poona. In terms of formal organizations, there seems to be an important relationship between the commercial activities of the municipal fruit and vegetable market in that city and the Congress Party. All of these aspects of economic and social activity remain to be explored for their political content.

In Agra, too, a series of betterment associations located in the wards—sometimes organized along caste lines, sometimes not—and groups which engage in singing and poetry recitals simply add to the variety of associational activities that involve persons either directly or indirectly in municipal life. The significance of such groups becomes clearer when it is pointed out that several politically active persons in Poona are equally respected for their literary abilities.

Alongside the voluntaristic activities of the cities are the quasi-ascriptive associations: the schools, temples and mutual-aid societies which are a regular feature of city life in India. It is through a proper understanding of the interplay of these ethnic and voluntary groups and the municipally relevant formal associations that we can better understand the nature of politics in India.

Yet, it is not clear that an adequate job of understanding the place of these organizations has been accomplished even in American life. Much more work has been done on the relationship of local businessmen to municipal decision-making than has been devoted to a study of social accommodation in the same cities. Indeed, the concern that some social scientists have shown for "decisions" in a narrow sense contrasts with their interest in detailing successes or failures in conflict-management, which has constituted an equally important aspect of political behavior in the United States.

In that sense, the phenomenon of "non-decisions" which Bachrach and Baratz (1962) seem to equate with the suppression of demands may actually represent a strength of democratic politics when it submerges potentially volatile inter-group conflicts.[18] Demands expressed in the form of "open housing" marches or school desegregation decisions made by school boards under siege reveal the weaknesses as well as some of the stronger features of a political order.

It is curious, therefore, that Dahl's history of ethnic conflicts in New Haven has received less attention than his focus on three rather low-conflict "issues." His discussion of the status ladder involved in ethnic mobility in New Haven provides an interesting model to compare systems cross-nationally, whatever its shortcomings.[19] Considerable interest in ethnic

---

[18] See also Clark (1967b) for discussion of dimensions of power related to "non-decisions."

[19] One of these shortcomings is the failure to clearly lay out any picture of the end-point of the assimilation process which he posits. Dahl's model (1961, pp. 34–36) appears to end in total obliteration of sub-group differences. In fact, this situation does not seem to be happening for some major groups in American life. In the United States, of course, high-status groups could opt out of political life without it having a great impact upon the local system; in India, their position is more complicated. Given their post-Independence minority status, the Poona Brahmans might well have withdrawn from politics; some Brahmans who did this harbor considerable resentment against the regime. That a substantial number continued to be active in politics and to form a base for opposition to the Congress, as well as a haven for Congress dissidents, built considerable flexibility into a national system dominated by one political party

politics has been generated by the work of Glazer and Moynihan (1963), but the several studies which have appeared since that time merely point up the need for continued investigation of the assimilation process and its place in American politics.[20]

Obviously, not all of the political cross-currents detailed in our consideration of two Indian cities are attributable to status demands alone. Economic, personal and situational factors shape many aspects of city government.

What I am arguing, however, is that for the purposes of cross-national analysis it is necessary to learn much more than we presently do about the political functions of ethnic and voluntary associations both in our own society and in other nations. Too often, a study of "interest groups" ceases when a list of unions, businesses, and agricultural groups has been provided. Much more emphasis must be placed on the kinds of organizations which a man encounters in his rounds of the city—those informal groups which make up his non-working hours. One ultimate task would be to plot the political life of a city through the ends sought by its associations; work of this kind, of course, needs to be tied in properly to our understanding of the general implications of stratification systems for political behavior. Thus, the Indian materials confirm the importance of the point made nearly a decade ago by David Apter, when he wrote:

Members of the public join in political groups in order to expand mobility opportunities and, in this respect, make representations to government or to influence or control government in some manner. Government policy must then in part be responsive to the interests of political groups. Depending upon who the group represents, we see that government policy is geared as well to the ultimate alteration of social stratification or aspects thereof. . . . Assuming that no one is ever truly satisfied with the system of social stratification other than conservatives, we find that the basic motive of politics then is a striving motive to expand mobility opportunities, either for some special group or for large segments of society [1958, p. 221].

Stated in a slightly different way, an important dimension of any kind of analysis of political systems—including the local—is the nature of

---

from 1947 to 1967. An outstanding example of this kind of relationship was the alliance recently formed between the Brahman-led Swatantra Party and the virulently anti-Brahman DMK which swept the Congress out of power in the state of Madras.

[20] In particular, articles by Wilson and Banfield (1964) and Wolfinger (1965) argue for more systematic data collection with respect to the effects of these group identifications on political behavior. Also see, Gerald Pomper's study of ethnic voting in a New Jersey city (1966).

attempts to enhance status and the responses to these efforts by existent elites. Such conflicts may be particularly apparent at the local level, where distinct individual and group actors may be less numerous and where powerful economic interests may be only marginally concerned with the activities of the municipality—as appears to be the case with many business interests in the United States. In many of the new nations, of course, the government is the chief organized economic interest, which means that advancement through politics is not so much a lesser alternative to the pursuit of business success as it is the major channel itself.

At the same time, governmental employment is such an important aspect of the economy that one must look more carefully at the choice structures built into local bureaucracies to see how they influence outcomes; greater concern with the implications of administrative procedures for political development than has heretofore been the case could result. More narrowly, it points to the need to be as concerned with rule-application as with rule-making.

Ultimately, of course, decisions are made for the municipality, even if they are not made locally or within the framework of democratic politics. How such decisions for the locality are made at higher levels is a subject requiring additional study; the bureaucratic network of state, district, and local officials must also be explored more systematically for both the latent and manifest consequences of its activities.[21] Such a multi-level analysis would shed greater light on the extent to which local demands are successfully articulated and local pressures mobilized in order to influence the distribution of political values in a society.

REFERENCES

Agger, Robert E., Daniel Goldrich, and Bert E. Swanson
1964   *The Rulers and the Ruled.* New York: John Wiley & Sons.
All-India Institute of Local Self-Government
1964   *Directory of Municipal Corporations in India.* Bombay.
Almond, Gabriel A.
1960   "Introduction," in Gabriel A. Almond and James S. Coleman (eds.), *The Politics of the Developing Areas.* Princeton: Princeton University Press.
Apter, David E.

---

[21] Some preliminary efforts have been made in this direction by the case studies of local decision-making conducted as part of the International Studies of Values in Politics by Messrs. Sheth, Attarde, and Chaturvedi.

1958 "A Comparative Method for the Study of Politics," *American Journal of Sociology*, 64, 221–237.

Bachrach, Peter, and Morton S. Baratz
1962 "Two Faces of Power," *American Political Science Review*, 56, 947–952.

Bailey, F. G.
1964 *Politics in Village India*. Mimeograph.

Beteille, Andre
1965 *Caste, Class and Power*. Berkeley: University of California Press.

Bendix, Reinhard
1964 *Nation-Building and Citizenship*. New York: John Wiley & Sons.

Brass, Paul R.
1965 *Factional Politics in an Indian State*. Berkeley: University of California Press.

Clark, Terry N.
1965 "Power and Community Structure: Who Governs, Where, and When?" presented at the 1965 annual meeting, The American Sociological Association, Chicago, Illinois; also in revised form in *The Sociological Quarterly*, Spring 1967.

1966 "Comparability in Community Research," presented at the session on Comparability in Community Research, Sixth World Congress, International Sociological Association, Evian, France, September, 1966.

1967a "Community or Communities—A Dilemma for Studies of Community Power," *Kansas Journal of Sociology*, Winter 1967.

1967b "The Concept of Power: Some Overemphasized and Underrecognized Dimensions," *Southwestern Social Science Quarterly*, December 1967.

Crain, Robert L., Elihu Katz, and Donald B. Rosenthal
1968 *The Politics of Community Conflict*. Indianapolis: The Bobbs-Merrill Co.

Dahl, Robert A.
1961 *Who Governs?* New Haven: Yale University Press.

Daland, Robert T.
1966 "A Strategy for Research in Comparative Urban Administration," Paper for a Conference of the Comparative Administration Group. Mimeograph.

D'Antonio, William V., William H. Form, Charles P. Loomis, and Eugene C. Erickson
1961 "Institutional and Occupational Representations in Eleven Community Influence Systems," *American Sociological Review*, 26, 440–446 [republished in this volume].

Form, William H. and William V. D'Antonio
1959 "Integration and Cleavage Among Community Influentials in Two Border Cities," *American Sociological Review*, 24, 804–814.

Glazer, Nathan and Daniel P. Moynihan
1963 *Beyond the Melting Pot*. Cambridge, Mass.: Harvard University Press and The M.I.T. Press.

Greenstone, J. David
1966 "Corruption and Self-Interest in Kampala and Nairobi," *Comparative Studies in Society and History*, 8, 199–210.

Gupta, Ram Ratan
1961 "Growth and Functioning of the Kanpur Municipality (1861–1960)," Ph.D. dissertation, Agra University.

Hart, Henry C
1961 "Bombay Politics: Pluralism or Polarization?" *Journal of Asian Studies*, 20, 267–274.

Hoskin, Gary
1966 "Patterns of Power and Politics in a Venezuelan City." Mimeograph.

Hunter, Floyd
1953 *Community Power Structure*. Chapel Hill: University of North Carolina Press.

Indian Institute of Public Administration
1959 *Improving City Government*. Delhi.

Institute of Public Administration (Lucknow University)
1963 "The Working of Municipal Corporations in UP," Background Papers for a Seminar at Lucknow University. Lucknow.

Kammerer, Gladys M., Charles D. Farris, John M. DeGrove, and Alfred E. Clubock
1962 *City Managers in Politics*. Gainesville: University of Florida Monographs.

Kesselman, Mark
1966 "French Local Politics: A Statistical Examination of Grass Roots Consensus," *American Political Science Review*, 60, 963–973.

Klapp, Orrin E. and L. Vincent Padgett
1960 "Power Structure and Decision-Making in a Mexican Border City," *American Journal of Sociology*, 65, 400–406.

Lynch, Owen M.
1966 "The Politics of Untouchability," Ph.D. dissertation, Columbia University.

Maheshwari, B.
1963 *Studies in Panchayati Raj*. Delhi: Metropolitan Book Co.

Miller, Delbert C.

1958 "Decision-Making Cliques in Community Power Structures: A Comparative Study of an American and an English City," *American Journal of Sociology*, 63, 299–310.

Miller, D. F.

1965 "Factions in Indian Village Politics," *Pacific Affairs*, 38, 17–31.

Pomper, Gerald.

1966 "Ethnic and Group Voting in Non-Partisan Elections," *Public Opinion Quarterly*, 30, 79–97.

Potter, David C.

1964 *Government in Rural India*. London: London School of Economics.

1966 "Bureaucratic Change in India," in Ralph Braibanti, ed., *Asian Bureaucratic Systems Emergent From the British Imperial Tradition*. Durham, Duke Commonwealth-Studies Center.

Retzlaff, Ralph

1962 *Village Government in India*. Bombay: Asia Publishing.

Riggs, Fred W.

1962 "Convergences in the Study of Comparative Public Administration and Local Government," *Studies in Public Administration*, No. 23, Gainesville, Florida.

Robson, William A., ed.

1954 *Great Cities of the World*. London: Allen and Unwin.

Rosenthal, Donald B.

1966a "Friendship and Deference Patterns in Two Indian Municipal Councils," *Social Forces*, 45, 178–192.

1966b "Factions and Alliances in Indian City Politics," *Midwest Journal of Political Science*, 10, 320–349.

Rudolph, Lloyd I.

1961 "Urban Life and Populist Radicalism: Dravidian Politics in Madras," *Journal of Asian Studies*, 20, 283–297.

Sharma, B. A. V. and R. T. Jangam

1962 *The Bombay Municipal Corporation: An Election Study*. Bombay: Popular Book Depot.

Shrader, Lawrence and Ram Joshi

1963 "Zilla Parishad Elections in Maharashtra and District Political Elite," *Asian Survey*, 3, 143–155.

Sirsikar, V. M.

1965 *Political Behavior in India*. Bombay: P. C. Manaktala.

Smallwood, Frank

1965 *Greater London: The Politics of Metropolitan Reform*. Indianapolis: The Bobbs-Merrill Co.

Srinivas, M. N.

1966 *Social Change in Modern India.* Berkeley: University of California Press.

Srinivasan, R. and B. A. V. Sharma
1965 "Politics in Urban India: A Study of Four Corporations," in S. P. Aiyar and R. Srinivasan, eds., *Studies in Indian Democracy.* Bombay: Allied Publishers.

Steiner, Kurt
1965 *Local Government in Japan.* Stanford: Stanford University Press.

Taylor, Carl C., Douglas Ensminger, Helen W. Johnson, and Jean Joyce
1966 *India's Roots of Democracy.* New York: Frederick A. Praeger.

Tinker, Hugh
1954 *The Foundations of Local Self-Government in India, Pakistan and Burma.* London: Athlone Press.

Weiner, Myron
1959 "Changing Patterns of Political Leadership in West Bengal," *Pacific Affairs*, 32, 277–287.

1967 *Party-Building in a New Nation: The Indian National Congress.* Chicago: University of Chicago Press.

1961 "Violence and Politics in Calcutta," *Journal of Asian Studies*, 20, 275–281.

———— and Kothari, Rajni (eds.)
1965 *Indian Voting Behaviour.* Calcutta: Firma K. L. Mukhopadhyay.

Werlin, Herbert
1966 "The Nairobi City Council: A Study in Comparative Local Government," *Comparative Studies in Society and History*, 8, 181–198.

Wilson, James Q., ed.
1968 *City Politics and Public Policy.* New York: John Wiley & Sons.

———— and Banfield, Edward C.
1964 "Public-Regardingness as a Value Premise in Voting Behavior," *American Political Science Review*, 58, 876–887.

Williams, Oliver P. and Charles R. Adrian.
1963 *Four Cities: A Study in Comparative Policy Making.* Philadelphia: University of Pennsylvania Press.

Wolfinger, Raymond E.
1965 "The Development and Persistence of Ethnic Voting," *American Political Science Review*, 59, 896–908.

V

COMMUNITY STRUCTURE
AND PATTERNS
OF LEADERSHIP

13

THE PROCESS OF
DECISION-MAKING WITHIN
THE CONTEXT OF
COMMUNITY ORGANIZATION *

PAUL A. MILLER
Department of Health, Education, and Welfare

[A process important in understanding community action is that of decision-making. This paper presents certain theoretical considerations relevant to research in community organization and action. A study of community efforts in the promotion of 218 small hospital projects and case studies of a representative community hospital project in the Southeast and one in the Northeast reveal differences in decision-making processes. The .Southeast projects developed more amidst arrangements made through constituted authority; while in the Northeast, community organizational arrangements seemed related to the social psychological components of influence. For the comparisons, use is made of the occupational positions of decision-makers in the projects, the types of sponsoring groups and practices, and the internal structure of the decision-making system of relationships.]

PURPOSES AND METHOD OF THE STUDY

The present paper treats an aspect of a study that has recently engaged the Social Research Service at Michigan State College.[1] Sponsored by the

---

* A paper read at the annual meeting of the Rural Sociological Society, Madison, Wis., Sept. 4, 1951.

[1] The following members of the project committee, although not responsible for the content and organization of this paper, must be acknowledged in that the paper is but one by-product of a larger interdisciplinary effort: Charles P. Loomis, Charles R. Hoffer, Duane L. Gibson, J. Allan Beegle, Christopher Sower, David G. Steinicke, and

Farm Foundation, this study has aimed to appraise the manner in which contemporary small American communities go about mobilizing their resources toward three major health goals: (1) obtaining a hospital, (2) securing a local health department, and (3) organizing a consumer-sponsored prepayment plan for medical care.

Consultation with officials of national agencies, and a perusal of their filed materials, yielded an original inventory of 618 communities. Beyond the fact that each state was represented, these communities had trading-center towns of not more than 7,500 population, had made substantial progress toward one or more of the above health goals, and community action had occurred since 1940. The inventory listed 282 new general hospitals assisted by funds of the Hill-Burton Hospital Survey and Construction Program, 79 cooperative hospitals, 116 consumer-sponsored prepayment plans, and 141 local health departments.

In addition to an extensive bibliographical analysis and correspondence with community workers in the respective communities, two broad methods have been employed in this study: (1) the development of detailed questionnaires for each of the three categories of communities, to be completed by the respective official sponsoring bodies; and (2) case studies of selected communities representing the different regions.

The selection of hospital cases for field study was made on the basis of the preponderant hospital community type found within each region, the types having been determined on the basis of four factors: high or low need for a hospital, expressed by the ratio of needed beds to available beds; rurality, as measured by rural-urban population ratios; high or low population in the hospital service area; and size of hospital goal, operationally defined as the money cost of the hospital. For instance, 62 per cent of the cases in the Northeast represented low need for a hospital, were relatively less rural, contained a large population in the service area, and reported relatively high-cost hospitals. In addition to selecting on the basis of preponderant community type and principal fund-raising method used in each region, there was the requirement that the cases represent county-seat towns. For fund-raising, the Southeast [2] used bond issues predominantly; the Middle States, both bond issues and voluntary subscription;

research assistants Wayne C. Rohrer, Joseph H. Locke, and Sheldon G. Lowry. Acknowledgment is also due Professor John Useem, who has repeatedly assisted this writer and other members of the project committee to a growing awareness of the potential efficacy of decision-making as a conceptual framework for the study of community action.

[2] Odum and Moore's regions, the Northeast, Southeast, Middle States, Far West, Northwest, and Southwest, were employed: cf. Howard W. Odum and Harry E. Moore, *American Regionalism* (New York: Holt, 1938), p. 436.

the Northeast, professional fund-raising; the Northwest, voluntary sub-scription; and the Far West, the Hospital District with a governing body to levy taxes. The foregoing may indicate the raw materials available regarding small hospital developments.

DECISION-MAKING AND COMMUNITY ORGANIZATION

Few areas of sociological endeavor have presented such a variety of theoretical and practical opportunities as that of community organization. The focus of the study, of which this paper represents one aspect, was determined partly by certain impressions gained through bibliographical analysis.[3] Crucial among them were: (1) The functional and structural requisites of communities within a *specific* action context usually are not emphasized. (2) The communities have usually been considered discretely, with little attention to their relationship to larger social or cultural areas, such as the region, state, and nation. [As Julian H. Steward has recently stated, "The Lynds were the first to recognize that one of its (Middletown) principal shortcomings was its failure to relate the town more explicitly and completely to the larger extracommunity society. How to remedy this deficiency in such studies has not yet been resolved: the theoretical and methodological bases for placing any community in its larger setting have yet to be worked out." [4]] (3) The preoccupation with an individual community, or at best a small number of communities, has tended to prevent sufficient quantitative analysis and has retarded a comparative approach.

Acquiring an expensive hospital is an event of considerable implication for the community. Given people and leaders, community needs and resources, the hospital will not become a reality until some one or some group acts; and to act is to decide. The decisions that result channel the efforts of the people, limit them to specific courses of action, and prescribe certain organizational methods. Accordingly, the general purpose of the parent study was to focus on community action with special reference to the decision-making process, or the deployment of authority and influence in social situations of goal-oriented behavior. The decision-making process, within the context of community organization, refers to three phases: (1) the making of decisions, (2) the manner in which they are given approval and made legitimate, and (3) the execution of the decisions in the sense of

---

[3] See the following for one classification of community studies and a supplementary critique: Julian H. Steward, *Area Research: Theory and Practice*, Social Science Research Council, Bulletin 63 (1950).

[4] *Ibid.*, p. 31.

an allocation and/or manipulation of the means at the disposal of the community.

The making of decisions in an ongoing social process would appear to be the reduction of alternative courses of action to persons or groups by an actor or actors in a decision-making system of relationships.[5] Legitimacy refers to (1) the sanctioned rights of some persons to make decisions, and draws on certain capacities of "rightfulness" possessed by the maker of decisions; and (2) to the approval rendered by certain groups in the community, by certain persons, or by all the people—i.e., referendum.[6] The execution phase simply refers to the organizational and administrative consequences evoked by the decision process, and introduces into the process those to whom the decisions apply.

Four interrelated concepts form the conceptual bulwark for the field studies: (1) position, (2) authority, (3) property, and (4) influence. *Authority* consists of the rights and privileges given certain positions within the formal associational life of the community, with specific reference to incumbency in political and associational office and the positional elements of family, kinship, and status. *Influence* refers to the possession of social property, or combinations of sociologically significant resources and proficiencies. By *resources* is meant the incidence of such capacities as wealth, time, respect, moral rectitude, reciprocal obligations, and access to intra- or extra-community persons and groups of prestige. By *proficiency* is meant the incidence of subject-matter competence, organizational skill, and the abilities to know and manipulate appropriate symbols.[7] Influence, thus,

---

[5] See Harold D. Lasswell and Abraham Kaplan, *Power and Society* (New Haven: Yale University Press, 1950) : "Since a decision is an effective determination of policy, it involves the total process of bringing about a specified course of action" (p. 74) ; Robert M. MacIver, *The Web of Government* (New York: The Macmillan Co., 1947) : "Policy-making depends on the assessing of alternatives with a view to translating one of them into action" (p. 9) ; for the relation of the manipulation of courses of action to the application of force, see Robert M. Bierstedt, "An Analysis of Social Power," *American Sociological Review*, Vol. 15 (1950) : "Force, again in the sociological sense, means the reduction or limitation or closure or even total elimination of alternatives to the social action of another person or group" (p. 733).

[6] See Robert M. MacIver, *op. cit.*, p. 225, who views legitimacy in decision-making as the justification of authority; M. J. Hillenbrand, *Power and Morals* (New York: Columbia University Press, 1949), who speaks of the "ethical sanction" for authority (pp. 134–191).

[7] See Charles E. Merriam's chapter on "Political Power," in *A Study of Power* (Glencoe, Illinois: The Free Press, 1950), for a reference to "facility in group combination" (p. 41) ; Paul Pigors, *Leadership and Domination* (New York: Houghton Mifflin Co., 1935), in reference to "administration as a function of leadership" (pp. 248–252) ; Harold D. Lasswell, *The Analysis of Political Behavior* (New York: Oxford University Press, 1947), who states: "Each public policy calls for two types of intelligence: ideological and technical. By ideological intelligence is meant facts about

is concerned with social property within the community, and the person who owns portions of this property may be a decision-maker through influence, which may not necessarily be related to his position within the community.

In one sense, a role of influence is a role of authority; but the assumption, as indicated by these definitions, is that the decision-maker of influence must reckon with and direct his activity through the interpersonal system that vests a portion of the community's social property in him. Authority, as used here, is constituted within strict associational limits. Thus, authority does not depend on the social property vested in the person, but on the explicit rights of position or office.

The concept of legitimacy is also useful in describing the socially derived bases of authority and influence. Consideration of how decisions are made legitimate in the community has led to a concern with the relevant formal associations as they relate to the institutionalization of authority, and the informal life of the community as it affects the investment of social property in specific decision-makers. Likewise, the informal organization of the community may provide the means by which decision-makers may reckon with and negotiate with competing centers of authority and influence, and through which strategy is made possible.

The remainder of this paper is devoted to a specific aspect of the decision-making process. The data are for the 218 Hill-Burton hospital communities for which questionnaires were returned. Special attention will be given to 24 communities in the Northeast that returned questionnaires, plus a field study in a western New York community; and to 52 Southeast communities returning questionnaires, plus a field study in the Black Belt region of Alabama.[8] The specific data to be discussed here pertain to the hypothesis that decision-making within the context of community organization may operate at times on a basis of position, and hence subsequent roles of authority; while, at other times, decision-making may take place on a basis of property, or community resources and proficiencies vested in certain decision-makers of influence. The theoretic interest here is that such differential operations may lead to a dynamic distinction in commu-

---

the thoughts, feelings, and conduct of human beings. Other facts are technical. It makes no difference whether the policy goal is phrased in ideological or technical terms; both kinds of information are involved in any complete consideration of goals or alternatives" (pp. 123–124).

[8] Field studies, conducted by three- or four-man research teams, have been completed in California, Wyoming, Indiana, New York, and Alabama. Field workers in the Northeast and Southeast communities were John B. Holland, Joseph H. Locke, Wayne C. Rohrer, Benjamin Thompson, and the author.

nity types, insofar as community action toward certain major goals is concerned.

OCCUPATIONAL POSITION OF DECISION-MAKERS

The questionnaire data on the 218 hospital projects yielded 670 persons named "most active." [9] They are almost entirely male and middle aged, and for the most part they reside in the towns that are the sites for the hospitals. Thirty-four per cent of the 670 "most active" persons are self-employed businessmen; 28 per cent are professionals, including 9 per cent who are medical doctors. Sixteen per cent are employed executives or managers, and 10 per cent are farmers.[10]

Reference to Table 1 will indicate that the Southeast is higher than the

TABLE 1. OCCUPATION OF PERSONS "MOST ACTIVE" IN SMALL-TOWN HOSPITAL PROJECTS

Occupation	Southeast (N—158)	Northeast (N—75)	All regions (N—670)
	Per cent	Per cent	Per cent
Self-employed businessmen	32.3	35.6	34.1
Professionals	30.4	24.7	27.9
Employed executives or managers	13.9	27.4	15.8
Farm owners or operators	9.5	5.5	10.0
Civil officials	10.1	2.7	8.2
Nonsupervisory employees	3.8	4.1	4.0
All persons	100.0	100.0	100.0

Northeast in farmers, civil officials, and professionals among the persons called "most active." The Northeast has a somewhat higher proportion of employed managers and self-employed businessmen. This suggests that the Northeast decision-makers for hospitals are oriented to the town sites of the hospitals, while in the Southeast larger systems are relevant, i.e., the county.

---

[9] Case-study checks have assured these nominations to be valid in a decision-making sense.

[10] For an intensive analysis of the occupational characteristics of the "most active" (decision-makers) in these 218 Hill-Burton hospital projects, see Joseph H. Locke, "The Participation of Occupational Groups in Local Efforts to Obtain Hospital Services," M. A. thesis, Michigan State College, 1951.

SPONSORING GROUPS AND PRACTICES

The following figures and comments for the two regional groups of projects indicate the incidence of sponsorship by constituted agencies of authority, i.e., county or municipal governing bodies, and of associated practices. In response to questions about the nature of the official sponsoring group for the hospital projects, eight out of ten Northeast communities reported the boards of previously established small hospitals, while the Southeast reported such groups in five out of ten cases.[11] Four out of ten cases in the Southeast reported municipal or county civil governing bodies as sponsoring groups. Not a single Northeast community reported a civil body as a central sponsoring group.

Four out of ten of the Southeast cases reported that the selection of members of hospital-operating groups was accomplished through appointment by local officials, as compared with less than one in ten of the Northeast cases. Two in ten of the Southeast cases reported that selection was made by election or appointment from community organizations or at community meetings, while about five in ten of the Northeast cases reported selection in this way.

As to ownership of the hospital, 50 per cent of the Southeast hospitals were listed as owned by county or city, 36 per cent by community or memorial associations, and the remainder by special associations or commissions of county or city. The Northeast had 12 per cent ownership by the county and 88 per cent by community or memorial associations.

In the hospital-getting process itself, it appears that concern with communicating to the community was less in the Southeast than in the Northeast. For example, 21 per cent of the Northeast communities and 54 per cent of the Southeast communities reported the opposition of persons who feared higher taxes, but in meeting this opposition 64 per cent of the Southeast cases reported the use of face-to-face discussion and persuasion, as against 96 per cent of the Northeast group.[12] Significantly, 48 per cent of the Southeast cases utilized "speeches to organized groups," while 79 per cent of the Northeast cases reported using this medium. Although there apparently was a higher incidence of opposition in the Southeast and

---

[11] Since the Southeast had fewer hospitals to start with, it is only natural that the board of an existing hospital should appear less often as a sponsoring body.

[12] It is possible that the Northeast respondents were more apt at completing the questionnaires than the Southeast respondents, which may show the latter to a disadvantage in terms of full reporting.

appeals to the community were used less often, nevertheless almost three-fourths of the Southeast cases were successful after the first attempt or campaign, while but one-half of the Northeast cases were as successful. Only two in ten of the Southeast cases required two campaigns, as compared with four in ten in the Northeast. One explanation of these differences in the two regional groupings of hospital projects is that, in the Southeast, decision-making operated more frequently within the limits of constituted authority, with less opportunity for recourse to decisions by those whom the decisions affected.

In promoting the hospital, the Northeast used appeals that had a personal content, while the Southeast used more general appeals, such as "Health is a community responsibility," and "A hospital will bring more doctors." Contrast these Southeast examples with the prevalent Northeast appeals that emphasized "community memorials," "fear of family ill health and disaster," "Everybody is helping, why not you?" One slogan used in the Northeast community studied intensively was, "Let the memory of our loved ones be a blessing to the living."

The foregoing suggests the conclusion that building hospitals in the small-town communities of the Northeast calls forth decision-makers who, first of all, occupy less of an authoritative position in the community than do those in the Southeast; secondly, operate in settings that are more organizationally diverse than in the Southeast; and thirdly, devote greater attention than corresponding persons in the Southeast to appealing to the community, although the incidence of opposition is less.

CASE STUDY DATA

Six basic procedures or steps were employed: (1) By means of a newspaper-file analysis, a detailed list of the sequence of events was secured and used in constructing a schedule. (2) This schedule was administered to members of the official sponsoring group to secure an accurate descriptive profile of the process. (3) Next, a schedule was constructed, on the ground, to secure data reflecting the general community setting relevant to the hospital process—beliefs about previous community hospitals, attitudes regarding methods of financing, recommendations to other communities, and the images held by the informants of the roles played by various persons in the hospital project. (4) This schedule was administered to 40–50 informants representing all members of the sponsoring group, finance campaign leaders, rural leaders selected by the local county agent, and heads of relevant organizations. (5) Intensive interviews were conducted with high-ranked decision-makers to discover the specific tactics, strategies, negotiations, and symbols that had been employed. (6) A post-card questionnaire was mailed to a sample of the voters in the hospital service area to elicit attitudes about the process from representatives of the community-at-large.

A major step in the analysis of the case materials has been to develop profiles for each principal decision-maker, which set forth important positional characteristics, and the resources and skills which the community imagery vests in him. Although it is not possible to elaborate on this analytical tool here, following are some summary comments which reflect on the authority-influence differential hypothesis. It should be noted that the Northeast community, located in western New York, has a town-center of 4,800 population; while the Southeast community, located in Alabama, has a town-center of 2,200 people. In these comparisons, reference will be made to the four highest-ranked decision-makers in each case.

In the Northeast community, the four highest-ranked decision-makers were linked together through twenty years of friendship, reciprocal relations and obligations, and experiences together on other community projects. They participated similarly in important community associations. The imagery of the community held them as "the team"; in more technical terms they form a "symbolic behavioral set." In the Southeast community, no reciprocal ties in the above sense could be found among the four central persons. Indeed, the leading person here was held, by several other decision-makers, to be a man "using the hospital to get into politics," who "always wants to do the telling," and "will see anything he starts through, but is a driver." The leading decision-maker in the Northeast community had the kind of imagery indicated in the following quotations: "anything he is connected with is honorable," "he is the personification of the town," "he knows more about hospitals than the most of us," "he has helped everyone in town," "he wants to always reach a goal, but won't step on you to do it," "he knows how to 'weave' people in." The leading actor in the Southeast had no legendary personality, but the Northeast imagery held the number-one man as legend, i.e., ". . . when (A) gets nervous, something is going to happen." [13]

In the Northeast community, of the four leading decision-makers, one was a printer having state-wide business, another was a wealthy gentleman-farmer with major contacts in town, another the local banker, and the fourth a wealthy farm-produce broker. In the Southeast community, one was the probate judge, two were big landowners and storekeepers, and the

---

[13] It is assumed that the presence of community legend in regard to personal eccentricities is the beginning, at least, of charisma for the influential person.

fourth was an oil-company representative in town. In the Northeast community, three of the four decision-makers had major influence in the town itself, and the associations relevant to the hospital process had their locus in the town. In the Southeast community, three of the four persons, through offices held, were county-oriented. In the Northeast case, the town seemed to be the crucial "community" for decision-making, while the two towns within the Southeast hospital-project area appeared, as it were, to be islands of decision-making, which had to be captured for purposes of votes but were not of crucial importance in an initiating and innovating sense.

In the Northeast community, no one of the four high-ranked decision-makers was a political officeholder or a political leader. In the Southeast community, one was the probate judge, one had recently been defeated for county commissioner, another was a town councilman, and the fourth was a political leader. Opposition in the Northeast community was centered in a few "old pioneer" upper-class families, who used the argument that the hospital project was not sound financially to disguise their inability to compete in contributions with the more wealthy decision-makers. Opposition in the Southeast case centered on the same argument, but it was used as an instrument to further traditional political alignments.[14]

Decision-making in the Southeast community revolved around two structural axes: (1) a vertical hierarchy of authority moving downward from the probate judge, and (2) a county-wide horizontal, informal, political organization operated by a small number of large landowners and storekeepers—this informal organization functioning, in part, through a politically acute farm organization.[15] The inner circle of hospital decision-making in this community was made up of a few big landowner-storekeepers and the directors of the farm organization. In the Northeast

---

[14] An analysis of the votes for the hospital bond issue by "beats" revealed that the opposing leaders (identified as "beat leaders") were associated with beats that voted the bond issue down, and that these same leaders were in opposition to the present political regime.

[15] See V. O. Key, Jr., *Southern Politics* (New York: A. A. Knopf, 1949): "The chief figure in the governments of about two-thirds of the counties of Alabama is the probate judge. . . . The probate judge generally is leader of the dominant faction within the county and often becomes the patriarch of the county. In many counties the potency of the probate judge demonstrates itself by a long string of re-elections" (p. 53). See also K. A. Bosworth, *Black Belt County* (University: Bureau of Public Administration, University of Alabama, 1941), who states: "The term [probate judge] derives meaning in part from the statutory duties of the judge, who from the very nature of his office knows intimately the county and its people. It takes added substance from the established pattern of political and governmental leadership, which is facilitated by the law but goes far beyond it" (p. 38).

community, the inner circle of decision-making consisted of four men, linked together by past events, who, through diverse reciprocal obligations and a positive community imagery, controlled the prestige associational life of the town.

Community imagery of the four leading decision-makers in the Southeast community was cast largely in terms of position. The crucial distinction was whether one was "refined and educated" or "narrow and uneducated." Two of the four central decision-makers here were termed "narrow" (had a "narrow streak" in terms of family, kinship, or education) but, nevertheless, were credited with making the hospital project a success. Three of the four in the Northeast community enjoyed a positive imagery of resources and proficiencies—"honor," "success," "vigor," "competence," "friendship," "loyalty," "Christian living." One person in the Northeast was given a negative imagery precisely because, as a banker, he had position but, according to community imagery, not enough resources to support it.

Finally, the involvement of needed persons in these two hospital projects appeared different. In the Northeast community, the four decision-makers followed their lines of reciprocal obligations and capitalized on the community imagery in community-wide involvements. In the Southeast community, the involvement of needed persons was accomplished largely through positional attachments. For instance, several large landowners appointed to the first hospital committee confessed that they had not personally favored the hospital project (due to its financial magnitude, the threat of heavy taxes, and political alignments), but that their position as an "old Black Belt" family and the need to be "educated and refined" forced them to approve the project publicly (by accepting the committee appointment) because the hospital had a high symbolic value of "being good for the community."

One of the important early decisions in the hospital-getting process is who must be involved for sponsorship. In the Northeast case, two persons secretly developed the idea and, although both were officers of the hospital board of an old hospital, did not report their early negotiations to the board. Instead, they contacted two other persons who refused to go along because of financial pessimism. The tactic employed by the first two decision-makers here was to state that, in the event of community default, they personally would supply the deficit. In the Southeast community, the directors of a farm organization went directly to the probate judge and obtained the appointment to a temporary hospital committee of all the principal large landowners in the county, including the directors of the farm organization.

CONCLUSIONS

In the present hasty treatment, many necessary aspects of decision-making have not been considered: the decisions, tactics, and strategies employed, form and content of negotiations made by decision-makers, symbols and their manipulation, legitimacy, the execution of decisions, and extra-community influences. However, the tentative conclusion is: to understand decision-making and community action in the Southeast one is forced to veer more toward an inquiry into community structure and subsequent offices of constituted authority; while, in the Northeast, more attention to the social psychological components of influence is required. Although both sets of decision-makers had strong positional attachments, it appears from both quantitative and qualitative evidence that the Northeast communities functioned, in decision-making, more squarely on a basis of social property, or resources and proficiencies vested in persons of influence; while the Southeast communities were characterized by a structural setting in which positional elements led to roles of authority.

14

INSTITUTIONAL AND OCCUPATIONAL REPRESENTATIONS IN ELEVEN COMMUNITY INFLUENCE SYSTEMS *

WILLIAM V. D'ANTONIO
Notre Dame University

WILLIAM H. FORM, CHARLES P. LOOMIS, and EUGENE C. ERICKSON
Michigan State University

In a recent study, Delbert C. Miller demonstrated the necessity of using the comparative method of community study to test even the simple proposition that "businessmen exert predominant influence in community decision-making." [1] For his test he selected an American and an English city with similar economic structures. The characteristics of the decision-makers of these two cities were compared with those found by Hunter in Southern City. [2] Miller concluded that the hypothesis that businessmen predominate in community decision-making could be accepted for

* We should like to express our appreciation for support by funds made available by the Division of Hospital and Medical Facilities of the United States Public Health Service for project W-108, "Anglo-Latino Relations in Hospitals and Communities," and the Carnegie Corporation for a project dealing with the United States-Mexican Border. Both projects are under the general direction of Charles P. Loomis. We should also like to acknowledge the work of the following persons for data collection: William V. D'Antonio and James Officer—Juarez; R. Clyde McCone and Eugene C. Erickson—El Paso; Sigurd Johansen and Laiten L. Camien—Las Cruces; Orrin E. Klapp and L. Vincent Padgett—Tijuana; Aubrey Wendling—San Diego; Robert C. Hanson—Denver; Edward H. Spicer and James Officer—Tucson; and Frank and Elizabeth Nall—McAllen. D'Antonio was also the field director of the entire project.

[1] Delbert C. Miller, "Industry and Community Power Structure: A Comparative Study of an American and an English City," *American Sociological Review*, 23 (February, 1958), pp. 9–15.
[2] Floyd Hunter, *Community Power Structure*, Chapel Hill: University of North Carolina, 1954.

the two American cities but had to be rejected for the English City.[3] The crucial and differentiating community variables seemed to be differences in occupational prestige systems and differences in articulation between local government and other elements in the community power complex.

RESEARCH DESIGN

The aim of this research note is to extend the search for crucial community variables in community influence systems by comparing the findings from recent research in six Southwestern American communities and two Mexican communities with the communities studied by Miller. This comparison will be concerned primarily with the relative "contribution" of different institutional and occupational sectors to the group of "top decision-makers" in the community. Since the method of identifying these persons was primarily by reputation rather than by direct observation, it may be more accurate to refer to them as "influentials."[4]

Following the suggestion by W. H. Form and D. C. Miller, the influentials are considered in two categories: top and key influentials. Top influentials (T.I.) are persons from whom particular members are drawn into various systems of power relations according to the issue at stake; the key influentials (K.I.) are sociometric leaders among the top influentials. As in the case of Miller and Hunter, the TI in this study were 30 to 50 consensual nominations obtained from panels of knowledgeables who represented the main institutional sectors in the city and the KI were the ten most influential persons selected by the TI in personal interviews.

RESEARCH SITES

The communities selected for study represent a wide range in size, industrial structure, and ethnic composition, the three most important variables for the purposes of the wider study. This range enabled us to

---

[3] See Miller, *op. cit.*, pp. 10–11 for a description of his technique to identify top decision-makers. Both Miller and Hunter utilized a reputational approach to identify community decision-makers.

[4] See Peter W. Rossi, "Community Decision Making," *Administrative Science Quarterly*, 1 (March, 1957), pp. 415–443. A central focus of the broader research is to test whether the influentials in these eight cities are indeed the key decision-makers in hospital issues which develop in the communities. Every effort was made in interviews with panel members to obtain nominations of persons who were key decision-makers in a range of concrete issues.

probe the question whether such community variables affect the social composition of local influentials.[5]

Table 1 displays for each city data on the main industries, estimates of their populations, and the percentage of persons with Spanish surnames. The task of making the data on industrial composition comparable for cities in the three countries was difficult. Nelson's service classification of American cities was used,[6] and an effort was made to apply his method to arrive at a comparable classification for the Mexican cities.[7]

Brief descriptions follow for the six American and two Mexican cities which were selected for the broader study. The two Mexican cities chosen for study are the two largest Mexican cities on the border.

Ciudad Juarez, Chihuahua is a commercial and distributive center of North Central Mexico. It is also a minor manufacturing center. As a transportation center, it probably reflects the extensive tourist trade which comes to Mexico through El Paso and Juarez. In addition, it is the largest of the Mexican border cities.

Tijuana, Baja California is also a commercial and distributive center for the Northwesternmost corner of Mexico. It is a minor manufacturing center. It is also a transportation center and attracts tourist trade from the western states, particularly from the San Diego environs.

Denver is a commercial, financial, and distributing center for most of the mountain states. It is the center of vast mining activities. It manufactures tires, rubber accessories, porcelain, serums, fishing equipment, saddlery, and other

---

[5] The variables of size and, more indirectly, industrial structure will be considered in this paper. The variable of ethnic composition will be reported separately.

[6] The Nelson classification considers the proportion of the labor force engaged in performing a service for the 897 urban concentrations of 10,000 or more persons in the United States. The mean proportion of persons engaged in a particular service in all 897 cities is calculated for each service group and standard deviations in excess of the mean are calculated. The classification of a city in one group arbitrarily reflects an excess of at least one standard deviation of the labor force employed in that service group. The service data are taken from the *1950 U.S. Census of Population Classification of Industry Groups* (Vol. 2, Table 35, "Economic Characteristics of the Population . . ."). See Howard J. Nelson, "A Service Classification of American Cities," *Economic Geography*, 31 (July, 1955), pp. 189–210.

[7] The classification of Mexican cities was based on a service classification of Municipios of over 10,000 population which includes a city of over 10,000. There were 37 municipios which fell within our criteria from the six border states. The Mexican and U.S. Census have non-comparable categories for "trade" and "service." For this reason two different categories were made for the Mexican cities. The commercial (C) includes Nelson's Retail and Wholesale Trade, Finance, Insurance, and Real Estate. The Service (S) includes Nelson's professional and personal service, and public administration.

TABLE 1. SERVICE CLASSIFICATION, ESTIMATED POPULATION, AND PERCENTAGE OF PERSONS WITH SPANISH SURNAME OF ELEVEN CITIES

City	Service Classification [a]	Estimated Population of Central City at Time of Study [b]	Percentage of Spanish Surname Population in 1950
		N	Per Cent
Pacific City	F2	552,200 [d]	N/A [c]
English City	[e]	444,200 [f]	N/A
Southern City	F2	331,300 [g]	N/A
Denver, Colorado	WF	527,500	6.0
San Diego, California	Pb2PsF	522,600	4.6
El Paso, Texas	T	263,000	49.0
Tucson, Arizona	Ps2PfF	110,000	21.1
McAllen, Texas	RWF	32,000	57.1
Las Cruces, New Mexico	Pb2R	22,500	48.7
Ciudad Juarez	CS [h]	250,000 [i]	96.0 [j]
Tijuana	CS [h]	160,000 [k]	97.0 [j]

[a] Taken from Howard J. Nelson, "A Service Classification of American Cities," *Economic Geography*, 31 (July, 1955), pp. 189–210. Key: Mf, Manufacturing; R, Retail Trade; Pf, Professional Service; T, Transportation and Communication; Ps, Personal Service; Pb, Public Administration; W, Wholesale Trade; F, Finance, Insurance, and Real Estate. A "2" after the symbol signifies the city fell two standard deviations from the mean.

[b] Except where noted differently, these estimates are taken from *Sales Management*, "Survey of Buying Power," 82 (May 10, 1959), and are the estimates as of January 1, 1959, pp. 201–780.

[c] Non-ascertainable.

[d] Estimate as of January 1, 1955 taken from *Sales Management, op. cit.*, 74 (May 10, 1955), p. 732.

[e] The city is described as "commercial, financial, and distribution center of the West of England. . . ."

[f] Estimate as of June, 1953 as noted in *Whitaker's Almanac*, (1955), p. 663.

[g] Estimate as of January 1, 1951 taken from *Sales Management, op. cit.*, 66 (May 10, 1951), p. 212.

[h] See footnote 7, *supra*. Key: C, Commercial; S, Service.

[i] Estimate based on census taken by municipio government, January, 1959.

[j] The percentage of Mexican persons in the population in 1950; from *Septimo Censo General de Poblacion, 6 de Junio de 1950.*

[k] Estimate obtained by researchers in the area.

products. Sugar refining, meat packing, and flour milling are major industries. It is a transportation center for rail, air, bus, and truck lines. Six colleges and universities are located in the city.

San Diego is a commercial and financial center of southern California with especially large proportions of its population employed in public administration and personal service. Its industries include fishing, fish packing, and aircraft. It is an important transportation center with an ocean port. One major college is located there.

El Paso is a transportation and communication center and a major tourist port of the southwestern United States. Its industries include clothing manufacturing, metal and oil refining, and meat packing. It houses two major military installations and a small college.

Tucson is a financial and commercial center of southern Arizona. A high proportion of its population is employed in personal and professional service. Its favorable climate attracts considerable tourist trade and a number of state, federal, and private hospitals. It has a major state university.

Las Cruces serves as a commercial center of a district rich in cotton, corn, fruit, alfalfa, truck and dairy products. A high proportion of its population is employed in public administration. It houses a state university.

McAllen is a financial and commercial center for its area. It is an important gateway to Mexico and popular winter resort. It distributes the vegetables and citrus production from the Lower Valley of the Rio Grande. It has a small college.

FINDINGS

Table 2 provides data on the institutional affiliation of the top influentials of ten cities.[8] As in the cases of the Miller and Hunter studies, the sector which provided the largest number of top influentials was business. This was true not only for the seven American cities, but also for the two Mexican cities. In fact, with the exception of San Diego, Tijuana had the largest proportion of businessmen among the top influentials of the ten cities studied. Apparently size of city is not related to the proportion of businessmen found among the top influentials of the community.

Along with business only government and the independent professions were the sectors which had representation in all of the cities. San Diego had the least broad representation of institutions among the top influentials, with only five sectors represented, and Denver, the broadest, with all sectors represented. Six to ten institutions were represented in the other cities, a situation quite similar to Miller's findings. Yet none of the Southwestern or Mexican cities had as high a percentage of representation from non-business sectors as Pacific and English cities.

The two Mexican cities give the strongest evidence of a challenge to business by another sector of the community, namely government. This should be expected because of the different institutional arrangements that

---

[8] Data for McAllen are not included here because only information on key influentials is available.

TABLE 2. INSTITUTIONAL IDENTIFICATION OF TOP INFLUENTIALS IN TEN CITIES

Institutional Affiliation	Pacific City[b] (N = 44)	English City[b] (N = 32)	Southern City[b] (N = 40)	Denver (N = 50)	San Diego (N = 30)	El Paso (N = 62)	Tucson (N = 45)	Las Cruces (N = 43)	Cd. Juarez (N = 50)	Tijuana (N = 30)	Total (N = 426)
	%	%	%	%	%	%	%	%	%	%	%
Business	33	34	58	50	80	57	58	44	46	67	52
Government	17	9	5	8	3	10	4	9	40	20	13
Independent professions	12	13	15	8	3	15	11	12	4	3	10
Education	10	9	5	8	0	0	7	7	2	3	5
Communications[a]	—	—	—	6	9	8	11	7	0	3	5
Labor	14	19	5	2	3	0	0	0	2	3	4
Religion	7	9	0	6	0	8	2	2	2	0	4
Welfare and cultural (Civic leaders)	7	0	0	8	0	2	2	9	4	0	4
Society and wealth	0	7	12	2	0	2	4	0	0	0	3
Agricultural[a]	—	—	—	2	0	0	0	9	0	0	1
Total	100	100	100	100	98	102	99	99	100	99	101

[a] Two institutions, "Communications" and "Agriculture," are not mentioned by Miller in "Industry and Community Power Structure," *American Sociological Review*, 23 (February, 1958), pp. 9–15, or in "Decision-Making Cliques in Community Power Structures: A Comparative Study of An American and An English City," *American Journal of Sociology*, 64 (November, 1958), pp. 299–310. However, in Miller, "Industry and Community . . .," *op. cit.*, p. 14, the members of the Pacific City Council are classified according to their institutional affiliation. Therefore, his "top influential" category *may* include some representatives from communications since newspaper owner-editors were classified as "Business." Agriculture has been added as a separate category.

[b] Miller, "Industry and Community . . .," *op. cit.*, Table 1, p. 11.

arose out of the Mexican Revolution. The latter, which began in 1910, was "one of the most significant and far-reaching Latin American social movements the twentieth century has seen." [9] As a result, a single political party, the *Partido Revolucionario Institucional* (PRI) came into power and has dominated the institutional life of Mexico ever since. Only recently have business and religion begun to reassert their independence or autonomy. In fact, the predominance of business over government representatives among influentials in Cd. Juarez and Tijuana may be a reflection of the proximity of these cities to the American border, and with this location a more rapid rate of social change compared to other Mexican cities.[10]

Let us now shift our attention from the Top Influentials to the Key Influentials in the eleven cities. A comparison of institutional representation among the key influentials is found in Table 3. As in Pacific and Southern City, business representation is dominant in all the American cities as well as in Tijuana. Cd. Juarez presents the only exception, namely that, like English City, it contains a sector (government) which has a greater or equal representation with business. The fact that this is not true of the other Mexican city calls for an explanation.

The states of Chihuahua and Baja California, in which Cd. Juarez and Tijuana are respectively located, have been among the main centers of the growing minority party, *Partido Accion Nacional* (PAN), the Party of National Action. Much of the strength of PAN in the presidential elections of 1958 came from these two border regions. In fact, the PAN presidential candidate is a citizen of Cd. Juarez and a key influential. Three other PAN leaders were also chosen as KI. All four became politically active in the last six years and ran for public office, with one of them winning a surprise victory in 1955. In an earlier study of business and politics in Cd. Juarez during 1954–55,[11] three of these men were listed as key business influentials. In view of their newly acquired political identity it is not surprising that they remained key influentials. The PAN leaders in Tijuana, however, were not among the top influentials in that city.[12]

It may be necessary to include in this kind of analysis the sector of

[9] George I. Blacksten, "Revolutions," in Harold E. Davis, editor, *Government and Politics in Latin America*, New York: The Ronald Press Company, 1958, pp. 131–132.

[10] See William H. Form and William V. D'Antonio, "Integration and Cleavage Among Community Influentials in Two Border Cities: A Comparative Study of Social Relations and Institutional Perspectives," *American Sociological Review*, 24 (December, 1959), pp. 804–814.

[11] William V. D'Antonio, "National Images of Business and Political Elites in Two Border Cities," unpublished Ph.D. dissertation, Michigan State University, 1958.

[12] This type of analysis has been urged by Robert A. Dahl, "Business and Politics: A Critical Appraisal of Political Science," *The American Political Science Review*, 53 (March, 1959), pp. 1–34.

TABLE 3. OCCUPATIONAL-INDUSTRIAL IDENTITY OF KEY INFLUENTIALS IN ELEVEN CITIES

Occupational Categories	Pacific City [a]	English City [a]	Southern City [a]	Denver	San Diego	El Paso	Tucson	McAllen	Las Cruces	Juarez	Tijuana	Total
Business												(83)
Finance	4	—	1	5	4	3	3	7	—	2	1	30
Merchant	3	—	3	2	3	—	5	4	3	1(1) [b]	5	29
Manufacture	1	3	2	1	2	2	—	1	1	2(3) [b]	4	19
Transportation and utilities	—	—	3	1	—	—	—	—	1	—	—	5
Government												(14)
Political	2	—	—	—	—	—	—	—	—	4	—	6
Mayor	1	—	1	—	—	1	—	—	—	1	1	5
Other government	—	—	—	—	—	1	—	—	—	1	1	3
Professional												(20)
Independent												
Lawyer	1	1	2	—	1	1	—	1	1	—	—	8
Physician	—	—	—	—	—	—	—	—	1	—	—	1
Dependent												
Education	1	2	—	1	—	—	1	—	2	—	—	7
Religion	1	1	—	—	—	—	1	—	—	1	—	4
Communications	—	—	—	1	2	3	2	—	1	—	—	9
Agriculture	—	—	—	—	—	—	—	—	3	—	1	3
Welfare and culture	—	2	—	—	—	—	—	—	—	—	1	2
Labor	—	1	—	—	—	—	—	—	—	—	—	1
Totals	12	12	12	11	12	11	12	13	13	12	12	132

[a] Delbert C. Miller, "Industry and Community Power Structure," *American Sociological Review*, 23 (February, 1958), Table 2, p. 12.
[b] Alternate classification of politicos.

mass communications that was omitted by Miller and Hunter. Newspaper editors or owners were found among both the top and key influentials in four of the five Southwestern U.S. cities studied. In the study of issues it appeared that understanding the local decision-making process may not be possible without giving adequate attention to the strategic position of the newspaper editor. Evidence from our present study demonstrates that major issues have been successfully resolved or blocked by the position taken by the newspaper editor. On the other hand, Miller's data suggest a relative absence of access to top influential circles by representatives of other communications media, such as radio and television. The fact that newspaper editors were not listed as top influentials in either Mexican city deserves comment. The major papers in these cities are owned by a chain whose chief is a strong supporter of the PRI (ruling) party. While local editors in Mexico may have some independence, their residence in a particular city is often relatively short, preventing their developing stable relationships. Since they are generally not perceived to be free and independent spokesmen, long tenure in the city may be necessary before they become community influentials.

It is noteworthy that though publishers or editors are in the list of key influentials in El Paso, Tucson, San Diego, and Las Cruces, they are completely absent in Pacific, English, and Southern cities. Could it be that short tenure in these communities also explains their absence from influential circles? Long tenured editors often establish themselves as spokesmen for the public; indeed, they often develop public opinion. Whether the editors' positions are their own or whether they reflect those of other "influentials" is, of course, problematic.[13] Since community projects are always of concern to editors but not always the concern of other influentials, it is not surprising that newspapermen are often considered to be top influentials in American cities.[14]

The dominance by financiers, merchants, and manufacturers of the key influential positions in the Southwestern cities is amply demonstrated.

---

[13] In a private communication, Delbert C. Miller indicated that in his studies newspaper editors were considered by the KI to be captive rather than independent. For this reason he placed them in the business sector. While Floyd Hunter tends to agree, publishers were found among the first, second, and third raters in *Top Leadership, U.S.A.*, Chapel Hill: University of North Carolina Press, 1959, pp. 177–179.

[14] Though his focus is the relation of mass media to mass society, C. Wright Mills has made similar observations in *The Power Elite*, New York: Oxford University Press, 1956, p. 315. He notes, "They [the mass media] are also among the most important of those increased means of power now at the disposal of elites of wealth and power; moreover, some of the higher agents of these media are themselves either among the elites or very important among their servants."

Nine out of the eleven cities reported at least one financier among the KI; these financiers constituted almost one-quarter of all the KI. Only English City and Las Cruces failed to list a financier. Merchants and manufacturers were represented in nine of the eleven cities. The merchants (both wholesale and retail) constituted almost one-quarter and the manufacturers constituted one-seventh of all the KI. Only English City and El Paso failed to list a merchant and only Tucson listed no manufacturers among the key influentials. While the peculiar industrial structure of the city may account for the latter, the absence of a financier in English City or Las Cruces cannot be explained in terms of absence of that function.

The most frequently found occupations next to business were those in communications and law. Lawyers were represented eight times in seven cities. It may well be that the lawyer is becoming or has been an effective link between business and other sectors, if he is not in fact a businessman himself.

Mayors were chosen as KI in five of the eleven cities, as were other governmental officials and political leaders. While it may be argued that the central role of government in resolving local issues should result in the mayor being among the key influentials, mayors were not represented in six cities and they were outnumbered by other governmental officials and politicians. This situation points to the need for extensive exploration of the relations between the governmental and other power structure variables in the city.[15] Labor union officials lacked representation in the key influence structure of all cities except English City. In like manner, agriculture was represented only in Las Cruces. Religion, education, welfare and "society" had scattered representation. Only one medical doctor was found among the KI, namely, in Las Cruces, the smallest of the cities in the study.[16] With lawyers excluded, educators, clergymen, and physicians are represented in six of the eleven cities, with educators having the largest numbers. There appeared to be no relationship between the number and distribution of professions among the KI and city size and industrial composition.

CONCLUSION

This note compares data on top influence structures of several Southwestern and Mexican border cities with those presented by Miller. Our data

---

[15] Dahl, *op. cit.*

[16] The place of physicians in the general influence structure and in the decision-making process revolving around hospital issues is a central theme of the broader study. These findings will be reported elsewhere.

lend additional weight to his hypothesis that businessmen tend to be most highly represented among top and key influentials. Moreover, the data from the two Mexican cities further support his contention that differences in the articulation of government to other elements of the community power complex results in rejecting the model of general business dominance. We tentatively suggest more information is needed on the place that newspaper editors and publishers occupy in the community influence structure. The explanation we suggested calls for further testing.

Further, although the cities studied were not drawn with the explicit view of determining the effect of size on representation of particular sectors of the community, there seems to be no consistent difference as one moves across this variable. Only in extreme cases did we find that the economic base of the community seemed to supply (and therefore effect) the composition of the top influence structures. We were unable, at this stage, to check other variables which might explain variations found in the representations of certain professions.

VI

POWER, RESOURCES, AND DECISION-MAKING

15

REPUTATION AND RESOURCES
IN COMMUNITY POLITICS

☯

WILLIAM A. GAMSON
University of Michigan

[This paper focuses on the role of reputational leaders in influencing the outcome of issues in eighteen New England communities. When such leaders are both active and united, they are on the winning side three-fourths of the time. This is not merely a function of their participation on the more active side, for they have as high a proportion of victories when they support the less active side. Furthermore, the side supporting change wins only 30 per cent of the time without the united support of reputational leaders but two-thirds of the time with it. There seems to be some reality to reputation, and this reality is consistent with a theoretical interpretation of reputation as a resource.]

In the post mortem which accompanies any political defeat, the losing group will typically take itself to task for various failures. There is, in such analyses, a tendency to assume that the exercise of influence alone determines the outcome of a decision. The other side is seen as having been more effective—as having spent more resources or as having used its resources more efficiently. While this may be true, it is also possible in such cases that the losing side was quite effective while the winning side did little or nothing to further their cause. The exercise of influence is only one element in the outcome of political issues.

It is helpful, in speaking of influence, to start with the notion of a decision to be made. Influence can then be handled very well, as Dahl has suggested,[1] using the notion of conditional probability. The amount of influence a social unit has had on a decision is represented by the difference between the probability of the desired outcome before and after the influence attempt. To say that one has influenced a decision means simply

---

[1] Robert Dahl, "The Concept of Power," *Behavioral Science*, II (July, 1957), 201–15. Herbert A. Simon and James G. March have suggested similar formulations.

that he has changed the probability of the desired outcome in the intended direction.[2] By such a definition, the presence or absence of influence cannot be clearly inferred from whether or not the would-be influencer is on the winning side of a decision. A partisan group in a community may start with little chance of an alternative being accepted. By waging a vigorous fight they may reach a point where acceptance or rejection is touch and go. Ultimately, of course, the measure will either pass or fail, but we should not judge this group to have had influence only if it passes. The move from an almost certain failure to a near-miss is a mark of their influence. Similarly, a victory cannot be taken as prima facie evidence of influence since a narrow victory by a partisan group in a situation in which they would have won doing nothing is no indication of influence.

This paper is concerned with understanding the outcome of community issues and, in particular, with the role that those with a general reputation for influence play in such outcomes. Factors other than influence may, in some cases, put severe limits on the possible effects which partisan groups or individuals may have. Accordingly, it seems useful to take as a working assumption the asymmetry of the influence task for different partisan groups. Those on one side of an issue are likely to have a natural advantage over those on the other side, an advantage which will enable them to win if they simply hold their own in an influence contest.

What is the nature of this "natural advantage"? Most broadly, it is the advantage that falls to those who do not carry the burden of proof. In relatively stable situations, this advantage is held by those who would maintain a present arrangement against those who would alter it. Many community issues arise from the presentation of a proposal to alter some existing facility or service or to add some new facility. The burden of proof in such cases generally rests with the side proposing the change. For example, if a new school is proposed, those who oppose it may raise any number of questions about need, cost, design, site, and so forth. It is not necessary to resolve such questions in order to block action on this proposal; if they remain unanswered, this is generally sufficient.

The communities studied here are not undergoing acute crises. They are, then, a special case in which the natural advantage falls to those who would maintain existing conditions. To admit the existence of such an advantage is not to argue that those who desire change will fail but only that they will fail in the absence of influence no greater than that exercised

---

[2] One might wish to talk of changes in an unintended direction as "negative influence," but this issue is not relevant for the discussion here.

by the other side. In the discussion which follows, special attention is given to the role of "reputational leaders" in such an influence process.

REPUTATION AND RESOURCES

A number of investigators interested in the operation of power in the community have elicited lists of names of community "leaders." Typically, a panel composed of heads of civic associations or some other group actively involved in public affairs is asked to nominate individuals and the nominees are in turn interviewed.[3] This "reputational method" of studying community power has been sharply attacked both for the interpretations that are made of the list of names obtained and, in more basic ways, for the use of such questions at all. To quote Polsby, "asking about reputations is asking, at a remove, about behavior. It can be argued that the researcher should make it his business to study behavior directly rather than depend on the opinions of second hand sources."[4]

What does it mean, we may ask, when an individual or group of individuals is frequently named as "influential" by those involved in community political affairs? Are such reputations meaningless in themselves, telling us no more at best than we might more efficiently learn from studying actual influence over decisions? Reputation, I will argue, is a resource; as such, it refers to potential influence rather than influence in use. Reputation is not simply the manifestation of the possession of large amounts of resources but is, itself, a resource in the same sense that money, wealth, or authority might be. This argument requires some discussion of the concept of resources.

What is it that an influencer uses to exercise influence? In any decision, there exists some "thing" or "weight" such that if enough of this weight is applied to the decision-makers the probability of an alternative being accepted or rejected will be changed. This thing must satisfy two important conditions to be considered a resource. First, it must be possessed by or, more accurately, *controlled* by the influencer. He must be able to determine its use. Second, he must be able to bring it to bear on decision-makers in interaction with them.

Since in any society certain things are widely valued, certain re-

---

[3] It is not my intention to review or even cite such studies here. Nelson Polsby's *Community Power and Political Theory* (New Haven, Conn.: Yale University Press, 1963) has a reasonably complete list of citations and a highly critical review of these studies. See esp. pp. 45–68.

[4] *Ibid.*, p. 51.

sources are both of high applicability across a variety of decision-makers and of high stability of value over time within a particular set of decision-makers. It is the possession of such general resources rather than of more idiosyncratic ones that is of significance for understanding the stable potential to influence the outcome of decisions.

Many authors have distinguished among the ways that resources are used to produce influence.[5] The most relevant distinction for the present argument is implicit in a number of these discussions, but it is made most .explicitly by Parsons. In the terms which will be used here, *sanctioning* influence is the addition of new advantages or disadvantages (conditional or not) to the situation of the decision-maker. *Persuasion* influence operates on the orientation of the decision-maker, changing the connection he sees between a decision outcome and his goals without the addition of any new advantages or disadvantages to the situation.

It is not difficult to conceive of sanctioning resources of high stability and generality. A person who holds a position of great potential influence in an elaborate network of institutional and interpersonal relationships possesses a powerful set of inducements. It is virtually certain that there will be some present or future alternative that he can influence that present decision-makers care about. Furthermore, it is a valuable political asset to have such a potentially influential person obligated to oneself.

Is it possible to talk about a similarly general basis of persuasion? Clearly, we can conceive of persuasion resources which are highly limited in scope. Expertness, for example, is only a resource for those areas in which the influencer is considered knowledgeable. Are there more generalized and stable persuasion resources?

A generalized reputation for "wisdom" or "good sense" is just such a stable persuasion resource. There are individuals who are respected by particular groups in a community not because of any *specific* expertness they may have on the issue at hand but because they are believed to be

---

[5] These include John R. P. French, Jr., and Bertram Raven, "The Bases of Social Power," in Dorwin Cartwright (ed.), *Studies in Social Power* (Ann Arbor, Mich.: Institute for Social Research, 1959), pp. 150–67; Herbert Kelman, "Processes of Opinion Change," *Public Opinion Quarterly*, XXV (Spring, 1961), 57–78; Amitai Etzioni, *A Comparative Analysis of Complex Organizations* (Glencoe, Ill.: Free Press, 1961); Franz L. Neumann, "Approaches to the Study of Political Power," *Political Science Quarterly*, LXV (1950), 161–80; Morris Janowitz, *The Professional Soldier* (Glencoe, Ill.: Free Press, 1960); Herbert Goldhamer and Edward A. Shils, "Types of Power and Status," *American Journal of Sociology*, XLV (September, 1939), 171–82; John Harsanyi, "Measurement of Social Power, Opportunity Costs, and the Theory of Two-Person Bargaining Games," *Behavioral Science*, VII (January, 1962), 67–80; and Talcott Parsons, "On the Concept of Influence," *Public Opinion Quarterly*, XXXVII (Spring, 1963), 37–62.

generally "knowledgeable," "sound," "reliable," "unselfish," "intelligent," and so forth. In other words, they are believed to possess certain stable personal qualities that transcend any given issue and make their opinion more convincing. A highly successful lawyer, for example, who actively participates in community affairs may find that his success is regarded by public officials as a sign of grace. While his persuasion resources on issues involving legal matters may be particularly great, he will carry with him a generalized reputation which acts as a resource—even on issues for which he has no special qualifications.

He has no persuasion resources, of course, among those who do not accept his reputation. Resources are categorized here in terms of their applicability to decision-makers. A spokesman who enjoyed the complete confidence of members of some solidary group would have a persuasion resource with respect to decisions made by his followers. However, his influence over this group might in turn be used as an inducement for public officials who wish the group's votes in an election.

A theoretical justification for identifying reputational leaders is being offered here. One asks about reputation simply to identify those who have reputation; such reputation is significant because it is a stable and generalized persuasion resource. Of course, we may quarrel with the method used to identify such people. One technique is to ask community decision-makers a question such as: "In many communities, there are people who are generally listened to when they take a position on community issues because they are believed to have good judgment. Are there any such people in ——?" Those who are frequently named form an operational definition of "people with stable persuasion resources." The validity of such a question concerns how well it measures reputation, not its connection with influence behavior.

Those who are named as "reputational leaders" simply comprise a pool of individuals with resources. No claim is made that they form a ruling elite or even a cohesive group of any sort; such claims must rest on demonstration of a number of additional characteristics. Those with resources may or may not be friendly with each other socially. If they all belong to the same clubs and organizations, this is an important additional fact about the organization of resources in the community. The list by itself tells us nothing about this fact.

Similarly, agreement on policy among reputational leaders is an empirical question. The list might contain, for example, political rivals who are never found on the same side. Or, it might contain individuals with different spheres of interest who tacitly or explicitly agree to remain neutral on issues outside of their major province. The only thing we wish to maintain about the list of reputational leaders is that, because they possess significant amounts of resources, their social organization is significant for the understanding of stable power relations in the community. The relations among members and their actions is a variable which will be related to the outcome of decisions in a variety of important ways.[6]

THE STUDY

The data to be presented here are drawn from a study of fifty-four issues in eighteen New England communities. The towns were generally small, ranging in population from 2,000 to 100,000 with the median size about 10,000. Seven of the communities were essentially suburbs of Boston, three were resort towns, and the remaining eight were more or less independent cities with some industrial base of their own. All but two of the communities were in Maine or Massachusetts.

Material on these communities was gathered through interviews with 426 informants, an average of twenty-four per town, supplemented by information from a variety of documents. Interviewing was done by teams of three or four individuals who stayed in each community for several days. Three issues were studied in each town, one of which—fluoridation—was common to all eighteen. The presence of a decision on fluoridation was, in fact, the basis of selection of these communities, and the eighteen include all those New England communities which made a fluoridation decision during an 18-month period of data collection.

Respondents were asked to name the most important issues that had arisen in their town in the previous 5 years. Of the fifty-four issues studied, twenty-six were mentioned by a majority of the respondents in the town.[7]

---

[6] The argument above focuses on persuasion resources. Most studies using the reputational method have not had such purposes in mind, and a variety of wordings have been used. What of asking for the names of people "who run the town," "who would be needed to get a new project across," or "who have a lot of influence on the outcome of decisions"? The responses to such questions may frequently include those who possess persuasion resources, but some individuals might be included for other reasons. It seems likely, although one would have to demonstrate this, that those frequently named individuals who do *not* possess persuasion resources do possess sanctioning resources. If this is true, then those who are named would still comprise a pool of individuals with resources and all of the above arguments for studying reputational leaders would apply.

[7] Issues were selected for study through examination of community newspapers and some informal checking with newspaper editors and city clerks. It was possible to miss issues on whose importance there was considerable concensus since this could not be discovered until the interviews were completed. Thus, five issues named by a majority of respondents were not studied.

In eleven of the eighteen towns, a majority mentioned a particular issue first or as most important and in all but one of these the issue was included in the fifty-four studied. Besides the eighteen fluoridation issues, eleven concerned schools, eleven were issues over the development of some new community facility or service, eight were zoning issues, and the final six were a miscellaneous assortment which included changes in the form of government and urban renewal.

The interviews themselves were with two categories of respondents—with active partisans on both sides of each of the three issues and with reputational leaders. The active partisans on the three issues studied were asked to name people in response to the following question: "In many communities, relatively few people are able to affect the outcome of issues sometimes because they are in a position to make key decisions or because they have the ability to persuade others to follow their leadership. Would you tell me the names of the most important and influential leaders in this community even if they do not hold public office?" [8] Those dozen individuals most frequently named were also interviewed and, in the course of the interview, asked this same question.

The criteria for inclusion on the list of reputational leaders should control for certain irrelevant variables between towns. Interviewers differed in the amount of probing they did for names, the total number of respondents interviewed in a town varied from nineteen to thirty-one, and the average number of people mentioned by respondents varied from town to town depending on the degree of consensus that existed and the volubility of respondents. By using as a base the total number of mentions,[9] we can control for all of the above variables. In communities where (1) the interviewers probed vigorously, (2) a large number of interviews were taken, and (3) the respondents were prolific in their naming, a large number of total mentions will emerge. Requiring a fixed proportion of the total for eligibility means that an individual must be named more frequently in such a town than in one where few names are mentioned over all.[10]

---

[8] Unfortunately, this question is not the one called for by the theoretical argument above nor is it directed, as it should be, to a sample of decision-makers. Thus, to treat our reputational leaders as a pool of resource holders we must assume that those named have some kind of stable and general resources, though not necessarily persuasion resources.

[9] That is, Σm_i, where m_i is the number of times the ith individual is mentioned.

[10] To be included, an individual must be mentioned more than some fixed proportion of the total mentions. The setting of such a fixed proportion is rather arbitrary, and I have set it here at 3 per cent of the total because such a figure yields an average of about 10 people per community. The number per town ranges from 6

Before we can assess the influence of reputational leaders on the outcome of the fifty-four issues, we must examine other aspects of these issues. Each is characterized by campaigns by one or both sides, but the intensity of these campaigns varies considerably. Furthermore, some of these efforts have as their object the adoption of some new proposal while others have the maintenance of existing arrangements as their goal. It is only against this backdrop that we can meaningfully connect winning efforts with influence. We must show that the active participation of reputational leaders on a side has some effect over and above the sheer amount of campaign activity and the natural advantage of defending the status quo.

CAMPAIGN ACTIVITY

All of those who were active on either side of an issue were asked a series of questions about the nature of campaign activities. These questions varied from such open-ended ones as "What did those in favor (opposed) actually do to promote their side, that is, what kinds of activities?" to a specific check list of sixteen activities. On several items respondents were asked to compare the campaigns of the two sides. From these descriptions of activities, we characterized each side's campaign on two dimensions—the magnitude of total activity and the degree of organization.

For the first of these dimensions, each respondent's description was culled for statements characterizing the extent of particular activities or characterizations of the campaign as a whole (e.g., "they spent a tremendous amount of money on advertising and literature," "we spent a whole year trying to convince people with a tremendous campaign in the last four weeks"). Independent coders were asked to classify the amount of activity for each partisan group as either "great," "some," or "little." [11]

For the degree of organization, heavier reliance was placed on the check list of activities. Many of the activities, such as holding meetings to decide and plan what to do, distribution of literature to the general public,

---

people at the low end to 13 at the other extreme. The number of mentions required for inclusion ranges from 3 to 8, with an average of about 4½. Since the average number of respondents per town is about 24, this means that a reputational leader is named by a minimum of about ⅕ of the respondents in his town, a figure obtained by dividing the average number of mentions required for inclusion (4.6) by the average number of respondents (24). This figure of ⅕ of the respondents provides some interpretation for the, by itself, meaningless criterion of 3 per cent of the total mentions.

[11] Initial coding plans were more ambitious, but difficulties in achieving satisfactory reliability forced resort to this crude classification. Intercoder agreement for these three categories was above 80 per cent for the 108 campaigns being coded.

circulating petitions, and raising money to support activities, require some degree of formal organization. They are typically carried on by groups that establish an ad hoc organization for the purpose with publicly identifiable leaders or else are carried on by some existing organization in the community. Other kinds of activities require less formal organization but do require interaction among those implementing them. These include telephone campaigns, selective distribution of literature, and participating at meetings or discussions. Finally, there are activities that require neither formal organization nor interaction—for example, writing and answering letters to newspapers, attending or testifying at council meetings or other official proceedings, or simply talking informally to people one encounters. Each campaign was characterized by the highest degree of organizational activity carried on. If the first category of activities occurred, then the campaign organization was characterized as formal regardless of what semiformal and informal activities occurred as well. Thus, an informal campaign was one in which *only* informal activities occurred. Each of the 108 campaigns was coded as either formal, semiformal, or informal.

With each partisan group's campaign characterized in this way, it is possible to compare the two sides on each issue. Interestingly enough, the winning side has only a modest advantage in amount of activity and organization; it had either more activity or more organization on only 48 per cent of the issues while the losing side had more on 33 per cent.[12] For the remainder, the two sides were equal in activity and organization or, in one case, the winning side was higher on one criterion while the losing side had the advantage on the other.

On forty-eight of the issues it was possible to identify one side with an effort to change the status quo in some fashion while the other side favored postponement of action, further study of need, a counter alternative requiring less change, or simply the maintenance of existing arrangements. The side identified with change was victorious in 42 per cent of these cases against 58 per cent for those who opposed the immediate action proposed.

It was hypothesized above that it takes more effort[13] to change the status quo than to maintain it, and Table 1 supports this. In almost two-thirds of the cases in which the side supporting change won, they made

---

[12] The base for these figures and for the subsequent analysis is actually 52 rather than 54 issues. Two of the issues are excluded because of ambiguity over the outcome, which made it impossible to designate a winner.

[13] The phrase "campaign effort" refers to the measure of amount of activity and degree of organization taken in combination. A side will be characterized as having greater effort if it is at least equal on one of these measures and greater on the other.

a greater campaign effort than the other side. However, when the side supporting no change won, they made a greater effort only a third of the time; two-thirds of the time they were able to win with no more effort than the losing side.

REPUTATION AND SUCCESS

There are two prior questions which we must ask about reputational leaders before we can examine their impact on issue outcome. First, to what extent are they actively involved as partisans on the issues studied? Second, to what extent do they act in unison when they are active; that is, how often are they predominantly on the same side? Having answered those questions, we can examine their impact when they are both active and relatively united.

TABLE 1. Campaign Effort and Success in Changing
the Status Quo

Winning Side	Supported Change		Supported Status Quo		Change Issue Irrelevant
	Per Cent	(N)	Per Cent	(N)	(N)
Made greater campaign effort	65	(13)	32	(9)	(3)
Made same campaign effort *	10	(2)	29	(8)	(0)
Made smaller campaign effort	25	(5)	39	(11)	(1)
Total (N = 52)	100	(20)	100	(28)	(4)

* Includes one case in which the winning side was higher on amount of activity but lower on amount of organization.

Activity.—Activity is measured in two ways. Respondents were asked, for each issue studied, if they were at all active. If they answered affirmatively, they were asked to describe such activity; only efforts to affect the outcome are included here or, in other words, non-partisan activities are excluded. Respondents were also asked for the names of the people "who have done most of the work in favor (against)." There were some individuals who, out of circumspection or modesty, did not rate themselves as active but were named as active by others. An individual will be considered active on an issue either if he rates himself as active and can describe some confirming partisan activity or if two or more other people rate him as active in favor or against.

A total of 161 reputational leaders were interviewed, 92 per cent of those identified as such. How frequently are they active? First, it is worth asking what a finding of inactivity might mean. Only three issues were studied in each town. These were salient and controversial issues, but many decisions which affect large numbers of individuals never become controversial or attract widespread interest. Thus, the absence of signs of activity by reputational leaders does not preclude their activity on many other issues which were not studied. As it turns out, however, these cautions are largely unnecessary because 82 per cent of the reputational leaders were active on at least one of the issues studied! Enlarging the number of issues studied per town could only have the effect of further cutting the already small pool of non-active reputational leaders. Furthermore, 41 per cent of the reputational leaders were active on a majority of the issues studied. All in all, there can be little doubt that reputation for influence is highly associated with activity on issues in these communities.

Unity.—Do those reputational leaders who engage in partisan activities act as a cohesive force or do they compete to determine the outcome of the issue? There were thirty-four issues on which at least three reputational leaders were active; with less than three, it makes little sense to ask about the extent of agreement. The active reputational leaders are unanimous on only nine of the thirty-four issues. If we use a less stringent criterion than unanimity, we still find that there is two-thirds or less agreement on eleven of the thirty-four issues.

Caution is necessary in interpreting this evidence of disagreement among reputational leaders. Among the many decisions that arise in a community, it is those few which produce serious competition that are likely to become salient. A proposal on which reputational leaders were united in opposition might have difficulty reaching a stage where it would become salient enough to be cited as an "important" community issue. Similarly, a proposal on which reputational leaders were united in favor with no significant amounts of competing resources arrayed on the other side is also unlikely to have high salience or high ratings of community concern. Thus, our method of selecting issues may contain a heavy bias toward those issues in which there is a substantial amount of disagreement among major resource-holders.

Nevertheless, the amount of disagreement revealed here tends to discourage any view of the reputational leaders as a cohesive group united behind common objectives. While there may be unstudied issues on which unanimous agreement existed, there are also likely to be others on which significant disagreement existed. There were only two among the eighteen communities studied in which active reputational leaders were undivided on all three issues; in only five of the eighteen towns was there as much as 80 per cent agreement on all three issues.

There is other evidence that the reputational leaders fail to comprise any sort of cohesive political force. In twelve of the eighteen towns, the list of reputational leaders contains individuals who are known to be political rivals or even political enemies. In some cases, there are individuals with a long history of political combat; in others, there are spokesmen for rival solidary groups. In the remaining six communities where the pool of reputational leaders did not contain clear protagonists, there were many instances of no more than casual acquaintance among members of the list. All in all, with the exception of three towns with both issue agreement and no evidence of sustained political rivalry among members of the pool, reputational leaders fail to form anything resembling a cohesive united political clique.

TABLE 2. REPUTATIONAL LEADER SUPPORT AND CAMPAIGN EFFORT

Winning Side	Made Greater Campaign Effort		Made Same Campaign Effort		Made Smaller Campaign Effort	
	Per Cent	(N)	Per Cent	(N)	Per Cent	(N)
Had reputational leader support	36	(9)	20	(2)	35	(6)
Had divided or inactive reputational leaders	56	(14)	80	(8)	41	(7)
Had reputational leader opposition	8	(2)	—	—	24	(4)
Total (N = 52)	100	(25)	100	(10)	100	(17)

Success.—When the reputational leaders are active and united, do they end up on the winning side? They do about 75 per cent of the time on the issues studied here (17 of 23 issues). But perhaps they are simply fellow travelers, joining with the more active and organized side. It turns out, in fact, that they support the more active side only 56 per cent of the time but are on the winning side about three-fourths of the time. Furthermore, as Table 2 shows, when the side with the smaller effort is victorious, it is just as likely to have reputational leader support as is the side with greater effort when it wins (35 per cent versus 36 per cent).

It might be argued that reputational leaders are associated with successful outcomes mainly because they support the status quo and thus gain the natural advantage of such support. This is decidedly not the case;

reputational leaders, when united and active, support the side favoring change more than twice as often as they support the side favoring the status quo (15 versus 6 times). This means that, to achieve victories, they must typically overcome the natural advantage of the other side. As Table 3 indicates, they are able to do this with some success. In fact, the side proposing change has considerable difficulty without the active support of the reputational leaders and their opposition amounts to a virtual veto. In half the cases where the winning side supported change, they had the

TABLE 3. REPUTATIONAL LEADER SUPPORT AND SUCCESS
IN CHANGING THE STATUS QUO

Winning Side	Supported Change		Supported Status Quo		Change Issue Irrelevant
	Per Cent	(N)	Per Cent	(N)	(N)
Had reputational leader support	50	(10)	18	(5)	(2)
Had divided or inactive reputational leaders	45	(9)	64	(18)	(2)
Had reputational leader opposition	5	(1)	18	(5)	. . . .
Total (N = 52)	100	(20)	100	(28)	(4)

support of the reputational leaders and only one success occurred against reputational leader opposition. When the winning side supported the status quo, they had the support of the reputational leaders only 18 per cent of the time.

Is the support of reputational leaders or a stronger campaign effort more likely to produce a victory for the side favoring change? With so few cases, it is not easy to disentangle variables. However, Table 4 has some suggestive evidence that reputational leader support may be most critical. With such support, the side favoring change is successful two-thirds of the time *regardless* of relative campaign effort. However, such campaign efforts clearly make an important difference when reputational leaders are divided or inactive. The side favoring change wins almost half the time with a greater campaign effort but only one-sixth of the time when it fails to make a greater effort.

It is instructive to look at the six cases in which the reputational leaders were united and active on the losing side. Two of these were efforts to have comprehensive zoning plans adopted, one involved the approval of a new high school, one a major change of land use in the central business district, and one an ambitious and expensive harbor-development project. In four of these five cases, the leaders of the defeated forces felt that they had lost a round but that the fight was not over. However, they spoke of modifying the alternative in important ways—of asking the town for half a loaf or of toning down the proposal in various ways.

None of the variables discussed here illuminate the sixth defeat. It

TABLE 4. REPUTATIONAL LEADER SUPPORT AND CAMPAIGN EFFORT
BY SUCCESS IN CHANGING THE STATUS QUO

| Side Favoring Change | Had Reputational Leader Support | | | | Had No Reputational Leader Support * | | | |
| | Had Greater Effort | | Had No Greater Effort † | | Had Greater Effort | | Had No Greater Effort | |
	Per Cent	(N)	Per Cent	(N)	Per Cent	(N)	Per Cent	(N)
Won	67	(6)	67	(4)	47	(7)	17	(3)
Lost	33	(3)	33	(2)	53	(8)	83	(15)
Total ($N = 48$ ‡)	100	(9)	100	(6)	100	(15)	100	(18)

* Cases where reputational leaders were opposed and where they were divided or inactive are combined here.
† Cases of equal effort and of smaller effort are combined here.
‡ Four cases in which change was not an issue are omitted here.

involved the rezoning of a considerable area of land from residential use to business use. Reputational leaders were active and united against the proposal, participated in a campaign which was apparently *more* extensive in both organization and activity than the other side, and were beneficiaries of the natural advantage of defending the status quo. I can do no more with this case than present it as evidence that the arguments above are not tautological.

CONCLUSION

Reputational leaders are not presented here as a ruling elite. They are presented as an aggregate of individuals with resources. In particular, I have argued that their reputation is itself a resource and not simply an indicator of resources. If this argument is correct, then we ought to find that they have some success in influencing the outcome of issues when they are active and united. Unfortunately, we cannot simply look at whether they are on the winning or losing side because other factors besides their influence are affecting the outcome. The factors focused on here were the amount of campaign effort and whether the campaign aimed at changing or preserving the status quo. The data indicated that a more active or more organized campaign was necessary to change the status quo than to maintain it.

Reputational leaders are, with few exceptions, active on at least one of the three issues studied in their respective communities. However, they are frequently active on opposite sides, although this may merely reflect a method of issue selection which emphasized controversy. When they are both active and united, they are on the winning side about three-fourths of the time. This is not merely a function of their participation on the more active side, for they have as high a proportion of victories when they support the less active side. Furthermore, they may be making a contribution to the campaign effort and thus exercising additional influence through their contribution to this variable. Nor is their success an artifact of the natural advantage gained from supporting the status quo. On the contrary, they achieve their success *against* this advantage. They are united and successful in support of change two-thirds of the time.

In short there seems to be some reality to reputation. This reality is consistent with a theoretical interpretation of reputation as a resource. I have no desire to defend the past uses and abuses of the reputational method, but neither am I inclined to heed Wolfinger's "plea for a decent burial." [14] A decent convalescence seems more in order.

---

[14] Raymond E. Wolfinger, "A Plea for a Decent Burial," *American Sociological Review*, XXVII (December, 1962), 841–47.

16

ON THE STRUCTURE
OF INFLUENCE*

☯

RONALD L. NUTTALL
Boston College

ERWIN K. SCHEUCH
University of Cologne

CHAD GORDON
Harvard University

[One section of a process model of community decision-making is explained as a conceptual tool with which to analyze the outcomes of particular decision-making events. A typology of influence positions is constructed in terms of two key properties of the actors concerned: (1) actual access to relevant resources (broadly defined) and, (2) whether or not others in the system credit him with this possession. This typology of manifest, potential, reputed, or non-existent influence is used to derive a number of rather general propositions concerning likely willingness to engage in conflicts, frequency of decisions moving to sanctioning and payoffs and the stability of the influence structure.]

The field of community decision-making has seen a great deal of controversy over concepts, methodology, and findings. A basic issue has been whether or not the urban community is characterized by a unified and enduring hierarchy of power rather than by a more amorphous and changing configuration which differs markedly from issue to issue. Associated with this controversy about substance is one of method, mainly between the "reputational technique" as introduced and typified by the

---

* This is a revision of a paper first presented at the Eastern Sociological Association's Annual Meeting, New York City, April 10, 1965. The research on which it was based was supported in part by Public Health Grant EF-00653, "Metropolitan Decision-Making." This support is gratefully acknowledged.

work of Floyd Hunter,[1] and the "issue approach" as exemplified by Robert A. Dahl's work in New Haven and Edward C. Banfield's studies of Chicago.[2] Unfortunately, the methods used to identify the influential figures of a community are not equally suitable for all types of structures. Thus, the issue approach tends to work best with a diverse structure and typically results in a greater number of people being identified as relevant for decision-making. Conversely, the reputational approach is best suited for delineation of an oligarchic structure, and if used uncritically makes it appear as if such a structure exists in every case. Often the results seem to be predetermined by the method of study: researchers select their techniques with the assumption of pluralism or oligarchy in mind, and they are usually confirmed by their results.

While the empirical literature of community decision-making continues to expand rapidly, there is little progress in theoretical analyses. In part, this situation is probably due to the alternate reification and abandonment of the concept of "power structure," and consequent small attention given to the general character of the *process* of decision-making; "power" proves to be very much an emotional concern of sociologists. While the current and the historical arrangements of decision-making may differ widely from one community to another, we feel that there are certain patterned regularities in the process of community decision-making *per se;* structural features of the particular situation are related to it as framework and input parameters.

The core of our analysis is a conceptualization of conditions of influence. Reflecting on the relation of actors to resources and assuming as an always present possibility a split between the consciousness of reality and reality, we arrive at a typology of influentials—or more precisely: of situations of influentials. This typology of influentials is derived by specifying two dimensions as principal: *access to resources,* and *belief of*

---

[1] *Community Power Structure* (Chapel Hill: University of North Carolina Press, 1953).

[2] Robert A. Dahl, *Who Governs?* (New Haven: Yale University Press, 1961); Edward C. Banfield, *Political Influence* (Glencoe: The Free Press, 1961). Critical analyses of both methods are contained in William V. D'Antonio and Howard J. Ehrlich, eds., *Power and Democracy in America* (Notre Dame: University of Notre Dame Press, 1961), and throughout a series of journal debates: Raymond E. Wolfinger, "Reputation and Reality in the Study of 'Community Power'," *American Sociological Review,* 25 (October, 1960), 636–644; Howard J. Ehrlich, "The Reputational Approach to the Study of Community Power," *American Sociological Review,* 26 (December, 1961), 926–927; William V. D'Antonio and Eugene C. Erickson, "The Reputational Technique as a Measure of Community Power: An Evaluation Based on Comparative and Longitudinal Studies," *American Sociological Review,* 27 (June, 1962), 362–376.

relevant others that such access exists. The sections which follow contain an explanation of these dimensions and certain propositions concerning their interrelations over time. The paper includes an attempt at a new conceptualization of "political resource." Decision-making in the urban community is the reality which the model is supposed to make more transparent.[3] In this paper we use only part of the more elaborate model which is outlined in Figure 1.

FIGURE 1. A DECISION-MAKING PROCESS MODEL

Process Step	*Related Informal Role*
I. *Structuring and Defining of Ideas as Proposals*	
A. Recognition of a discrepancy between a conception of the desirable and current conditions.	Critic
B. Identification of the case as potentially actionable.	Initiator
C. Formulation of "possible" alternatives "worth looking into."	Planner
II. *Identifying the Properties of Alternatives*	
A. Inherent merits of alternative cases as identified by experts at a given time and place.	Technical Expert
B. The values held by the individual actors.	Investigator
C. The factual effect on the resources of the individual actors and the collectivity.	Social-Emotional Expert
D. The presumed effect on the position of individuals in the social structure of the collectivity itself.	Investigator; Social-Emotional Expert
E. The presumed availability of social support for alternative courses of action.	Inside Dopester
III. *Structure of the Social Field*	
A. Identification of potential support and opposition: (1) Supporters, (2) opponents, (3) the uncommitted, (4) those not yet involved.	Strategist
B. Communication of own preferences and solicitation of support.	Spokesman; Advocate
C. Initial negotiation (offering the exchange of positive and negative sanctions).	Mediator; Negotiator
D. Definite structuring of alternatives for overt decision-making.	Planner
E. Planning strategy for overt decision-making.	Strategist

---

[3] Erwin K. Scheuch, Ronald L. Nuttall, and Chad Gordon, "A Process Model of Community Decision-Making," (as yet in mimeographed form, Social Relations Department, Harvard University, Cambridge, Mass., 1965) and as presented by Chad Gordon in the political sociology section of the Eastern Sociological Association meetings, Philadelphia, April 1966, "Decision-Making Processes in the Cambridge NASA Proposal."

FIGURE 1 *(Continued)*

Process Step   *Related Informal Role*

F. Organizing the necessary personnel and their resources.   Organizer
   Potential outcome: transformation of proposals into issues
   and planning of decision-making process.

   IV. *Engaging in the Overt Decision-Making
       Processes* (possibly repeated at several
       levels or in other systems)

A. Acknowledgement of overt commitment and   Spokesman; Public
   responsibility.   Leader; "Figure-
       head"

B. Involving the total relevant audiences including manipu-   Propagandist; Ana-
   lation of meanings: (1) "horrible consequences," (2) "glori-   lyst; Pundit
   ous benefits," (3) the "real meaning," (4) information up-
   dating.

C. Exchange of support and sanctions (including procedural   Arbitrator
   and administrative facilitation or block).

D. Final negotiation.   Negotiator

E. Situated contingent action, committing the collectivity to   Facilitator; Blocker
   course of conduct.

F. Legitimation—*Potential outcome:* Debate of issues in rele-   Formal Authority
   vant audiences, and involvement of the collectivity for one   Roles; Sanctifier;
   course of action (or decision not to act).   Symbolic Leader;
       [Father Figure]

   V. *Carrying out the Consequences of Decision Process*

A. Implementation by designated persons or institutions.   [Formal Roles]

B. Final application of positive and negative sanctions   Enforcer; Hatchet
   (payoff).   Man

C. Appraisal of actors and power relations.   Social-Emotional
     Expert

D. Appraisal of action and consequences.   Pundit; Analyst;

E. Re-appraisal of program—*Potential outcome:* Re-structur-
   ing the meaning of a decision and re-institution of the   Critic; Evaluator
   process.

ACCESS TO RESOURCES

First, this paper considers the constitutive features of social resources. For purposes of this paper, a *sanction* is conceived of as anything which can be applied to a person, group or collectivity (an actor) which the given actor subjectively defines as rewarding or harmful, as a benefit or burden, as a "good thing" or "bad." We use the term *resource* to mean anything which allows one actor to control, provide, or apply a sanction (positive or negative) to another actor. Thus *sanctioning* is the actual *use of resources to reward or harm another*. Resources can, of course, be further classified, and one of the most important distinctions is the difference between consummatory and instrumental resources. However, for our purposes, anything an actor wants to obtain or experience (or seeks to avoid) is (for that actor, in that situation) a sanction, regardless of its instrumental or consummatory character.[4]

Among the most important social resources are those to which a member of a collectivity has access by virtue of his incumbency in an institutionalized status or office. The clearest case of this situation is *authority*, the legitimated "right" of the certified incumbent of a position to make binding commitments regarding the collectivity's policies and resources, and to direct the activities of his subordinates. The day-to-day activities of such officials are presumed to center on the application of positive sanctions (hiring and promotion, salary increases, praise and recommendations, allocation of funds, materials, and the like). But there is always the right of applying negative sanctions for noncompliance with the directives of those in a position of authority. These sanctions may vary in intensity from gentle reproofs through "firing" the subordinate to "taking legal action" or even to calling on those who in our societies have the authority to use physical coercion.

In addition to these resources, a person in a position of authority often has access to a frequently overlooked type of resource: *information* which an actor without this official position would have trouble obtaining. In many cases such privileged information can be a resource of great importance even in areas far from the position-holder's realm of authority. Other resources often associated with the incumbency in a position are the growth of *networks of friendship* and mutual cooperation with other actors.

It should be pointed out that the term authority is not restricted only to those at or near the top of the structure of a collectivity. Even the "underlings" in any collectivity have some measure of power, to the degree that they have legitimated authority (such as votes) even of narrow scope, informal support resources (such as cooperation and "effort") which they

---

[4] Important conceptualizations of the processes of exchange are found in the work of George C. Homans, *Social Behavior: Its Elementary Forms* (New York: Harcourt, Brace, 1961); Peter M. Blau, *Exchange and Power in Social Life* (New York: John Wiley & Sons, 1964); and Talcott Parsons, "On the Concept of Influence," *Public Opinion Quarterly*, 27 (1963), 37–62; and "On the Concept of Political Power," *Proceedings of the American Philosophical Society*, 107 (1963), 232–262.

may give or withhold, or access to such resources as information, knowledge, or friendship networks.[5]

We conceive of *"influencing the outcome of decision-making"* (or, more generally, "achieving results in interaction") as the most general form of a phenomenon, and in all cases based on access to some form of resources. Frequently these resources can be *directly* used to sanction (positively or negatively); here the actor possesses *power* to directly control outcomes. If this power (control) is *legitimated* we understand it to be *authority;* if it is not legitimated (as in an "unauthorized" threat or use of force or restraint) we have *coercion* and *deterrence.*

By *"direct"* resources we mean that the actor himself commands the events relevant for the particular mode of action, as, for example, the authorization of funds as a part of the powers of office that a mayor or city manager has. Of course, unauthorized actions also exist involving direct resources.[6]

In a great many cases of political interest, however, the relevant actors do not command direct resources, and must attempt to influence those who do, so that desired authoritative (and perhaps coercive) commitments will be made. In so far as an actor can influence another actor who does have direct resources, we call the influence of the first actor *indirect.* The resources of the actor in question are of an *indirect* character with respect to the actual event which is intended to take place (for instance, "official" approval of a site for urban renewal, award of a city contract, and the like).

Some of the important strategies in influencing are: (1) *persuasion* such as using facts, presumed expertise, reputation, or friendship; (2) *inducement* via using money, favors, or other material rewards; and (3) *invoking obligation* by appealing to commitments and shared norms. Less obvious strategies are (4) the *structuring* of the actual behavior alternatives open to the others (usually by ignoring other courses of action); (5) *manipulating the perception* of these alternatives (by emphasizing certain aspects of a proposal at the expense of other aspects, or by actual deception); (6) *diverting the other's attention* by raising irrelevant issues so as to preclude his taking unwanted action. Even (7) *coercion* by threatening or actually applying force and violence can be conceived as a strategy of influence, given the generality of our formulation.

---

[5] Talcott Parsons, "The Political Aspect of Social Structure and Process," as yet in mimeographed form, Social Relations Department Harvard University, Cambridge, Mass.: 1965, esp. p. 10 ff.

[6] Blau, *op. cit.*, esp. Chapter 8.

A further property of a resource is its *generality*. This term denotes the number of situations (or contexts) and actors for which the very same resource is effective in influencing. Resources differ drastically in their generality, from money which is applicable in most situations—and can thus be called by Parsons a "generalized medium"—to a refusal to cooperate by a specific office holder, or the withdrawal of affection which is effective only between two specific actors. We believe that in community decision-making most resources are rather specific, and lead to complications in bargaining.

From a preceding consideration we derive the following empirical proposition about an inverse relation between the generality of influence and the degree of direct or indirect access to resources: *Direct access to resources usually means that for the actor having direct access the resources are of limited generality; indirect access to resources implies that the resources can be employed more generally.* While indirect access may be a less certain form of control over a resource, it may also be traded more freely—and in case of illegitimate use, with greater impunity.

It will be apparent that our formulations regarding the nature of influence and its components owe much to the work of Talcott Parsons and Edward C. Banfield.[7] However we do not follow Parsons' restriction of the concept of "influence" to being the special medium of persuasion based on generalized features such as the prestige or reputation of the source. We prefer to use the concept of "influence" as including Parsons' notion of persuasion by presumed expertise or standing, but include also the other modes previously mentioned. In our usage "power" would be the more special category, with "influence" being the more general and inclusive one. We will reserve a discussion of the conceptual issues underlying these differences in terminology, as well as an argument over the contexts in which it seems meaningful to speak of "generalized media" for a subsequent paper.

The notion of "resource" used here is intentionally general: it includes such diverse items as control over votes, the ability to destroy or enhance reputations, or money. Also included are personal characteristics such as intelligence, expertise, a likeable personality, or ascriptive attributes such as race or sex.[8] Resource needs to be defined generally and with reference to effects in view of the character of social bargaining. Bargaining usually means trading a resource of one kind for a resource of another

---

[7] Parsons, "Influence," and "Power," *op. cit.*, and Edward C. Banfield, *op. cit.*

[8] Of course, the extent to which actors use their resources is of great importance. See for example, Dahl, *op. cit.*, 273–275.

kind, and this ability to exchange may be limited to a particular time and situation. The very specificity with which resources are effective demands an unspecific definition.

In any analysis of a power relationship, the transformability of a resource—or its generality—is of central importance. The degree of generality is, however, not merely a function of a specific issue, but also of the characteristics of the actors.

Our conceptualization of resource includes at least two actors: one of whom *possesses* a resource which allows him to sanction (positively or negatively) the second actor. This second actor will be called the *receptor* of the sanction. Receptor in this sense means simply the target of a sanctioning—whether actually applied or merely invoked. Since in the absence of a receptor a resource loses its effect, the characteristics of the receptor are seen as the prime determinant of a sanctioning situation. The presence of a potential receptor for a resource determines whether the actor controlling a resource has anything to control; the actor controlling the resource has mainly the choice to apply or withhold a sanction.

In real life each actor will usually have more than one resource, and quite often more than one type of resource. In addition, each actor usually has a larger amount of one type of resource than he does of another.

Once an actor attempts to influence the outcome of a decision-making sequence, the amount of influence he can bring to bear will depend on the mode of the resource which is relevant for a decision, and upon the presence or absence of receptors for his various types of resources. Of course the presence and strength of the actor's commitment is also a crucial variable, but one which we will not explicitly deal with at present.

THE MODE OF THE DECISION SITUATION

In analyzing a concrete situation it is essential to consider the mode or type of resources relevant to the particular decision. According to our notion that the mode of a resource may be specific to the decision under consideration, an actor's position in this category system for one decision may differ from his classification for another decision.

A diagnostic question to appraise the mode of a resource is: for a concrete issue, what is the commodity for which there are receptors who are ready to declare that upon invocation of the commodity, the decision process is resolved. Usually this question can be decided by looking at the criteria which the actors themselves use in inferring when a binding decision has been reached.

Each issue may move through several modes of decision. Most decisions may be "forgone conclusions" and hence of little interest. In many cases the outcome of the decision was really "up for grabs" in an informal mode decision and is then followed by a formal mode of decision as a ritual of ratification. In an analysis one must appraise which decision is really the crucial one for a particular issue.

For each decision situation, certain modes of resources are intrinsically more relevant than other modes of resources. The relevance of a resource depends on whether it can be used directly or at least exchanged for a resource which can be used in the ultimate decision of an issue. It should be noted that a particular mode may preclude the use of certain resources. For example, in many situations in the United States the use of force is generally precluded. In saying that a particular resource is generally precluded we mean that if an actor attempted to invoke sanctions related to this resource, other actors in the decision-making situation would react so strongly to this very invocation as to make the use of this resource unprofitable.

When an actor is in a situation where—at a particular time and place—his strongest resources are in the wrong mode, he may try to transform them into a more effective mode. Such a transformation is usually done by "exchanging" the actor's resources for those of another actor who has the desired type. Sanctioning in social bargaining parallels a barter economy, but it also contains elements of exchange of a more generalized and symbolic character.[9]

An example should clarify further the use and usefulness of this conceptualization. Several years ago a major university very much wished to influence the city council of its community. This university had very few of its members actually living and voting within the city limits, and thus could not exert much direct political pressure through voters. However, the university did have an exceedingly high prestige and status. By making the city councillors members of the university faculty club, the university allowed these men and their guests to use these prestigious facilities, thus allowing the city councillors to invoke the university prestige for their own purposes. In this way the university traded certain of its own resources (prestige and socially acceptable facilities) for different resources (political influence) via a change in the mode of its own resource "prestigious faculty club"; and without changing the mode in which prestige became available, the prestige as such would have remained quite irrelevant.

The analysis of a particular decision-making process (whether in the

---

[9] Parsons, "The Political Aspect," *op. cit.*, esp. p. 26. A related but appreciably different formulation may be found in Blau, *op. cit.*, Chapter 5.

political sector or an urban community or in other areas of social life) should take into account: (1) the types of resources each actor possesses, (2) the presence of receptors for them, and (3) the type or mode of resources which is crucial for the decision being made.

The degree to which an actor's resources can be exchanged or transformed into other types of resources is most important for his influence. It may be expected that the actor who has a very general resource (a resource which finds many receptors in a variety of situations), will have impact on more situations than the actor with a very narrow resource. For example, friendship with a specific office holder is of relevance in many fewer decision-making areas (saying, of course, nothing about their importance) than would be access to a resource such as a large block of votes or large funds of money or credit. When the particular office holder dies or leaves office, friendship with him is no longer of much value.

The distinction made here between the concepts of sanctioning and invoking a resource allows us to deal better with actual decisions. Actual sanctioning is only one and an extreme case in which a resource becomes effective. Very often a particular time is set aside for the actual exchange of sanctions, called here "the payoff." We believe that quite often such a "payoff" time is clearly recognized by the actors as a potential, separate phase in a particular decision-making sequence. Tactics in some situations are influenced by beliefs whether such a payoff time is certain to occur, and the maneuvering may largely be aimed at forcing the sequence to a payoff or trying to resist this. Clearly, decision-making is not tantamount to actual sanctioning, nor does the use of resources require payoff in order for them to be effective.

BELIEFS OF OTHERS THAT ACCESS TO RESOURCES EXISTS

The *invocation* of a resource occurs when an actor claims that he possesses a resource which would allow him to sanction. The other actors involved in a decision-making situation (receptors) may or may not credit him with the actual ability to control this resource. When the time for payoff comes, the actor may or may not actually have the ability to sanction with a resource he has invoked. Actors often *invoke* resources they do not actually control (bluffing), and some actors may actually *sanction* with resources which the other actors did not believe them to possess.

Usually, actual sanctions—if they are applied at all—occur at a much later stage in the decision-making process than do invocations. Thus those actors who invoke resources *and* are believed to possess them are able to influence the decision-making process at an earlier point in time than those actors who are not credited with the resources they claim. In many decision-making situations the process is partially irreversible, and in these cases the actors who can bring their influence to bear early in the process have a definite advantage. Accordingly, those actors whose invocation of a resource is accepted are in a much stronger position than those actors who must actually sanction before their influence is accepted.

A TYPOLOGY OF INFLUENTIALS

Reputation for controlling a resource and actual ability to do so were two aspects of influence that we specified as independent dimensions. For each of these dimensions we identified a number of correlates and implications. The interaction of these dimensions can best be visualized by having them intersect in a four-fold table. In this way we arrive at the definition of four types of influence situations.

The four-fold table of Figure 2 presents these four types of influence

		Perceived Access to Resource	
		yes	no
Actual Access to Resource	yes	(A) Manifest Influence	(B) Potential Influence
	no	(C) Reputed Influence	(D) Without Influence

FIGURE 2. A TYPOLOGY OF INFLUENTIALS

as a combination of the objective and subjective factors. The two cross-cutting dimensions are: (1) the actual ability to apply a resource in sanctioning if payoff time comes, and (2) the belief of the other actors that the actor possesses or controls the resource which would allow him to sanction.

Of course, this simple table is a vast abstraction from what reality is believed to be. Thus, the kind and the quantity of resources are ignored here; actors that are lumped together in one quadrant of this table may differ in this respect—and consequently in their influence. However, the interaction between reputation and fact that this table specifies does help to resolve some of the argument over the so-called reputational approach; it also will enable us by a process of simple deduction to arrive at some predictions about the effects of decision-making on a power structure itself.

FOUR TYPES OF INFLUENCE

Referring again to Figure 2, the four types of influentials can now be treated in more detail. Having a resource and being credited with having it is the most simple case (A); it may be called *Manifest Influence*. The combination of having access to a resource (whether the actor himself is aware of it or not) but *not* being credited with its possession (B) is here called *Potential Influence*.

Potential Influence—here somewhat redefined in terms of an intersection between two dimensions—has been the object of some heated debates. Dahl has (correctly, in our opinion) argued that potential power is usually ignored in discussions of power structures, and that ignoring it often leads to incorrect predictions.[10] Others such as Bierstedt have maintained that unless power is actually felt (here "invoked" and credited) it does not exist.[11] Our position in this argument becomes more clear from an inspection of cell (C) of Figure 2, referring to actors who are believed to have a resource, but do not actually possess it. It seems that Bierstedt would have to credit this type of actor with a higher degree of importance than the actor with Potential Influence, which may indeed be the case for the immediate decision, but perhaps not for long-term processes or for many issues. This intersection of not actually being able to sanction with a resource, but being credited with this ability nonetheless, is termed *Reputed Influence*. From this simple distinction between the situation of an actor with Reputed Influence and of an actor with Potential Influence, some propositions can be derived which otherwise might not be obvious.

We predict that, in general, *the less crucial the decision,*[12] *the more likely will holders of Reputed Influence be able to act* (*invoke credited resources*). This follows if one assumes that other things being equal the demand for a payoff (the actual sanctioning with resources) will be weaker, the less crucial a decision. Since the merely reputational character of influence will not become obvious until a payoff is required, actors with

---

[10] Robert A. Dahl, "The Concept of Power," *Behavioral Science*, 2 (1957), 201–214.

[11] Robert Bierstedt, "An Analysis of Social Power," *American Sociological Review*, 15 (1950), 730–738.

[12] How "crucial" a decision becomes depends on the properties of the issue and its relationship to the decision-making structures. The dimensions of the issue-properties and their inter-relationships cannot be treated in the present paper.

Reputed Influence will be able to invoke resources which they do not possess, and will be able to influence the decision process as if they had Manifest Influence. On the other hand, when decisions of a more crucial nature arise, all actors are more likely to be driven to the payoff stage. "Crucial" decisions will be those decisions which are perceived as setting precedents for further decisions. In these crucial situations, actors with Potential Influence, who did not invoke their resources (or whose invocations were not credited), *do* sanction with them. At this payoff stage it is *they* who are able to act (sanction) in a manner similar to those actors with Manifest Influence while actors with Reputed Influence must act like those Without Influence (cell D).

It was found that at a particular point in time and with respect to a particular decision-making event, each actor may be classified along these two dimensions: actual ability to sanction with resources, and perceived ability to sanction. When all important actors are so classified, the state of the decision-making system at that point in time is specified. When a decision comes up, each actor in three of the quadrants (A,B,C) are faced with two choices: they may invoke their resources or they may not. At a (usually) later point in time the actor may want to, or be asked to, "payoff" or actually apply sanctions. As a result of these actions (and in this context, inaction amounts to a form of action) a change of position of the actor within the category system may occur, in addition to influencing a decision.

ACTORS WITHOUT INFLUENCE

Apparently, the most simple case is that of actors Without Influence: for a given decision-making situation or decision-making structure he must remain without influence. However, through activities outside the immediate decision-making situation he can change his position by gaining resources or by shifting the issue (the more promising strategy) into another decision-making structure, or into another mode of decision-making. An example would be for a local person without influence to try involving Federal authorities in settling an issue. We predict that *it will be primarily the actors without influence who will try to change the mode or structure of a decision-making system.*

ACTORS WITH REPUTED INFLUENCE

The diagnosis of the consequences for an actor with Reputed Influence is now obvious. If an actor with Reputed Influence (cell C) does not attempt to sanction at payoff time, his position remains unaffected, and he can continue to invoke resources just as can an actor with Manifest Influence. However, if the actor with Reputed Influence is asked to or tries to use his resources at payoff time, their absence becomes manifest, and his position will change to that of an actor Without Influence (cell D).

By introducing as an additional variable the concept of "self-diagnosis of access to a resource," a simple prediction can be derived from this analysis: *if an actor is aware that his influence is essentially illusory, he will try to avoid a demand for pay-off sanctions.* This tendency to try to avoid payoff situations can often be noted when heretofore very powerful-seeming actors suddenly give in and make concessions rather than force the issue to where sanctions would have to be called in. If an actor with Reputed Influence sees himself as having a real choice between sanctioning and non-sanctioning, he is simply in error and does not realize his lack of resources.

The normative system with regard to acts of influence (sanctioning or invocation) is of course relevant for predicting concrete actions. We propose to include norms as one aspect of "access" to resources or as a resource themselves (for instance, pointing out past norm violations of an opposing actor; deciding to seek help by appealing to the courts). Rather than taking the normative system as only a system of constant coordinates in which the decisions are seen to occur, a concrete set of norms can be treated as one aspect that actors have to consider in a specific decision situation—or can even be viewed as a resource.

Given decision-making systems where crucial decisions occur frequently, we expect that few actors with Reputed Influence will be able to keep from being asked to payoff. Hence we predict: *the more numerous the crises, the lower the percentage of actors with merely Reputed Influence.*

A corollary of this proposition is that *in a decision-making system where few crucial decisions have occurred in the recent past, many actors will have merely Reputed Influence.* Consequently, when and if a crisis does hit a decision-making system with a history of few recent crises, we may expect sudden changes in the power positions of many actors. An example is the sudden reshuffling which occurs in a company upon the appointment of new top executives; here, many more issues are forced to the payoff stage.

We may also expect that *actors with merely Reputed Influence who have a correct self-diagnosis of their influence situation will act as a conservative force in the community.* Above all else, these actors must avoid situations which "get out of hand" and call for an exchange of actual sanctions. Other things being equal, these actors will make more of an effort to calm down and sooth a crisis before it reaches a payoff stage. This implies that *decision-making structures with few recent crises will tend to avoid crucial decisions* because there are more actors with Reputed Influence who are able to invoke resources and thus have an influence in these systems.

ACTORS WITH POTENTIAL INFLUENCE

The effects of Manifest Influence and Potential Influence become clearer by introducing an additional concept: the *permanency* of a resource. Resources may be thought to differ by the degree to which they are consumed in the act of sanctioning. Thus, a political debt is a resource, but an impermanent one: when the debt is called, it is often paid off and no longer exists. However, the control of a block of votes may usually be invoked and used as a sanction again and again. This distinction becomes especially useful in a dynamic analysis of influence structures, for example, if we are studying the effects of one decision event on the influence positions of the various actors for the next decision-process. Depending on the permanency of the resource, the application of sanctions may result in four different states of the influence position of an actor. Looking only at his original position, his position after a payoff cannot be predicted. We must know the permanency of his resources.

Provided a resource is recognized as permanent, its use to sanction at payoff time will cause the actor with Potential Influence to move to a position of Manifest Influence for the next decision. On the other hand, should the resource actually be consumed in the sanctioning but this fact not be recognized, after applying his sanction the actor with Potential Influence will move into a position of Reputed Influence.

Two further outcomes are possible. (1) If the resource is consumed and other actors understand that it is now gone, the actor moves from a position of Potential Influence to one Without Influence—*even though he was able to apply his sanction*. And finally, the application of a sanction may change nothing at all. (2) If it is believed that the resource was consumed while actually the resource was permanent, the actor remains in his position of Potential Influence. At the next decision he will again be able to sanction but not to invoke resources.

This delineation of the effects of sanctioning on a position of Potential Influence should have made it obvious that the impact and results of actually present but unacknowledged resources are most difficult to predict.

ACTORS WITH MANIFEST INFLUENCE

For actors with Manifest Influence, it is relatively easy to predict the consequences both for the decision-making process and for the categorical position of the actor himself when sanctions are not applied. Actors with Manifest Influence will affect the decision by invocation of resources; if no sanction need be applied, these actors will simply retain their position of Manifest Influence. A prognosis becomes more complicated if actors with Manifest Influence are asked to actually sanction at payoff time:

(1) If the resources of the actor with Manifest Influence are permanent and are recognized to be such, then their use to sanction will leave the actor with Manifest Influence.

(2) If the resource is permanent, but other actors believe it to have been consumed in the sanctioning, the actor with Manifest Influence moves to a position of Potential Influence after applying his sanction.

(3) If the resource is consumed but not known to be, the actor is left with only Reputed Influence.

(4) If the resource is used up and this is known, the actor moves directly from having Manifest Influence to being Without Influence.

Thus, depending on whether the resource is dissipated or not, and whether this information is known or not, the actor with Manifest Influence will be in any of the four influence positions after actual sanctionings are exchanged. Given a knowledge of the actor's self-diagnosis of his resource position, we may be able to predict his strategy in a given decision process. Given a knowledge of communication patterns in a decision-making structure, we may be in a position to predict the definitions and perceptions of other actors.

GENERAL HYPOTHESES ABOUT
ACTUAL SANCTIONING

If certain restrictive assumptions are introduced, further propositions can now be formulated. Let us assume for the moment that actors are primarily motivated not to increase their influence but merely to maintain it. We can then predict that *whenever there is a choice to sanction or not, the rank order of readiness to sanction would be: (1) actors with Potential Influence, (2) actors with Manifest Influence, and (3) actors with Reputed Influence. For all actors, the tendency to sanction will be lower the less permanent are their resources.*

Let us now recall the earlier observations about actors with Manifest Influence and with Reputed Influence. For these influence positions a prognosis was much easier if sanctions merely needed to be invoked; a prognosis required more information about self-diagnosis of actors, and about the perceptions of alters whenever actual payoff occurred. Actual sanctioning was a situation to be avoided anyway by actors with merely Reputed Influence. From this follows: *except for actors with the goal to increase influence, all actors will tend to avoid payoff, unless an avoidance of sanctioning would imply a loss of influence.* And, *the main condition under which payoff is chosen as the normal strategy by all other types of actors is against actors who are suspected of having only Reputed Influence.* Other things equal, *the suspicion that the influence of other actors may be merely Reputed will increase, the longer the time since the previous payoff.*

In all these propositions we did not specify the permanency of resources. *If there is a mutually perceived asymmetry in the permanency, then the actor with the more permanent resource will tend to push sanctioning to the payoff state.*

Whether payoff occurs or does not occur is also dependent on the generality of a resource. The less general a resource, the fewer the options. Given the fact that not to sanction may often mean that henceforth an actor's influence is suspected of being Reputed, his inaction after having invoked a resource may cause other actors to force him to a payoff next time. The loss of influence resulting from not accepting a challenge to actually sanction is greater, the less general a resource. An actor with a narrow resource who could actually sanction this time may find that next time his resource may not cover the new decision-making situation. Therefore we conclude: *The more general a resource, the greater the chance that a challenge to actually pay-off will not be accepted; the more specific a resource, the more likely the actual sanctioning after a challenge has been extended.*

Our classification is based on a distinction between perceived and actual access to a resource. Errors in perception do not merely occur in the diagnosis of an influence situation; they are just as likely in judging the permanency of a resource. This type of error modifies the earlier proposition that a change in the power status of actors after payoff is more likely if there has been a time-lapse since the last open conflict. The variable "perception of permanency" makes it possible that the outcome of a payoff is a new disparity between perception and actual access to resource. This likelihood depends on the extensiveness with which sanctions are exchanged. Therefore: *the longer the exchange of sanctions continues in a given conflict situation, the more likely is the reduction of influence positions to the two positions of Manifest Influence and Without Influence.* And: *A single round of exchange of sanctions does not increase the stability of an influence structure; an extended exchange of sanctioning does.*

Finally, the readiness to engage in actual payoff depends on the readiness of all involved to perceive a chance that they may benefit from an exchange of actual sanctions. Under the condition of complete information, an actual exchange of sanctions becomes largely unnecessary since all concerned agree on the outcome. Conversely, the readiness to engage in payoff is heightened by actual ignorance or error due to a lack of information. Therefore we conclude: *Other things equal, the better the communication in a given decision-making structure, the less likely is the occurrence of actual pay-off. Lack of communication and lack of actual precision in a situation increase the likelihood that challenges to actually engage in sanctioning will occur.*

INCOMPLETENESS OF THE MODEL

In discussing this scheme of types of influence, reference has been made to whether an actor was "believed" or "not believed" to have access to resources. However, *who* does the believing has not been specified. There may, in fact, be considerable disagreement among the actors about the influence status of a particular individual, organization, or group. Moreover, by the nature of the resources involved and the mode of the decision-making situations, an actor can have a resource for some actors in some conditions, but not have a resource wanted by other actors or in other conditions.

The spelling out of the implications of the full model cannot be done in one paper. This paper is merely intended to suggest an approach in a relatively simple form.

This approach has advantages for empirical research on decision-making. One advantage is the clear distinction between variables referring to objective conditions (access to resource, nature of resource, mode of decision-making), and those variables which are part of the belief systems of the actors (credibility of resource, self-diagnosis of access to resources).

The outside investigator must determine these variables as best he can and will generally have less precise measures of the belief system variables.

It should be emphasized that this typology of influence is only one aspect of our developing theory of community decision-making. Decision-making can be seen as a process with a proposal or *issue* passing through many stages before being finally accepted and acted upon, rejected, or left dormant and unresolved. Accordingly, a model of stages in decision-making has been specified plus a system of properties of issues.

Moreover, we see the community as being faced with many issues at any one time, and with each issue continuing for a period of time. Thus decisions are being made often and are being made at various stages in the development of several issues. Who is involved in each decision varies greatly with the issue and with its stage in a decision process. The model presented in this paper is useful in the analysis of each decision on each issue at each stage. However, the model is far from complete. Its use and potential usefulness even in the simple form in which it was presented here—together with a number of propositions following more or less tautologically—shall now be shown by applying it to a concrete case.

AN APPLICATION OF THE MODEL: The Defeat of Urban Renewal in Cambridge, Massachusetts

This model will now be applied to our work on the community decision-making structure of Cambridge, Mass. During the summer of 1962, an urban renewal proposal was defeated in the Cambridge City Council by a tie 4–4 vote. The analysis of this defeat and of the surrounding issue of urban redevelopment can exemplify the use of the present model.

This particular urban renewal issue involves four separate decision processes. These four stages have been called the Planning, the Defeat, Reformulation, and Acceptance. The first stage was the planning and development of the particular proposal, the Donnelly Field project. Plans for this project originated in the later part of 1957. Yet the first public hearing was held on June 2, 1961. During the three and a half years before this public hearing and during the year following this first hearing, the Donnelly Field urban renewal plans were worked out by the Cambridge Redevelopment Authority. The actors whose invocations of resources were accepted and who thus were able to influence the development of these plans were, in addition to the Cambridge Redevelopment Authority, the federal Housing and Home Finance Agency, the Mayor and City Manager, and the union which was to own and operate the new buildings. However, the people living in the area concerned were not included in these deliberations and indeed their attempts to invoke their resources and influence were rebuffed.

In terms of the model, this decision process was officially defined as administrative, with the generally relevant resources being those of official position, legitimate authority, expert knowledge, and legal sanction. Political resources were allowed to enter only by accepting the invocations of the resources of the Mayor and the City Manager. The support of the Mayor, who was reputed never to have lost a vote in the City Council, was deemed sufficient political backing. All other actors who attempted to invoke political resources were not credited with sufficient resources to bring any relevant sanctions to bear.

The actors then, who were allowed to have an influence on the decision process (having manifest influence or reputed influence) were the Cambridge Redevelopment Authority, the CIO union which was to build and own the redevelopment housing, several major businessmen and bankers in Cambridge, the City Manager, and the Mayor. As will be seen later, the latter two actors actually had part or all of their influence based on reputation, not on control of resources.

Those whose invocations were not accepted were the small businessmen whose stores and shops were in the area to be renewed, the people who lived in the area, a small Lithuanian Catholic church whose parish was included in the renewal area, and most members of the City Council. All of these actors did indeed have the ability to sanction with their resources and thus were, at this point, actors with potential influence. As it became apparent this group was quite large.

We consider the first stage of the decision-making process to have been completed with the formal presentation of the developed plans for the Donnelly Field urban renewal project. Figure 3 illustrates the categorization of the various actors.

The exchange of sanctions began with the formal presentation of the plans. The small businessmen, homeowners, and religious leaders of the area began a public campaign against the announced plans. Of those supporting the plans, only the Mayor and the City Manager had any political resources with which to return the fire of the opponents. The resources of expertise, authority and money of the other actors who had had influence in the development of the plans found no receptors in the public debate. As the public controversy continued and as the dissident actors began to involve new publics and to gain allies in other parts of the city, the Mayor came out strongly for the renewal plans, thereby placing

		Other's Perceptions	
		Actor was believed to have resources.	Actor was *not* believed to have resources.
Actual Access	Actor had the resources.	(A) *Manifest Influence* Cambridge Redevelopment Authority Federal Housing and Home Finance Agency CIO Union	(B) *Potential Influence* People in area Small businessman in area Lithuanian Priest City Councillors
	Actor did *not* have the resources.	(C) *Reputed Influence* Mayor City Manager	(D) *Without Influence* People in other parts of Cambridge

FIGURE 3. The Planning Stage. The Influence Position of Actors Involved in Planning the Urban Renewal Project

his prestige on the line. During the development of the plans the resources of time, effort, and political organization of the dissident actors were in the wrong mode to affect the administrative decision process. Now, however, the issue had moved out of the administrative mode and into a new mode for the next decision.

Federal law requires that the urban renewal plans in each community be approved by the governing body of the locality. For Cambridge this body was the City Council. For a decision-process involving a City Council, it is only resources which can be brought to bear on the votes of the councillors which can have an influence. This second decision process allowed much greater scope to the political resources of the opponents of the urban renewal project, and the opponents began to invoke these resources to influence the vote of the councillors. Protest meetings were held, public statements were made, and meetings of the City Council were thronged with residents and businessmen from the area, almost all strongly opposed to the plans.

One of the most powerful pleas against the urban renewal plan was made by a priest from the small Lithuanian Catholic church. Arguing on moral grounds, the opponents of the renewal plan noted that the present residents of the area were paying average rents of about $42 per month, while the lowest rents for the new units to be built would be $55 with the majority of the new rents near $75 per month. Obviously the people displaced by the renewal program would not be able to return and live in the new apartments. Small businessmen would be given only a small amount of money to move and many would be forced out of business by the project.

The Cambridge City Council has two major factions, the "Independents" and the Cambridge Civic Association (CCA) councillors. The CCA is a non-partisan political action group committed to "good government." Although the city operates on a proportional representation system and all councillors were elected at-large, various councillors do in fact represent various areas in the city. The councillors allied with the CCA in general hold the viewpoints of the upper socioeconomic groups, the Protestants, and of the universities (M.I.T. and Harvard). The "Independent" councillors usually represent various ethnic and working-class constituencies. At this time there were among the Independents two councillors representing working-class Irish-American constituents, one representing working-class Italian-American people, and one Jewish councillor. Among the CCA-endorsed councillors were an Italian-American and an Irish-American, both Harvard graduates and both representing predominently middle class points of view. In addition, a middle class Jewish housewife and two other councillors were endorsed by the CCA. Because the Jewish population of Cambridge is too small to support two councillors, they both depended on other minority groups, especially the Negroes, for electoral support.

Since five of the councillors were associated with the CCA and part of the ideology of the CCA's "good government" platform was that urban renewal was "a good thing," it was confidently expected by most observers that the Donnelly Field proposal would pass with little trouble. However, the public outcry following the final presentation of the plans put considerable political pressure on the council. The pressure came not only from the people to be immediately affected by the proposal, but also from Negroes and low income groups in other parts of the city. These other people were afraid that they too would be displaced out of the city by future urban renewal programs. The two Jewish councillors received the strongest pressure since they depended on the Negro vote as well as the vote of other minorities. In addition, the moral appeal by the Lithuanian priest was said to have been very persuasive for these two councillors.

Counter invocations of resources were built up as the day of the final vote approached. The CCA threatened not only to stop supporting but to actively oppose anyone who voted against urban renewal. The Federal Housing and Home Finance Agency threatened to withdraw its support for all urban renewal programs in the city if the Donnelly Field proposal was defeated. This move, it was widely pointed out, would cost the city twenty million dollars in federal funds.

The final decision rested on the vote of one councillor, the CCA-endorsed Jewish housewife; she finally voted against the urban renewal plan. After the defeat of the proposal the sanctions invoked were applied. The deciding councillor chose not to run for office again, since to do so would involve running against the CCA organization and would have resulted in almost certain defeat. The federal agency withdrew its twenty million dollars from Cambridge.

Analysis of the then surprising defeat of urban renewal in terms of the model reveals that one of the causes was that the Federal agency's resources were in the wrong mode. Expertise and large funds did not impress the councillors, who were more concerned with the votes of their constituents in the coming election. The agency had money, but was prevented by law from using it to buy votes; no receptor, other than the city as a whole, existed for their sanction.

The political resources of the CCA were counter-balanced by the political force of the working-class Irish, Italians and especially the working-class Negroes in the city. Had the crucial councillor voted *for* urban renewal, she probably would have been as equally certain of defeat at the polls. Given this political balance, it is said that the moral suasion of the Lithuanian priest, invoking the norms of fairness and good will to the poor, finally carried the day. In this instance, access to the resource of the moral norms of the community was decisive.

Because the decision was in the City Council, the official support by the City Manager (who could not vote) was worthless, as was the technical knowledge of the staff of the Cambridge Redevelopment Authority. These actors were Without Influence on this decision. The most important outcome, however, was that the Mayor, reputedly always able to carry the City Council, was shown to have part of his influence only reputed. Indeed it was said that this defeat was the greatest he had ever suffered.

The influence positions of the various actors for this vote in the City Council are presented in Figure 4. As indicated, the Cambridge Redevelopment Authority, the Federal Housing and Home Finance Agency, and the CIO Union were all Without Influence in this decision because their resources were in the wrong mode. They could not find acceptors for their resources in this situation. Many actors whose claims of resources and whose influence attempts had been turned down in the previous administrative decisions now had Manifest Influence. Their resources were seen to exist and many of the councillors were receptors for these political resources. The usually powerful Cambridge Civic Association had, in this

| | | Other's Perceptions | |
		Actor was believed to have resources.	Actor was *not* believed to have resources.
Actual Access	Actor had the resources.	(A) *Manifest Influence* City Councillors People in area; Lithuanian Priest Small businessmen in area People in other parts of Cambridge, especially Negroes	(B) *Potential Influence* Large businessmen in area
	Actor did *not* have the resources.	(C) *Reputed Influence* Cambridge Civic Association Mayor	(D) *Without Influence* Cambridge Redevelopment Authority Federal Housing and Home Finance Agency CIO Union

FIGURE 4. The Defeat. The Influence Positions of Actors Involved in Cambridge City Council Vote on the Urban Renewal Project in Summer 1962

particular situation, only reputed influence. Their support caused an automatic opposition by other groups in the electorate, and the opposition of the CCA was automatically countered by the support of others. Given this situation, the CCA found itself unable to actually deliver their sanctions, defeat or election at the polls.

The large businessmen in the area to be renewed were still ignored in the proceedings. It will be noted that these businessmen with potential influence were able to have influence only in the fourth phase of the urban renewal issue.

After the defeat of the urban renewal proposal the second decision on this issue had been made. The issue was then returned to the Cambridge Redevelopment Authority for redrafting and replanning. This reformulation consumed the next three years and constituted the third decision process for this issue.

During this third decision-making process the actors had very different influence positions from those they held during the first. Now the people in the area, the Lithuanian Priest, and the small businessmen of the area were in positions of Manifest Influence. These people or their representatives sat on a newly created Citizens Advisory Committee which worked with the Cambridge Redevelopment Authority in the replanning process. The people in the area were regularly polled on the urban renewal plans and the effects they would have on each house were discussed with the owner and/or resident of the house. The plans themselves were much modified in this process. Emphasis was given to repairing and restoring houses wherever possible. Great efforts were made to tear down only buildings which were beyond repair and only where the owner was willing. Not all wishes of all people were respected, of course, since some owners did object to the plans for their property. This dissatisfaction was kept to a minimum however, and the great majority of the people in the area supported the revised plans.

Most heavily hurt by the new plans were the several large warehousing and manufacturing properties in the area. Small retail shops, however, were unmolested. One area alongside a railroad track was owned by a few large businessmen who had their own redevelopment plans. This area was intended to be taken to be given to the businessmen displaced from the residential areas of the project.

The actors involved in this third decision were categorized in Figure 5. It should be noted that the City Councillors and the large businessmen were not allowed to invoke their resources during this re-formulation stage even though an observer would have concluded that they really did have the resources to sanction if necessary.

In the summer of 1965 the redrafted plans were again submitted to the City Council for approval. Several public hearings were held. At these hearing the Citizens Advisory Committee took the center of the stage in support of the new plans, and the men of the Cambridge Redevelopment Authority kept well in the background. The opposition to the new plans consisted mostly of the large businessmen whose property along the railroad tracks was to be taken, and two councillors from other parts of Cambridge whose constituents were still concerned that future urban renewal plans would affect them. The two opposing councillors had Manifest Influence to the extent of their own votes and in their ability to summon hostile witnesses and to sharply question favorable witnesses.

However it was only the large businessmen who were really concerned. They came to the hearing room well supported with their lawyers. These actors realized that according to the federal law the legality of taking these businessmen's lands could be contested. In fact the businessmen

		Other's Perceptions	
		Actor was believed to have resources.	Actor was *not* believed to have resources.
Actual Access	Actor had the resources.	(A) *Manifest Influence* Cambridge Redevelopment Authority Mayor; City Manager People in area Lithuanian Priest Small businessmen in area Federal Housing and Home Finance Agency CIO Union	(B) *Potential Influence* City Councillors Large businessmen in area People in other parts of Cambridge
	Actor did *not* have the resources.	(C) *Reputed Influence*	(D) *Without Influence* Cambridge Civic Association

FIGURE 5. THE REFORMULATION. THE INFLUENCE POSITIONS OF ACTORS INVOLVED IN REFORMULATION OF THE URBAN RENEWAL PROJECT

invoked this legal resource and said that if the plans were not changed, they would take the matter to court. With respect to the council vote the businessmen were in a very weak position because these businessmen did not have control of very many votes while the supporters of the proposal now had the great support of the voters.

In this case, however, the businessmen were able to find a receptor for their sanctions. The mayor, who had seen his mistaken political judgment delay the project for three years, did not wish to see the issue carried to yet another decision process especially not one in the new mode of court action. While there were thus votes enough to carry the issue as it was formulated, the mayor delayed the final vote for a week to work out a compromise with the large businessmen. According to our model this final compromise may be seen as a fifth phase of the decision-making process on this issue and will not be analyzed here. In essence the mayor's compromise involved bringing in the large businessmen into the deliberations for actually implementing the plans. Thus these businessmen, by invoking their legal resources, were able to have their status shifted from Potential

		Other's Perceptions	
	Actor had the resources.	Actor was believed to have resources.	Actor was *not* believed to have resources.
Actual Access		(A) *Manifest Influence* Mayor City Councillors People in area Lithuanian Priest Small businessmen in area People in other parts of Cambridge	(B) *Potential Influence* Cambridge Civic Association
	Actor did *not* have the resources.	(C) *Reputed Influence* Cambridge Redevelopment Authority	(D) *Without Influence* Federal Housing and Home Finance Agency

FIGURE 6. The Acceptance. The Influence Positions of Actors Involved in Cambridge City Council Vote on the Replanned Urban Renewal Project in Summer 1965 (Stage 4)

Influence to that of Manifest Influence even though they could not have influenced the City Council vote. The positions of the actors before the mayor's final action are presented in Figure 6.

DISCUSSION AND CONCLUSION

We have presented a model of influence for actors involved in decision processes. This model has been applied to one issue in Cambridge, Massachusetts. This example has illustrated how actors can change their influence positions as an issue moves through several decisions and how the mode of the decision process greatly affects the influence of various actors. When actors demonstrate that they have resources, such as the public campaign against the urban renewal project waged by the residents of the area, they can move from potential to manifest influence. When sanctions fail or become unworkable, such as was the case for the Cambridge Civic Association and the federal Housing and Home Finance Agency, the actor can move from his Manifest or Reputed Influence position to one of being Without Influence.

The analysis of the example also illustrates how the actors can use the threat of shifting an issue into another decision situation, such as the courts, as an invocation of a resource. It should be noted that the expectation of the likely effects of such a shifting of the issue can be a powerful resource in itself.

This example also enabled us to test certain propositions. We noted in the description that the mayor was reputed for a long period not to have lost any important vote in the city council; in addition, for a long time there had been no major issue in the city council involving several segments of the social structure. From this information we postulated that the influence position of many actors (or action groups) would be incorrectly assessed. Indeed, the real test of strength resulted in a change of the power position of a great number of actors. It is our expectation that the manifest influence and the without influence positions are usually the most stable and that over time more actors will be found in those two categories than in the potential and reputed influence positions.

This proposition can be further generalized to the notion of a "life cycle" for actors. It begins with the emergence from a position without influence into a position of potential influence; potential influence turns into manifest influence when a properly chosen test of strength arises; manifest influence turns into reputed influence as the strength is declining or incorrectly generalized from successful applications; and reputed influence changes to a position of without influence as the illusory character of influence becomes apparent. We suggest that this general counter-clockwise drift will go faster in decision-making systems with many crucial decisions, with many payoff times, and more slowly in less hectic times with fewer forced payoff times. These propositions will be tested in further application of the model.

APPLICATION OF THE INFLUENCE MODEL
IN COMPARATIVE ANALYSIS

This model is basically a framework to guide the empirical study of specific communities. Given a community and an issue the investigator can then examine the resource positions of the various actors and the perceived resource positions and reach a classification of the actors in that community with respect to that decision-making process.

Our own work is continuing in the development and use of instruments and techniques for analyzing issues in different communities. Of special interest to us are the development of procedures for informant selection. At present we use a combination of positional, snowball, and random selection. In brief, people in positions of knowledge such as editors or city reporters on newspapers, and office holders, especially past office holders are interviewed. They mention people whom we follow up in a second and subsequent waves of interviews (the snowball technique). To check the possible bias of our original positional informants we also select a small random sample as an alternate base for our snowball technique.

In our interviews great attention is paid to the resources which the variously mentioned people or organizations can bring to bear. We specifically attempt to find out how the resources match up with the modes of the decision-making situations which the issues of interest go through. The greatest difficulties are in identifying the potential influence actors.

However it is possible to use the model in a much less detailed fashion. When nationwide policies are being considered, such as the Office of Economic Opportunity Community Action Programs, where many communities are involved it is too expensive to study more than a few of them in great detail. We believe that certain expectations can be held with respect to some of the parameters of the model using only the data from the communities which is readily available.

Starting with the data from the 1960 Census as recorded in the *City and County Data Book 1962*, Hadden and Borgatta have constructed a twelve dimensional typology of American cities based on a sequence of factor analytic studies.[13] These twelve dimensions are: (1) Total Population, (2) % Single dwelling units, (3) Density, (4) Median Income, (5) Deprivation Index, (6) % Nonwhite, (7) % Foreign Born, (8) Median Age, (9) % Population Increase, 1950–1960, (10) % Same House 1955–1960, (11) % Migrants, and (12) Educational Center. All of these variables are single items chosen to represent aspects of the factorial structure except for the Deprivation Index and the Educational Center dimensions. These indices are obtained by equally weighting other variables, per cent living in group quarters and per capita employed in education for Educational Center for example.

Decile position on each dimension of some 679 cities on the twelve dimensions are presented by Hadden and Borgatta. From these tables it is possible to find the twelve-dimensioned profile of any of these cities. Using the Influence Model it is possible to make predictions about the decision-making processes in communities with different profiles.

Probably the most important dimension is that of size, or total population. For community decision-making processes we can assume that the

---

[13] Jeffrey K. Hadden and Edgar F. Borgatta, *American Cities: Their Social Characteristics* (Chicago: Rand McNally & Co., 1965), Chapter IV, pp. 67–100.

larger the city the more will the influence wielders draw their resources from within the community itself. That is, people with contacts to the state, federal, or other nearby cities will be relatively less important in the larger cities than in the smaller. Conversely, in the smaller cities and towns many of the most important actors will be liaison men with outside governments, industries, or other resource bases. This is most likely to be the case for the initiation of issues. Ideas are more likely to come from outside in the smaller communities, more likely to be indigenous to the larger communities.

A curvilinear relationship between the adequacy of the communication networks and total size can be expected. The larger communities will have well developed mass communication networks of radio stations and local newspapers. The very small communities will have relatively good word of mouth networks. The medium size communities, with populations from 10,000 to 200,000, will have neither effective mass nor effective informal communication networks. Since our proposition is that "the better the communication in a decision-making structure, the less likely is the occurrence of actual payoff," crises can be expected to reach the stage of mutual exchanges of sanctions more often in the intermediate size communities than in either the larger or the smaller cities.

The complexity of the decisions to be made and the complexity of the decision-making structure is likely to increase with the total population. The result should be an increase in the number of receptors for resources of expert knowledge and technical expertise in the larger cities. The specialists should be having relatively more influence in the larger cities than in the smaller. Very often the experts available in the smaller communities will also be "outsiders" and hence have less impact on that account.

The second most important factor derived from the Hadden and Borgatta work was socioeconomic status, which is represented by the two dimensions of median income and Deprivation Index. Looking first at median income, those cities with a higher income should have a larger proportion of their population able to exert leadership. The implication is that many people will be potential influentials, that they will have the resources of organizational ability, wealth and education to be able to play important sanctioning roles if they become aroused. In the poorer communities there would be fewer potential influentials having these personal resources.

The manifest influentials and the reputational influentials who actively control the decisions in the wealthy communities are likely to be careful of arousing the concern of the large group of potential influentials. This concern can be expected to be translated into decisions which take greater account of "the public interest" in the well-to-do communities. In general the wealthier communities should be better managed because of this concern for the potential influence of the citizens. Obviously this major effect is likely to be contaminated by the wealthier community's greater ability to pay for good government.

However a similar effect, greater numbers of people with organizational ability and knowledge leading to potential influence, should also be true for communities which are high on the Educational Center dimension. Thus Educational Centers should also, in general, have decisions made more "in the public interest" and be better managed than similar communities which are not Educational Centers.

With increased numbers of potential influentials in wealthy or Educational Center communities we should expect that some will not remain merely "potential" but will move to the "manifest" category. With a plethora of people with high quality personal resources it should be difficult to maintain an oligarchic system of manifest influentials. Hence the Dahl type of community where leadership shifts with the issues and over time should be more likely in communities which are wealthy or are educational centers while the Hunter type of oligarchic control would be more prevalent in less well-to-do and less strongly Educational Centers. The total size of the community should enter here in an interactive fashion with the smaller communities more influenced by the wealth or educational center factors than the larger communities, but the very smallest communities would perhaps be able to maintain oligarchic control even if they were well-to-do or educational centers.

One of the areas in which the model is incomplete is in the specification of the "interest" of the actors in a community. Obviously if all actors in the community were in agreement as to which way decisions should go there would be very little to study. However, when and why actors will oppose each other has not been dealt with. At a very elementary level it can be argued that when people differ from each other on one set of variables, they are likely to differ on others as well. So when a community has a high proportion of nonwhites or a high per cent foreign born, we can expect that it will be more likely to have built-in conflicts of interest than communities which are more homogeneous. Similarly, when the Deprivation Index of a community is high it can be expected that there will be stronger built-in conflicts of interest than when the Deprivation Index is low. It can be argued that conflicts of interest based on race, national origin, or economic deprivation are likely to be relatively intractable.

Intractable conflicts of interests should result in more issues being pushed to the payoff stage. Community conflicts are likely to be more intense and there should be relatively few actors with reputed influence. In communities with high proportions of nonwhites, foreign born, or with high Deprivation Indexes, we can expect periodic crises and exchanges of sanctions. The people with influence are likely to have demonstrated that they had the resources to sanction. These communities are also likely to be composed of many people without influence, who have conflicts of interests with those who do have influence. When conditions, such as outside help or economic or educational improvement give these people resources, there is likely to be a series of confrontations. Unlike communities with high median incomes or Educational Centers, there should be few actors with potential influence or with reputed influence but many without influence or with manifest influence in direct proportion to the control of resources.

The issues around which community tensions develop should be specific to the nature of the minority group, nonwhites, foreign born, or economically deprived.

Three of the Hadden and Borgatta dimensions can be seen as related to the stability of the community. The greater the per cent of migrants, the greater the population increase and the fewer people in the same house in the last five years the less stable the community. Communities which are stable should have fewer issues carried to the payoff stage of exchanging sanctions. Thus, in communities with only moderate population increase, or a population decrease, communities with few immigrants, and communities with few people shifting their residences should have few community conflicts. The implication is that many actors have only reputed influence, so if and when a crisis hits, these communities are likely to see a radical sweeping out of familiar influentials.

The less stable communities should have many more and much more frequent exchanges of sanctions but each one will find few reputed influentials to discredit and so the decision-making structures will be more stable. Thus elections can be expected to be more vigorously contested in communities with rapid increase in population, with much home switching, and with many migrants. However, after a period of time the same manifest influentials will continue to be presesent, each with his influence closely related to his resource position.

In brief, this section has indicated how the Influence Model can be used to make predictions in a comparative analysis of communities. The empirical confirming or infirming of these hypotheses awaits further work.

VII

COMMUNITY STRUCTURE AND
DECISION-MAKING OUTCOMES

17

A COMPARATIVE STUDY
OF DECISION MAKING
IN RURAL COMMUNITIES

KENNETH KAMMEYER
University of California, Davis

[This paper reports on a comparative study of community decision making. One hundred and ten small communities constituted the cases analyzed. All communities had voted on school district reorganization proposals which would have had the effect of discontinuing the local high school. Relationships were found between several demographic and ecological variables and the degree to which community members expressed opposition to the discontinuance of the local high school.]

Decision making on both the individual and group level has become an increasingly important area for social research.[1] Among rural sociologists the decisions of individuals to adopt new products and practices have received considerably more attention than decisions made by groups or collectivities. Encompassed in this latter category is the area of community decision making which we can define as the process of making choices among alternative courses of action which will change or maintain community-wide institutions.[2] The study reported in this paper focuses on the decisions made by a number of small communities located in an essentially rural setting.

From a methodological perspective it has been pointed out repeatedly in recent years that the comparative approach must be utilized more fully

---

[1] For a comprehensive interdisciplinary bibliography covering the work on this subject up to 1958, see Paul Wasserman and Fred S. Silander, *Decision Making, An Annotated Bibliography* (Ithaca, N.Y.: Graduate School of Business and Public Administration, Cornell University, 1958).

[2] Everett M. Rogers, *Social Change in Rural Society* (New York: Appleton-Century-Crofts, 1960), p. 145, and Peter H. Rossi, "Community Decision Making," *Administrative Science Quarterly*, I (1957), 415–417.

in the study of communities.[3] Through comparative community research it will be possible to develop generalizations about communities and, thereby build a systematic theory of communities. For example, Reiss has suggested that a number of communities which have faced or are facing a similar decision, such as fluoridation, school consolidation, or school desegregation, may be studied to determine whether or not there is any association between community attributes and the kind of decision made.[4] It was with this methodological consideration in mind that we studied the decisions of 110 small Iowa communities on the issue of high school district reorganization.

THE RESEARCH PROBLEM

In many states there has been a continuing effort by state educational authorities to eliminate existing small school districts, which are believed to be both inadequate and inefficient. In particular, efforts have been directed toward the elimination of the small, one-room-school district and the small rural community high school. The closing of the small high school has usually been effected through school district reorganization or consolidation. By combining two previously existing high school districts, it is frequently possible to eliminate the high school attendance center in one district. From the point of view of the members of one of the communities, the net result of such reorganization is the loss of their high school.

In this study the focus is on the community decision whether or not to discontinue the local community high school. This decision is made when community members vote on the question of whether to *accept* or *reject* a school district reorganization proposal which would, *if accepted*, have the effect of discontinuing their high school as an attendance center.

PREVIOUS RESEARCH

Through the years there have been numerous attempts to determine the factors which create opposition to school district reorganization. Educators, political scientists, economists, and sociologists have all given some

---

[3] Albert J. Reiss, Jr., "Some Logical and Methodological Problems in Community Research," *Social Forces*, XXXIII (1954), 51; Albert J. Reiss, Jr., "The Sociological Study of Communities," *Rural Sociology*, XXIV (1959), 126; Rossi, *op. cit.*; Robin Williams, Jr., Burton R. Fisher, and Irving L. Janis, "Educational Desegregation as a Context for Basic Social Science Research," *American Sociological Review*, XXI (1956), 582.

[4] Reiss, "The Sociological Study of Communities," p. 126.

attention to this question. Various lists of such "deterrent factors" have been compiled, sometimes on the basis of systematic research but more frequently on the basis of *Verstehen*. From a methodological point of view the empirical studies have not varied greatly. Either through the use of interviews or questionnaires variously constituted panels of "knowledge-able" people have been asked which factors they *perceive* as most impor-tant. The consensus of their *perceptions* has been taken as evidence of the relative importance of these factors.

THE RESEARCH PROCEDURE

Our objective was to analyze the relationships between a number of demographic and ecological characteristics of communities and the *degree* to which members of the community opposed high school district reorgani-zation proposals. The cases in this study include 110 Iowa communities, each of which voted on a reorganization proposal between 1956 and 1959. Each reorganization proposal provided for closing the high school in the community and sending the students to school in a neighboring town. In order to facilitate communication the community which was to close its high school will be referred to hereafter as the "losing community" and the community which was to receive the students from the closing high school will be called the "gaining community." To avoid confusion it should be noted that the term "losing community" refers to the proposed loss of the community's high school, and not to the actual election results.

The dependent variable in this study is the amount of opposition to reorganization in the "losing community." As an objective measure of community opposition we took the percentage of the total community vote that was negative. The "percentage of negative votes" indicates the percent-age of the voters in the "losing community" who voted against the reorgan-ization proposal. Among the 110 losing communities the range of the negative vote was from 0 to 76 per cent. The mean negative vote for all losing communities was 28.1 per cent and the median was 26 per cent.

The independent variables were derived from four aspects of the losing and gaining communities. These four characteristics are the distance in miles between the population center of the losing community and the population center of the gaining community, the high school size (number of students), the assessed valuation per resident child, and population center size (number of people in the town, village, or hamlet where the school is located).

At the beginning of the study we were primarily interested in the relationships that might exist between the characteristics of the losing community and that community's opposition to school district reorganization. It became apparent, however, that the nature of the issue called for a consideration of variables which expressed relationships between the losing and gaining communities. For example, there is reason to believe that the relative sizes of the high schools in the losing and gaining communities may influence the amount of opposition to reorganization in the losing community. To put this in concrete terms, a community with a high school of size 30 may react differently to combining with a high school of size 60 than with a high school of size 300.

Before the findings of this study are presented, one cautionary note must be added. The actual political unit from which most of the measures have been derived is the high school district. Whether or not this political entity has boundaries which are coterminous with the sociological or ecological community is, of course, problematic. It is our belief that at least minimally the school district constitutes a special purpose community.[5] Furthermore, the studies conducted by John Kolb and his associates at the University of Wisconsin have led them to believe that the high school district of today is perhaps the best indicator of community boundaries.[6]

FINDINGS

One of the factors which has frequently been cited as a deterrent to school district reorganization is the increased distance that school children will have to travel to reach their school. In fact, one study found that concern about the transporting of children is *the most* important factor inhibiting school district reorganization.[7] Thus we hypothesized that as the distance between the losing community and the gaining community increases the opposition to reorganization will also increase. Table 1 shows the distribution of cases above and below the median percentage of negative votes according to various categories of distance.

It is readily apparent from Table 1 that there is no relationship between the distance between communities and the percentage of the vote in the losing community that is negative. Thus the factor of distance, although it is *perceived* as an important cause of opposition to school

---

[5] John H. Kolb and Edmund deS. Brunner, *A Study of Rural Society* (4th ed.; Boston: Houghton Mifflin, 1952), p. 233.

[6] John H. Kolb, *Emerging Rural Communities* (Madison: University of Wisconsin Press, 1959), p. 109.

[7] William P. McLure and James E. Stone, *A Study of Leadership in School District Reorganization* (Urbana: Bureau of Educational Research, College of Education, University of Illinois, 1955), pp. 55–79.

district reorganization, appears to have little influence on the actual voting.

Another factor which is frequently cited as a cause of opposition to school district reorganization is the fear that children will receive less individual attention and be less able to win awards and honors in larger schools. To test the importance of this factor, we computed a ratio between the size of the high school in the losing community and the size of the high school in the gaining community. For example, a ratio value of 3.0 indicates that the gaining high school is three times larger than the losing

TABLE 1. The Distribution of Cases Above and Below the Median Percentage of Negative Votes on the Basis of Distance Between Population Centers of the Losing and Gaining Communities
($N = 110$)

Distance between the population centers of losing and gaining communities	Percentage of negative votes		
	No. of cases below the median	*No. of cases above the median*	*Total*
Less than 6 miles	8 (47%)	9 (53%)	17 (100%)
6 to 10 miles	31 (52%)	29 (48%)	60 (100%)
More than 10 miles	16 (48%)	17 (52%)	33 (100%)
	55	55	110

high school. We hypothesized that as the high school ratio increases the opposition to the reorganization will also increase. Table 2 shows the relationship between high school ratio values and the percentage of negative votes. Both variables have been dichotomized at the median. Table 2 indicates that there is a relationship between the high school ratio values and the percentage of negative votes, and it is in the direction hypothesized.

Economic factors have frequently been mentioned as obstacles to school district reorganization, particularly as these factors influence tax rates. In order to test the influence of possible increased tax rates on the negative vote, we computed a ratio between the assessed valuation per resident child in the losing district and the assessed valuation per resident child in the gaining school district. For this measure a ratio value of 3.0 means that the losing community has *three times as much* assessed value per resident child as the gaining community. We hypothesized that as the assessed valuation ratio increases the opposition to reorganization will also

TABLE 2. The Distribution of Cases Above and Below the Median Percentage of Negative Votes on the Basis of High School Size Ratio Values ($N = 110$)

High school size ratio	Percentage of negative votes		
	No. of cases below the median	No. of cases above the median	Total
Below 3.59	37 (67%)	18 (33%)	55 (100%)
3.59 and above	18 (33%)	37 (67%)	55 (100%)
	—	—	—
	55	55	110

$Q = .62.$

increase. Table 3 shows the relationship between the assessed valuation ratio values and the percentage of negative votes. Both variables are again dichotomized at the median values. Table 3 shows that there is a relationship between the assessed valuation ratio values and the percentage of negative votes, and it is in the direction hypothesized.

TABLE 3. The Distribution of Cases Above and Below the Median Percentage of Negative Votes on the Basis of Assessed Valuation Ratio Values ($N = 110$)

Assessed valuation ratio	Percentage of negative votes		
	No. of cases below the median	No. of cases above the median	Total
Below 1.17	34 (64%)	21 (36%)	55 (100%)
1.17 and above	21 (36%)	34 (64%)	55 (100%)
	—	—	—
	55	55	110

$Q = .45.$

As a fourth independent variable we considered the population center sizes of the losing and gaining communities. Although it was unanticipated, we found that the size of the town or village in the losing community was more highly related to the negative vote than was a ratio between the population center sizes of the losing and gaining communities. Table 4

TABLE 4. THE DISTRIBUTION OF CASES ABOVE AND BELOW THE MEDIAN
PERCENTAGE OF NEGATIVE VOTES ON THE BASIS OF THE POPULATION
CENTER SIZE OF THE LOSING COMMUNITY ($N = 110$)

Population center size of the losing community	Percentage of negative votes		
	No. of cases below the median	No. of cases above the median	Total
Less than 249 people	20 (36%)	35 (64%)	55 (100%)
249 or more people	35 (64%)	20 (36%)	55 (100%)
	—	—	—
	55	55	110

$Q = .51.$

shows the distribution of cases above and below the median percentage of
negative votes when they are cross-tabulated with the *size of the population
center of the losing community*. Table 4 shows that as the size of the
population center in the losing community decreases there is a tendency for
the negative vote to be above the median.

Tables 2, 3, and 4 have shown some moderate relationships between
three different independent variables and the percentage of negative votes.
It is now of some interest to know what the combined effect of these three
independent variables will be on the percentage of negative votes. In Table
5 we have divided the 110 cases into four groups. In Group I we have
placed all cases having values for the three independent variables which
would cause us to expect a high degree of opposition to school district
reorganization. The Group II cases have values for *any two* of the independent variables which would lead us to expect opposition to reorganization.[8] Group III cases have only one characteristic which would make us
expect opposition to reorganization, and Group IV includes those cases
which have such values for all three independent variables that we would
expect only a small amount of opposition to reorganization. The distribution of cases above and below the median percentage of negative votes
clearly indicates that the combined influence of the three independent
variables is quite great. While 88 per cent of the cases in Group I had a
negative vote above the median, only 15 per cent of the cases in Group IV

---

[8] Specific combinations of two of the three independent variables are not placed in
separate groups because the number of cases in each group would be too small to be
meaningful.

TABLE 5. THE DISTRIBUTION OF CASES ABOVE AND BELOW THE MEDIAN PERCENTAGE OF NEGATIVE VOTES ON THE BASIS OF THE VALUES OF THE HIGH SCHOOL SIZE RATIO, THE ASSESSED VALUATION RATIO, AND THE POPULATION CENTER SIZE OF THE LOSING COMMUNITY ($N = 110$)

	Percentage of negative votes			Group mean: Percentage of negative votes
	Below median	Above median	Total	
Group I: High school size ratio 3.59 & above				
Assessed valuation 1.17 & above	(12%)	(88%)	(100%)	
Population center size below 249	3	21	24	42.2%
Group II: (Any combination of two) High school size ratio 3.59 & above	(52%)	(48%)	(100%)	
Assessed valuation 1.17 & above	14	13	27	24.7%
Population center size below 249				
Group III: (Any one of the following) High school size ratio 3.59 & above	(54%)	(46%)	(100%)	
Assessed valuation 1.17 & above	21	18	39	28.4%
Population center size below 249				
Group IV: High school size ratio *below 3.59* Assessed valuation ratio *below 1.17*	(85%)	(15%)	(100%)	
Population center size *249 & above*	17	3	20	15.0%
	55	55	110	
			Grand mean 28.1%	

were above that central measure. Another indication of the influence of the three independent variables is the mean percentage of negative votes for each group. While the mean negative vote for the Group I cases was 42.2 per cent, the mean negative vote for Group IV was only 15.0 per cent.

CONCLUSIONS

A comparative study of community decision making which considers only ecological and demographic variables clearly has its limitations. The number of cases studied and their geographical dispersion precluded a consideration of a number of factors which are potentially important in the decision-making process. Such factors as community influence structures, traditional rivalries between communities, and community identification with the high school are all potential influences on the outcome of the issue considered in this study.

Nevertheless, the approach that was used allowed us to examine the influence of certain factors in a relatively objective manner. By testing the relationships between certain ecological and demographic variables and the actual opposition to reorganization proposals, we were able to avoid the necessity of relying on the perceptions of so-called knowledgeable people.

Using this approach, we find no support for the notion that the distance the children must travel to get to the new school influences the opposition to reorganization. Our findings support the contention that people oppose reorganization because they do not desire to send their children to high school where it will perhaps be more difficult for the student to win scholastic and athletic honors. Opposition also appears to increase when the proposed reorganization is with a school district possessing less taxable property and there is likelihood that taxes will be increased if the merger takes place.

The finding that opposition increases as the population center of the losing community gets smaller allows several possible interpretations. Perhaps the most reasonable is that for the very small village or hamlet the high school is the dominant institution of the community. The high school may be the only remaining service provided in the community. Thus the loss of the high school either symbolizes or actually is the end of the community. If this is the case, then it is not surprising that community members should cling tenaciously to the sole remaining function of their community.

18

COMMUNITY POWER AND
URBAN RENEWAL SUCCESS[1]

☯

AMOS H. HAWLEY
University of North Carolina

Power, in most sociological studies, is conceived as the ability to exercise influence in a decision-making process. It is viewed as a personal attribute that distinguishes leaders from followers. Working with that conception investigators normally proceed by inquiring into the reputations of members of a community, establishing juries to winnow the great from the small, constructing sociograms to determine who interacts with whom, and so on. No matter what the methodological apparatus, investigators are uniformly led to the discovery that managerial and proprietary personnel, with occasional exceptions, constitute the power figures.[2] Some of the more sophisticated start with the assumption that managers and proprietors are the principal power figures and use their sociometric tools to discover how members of an elite are grouped about various kinds of issues to form power centers. Both procedures, as Wolfinger has recently pointed out, often rest on certain unspoken and unwarranted assumptions.[3] They appear to assume, for example, that lines of influence are clearly perceptible to respondents. They also assume a static distribution of power among certain personalities. But the chief difficulty with the usual approach is that it is only applicable in a case study; it offers no facility for

---

[1] I am indebted to Professors Albert J. Reiss, Jr., and Robert Somers for helpful advice in the preparation of this paper.

[2] Representative studies include Floyd Hunter, *Community Power Structure* (Chapel Hill: University of North Carolina Press, 1953); Robert O. Schulze and Leonard U. Blumberg, "The Determinants of Local Power Elites," *American Journal of Sociology*, LXIII (1957), 290–96; Delbert C. Miller, "Decision-making Cliques in Community Power Structure," *American Journal of Sociology*, LXIV (1958), 299–309; Paul Miller, "The Process of Decision-making within the Context of Community Organization," *Rural Sociology*, XVII (1952), 153–61.

[3] Raymond E. Wolfinger, "The Study of Community Power," *American Sociological Review*, XXV (1960), 636–44.

quantitative and comparative studies of the phenomenon. And that, it seems to me, is a disability inherent in a social-psychological approach to the study of community structure.

Before turning to an alternative way of treating the matter, a prefatory comment on the nature of that which is in question seems to be appropriate. It should be obvious that power in the social sphere, as with energy in the physical world, is ubiquitous. It is like energy, too, in that it appears in many forms. Every social act is an exercise of power, every social relationship is a power equation, and every social group or system is an organization of power. Accordingly, it is possible to transpose any system of social relationships into terms of potential or active power. Perhaps such a transposition is nothing more than the substitution of one terminology for another. At the very least, however, it focuses attention on the instruments of control and causes a social system to be viewed as a control mechanism.

The community, for example, may be conceived as an energy system. That is, as a system of relationships among functionally differentiated units the community constitutes a mobilization of power—the capacity to produce results—for dealing with the environment, whether physical or social. Each unit or subsystem—family, church, store, industry—is also an organization of power for the conduct of a function. Both the system and its subsystems tend to approximate a single organization model. Moreover, since the performance of its function by any one part affects in greater or lesser degree the conditions under which other parts carry out their functions, the parent system and each subsystem is an arena in which a more or less continuous interplay of influence occurs. Power, then, is expressed in two ways: (1) as functional power—that required to execute a function; and (2) as derivative power—that which spills over into external relationships and regulates the interaction between parts. The two modes of manifestation are necessarily connected. The type of function performed determines the kind of derivative influence transmitted to other parts or subsystems. There might also be a quantitative association, though the magnitude of the derivative influence is a consequence not only of the scale to which a function has developed but also of its position in the system. Those subsystems that are most instrumental in relating the system to the environment doubtlessly exert a greater derivative effect than do subsystems one or more steps removed from the key position. Space does not permit a full exposition of a system conception of power. Perhaps enough has been said to indicate that power is a product of a system having developed, that it is lodged only in a system, and that it is most appropriately treated, therefore, as a system property.[4] Whatever power an individual might appear to possess is in effect attached to the office he occupies in a system. He acquires power by attaining to an office and he loses it when he is separated from the office. But the acquiring and losing of power is illusory; the property belongs rather with the office or, better still, to the system in which the office is a specialized function.[5]

In the conduct of its routine activities the system exercises its power through established and well-worn channels; the interplay of influence is institutionalized. But the structure of relationships through which power is communicated may leave various areas of interest or activity unattended, for example, private charity, religious digression and reform, the supervision of adolescents. When crises occur in such matters or when non-routine issues affecting the whole system arise, the existing structure is put to a test. It may or may not be effective in dealing with the exceptional circumstance. Whether it is effective would appear to be contingent on the way in which derivative power is distributed in the system. Where it is highly concentrated the community should be able to act as a unit in almost any emergency. On the other hand, where power is widely distributed a community may be able to act coherently only with great difficulty, if at all, when confronted with a novel problem.

This suggests a way of dealing with the variable quantitatively. A frustrating feature of studies of power has been the understandable failure to find a way to measure its amount. If, however, we can assume that an enduring system has sufficient force to regularly perform its normal functions, we can conclude that all systems of the same kind generate equivalent amounts of power. There remains a variable, namely, the way in which power is distributed. Any given amount may be in some instances concentrated in a small sector of the system or in other instances distributed more or less uniformly over all sectors or subsystems. The measurement of distribution appears to present fewer difficulties than does the measurement of the amount of power.

Now let me propose that the greater the concentration of power in a

---

[4] This position has been stated recently by Richard M. Emerson, though he objects to the assumption of generalized power that is adopted, at least for present purposes, in this study ["Power-Dependence Relations," *American Sociological Review*, XXVII (1962), 31–32].

[5] The conception of power developed here is interchangeable with the ecological concept of dominance. Ecologists, however, have been content to treat dominance as an attribute of location or type of place, though the concept has always carried overtones of organizational properties. They have neglected to exploit the concept as an entree into the general problem of organization.

community the greater the probability of success in any collective action affecting the welfare of the whole. This follows, if it be granted that (1) success in a collective action requires the ability to mobilize the personnel and resources of the community and (2) that ability is greatest where power is most highly concentrated. The proposition does not say that a concentration of power assures success in any community venture. Various factors might intervene to defeat a collective project. Moreover, a concentration of power might be used to block a course of action. Power concentration, however, is not needed to defeat an action on the part of a community. That might occur as a result of power being so diffusely held that mobilization of the community cannot be accomplished.

Proceeding from the notion that system power resides in the subsystems or functional units of a community, we can infer that it must be exercised through the managerial functions of the subsystems. For it is those functions that co-ordinate the several other functions in their respective subsystems and articulate the latter with the larger system. In the absence of data on the number of managerial functions, I shall use the number of managerial personnel, that is, the number of people who reported occupations as manager, proprietor, or official in the Population Census, to measure concentration of power. Personnel, it should be stressed, is used only as a substitute for, and as an index of, functions.[6] Since the significance of the number of functions varies with the number of all other functions (i.e., the size of the employed labor force), it should be expressed as a ratio to the latter. Hence the lower the ratio of managers, proprietors, and officials [7] to the employed labor force the greater is the concentration of power. (This measure will hereafter be called the MPO ratio.)

As the dependent variable, that is, an example of collective action, I shall use success in urban renewal. Urban renewal, programed and administered by the Housing and Home Finance Agency, has the advantage of involving a standard procedure to which all participating communities must submit in like manner. Participation in the program by a municipality involves passage through a series of stages, differentiated by the extent

---

[6] A similar notion appears in the introductory remarks of C. Wright Mills in his book on *The Power Elite* (New York: Oxford University Press, 1956). Nevertheless it soon becomes apparent that Mills is mainly concerned with the personal characteristics of the occupants of such positions.

[7] For present purposes only managers, proprietors, and officials "not elsewhere classified" are used, this eliminating technical positions that have no management or policy-determining functions. The category, it should be noted, is not limited to management positions in pecuniary establishments. It includes managers of art galleries, libraries, community funds, welfare agencies, and others.

to which the planning and other local arrangements required for federal financial support have been fulfilled. The stages are *planning, execution,* and *completion.* Arrival at the completion stage is unquestionably the best measure of success. Unfortunately only eighteen cities in the continental United States had by the end of 1959 advanced so far—hardly enough for statistical purposes. The next best indication of success in urban renewal is arrival at the execution stage. At that stage a city has completed its planning and has satisfied all administrative requirements for the receipt of a capital grant from the Housing and Home Finance Agency. The city is then either at the point of, or has embarked upon, the acquisition of land, the relocation of current occupants, and clearing and improving the land. At the end of 1959, ninety-five cities with population of 50,000 or more (in 1950) had advanced to the execution stage.[8]

For control purposes data on two other classes of cities of 50,000 or more population are employed. One class includes cities that entered the urban renewal program but for one reason or another abandoned their efforts sometime between 1950 and 1960. The thirty-eight cities that had that experience are called "dropouts." The second control class is made up of all cities, in states where urban renewal is legally permissible, that have not attempted urban renewal at any time. There are sixty-one such cities. All the members of this class, it is to be noted, are eligible for urban renewal assistance from the federal agency. There remains a sizable group of cities that are still in the planning stage. Eventually they will either pass into the execution stage or terminate their efforts; but at present their status is indeterminate. For that reason they are not included in the present study.

Whether urban renewal is a form of collective action that would call into operation the organization of the entire community may be debatable. The general scale of urban renewal projects is clearly relevant to the question. The average acreage involved in urban renewal projects in the 253 cities that were in the program in mid-1959 was 78.6 per city, or about one-eighth of a square mile. But one-fourth of all urban renewal acreage was contained in five cities; half the total was in nineteen cities. In the remaining cities the average acreage per city was 42.5, or a little over one-sixteenth of a square mile. That urban renewal, in the light of these magnitudes, represents a significant challenge to a community must be left as an unanswered question for the present. If it is regarded as a major

---

[8] Data on cities that have had urban renewal experience have been obtained from the *Annual Report of the Housing and Home Finance Agency,* 1951 through 1960 (Washington, D.C.).

undertaking in a community, it should certainly involve the local power structure. If it is considered to be a rather insignificant form of collective action, then as a dependent variable it provides a fairly severe test of the hypothesis.[9]

It seems advisable to restate the hypothesis in the operational terms set forth. The hypothesis is: MPO ratios are lowest in urban renewal cities that have reached the execution stage and highest in cities that have never attempted urban renewal. Dropout cities are expected to occupy an intermediate position between the polar classes.

The hypothesis is to be examined with reference to cities of 50,000 population or more. The abundance of data available for cities in that size range offers considerable latitude for refining the measure of power concentration and for the development of controls. In the following, however, the analysis of power concentration as an independent variable is confined primarily to ratios for the entire class of MPO's. Differentials within that class will be investigated in a later report.

As a preliminary test of the representativeness of cities of 50,000 population or more, their MPO ratios, for each urban renewal status class, are compared with those for all cities of 15,000–50,000 population, in Table 1. Observe that the two series of ratios are very similar. Thus it seems possible that findings for large cities might apply to all cities regardless of size. Further, though somewhat tangential, support of that conclusion is found in the fact that the number of years spent in the planning stage before reaching the execution stage is unrelated to size of city. No further attempt to ascertain the representativeness of large cities has been made.

It is also to be noted in Table 1 that the ratios conform to the hypothesis. Power is most highly concentrated in the execution-stage cities and most diffusely distributed in the never-in-program cities. That the concentration of power, as represented by the ratio of all MPO's to the employed labor force, is significantly greater in cities that have reached the execution stage in urban renewal than in the other classes of cities is apparent in Table 2. The probability that the association shown there is due to chance is less than 1 in a 100.

The quintile distribution of cities shown in Table 2 displays a considerable spread over the ratio range in each urban renewal status class. That raises a question of how some cities manage to get to the execution stage without a concentration of power. The complementary question of

---

[9] *Urban Renewal Project Characteristics* (Washington, D.C.: Housing and Home Finance Agency, Urban Renewal Administration, June 30, 1959).

TABLE 1. Number and MPO Ratios, Cities by Size Class and
by Urban Renewal Status

Urban Renewal Status	All Cities of 15,000 Population and Over		Cities of 50,000 Population and Over		Cities of 15,000–50,000 Population	
	No.	MPO Ratio	No.	MPO Ratio	No.	MPO Ratio
Execution stage	136	9.0	95	9.0	41	9.1
Dropout	79	10.0	38	10.1	41	9.8
Never in program	402	11.0	61	10.8	•341	11.1
Total	617	10.4	194	9.5	423	10.7

TABLE 2. Quintile Distribution of Cities (MPO Ratios),
by Urban Renewal Status *

Urban Renewal Status	1st (Under 7.7)	2d (7.8–8.9)	3d (9.0–9.9)	4th (10.0–11.7)	5th (11.8 and Over)
Execution stage	27	22	21	17	9
Dropout	3	9	8	8	7
Never in program	9	9	8	13	22

* $X^2 = 23.516$, $C = .330$, $P < .01$.

how other cities with marked concentrations of power escape urban renewal may be given a tentative a priori answer: that is, they are susceptible and may yet enter the program. In any event, it is doubtlessly true that factors other than the distribution of power operate on urban renewal experience or the lack of it.

For example, the probability that urban renewal might recommend itself to a community as a course of action should be somewhat contingent on the state of its physical equipment. If the equipment, in this instance its buildings, is fairly new and in good condition, urban renewal would make little sense. But where buildings are old or dilapidated a proposal to renew or rehabilitate would appear to be appropriate. Two measures of the condition of buildings are used here: (1) the percentage of all residential units constructed before 1920, and (2) the percentage of all residential units reported as dilapidated. Cities are classified relative to the median for each characteristic, providing two dichotomies. "Young" cities have less than 65 per cent of their houses built before 1920, and "old" cities 65 per cent or more of their houses built prior to that data. Cities with less than 4.7 per cent of their houses dilapidated are described as "low" on that variable while those with 4.7 per cent and over are classified as "high."

It is conceivable, too, that some cities might have anticipated the problems that invite urban renewal by having established a well-financed and strongly supported planning agency. Cities that have done so might not have to seek federal assistance for improvements. A contrary argument can also be advanced. Perhaps cities with substantial commitments to planning are more prepared to enter into a renewal project than are cities in which planning has not been developed to any appreciable extent. Notwithstanding my inability to resolve this question, the size of the planning budget might prove to be a factor of some consequence. For the purpose of control, planning expenditures are expressed as a ratio to total government operating costs in 1955. Ratios of less than .4 are below the median and thus identify their respective cities as "low" with respect to planning budgets, while ratios of .4 and over indicate cities with "high" planning budgets.

There is a strong likelihood, too, that central cities of metropolitan areas might be more favorably disposed toward urban renewal than suburban cities. That should follow from the fact that central cities are generally older than are suburbs. But it should also derive from the deconcentration trend through which central cities have been losing population and industry to outlying areas. Many large suburban cities have also begun to experience declining growth rates, though in only a few cases has the trend reached a critical stage. Where substantial losses, real or threatened, have been encountered urban renewal might appear to offer a means by which to reverse the trend. There is a second factor that calls attention to the central city–suburb distinction. That is the peculiar residential distribution of managers, proprietors, and officials. Since members of those groups tend to live in suburbs while working in central cities their numbers as reported in the Census fail to reflect accurately the number of such positions in each place. The only practicable solution to this difficulty is to control for metropolitan status, that is, central city and suburb.

My operationalization of the concentration of power represents but one facet of a complex phenomenon. Other dimensions of that phenomenon should at least be admitted as control variables. For example, power may lie mainly in either the manufacturing or in the local service sector of a community's economy, whichever is most important. Relative importance is here measured by the ratio of manufacturing payroll to the combined payrolls in retailing, wholesaling, and service enterprises. Service cities have ratios of 1.5 or less and manufacturing cities have ratios of over 1.5.

The average size of manufacturing plant is another possible dimension of the distribution of power, especially if it may be construed as an indicator of the general scale of functional activities in the community. Size of plant is measured by the average number of employees per plant. Small-plant cities have averages of less than 70 employees; large-plant cities have over 70 employees per plant.

Still another expression of power distribution is found in the type of city government. In cities having a commission form of government, administrative responsibility is spread over a large number of non-elective officials. Such cities probably are unable to mobilize for action unless there is a fairly high concentration of power of the kind under study here. Administrative authority is more centralized where a mayor-council government exists. And in a city manager government administrative authority reaches its highest degree of centralization and articulation. Hence, contrary to the findings of another study that type of city government is not important in determining urban renewal success,[10] I shall employ it as a control.

Two other controls having to do with the socioeconomic level of the resident population are used. Both assume that where the socioeconomic level is high the community may be prepared to act in a matter such as urban renewal independently of a concentration of power. The first, education, is represented by the proportion of the population with four or more years of college completed. The second, income, is measured by median income. Cities are dichotomized on the median for each variable. Cities with less than 6.0 per cent of their residents with four years or more of college education are "low," and those with over that proportion are "high." The median position for the median income array falls at $3,450; cities below and above that figure are "low" and "high," respectively.

Finally, region is included among the controls. To some extent regional differences combine differences in age of cities, dilapidation, income, education, and possibly other of the control variables discussed above. Thus it is reasonable to expect that the association of power distribution with urban renewal success might vary by region. Four regions are recognized for control purposes; northeast, north central, south, and west.[11]

---

[10] George S. Duggar, "The Relation of Local Government Structure to Urban Renewal," *Law and Contemporary Problems*, XXVI (1961), 49–69.

[11] Two other controls were used with similar results: population size and income as represented by the proportion of families with incomes of $10,000 or more per year.

TABLE 3. Mean MPO Ratios in Cities, by Urban Renewal Status, with Selected Variables Controlled

Control Variable	Urban Renewal Status		
	Execution Stage	Dropout	Never in Program
Age of housing:			
Young	10.1	10.7	12.2
Old	8.2	9.5	9.5
Extent of dilapidation:			
Low	9.1	9.2	11.0
High	9.1	10.9	10.2
Planning budget:			
Small	8.8	9.3 *	11.0
Large	9.6	11.3	11.6
Metropolitan status:			
Central city	9.0	10.8	10.1
Suburban city	8.9	8.5	11.9
Government:			
Manager	9.5	9.7	12.3
Mayor-council	8.8	9.4	9.7
Commission	8.7	12.1	10.2†
Industry:			
Service	10.0	10.9	12.6
Manufacturing	8.1	9.2	9.7
Size of manufacturing plant:			
Small	9.5	11.0	12.0
Large	8.1	8.8	9.5
Median income:			
Low	8.8	10.7	9.6
High	9.2	9.7	11.4
Education:			
Low	8.2	9.8	8.6
High	9.8	10.5	12.4
Region:			
Northeast	8.5	8.1	9.8
North central	8.5	10.6	10.4
South	9.4	11.0	12.2†
West	11.9†	12.8 *	12.6

* *N* is 5 or less.
† *N* is less than 10.

MPO ratios for each urban renewal status class and with each of the ten controls applied successively are shown in Table 3. In no instance does the introduction of a control vitiate the association of power concentration with urban renewal success, though in a number of instances the dropout cities fail to hold an intermediate position between execution stage and never-in-program cities. Although the averages for dropout cities are affected by small numbers of cities in many cases, it is also possible that power concentration has been employed to defeat urban renewal in those cities. It is worth noting that even where the concentration of power is relatively great, as in old cities, mayor-council cities, manufacturing cities, large-plant cities, low-education cities, and cities in the northeast, the concentration varies with urban renewal success. There is no indication, in short, that the importance attached to the concentration of power is peculiar to any one type or class of city. Despite the fact that suburban cities are the preferred places of residence for a large proportion of the holders of administrative positions, urban renewal success seems to require as great a concentration of power in suburbs as it does in central cities. Also of interest is the evidence that manager cities appear to be able to achieve urban renewal with less power concentration than do cities of other government classes.

To better assess the closeness of the association of power concentration with urban renewal success I have employed rank correlation analysis, using Kendall's tau–c. For this purpose the three urban renewal status classes are assumed to constitute a scale. Evidence that such an assumption is reasonable is present in Tables 1 and 3. The independent variable is treated in a quintile distribution of cities by MPO ratios, as in Table 2. The results are shown in Table 4, for which data a one-tailed test of significance was used.

It is clear from the findings in Table 4 that the concentration of power is positively and significantly associated with urban renewal success under virtually all conditions of control. Several exceptions occur, however. The relationship is not dependable for cities with mayor-council governments, with a predominance of service industry, with small proportions of college graduates among their residents, and with locations in the northeast and the west. Some of these exceptions appear to be contrary to the positive findings involving variables known to be closely associated with them (education and income, northeastern location, and manufacturing industry). Had it been possible to refine the controls, some of the inconsistencies doubtlessly would have disappeared.

The category of all managers, proprietors, and officials is quite heterogeneous; it embraces the full range of both size and type of unit in which

TABLE 4. MEASURES OF ASSOCIATION OF MPO RATIOS WITH URBAN RENEWAL STATUS, WITH SELECTED VARIABLES CONTROLLED

Control Variable	Tau	χ/σ	P
All cities	.267	4.112	.00003
Age of housing:			
Young	.239	2.568	.00510
Old	.236	2.689	.00360
Extent of dilapidation:			
Low	.258	2.801	.00260
High	.267	2.951	.00160
Planning budget:			
Small	.243	2.159	.01540
Large	.305	2.430	.00750
Metropolitan status:			
Central city	.214	2.874	.00200
Suburban city	.402	3.337	.00048
Government:			
Manager	.429	3.711	.00011
Mayor-council	.134	1.387	.08230
Commission	.302	3.337	.00048
Industry:			
Service	.169	.998	.15870
Manufacturing	.220	3.175	.00068
Size of manufacturing plant:			
Small	.301	3.292	.00048
Large	.186	2.065	.01960
Median income:			
Low	.219	2.533	.00570
High	.266	2.833	.00230
Education:			
Low	.122	1.382	.08380
High	.363	3.995	.00003
Region:			
Northeast	.108	1.096	.13350
North central	.233	2.062	.01970
South	.388	2.805	.00260
West	.105	.649	.25780

such positions occur. Thus it is not unlikely that one or another subclass or industry group of managers, proprietors, and officials might be primarily responsible for the observed association. But the measures reported in Table 5 indicate that that is not the case. The correlation is statistically significant for every industrial class of managers, proprietors, and officials but one. The one, public administration, not only falls short of significance, it is negative. Why the prospects for urban renewal success should tend to increase with increases in the relative numbers of managers and officials in public administration poses an interesting problem. But that is not a question that can be pursued here. Nor is it possible to press the analysis of industry class of managers, proprietors, and officials further at

TABLE 5. MEASURES OF ASSOCIATION OF MPO RATIOS WITH URBAN RENEWAL STATUS, BY CLASS OF INDUSTRY, WITH SELECTED VARIABLES CONTROLLED

Industry Class	*Tau*	χ/σ	*P*
All industries	.267	4.112	.00003
Manufacturing:			
Salaried MPO's	.170	2.622	.00440
Self-employed MPO's	.209	3.229	.00137
Retail and wholesale trade	.214	3.300	.00097
Banking and finance	.209	3.229	.00137
Public administration	−.105	−1.612	.10740

present, though the fact that the relationship for each industry class taken separately responds differently to the application of controls clearly points to a need for a more intensive investigation.

While the findings reported in this paper should be regarded as exploratory, they clearly support the hypothesis that the lower the MPO ratio the greater the chance of success in an action program such as urban renewal. They also demonstrate the facility and the economy in research of a conception of power as a system property. Much remains to be done, however, to develop knowledge about that property. A factor of some importance is the composition of managerial positions in a city. The relative numbers in the key industry should prove decisive, if my initial argument is correct. What constitutes a key industry, of course, is contingent upon the function the city performs for the regional and national society. The pursuit of that question will doubtlessly suggest further lines of investigation.

19

PURPOSIVE COMMUNITY CHANGE
IN CONSENSUS AND
DISSENSUS SITUATIONS *

☯

ROLAND L. WARREN AND HERBERT H. HYMAN
Brandeis University

Studies of efforts at purposive social change at the community level are important for community mental health from at least two standpoints. First, the development of mental health programs, particularly those comprehensive approaches called for in the Community Mental Health Centers Act in itself, constitutes such a purposive change effort. Second, the manner in which change efforts are made in the community, and the manner in which they are received and resolved, the "style of issue resolution," as it were, is itself highly relevant to an inclusive concept of community mental health.

Recent years have seen a proliferation of studies of community action episodes. Many of these studies have concentrated on the total interaction process through which ideas are moved ahead from planning to action, with whatever outcome they encounter (Sower, *et al.*, 1957; Hunter, Schaffer, and Sheps, 1956; Kimball and Pearsall, 1954; Meyerson and Banfield, 1955). Other studies, especially numerous recently, have concentrated on the resolution of community issues on the basis of the differential distribution of power and influence (Bonjean & Olson, 1964).

While a few comparative studies have been made, particularly regarding the distribution and use of power (Miller, 1953; Polsby, 1963; Presthus, 1964), a large number of purposive social change studies at the community level have tended to pile up one upon another, each adding some more or less enlightening findings, but with little generalizability.

* The research on which this paper is based was supported by a Public Health Service research career program award (number K3-MH-21,569) and supplementary grant number MH-11085-01.

There have been few if any attempts to make systematic use of published reports of episodes of purposive social change at the community level for research purposes. On the one hand, such studies involve methodological problems caused by the difficulty that the data were not gathered and reported according to a unified conceptual scheme, and there are great difficulties in codification, even when the necessary data are present in the reports. In addition, though, there is little agreement as to what variables would seem to be most pertinent and feasible for research in comparative instances of purposive change at the community level.

The study reported here embodies an attempt to gain first-hand experience in utilizing published reports as a basis for systematic research in this area, as well as to test in preliminary fashion a hypothesis regarding two purportedly distinct types of purposive change situations. The variables employed in the study lend themselves to application in analyzing the published reports of change episodes. In addition, the authors believe that these variables have more than merely empirical significance, since they have been developed through systematic theoretical conceptualization. Hence, despite the implicit methodological difficulties, the authors believe it to contain theoretically important, though necessarily tentative findings, as well as to afford a possible method for mining the vast lode of published accounts of purposive change episodes which so far have received little systematic comparative attention.

This paper is based on a comparative study of 35 published episodes of purposive change at the community level. It uses as a primary consideration the "action environment"—whether or not the action episode developed within a consensus or a dissensus situation.

Three distinct but interrelated lines of speculation contributed to the rationale of this approach.

The first is related to the cleavage in social change theory between approaches which emphasize system maintenance and stability as the principal focus around which change is to be considered, and those which emphasize the dynamics of conflicting interests and unstable systems (Parsons, 1951; Moore, 1963; Neal, 1965; Martindale, 1965). It is widely believed that the equilibrium theory, emphasizing both system maintenance and the common values which are a basic part of such systems, tends toward conservatism in its implications (Hacker, 1961; Dahrendorf, 1959). Conflict theories, based on a fluid conception of society in the dynamic interplay of different interests, are often held to be more favorable toward change. The consensus situations considered in this paper fit more readily into the former model than the latter, while the reverse is true of the dissensus situations.

A second line of consideration comes from the field of community change today. A number of developments challenge the older conception of community action strategy based on consensus and inclusiveness of decision-making. On the one hand, such issues as birth control, civil rights, and fluoridation have presented situations where consensus models of change processes do not appear to be applicable (Coleman, 1957; *Journal of Social Issues,* 1961). At the same time, there has been a growing movement toward reinstating conflict as a "respectable" process, or strategy (Coleman, 1957; Keeton, 1960; Coser, 1956). Hence, a "contest" model for change has arisen as an alternative to the collaborative models.

The third line of convergence has to do with the senior author's own activity in attempting to relate empirical practice and social theory at the community level. In this connection, a model of "community action episodes" was developed, based on the following sequence of stages: 1) initial systemic environment, 2) inception of the action system, 3) expansion of the action system, 4) operation of the expanded action system, and 5) transformation of the action system (Warren, 1963). In the further testing of this model, including the research which is here reported, it was found that the model is of considerable usefulness in accommodating community action episodes which develop in consensus situations, but requires some modification for the analysis of episodes growing out of dissensus situations. *In these dissensus situations, there are usually two identifiable action systems rather than one.*

In the senior author's earlier paper on "Types of Purposive Social Change at the Community Level," (Warren, 1965) an analysis was made of the relation of value-interest consensus or dissensus to different change strategies currently in use in purposive change at the community level. These varied from "consensus-planning" at the one extreme to various types of "contest" strategy at the other extreme, including mass demonstrations, civil disobedience, and violence. Briefly, that paper presented an analysis of three different kinds of situation along the dimension of values and interests. Values were defined as "underlying, implicit bases for judgment and evaluation." By interest was meant "the relation of an actor to specific reality configurations. Presumably, interests are the specification of values in terms of evaluations of actual and potential social situations." Thus, values are denoted by such general terms as "equality," "freedom," "respect for human personality," etc.; interests, by "civil rights," "low taxes," "air pollution control" (Warren, 1965, p. 10). It was concluded that where there is a large measure of agreement among the principal parties to a proposed community action (value-interest *consensus*), the change agent can be expected to employ *collaborative* strategies in pursuing his objective. Where there is not a large measure of agreement, but where the change agent thinks that such agreement may be achieved (value-interest *difference*), he will tend to use persuasive or *campaign* strategies. Where value-interest agreement is not the issue, but rather simply support or acquiescence, various pressure techniques may be used, as well as bargaining. Where there is little basic agreement around the issue, and little likelihood of obtaining it through campaign strategies (value-interest *dissensus*), the change agent must either renounce his goal or utilize *contest* strategies (which may include conflict).

For the present research, it was hypothesized that action systems in consensus situations would tend to use collaborative strategies and action systems in dissensus situations would tend to use contest strategies. It was also hypothesized that action systems in these two different types of situations would differ systematically on a number of other relevant variables.

METHODOLOGY

Thirty-five detailed case studies of community action episodes in a variety of community settings were chosen for comparative analysis. They were deliberately selected so as to include large and small communities, task-oriented goals and integration-oriented goals, public and private auspices, collaboration and contest strategies. Thus, the cases represent a broad variety of settings and circumstances, even though they cannot be assumed to constitute a statistically representative sample.[1] Explicit classi-

---

[1] The cases were drawn from the following sources: Edward C. Banfield, *Political Influence* (New York: The Free Press, 1961), The Branch Hospital; The Welfare Merger; The Chicago Transit Authority; Severyn T. Bruyn, *Communities in Action: Pattern and Process* (New Haven: College & University Press, 1963), Eldorado Community; The Cobden Community; Chapin Community; Jacksonville Community; Jacqueline D. Goodchilds and John Harding, "A Case Study of Community Participation," *Journal of Social Issues*, vol. 16, no. 4, 1960; Floyd Hunter, Ruth Connor Schaffer, and Cecil G. Sheps, *Community Organization: Action and Inaction* (Chapel Hill: University of North Carolina Press, 1956), entire book; Floyd Hunter, *Community Power Structure* (Chapel Hill: University of North Carolina Press, 1953), Annexation (pp. 215–220) and International Trade Council (pp. 173–174); Martin Meyerson and E. C. Banfield, *Politics, Planning and the Public Interest* (Glencoe: The Free Press, 1955), entire book; Robert J. Mowitz and Deil S. Wright, *Profile of a Metropolis* (Detroit: Wayne University Press, 1962), Gratiot Redevelopment Project; Urban Renewal in Corktown; Detroit's City-County Building; Harper Woods vs. Ford Expressway; The Case of the Missing Port; Annexation in Farmington; Benjamin D. Paul and Walter B. Miller, *Health, Culture, and Community* (New York: Russell Sage Foundation, 1955), Mental Health Education; A Medical Care Program in a Colorado County; Mental Health in a Boston Suburb; An Alabama Town Surveys Its Health

ficatory definitions were made of all key terms used. Cases were analyzed in terms of the following variables:

Variable	*Variation*
Action environment	Consensus—Dissensus
Principal strategy	Collaboration—Contest
Type of goal	Task-oriented—Integration-oriented
Size of community	Over 50,000—Under 50,000
Origin of action system	From a formal organization—From an informal organization
Auspices of action system	Governmental—Non-governmental
Organization of action system	Formal—Informal
Key leadership stance	Supported—Opposed
Goal outcome	Accomplished—Not accomplished
Fate of action system	Continued—Discontinued

A word of caution should be taken regarding the validity of the case classifications using the operational definitions employed. These definitions were formulated explicitly and then refined as possible ambiguities in classification developed in the actual process. Careful consideration was given to cases where the two authors differed in their classification judgment. In these cases, definitions were refined until agreement was reached. The fact that most judgments were in agreement and that ambiguities were systematically pursued leads the authors to believe that the findings merit attention, despite the limitations of precision imposed by the data. They must, however, be considered as tentative and suggestive, rather than as definitive.[2]

Needs; Murray G. Ross, *Case Histories in Community Organization* (New York: Harper and Brothers, 1958), The West End; St. Peters; Bellville; The South Side Center; The Paarmount Area; Henshaw; Elmsville: Centertown; South Haven; Peter H. Rossi and Robert A. Dentler, *The Politics of Urban Renewal* (New York: The Free Press, 1961), Southeast Chicago Commission; Hyde Park-Kenwood Community Conference; Christopher Sower *et al.*, *Community Involvement: The Webs of Formal and Informal Ties that Make for Action* (Glencoe: The Free Press, 1957), entire book; Henry G. Tate, *Building a Better Home Town* (New York: Harper and Brothers, 1954), entire book.

[2] Subsequently, reliability tests were made using coefficients of intercorrelation. For this purpose, five additional judges were trained briefly in the application of the definitions, and their judgments along with the composite judgment of the authors, were intercorrelated, with coefficients as follows: Action environment, .60; type of goal, .49; size of community, .88; origin of action system, .39; principal strategy, .77, and goal outcome, .58. The two remaining variables did not involve completely discrete categories. It is believed that greater effort in training judges would yield higher correlations.

CHARACTERISTICS OF THE SAMPLE

The *action environment* in which a purposive change effort—such as developing a new exhibition hall or attempting to attract industry to the community—occurs, may be one in which important parties are in agreement on the matter, or where such agreement is readily attainable. This situation is called *consensus*, as distinguished from situations of *dissensus*, where there is basic disagreement, or interest conflict, and the likelihood of reaching consensus seems remote.

This variable, like some others employed here, is a dichotomized continuum. We had actually approached the study with an intermediate stage between these two types, a *difference* stage, characterized by situations where agreement is not immediately attainable, but where it is felt that a strategy of persuading the other party would yield eventual consensus. As the cases unfolded, those characterized by difference tended to change to either consensus or dissensus situations, and so for purposes of simplicity of design only these two extreme categories were employed. Of the 35 cases classified, 21 took place in a consensus environment, 14 in a dissensus environment.

By *principal strategy* we denote the dominant type of interaction which characterized the total community action. Twenty-four actions were of the collaboration type, 11 were of the contest type.

The *type of goal* reflected whether the principal purpose of the action was the accomplishment of some specific task, such as providing a number of low cost houses, or rather an attempt to strengthen the cohesiveness and vitality of the community. Twenty-two actions were primarily task oriented, 10 were integration oriented, and 3 were both.

Nineteen actions took place in communities of *over 50,000* and 16 took place in communities under that size.

In cases such as those studied, special *action systems* are developed to pursue the projected goals. Twenty-one action systems arose out of a formal organizational origin, while 14 action systems arose informally.

The variable, *auspices of action system* denoted whether private individuals or groups were primarily responsible for the inception of the action system, or whether a governmental unit played the principal role in its inception. Seven of the action systems were governmental in auspices, 24 were nongovernmental, and 4 were a combination of both.

By *organization of action* system we denote the formal or informal systemic structure that predominantly characterized the action system which was set up to achieve the desired goal. Because of classification difficulties, this variable was discarded.

By *key leadership*, we include only those persons mentioned in the case studies who were in positions of formal or informal influence or power in relation to the action system and its goal and whose action or inaction had a major effect on the outcome. Of the 61 leaders so clearly identified in the 35 cases, 34 were active in supporting the action systems, 9 were inactive, and 18 opposed the action system's activities and goals.

By *goal outcome* we refer to whether or not the action system's goal was substantially accomplished, regardless of whether the action system was task oriented or integration oriented. In 19 of the actions, the goal was accomplished, in 16 the goal was not accomplished, or only partly accomplished.

By *fate of action system* we refer to whether the action system which had been set up to accomplish a particular goal was still in operation at the time of the case report, whether it had been discontinued, or whether it had been transformed into a formal organization. Twelve of the systems were still in existence, 7 had been transformed into a formal organization, and 19 had been discontinued. (On this variable, the first two categories are not mutually exclusive, hence, the total is not 35.)

FINDINGS

The first relationship to be tested can be stated: *Action systems in consensus situations tend to use collaborative strategies; action systems in dissensus situations tend to use contest strategies.*

This hypothesis was based on the following line of analysis: If the party attempting to bring about a change can reasonably expect that there will be no major opposition, and that there is substantial agreement on the way the issue will be seen, he has much to gain by employing a collaborative strategy. He has the reasonable assurance that this strategy will lead to goal accomplishment. In addition, there may be tangible gains through enlisting the participation of other relevant parties in decision making and issue resolution. Through such participation, they may come to give the outcome more active support than they otherwise might. The potential donor may write a larger check; the hoped for clients may come in larger numbers; the climate in which the new achievement is brought about may augur well for its further success. In addition, there are strong cultural values which take the concept of "democracy" beyond mere majority rule to virtual unanimity—to the achievement of consensus-based decisions.

Thus taking advantage of the possibility of achieving decisions based on consensus, where this seems possible, would be expected.

On the other hand, where there is opposition to the goal, opposition which cannot be won over through alternative strategies, one must "fight" for it or give it up. Thus, various types of contest strategy will be employed, including debate, mutual propaganda campaigns, political campaigning, and demonstrations, as well as more specific conflict, in the sense of turning from the issue to attack or destroy one's opponent.

The findings showed a strong relationship in the expected direction. Collaborative strategies are used overwhelmingly in consensus situations, contest strategies in dissensus situations. The first ratio is 21 to 0, and the second is 11 to 3.

Thus, the first hypothesis would appear to be strongly supported by

TABLE 1. PRINCIPAL STRATEGY BY ACTION
ENVIRONMENT

Strategy	Action Environment		
	Consensus	Dissensus	Total
Collaboration	21	3	24
Contest	0	11	11
Total	21	14	35

the cases in this study. One suspects that at least part of this extraordinarily high association is caused by an actual spill-over in the attempt to operationalize the concepts of Action environment and Principal strategy. While they are fairly easy to define abstractly, they are difficult to operationalize without considerable overlap.

In assessing this finding, a related consideration is important. Whether or not a situation is classified as a consensus environment depends to a certain extent on the level of abstraction at which one defines that situation. Thus, at the most general level of proposed change (as in improving the quality of public transportation in Chicago) there may be broad agreement, but disagreement might surround the more specific implementing proposal—in the Chicago case, to do so by raising taxes. In most cases, however, judgments of consensus or dissensus could be based on relatively tangible proposals.

In summary, although there were important difficulties in classification, the most careful classification the authors could give indicated a close relationship between consensus and collaboration strategies, dissensus and contest strategies.

One may ask whether the choice of strategy might not possibly change the nature of the action environment, in the sense of a "self-fulfilling prophecy." There did seem to be some indication that this process operated—in both directions—in the cases under study, but the research was not specifically designed to explore this question.

The second hypothesis was *that action systems in consensus or dissensus situations would differ from each other on a number of other specified variables.* These will now be considered in sequence.

Action environment and type of goal. It seems plausible to expect that action systems with task oriented goals, such as the provision of new housing units or port facilities, or the planned renewal of a part of the city, would be likely to encounter opposition from those groups whose interests are threatened by the change. On the other hand, where the goal is oriented toward integration, as in developing "community spirit" or increasing communication between various segments of the community under circumstances which do not threaten to change the existing configuration of power, one might expect there would be relatively little opposition, though of course it may be difficult to enlist support because of apathy.

Changes brought about by deliberate intent may well have the effect of creating tension as strains are placed upon the previous balance of reciprocal adjustments. In his experimental group situations, Bales found that groups tend to go through alternating phases of instrumental and expressive activity, the latter made necessary by the tensions aroused by the former (Parsons and Bales, 1955). Long has pointed out that different groups in the community tend to play their own "games" as they pursue their own interests and engage the relevant parties in issue resolution. Each "game" has its own behavior norms, and the participants have their own goals. Occasionally, one game encroaches upon another, and in this circumstance, a power struggle ensues (Long, 1958).

The findings of this study indicate that consensus situations are associated with task oriented goals and integration oriented goals equally, while dissensus situations are characterized overwhelmingly by task oriented goals. In consensus situations, task goals appeared as often as integration goals (9 to 9, with 3 cases mixed), while in dissensus situations, task goals predominated (13 to 1).

In terms of our second hypothesis, it is modestly substantiated that there is a definite relationship between types of goals and action environments.

Action environment and Size of community. Much of the basic theoretical conceptualizing about social processes in communities has tended to take the lead of Simmel and Wirth in considering the size of the population to be an important variable affecting social relationships (Simmel, 1950; Wirth, 1938). It is therefore interesting to see whether differences in size are associated with purposive change episodes in consensus situations and dissensus situations. One might assume that the greater heterogeneity of social groups and of group interests, along with other conditions associated with large city life, might lead to a higher proportion of dissensus situa-

TABLE 2. TYPE OF GOAL BY ACTION ENVIRONMENT

Type of Goal	Action Environment		
	Consensus	Dissensus	Total
Task oriented	9	13	22
Integration oriented	9	1	10
Both	3	0	3
Total	21	14	35

tions surrounding change episodes in the large cities. On the other hand, the alleged conservatism of the small community and presumed greater cosmopolitanism of the large community and willingness to change might be expected to operate in the other direction.

In the 35 cases of this study, a modest association was found between consensus situations and small communities, dissensus situations and large communities.

TABLE 3. SIZE OF COMMUNITY BY ACTION
ENVIRONMENT

Size of Community	Action Environment		
	Consensus	Dissensus	Total
Large	9	10	19
Small	12	4	16
Total	21	14	35

Action environment and Auspices of action system. A number of considerations might lead one to expect that action systems characterized by dissensus would arise under nongovernmental auspices, while those characterized by consensus would arise under governmental auspices. Many types of activity are considered too "controversial" for government offices to initiate; by the same token, voluntary activities have traditionally been acknowledged as the free forum for controversial issues. Vidich and Bensman reported on the "paralysis" of local government in Springdale, a small New York community, and its abdication of all functions which might create controversy (Vidich and Bensman, 1958). On the other hand, many political scientists take the position that the major controversial issues of a community will sooner or later be decided in a political context. And many current actions by local government, often with federal initiative and financial support, proceed on the basis that government must enter important problem areas largely abandoned by voluntary groups.

Our findings from these 35 cases are that action systems originating under private auspices tend to be associated with consensus situations, while action systems under governmental auspices are associated overwhelmingly with dissensus situations. All but one of the governmentally sponsored action systems arose in a dissensus situation. In sharp contrast, most of the action systems arising out of consensus situations were initiated by private agencies alone.

TABLE 4. Auspices of Action System by Action Environment

Type of Auspices	Action Environment		
	Consensus	Dissensus	Total
Governmental	1	6	7
Non-governmental	19	5	24
Both	1	3	4
Total	21	14	35

As it happens, none of the cases in the sample involved contest actions by such activist organizations as the ADA, the NAACP, SNCC, etc. If they had, perhaps the findings would have been different. At least, though, this finding casts grave doubt on the assumption that government offices and agencies tend to be conservative, dodging the controversial actions, while non-governmental agencies are the fearless protagonists of conflicting points of view. Taken aggregately, governmental auspices in these cases are handling a much greater proportion of controverted issues than are the nongovernmental auspices.

One may raise the question whether the governmental auspices involved in dissensus actions might be principally elected political officials engaging in a loose, free-swinging type of contest activity, while the cases where governmental auspices were associated with consensus situations might be those of the presumably more conservative and cautious government bureaucracies. A check of the 6 dissensus cases started under government auspices did not substantiate this. Two of the controverted actions were clearly initiated by bureaucratic officials, two were by electorate-sensitive political leaders, and two were mixed.

Action environment and key leadership stance. Do top leaders tend to become involved in large community actions involving dissensus, or do they shy away from these in favor of the actions on which there is general agreement? Atlanta, Ga., Dallas, Tex., Pittsburgh, Pa., and many other cities have been reported to have a formally or informally organized top leadership group which irons out its differences in private, presenting a fairly united front to the community (Hunter, 1953; Thometz, 1963; Auerbach, 1965). On the other hand, many studies show a fragmentation of top leadership around specific interests and issues (Martin and Munger, 1962).

The cases studied here show a significant difference based on action

TABLE 5. KEY LEADERSHIP STANCE BY ACTION
ENVIRONMENT

Key Leadership Stance	Action Environment		
	Consensus	Dissensus	Total
Support	20	14	34
Oppose	4	14	18
Inactive	3	6	9
Total	27	34	61 *

* Leadership stance totals more than 35 because of multiple leadership factions.

environment. *In consensus situations, key leadership tends overwhelmingly to support the action system; in dissensus situations, key leadership tends to support the action or oppose it about equally, with a few remaining inactive.*

This finding should be considered in connection with the fact that only those leaders are included in the analysis whose position was specifically mentioned in the action episode reports. Nevertheless, the findings are not unexpected. In consensus situations, the principal obstacle to action is likely to be apathy. Hence, the leaders mentioned in these cases are primarily those who support the action system. In situations of dissensus, on the other hand, important controversial issues are at stake, and it is to be expected that leadership will range itself more actively on one side or the other of the issue.

Action environment and Goal outcome. Do community actions arising out of consensus achieve their goals more often than actions arising out of dissensus? One might anticipate that they would, for agreement might be presumed to be a more favorable circumstance for eventual goal accomplishment than dissensus. Risking oversimplification, the question at stake here is whether in community actions such as these, apathy or opposition is the more formidable obstacle.

In this study, there was *a moderate tendency for actions arising in consensus situations to accomplish their goals and for those arising in dissensus situations to fail to accomplish their goals.*

TABLE 6. Goal Outcome by Action
Environment

Goal Outcome	Action Environment		
	Consensus	Dissensus	Total
Accomplished	14	5	19
Not accomplished	7	9	16
Total	21	14	35

Here, the association is between action environment and goal accomplishment. It is interesting to examine the association between the highly related variable of principal strategy and goal accomplishment. Table 7 shows the relationship:

TABLE 7. Goal Outcome by Principal Strategy

Goal Outcome	Principal Strategy		
	Collaboration	Contest	Total
Accomplished	16	3	19
Not accomplished	8	8	16
Total	24	11	35

This association would at first glance seem to support the often-voiced tenet that strategies of collaboration are more likely to accomplish their goals because people who collaborate in decision making are more likely to support—or at least not oppose—the final decision than as though they had not been a party to the decision. Actually, though, a different interpretation of this finding is also possible. This is the interpretation that the vast majority of change efforts using a collaborative strategy involved change goals which were relatively "safe bets," which did not raise major issues or threaten the existing power configuration of the community. The high association between collaborative strategies and consensus situations (See Table 1) tends to support this interpretation, as does a preliminary assessment of the change goals on the basis of whether they involved basic structural change or rather merely an incremental kind of expansion of already existing types of behavior or facility. Preliminary assessment indicates that the latter were those which tended to use collaborative strategies and preponderantly to accomplish their goals, while the former tended to be those which used contest strategies and accomplished their goals less frequently.

On two of the variables investigated, little association was found with consensus or dissensus. These were the origin of the action system, whether from a formal organization or an informal organization, and fate of the action system, whether continued, transformed into a formal organization, or discontinued.

A third variable, the organization of the action system, whether formal or informal, presented great difficulty in definition and classification. The authors were quite confident of being able to conceptualize operational definitions which would be both meaningful and on which they could agree in their classification. Actually, this was found possible in assessing the origin of the action systems (whether out of a formal or informal organization), but not in classifying the action systems themselves.

CONCLUSIONS

In this study, an attempt was made to examine 35 purposive change episodes in terms of a number of variables which appear to be important dimensions of such efforts. A principal interest was to discover whether change efforts characterized by consensus differed systematically from those characterized by dissensus. There were two principal hypotheses. The first was that action systems in consensus situations would tend to employ collaborative strategies, while those in dissensus situations would tend to employ contest strategies. This relationship was strongly suggested by the data.

The second hypothesis was that action systems in consensus or dissensus situations would differ from each other on a number of other relevant variables. Although severe limitations are imposed on generalizations because of the methodological difficulties, the differences found, though modest, would seem to indicate that these two types of episode actually do differ from each other in a number of important respects.

In the 35 cases studied, the 21 which took place in a consensus environment differed from those taking place in a dissensus environment. They employed collaborative strategies for change rather than contest strategies. They tended to have task oriented and integration oriented goals about equally; to occur in small communities somewhat more than the large ones; to be almost exclusively non-governmental in auspices; to involve key leadership in active support, rather than opposition, and to accomplish their goals in most cases.

By contrast, the 14 cases which took place in a dissensus environment tended to employ contest strategies; to have task oriented goals only; to predominate in larger communities; to have a higher proportion of governmental auspices; to involve key leadership actively in both support and opposition, and to fall short of goal accomplishment in most cases.

In the case of two variables, the formal or informal origin of the action system, and whether it was continued, transformed, or discontinued at the completion of the episode, no meaningful relationship was found to the action environment variable.

The systematic differences found between action systems characterized by consensus and those characterized by dissensus has certain inherent significance in terms of the contrasting patterns of strategies, goals, auspices, key leadership involvement, and goal outcome. They suggest that *however desirable may be the comparative study of purposive change efforts at the community level, the findings may be greatly blurred unless a distinction is made between two substantially different types of change effort:* those which involve important opposition to the proposed change and those which do not. It has been suggested, loosely, that the former type have opposition as their principal obstacle, while those of the latter type have apathy as theirs. Further study of these contrasting types of purposive change effort would seem to be justified.

In connection with further study, there is reason to believe that the multitude of accounts of individual change efforts at the community level can be assessed and objectively classified according to variables or attributes such as those employed in this exploratory study. In this connection, it is suggested that some, though perhaps not all of the methodological difficulties of this exploratory study can be attenuated by a more systematic basis for assuring the representativeness of the sample of cases, by further conceptual refinement and by the measurement and improvement of reliability of classification judgments.

The sampling of cases can be improved by developing as large as possible a universe of case records of the consensus type, and another of the dissensus type, and then sampling randomly or by some stratified method from these clearly defined universes, respectively.

Further conceptual refinement in the variables of action environment and principal strategy will indicate whether these can be more rigorously distinguished operationally for further research purposes.

The problem of judgment reliability can be approached through revision of classificatory definitions based on instances in which cases are classified differently by different judges, and the employment of statistical measures of interjudge reliability, attempting further conceptual refinement of those variables on which reliability remains low. If sufficient interjudge reliability can be attained in this manner, the use of more sophisticated statistical techniques, would appear to be feasible.

Meantime, on the basis of the findings of this preliminary study, it would appear that persons interested in bringing about community change would do well to examine their proposed strategy in the light of the different situations they may confront if they are dealing primarily with apathy or with opposition.

REFERENCES

Auerbach, Arnold J. "Power and Progress in Pittsburgh," *Trans-action* 1965, vol. 2, no. 6, 15–20.

Bonjean, Charles M., and David M. Olson. "Community Leadership: Directions of Research," *Administrative Science Quarterly*, 1964, vol. 9, no. 3, 278–300.

Coleman, James S. *Community Conflict*. Glencoe: Free Press, 1957.

Coser, Lewis A. *The Functions of Social Conflict*. New York: Free Press of Glencoe, 1956.

Dahl, Robert A. *Who Governs? Democracy and Power in an American City*. New Haven: Yale University Press, 1961.

Dahrendorf, Ralph. *Class and Class Conflict in Industrial Society*. Stanford: Stanford University Press, 1959, p. 157 ff.

Hacker, Andrew. "Sociology and Ideology," in Max Black (ed.), *The Social Theories of Talcott Parsons*. Englewood Cliffs: Prentice-Hall, 1961, p. 290 ff.

Hunter, Floyd. *Community Power Structure*. Chapel Hill: University of North Carolina Press, 1953.

Hunter, Floyd, Ruth Connor Schaffer, and Cecil G. Sheps. *Community Organization: Action and Inaction*. Chapel Hill: University of North Carolina Press, 1956.

Journal of Social Issues, 1961, vol. 17, no. 4.

Keeton, Morris. *Values Men Live By: An Invitation to Religious Inquiry*. New York: Abingdon Press, 1960.

Kimball, Solon T. and Marion Pearsall. *The Talladega Story: A Study in Community Process*. University: University of Alabama Press, 1954.

Long, Norton E. "The Local Community as an Ecology of Games," *American Journal of Sociology*, 1958, vol. 64, 251–261.

Martin, Roscoe C. and Frank J. Munger, *et al. Decisions in Syracuse*. Bloomington: Indiana University Press, 1962.

Martindale, Don (ed.) *Functionalism in the Social Sciences*. Philadelphia: American Academy of Political and Social Science, Monograph 5, 1965.

Meyerson, Martin and Edward C. Banfield. *Politics, Planning and the Public Interest*. Glencoe: The Free Press, 1955.

Miller, Paul A. *Community Health Action: A Study of Community Contrast*. East Lansing: Michigan State College Press, 1953.

Moore, Wilbert E. *Social Change*. Englewood Cliffs: Prentice-Hall, 1963.

Neal, Sister Marie Augusta. *Values and Interests in Social Change*. Englewood Cliffs: Prentice-Hall, 1965.

Parsons, Talcott. *The Social System*. Glencoe: The Free Press, 1951.

Parsons, Talcott and Robert F. Bales. *Family, Socialization and Interaction Process*. Glencoe: The Free Press, 1955.

Polsby, Nelson W. *Community Power and Political Theory*. New Haven: Yale University Press, 1963.

Presthus, Robert. *Men at the Top: A Study in Community Power*. New York: Oxford University Press, 1964.

Simmel, Georg. "The Metropolis and Mental Life," in Wolff, Kurt H. (ed.) *The Sociology of Georg Simmel*. Glencoe: The Free Press, 1950.

Sower, Christopher, et al. *Community Involvement: The Webs of Formal and Informal Ties that Make for Action*. Glencoe: The Free Press, 1957.

Thometz, Carol Estes. *The Decision-Makers: The Power Structure of Dallas*. Dallas: Southern Methodist University Press, 1963.

Vidich, Arthur J. and Joseph Bensman. *Small Town in Mass Society: Class, Power and Religion in a Rural Community*. Princeton: Princeton University Press, 1958.

Warren, Roland L. *The Community in America.* Chicago: Rand McNally & Co., 1963.

Warren, Roland L. "Types of Purposive Social Change at the Community Level," *Brandeis University Publications in Social Welfare*, No. 11. Waltham, Mass.: The Florence Heller Graduate School for Advanced Studies in Social Welfare, 1965.

Wirth, Louis. "Urbanism as a Way of Life," *American Journal of Sociology*, 1938, vol. 44, no. 1.

VIII

INTER-COMMUNITY RELATIONS AND DECISION-MAKING

20

LIFE-STYLE VALUES AND POLITICAL DECENTRALIZATION IN METROPOLITAN AREAS*

OLIVER P. WILLIAMS
University of Pennsylvania

[Essentially three models—international relations, power structure, and service marketing—have been developed to explain the proliferation of governments and inter-governmental relations in metropolitan areas. Building on the latter of these, an alternative model stressing municipal life styles is proposed. This model emphasizes the specialized nature and differentiated character of municipalities in the metropolitan milieu.]

Through the second quarter of this century many political scientists were writing on why metropolitan areas needed to be politically integrated through local government consolidation. Thus far, in the third quarter, a major theme has been to document how thoroughly this advice is rejected by the American people. Assuming that the present decentralized metropolitan political structures are durable, rather than transitory, phenomena, it is useful to develop models which enable us to understand them as well as to evaluate their social consequences. A substantial beginning has been made with respect to both of these concerns. This paper seeks to improve on existing analytical models of metropolitan politics as a step toward guiding empirical research and sharpening our perceptions of the social values served by the new metropolitan urban form.

EXISTING MODELS AND THEIR SHORTCOMINGS

There are essentially three models which have been developed to explain the proliferation of governments and the relationships among them

---

* An earlier version of this paper was delivered at the Conference on Comparative Research in Community Politics at Athens, Georgia, November 16–19, 1966 under the sponsorship of the National Science Foundation and the University of Georgia.

in metropolitan areas. These three—international relations, the market place, and power structure—will be briefly reviewed, and then an alternative will be suggested. The eclectic approaches which list separate sets of "political" considerations to explain events in each metropolitan area will be ignored here. It is assumed that theories which promise a higher level of generality should be explored before we resign ourselves to *ad hoc* explanations.

The international relations model was probably first suggested by Victor Jones,[1] then restated by Matthew Holden [2] and given an operational test by James V. Toscano.[3] The model relies primarily upon analogies between the relationships among nation states and those among municipalities in a metropolitan area. Parallels are seen between alliances and special districts, international organizations and councils of governmental officials (such as the Association of Bay Area Governments), and imperialism and annexation. The problem of any analogy is that it glosses over dissimilarities. For example, one of the old saws of international relations is that economic integration precedes political integration among nations. But metropolitan areas are economically integrated; that is what gives them their identity. Furthermore, most metropolitan areas were once more fully politically integrated than they are now. Despite economic integration, metropolitan areas have become politically decentralized.

The real test of the usefulness of international relations analogies lies, however, in concrete analysis. One such attempt was made by Toscano,[4] who employed several transaction flow theories, taken from the literature on integration among nations. One hypothesis he tested was derived from spill-over theory. According to this theory, if municipalities learn to agree in one area, they are likely to agree in others. Thus, the experience of successful cooperation will have cumulative effect, and the areas of cooperation will have a cumulative effect, and the areas of cooperation will be extended. Toscano's findings did not substantiate this hypothesis, for the substantive content of the service in question, rather than the experience of interacting, appeared to be the controlling variable.[5] Communication, as such, was not the key.

---

[1] "The Organization of a Metropolitan Region," *University of Pennsylvania Law Review*, 105 (February, 1957), 538–552.

[2] "The Governance of the Metropolis as a Problem in Diplomacy," *Journal of Politics*, 26 (August 1964), 627–647.

[3] Philip E. Jacob and James V. Toscano, eds., *The Integration of Political Communities* (Philadelphia: J. B. Lippincott Co., 1963), Chapter IV.

[4] *Ibid.*

[5] See also Oliver P. Williams, Harold Herman, Charles S. Liebman, and Thomas R. Dye, *Suburban Differences and Metropolitan Policies*, (Philadelphia: University of Pennsylvania Press, 1965), Chapter IX.

The market place model treats each municipality as an enterprise in the business of supplying services.[6] The core city, suburbs, and satellite cities each offer a different bundle of services which attract a different type of customer. Thus, families seeking good schools for their children go to suburbs that offer quality school services. Resistance to consolidations is an expression of a desire to preserve a particular service mix. However, all services cannot be provided on a small area basis. This problem is covered by the concept of "packageability" of Ostrom *et al.*[7] Special districts emerge when the municipalities prove too small to comprehend a problem. Air pollution control needs a different size "package" from police service.

The market place model does have certain attractive features which will be developed later. The fact remains, however, that there is a surprising incongruity between actual service areas and the technically required service area, such as, for example, in controlling pollution in most metropolitan areas. In addition there is some question as to whether the model conceives the time sequence properly. Which comes first, the specialized suburb or its specialized services?

The third model, power structure, raises the question of whether services, which are integrated on an area wide basis, coincide with the interest of a metropolitan wide political elite. Is there an elite which integrates those functions in which it has a particular stake and then ignores all others, which remain decentralized? The power structure approach was first suggested by Floyd Hunter,[8] who defined the Regional City political community in metropolitan dimensions. A specific effort was made to verify this model in the Syracuse study,[9] which concluded that no over-all elite existed and that political leadership varied from one functional service area to another. A more extreme statement rejecting the power structure model was made by Norton Long,[10] who saw the relationships among the metropolitan political structures as ecological in nature. He viewed the metropolitan governmental service pattern as resulting from unplanned and uncoordinated actions.

---

[6] Wilbur R. Thompson, *A Preface to Urban Economics*, (Baltimore: The Johns Hopkins Press, 1965), Chapter VII.

[7] Vincent Ostrom, Charles M. Tiebout, and Roland L. Warren, "The Organization of Government in the Metropolitan Area: A Theoretical Inquiry," *American Political Science Review*, 55 (December 1961), 835–837. The "polycentric" model presented in this article is not strictly an economic one.

[8] *Community Power Structure* (Chapel Hill: University of North Carolina Press, 1953).

[9] Roscoe C. Martin, Frank Munger, *et al.*, *Decisions in Syracuse*, (Bloomington: Indiana University Press, 1961).

[10] "The Local Community as an Ecology of Games," *American Journal of Sociology*, 64 (November 1958), 251–266.

The shortcoming of all three models, as valuable as some of their insights are, is the failure to perceive the characteristic differences between the services which are centralized and those which are decentralized, or to misconstrue the basis of the distinction where it is perceived. It is the thesis of this paper that a distinction does exist and that it can be identified in terms of values. Models which restrict their attention to economics, technology, or communications will fail to be sufficiently comprehensive, despite the relevance of each of these variables to a theory of metropolitan politics.

THE DEVELOPMENT OF MUNICIPAL LIFE STYLES

While the service-market place theory represents a sound observation, it starts too late in the process of metropolitan development. It is necessary to begin earlier and ask about the way the new metropolitan form emerged. This subject must be dealt with in a brief and suggestive manner here. Economic location theory and cultural ecology will be used as points of departure.

Locational theory endeavors to explain the urban land use pattern in terms of space friction costs and rent.[11] Every economic unit seeks that place in the urban environment where the cost of overcoming space friction is minimized. Space friction exists because of each unit's need for other units to carry out its own purposes. For example, a firm must assemble a labor force, obtain supplies, and deliver its product to customers. As more than one economic unit attempts to occupy the same site in their efforts to minimize the cost of overcoming space friction, rent becomes the determining factor in deciding site occupation. The unit which can exploit a given location most profitably will occupy it through paying higher rent. As similar units seek similar locations, certain homogeneous groupings emerge (such as, industrial areas, the CBD).

An attempt to explain the location of homesites in the same fashion, after scant analysis makes it abundantly clear that the family is not simply an economic unit. Urban ecologists discovered years ago that social values contribute to homesite selection.[12] More recent surveys find families moving to suburbs for a syndrome of child-rearing reasons. Despite the influ-

---

[11] A classic statement upon which many subsequent elaborations rest is R. M. Haig, *Major Economic Factors in Metropolitan Growth and Arrangements.* (New York: The Regional Plan of New York and Its Environs, 1928).

[12] Pioneering work in this area was contributed by Walter Firey. See his "Sentiment and Symbolism as Ecological Variables," *American Sociological Review.* (April, 1945), 140–148.

ence of social values, rent also acts as a constraining factor. Thus both the theories of land economics and cultural ecology must be used in explaining urban location decisions.

The use of a slightly different perspective can bring together the statements of the economic location theorists and the cultural ecologists, allowing discussion of all locational decisions with one set of references, minimizing confusion in our discussion. Lewis Mumford has characterized a city as a "special receptacle for storing and transmitting messages." [13] That is to say, a city is a device for overcoming space friction for a social purpose. The content of these messages and the relative importance of particular types of messages vary over time and from city to city. Economic message exchanges are very important in our contemporary cities, but they are not the only ones. Middle class families choose suburban locations with lots of grass, but more important, these locations are where the variety of home-related message exchanges are compatible with middle class values. These considerations are usually more social and educational than economic. Locational choices are made not only to increase the ease of exchanging rewarding messages, but also to minimize unrewarding and unwanted messages. This situation is particularly true of our homesite selection illustration. A middle class family chooses a suburb which will also reduce unpleasant message exchanges from lower class persons in the form of muggings, fistfights, and uncouth syntax.

Strategic locations, which afford the favorable message exchange arrangement, once acquired, must be safeguarded. The location requires protection, for the curse of urbanism is the instability of site advantages. A variety of social institutions, of which the municipality is one, help to protect the place of advantage for its constituents and to slow down the forces of change. Strategic locations can be maintained, in part, by policies which regulate who will occupy adjacent locations. The values of one household are affected by the values of adjacent ones, particularly if there are children, for modes of child-rearing become an issue. Viewed in these terms, zoning is a device for maximizing rewarding message exchanges and minimizing unpleasant ones, through assuring the spatial contiguity of compatible message generating units. This language may be a bit overwhelming for describing "neighboring," but it permits us to refer to such different social institutions as factories and homes with a common set of concepts.

The political unit in metropolitan analysis is a social unit which has a spatially definable domicile. These units (which will be called *socio-spatial*

---

[13] *The City in History* (New York: Harcourt, Brace & World, 1961), p. 99.

units) include households, factories, stores, churches, clubs, offices, and the like. Each one of these socio-spatial units possesses a hierarchy of values. For example, businesses generally wish to maximize profits, but the profit value subsumes intermediate values, such as a desire for expansion room, accessibility to a high class labor force, protection from pilfering, and so forth. Households may seek quality education, convenient shopping, pleasant neighbors, and a short trip to work. These sets of values may be called the unit's *life style values*. The realization of some of these life style values are enhanced by the locational choices of the unit; some require the support of local services for their realization. Those life style values which depend upon location for their realization are the major sources of metropolitan politics. Local government, in its various manifestations, is the governmental level which has primary control over the immediate physical and social environment of any given socio-spatial unit. The physical environment includes such factors as highway access patterns, parks, the location of facilities, and other mapable and physically describable appurtenances. The social environment includes the proximate social processes and institutions.

One of the important strategies commonly pursued by socio-spatial units in maximizing their possibilities for realizing life style values is homogeneous and complementary groupings. Jane Jacobs' importunings to the contrary notwithstanding, this remains a cardinal principle of most city planning.[14] Subdivisions, industrial parks, and shopping centers are the norm. Following the logic of this strategy, a decentralized (suburbanized) metropolitan governmental pattern appears to be superior to a centralized (consolidation) mode for the enhancement of life style values. Under the former arrangement, diverse groups need not constantly compete in the same political arena, a situation characteristic of heterogeneous units, such as the core city (particularly as it has existed traditionally). The more nearly the suburb specializes, the easier it is, politically, to maintain the primacy of the values prized by the dominant type of socio-spatial unit. This point brings up the question of why any specialized suburb would ever voluntarily consent to amalgamate with another whose life style was different.

The above analysis is not incompatible with the market place model; it is simply more inclusive. Location choices are made in relationship to

---

[14] *The Death and Life of Great American Cities* (New York: Random House, 1961). Mrs. Jacobs advocates a mixed land use pattern and feels that zoning as presently practiced leads to undesirable blocks of single usage land development patterns.

many factors, of which municipal services is one—how important a one, we do not know. It is certainly the case that once established, suburbs offer specialized service packages. Some offer good schools, large lot zoning, and a county squire physical setting. Some may be more predisposed to fitting parochial schools into the service set. A list of a few of the exotic types might include the suburb that caters to industries only, where night watchmen supply the required population to establish a voting citizenry; the vice suburb that services a metropolitan area in illicit entertainment by selective police enforcement policies. California even has its dairy farm suburbs, sort of anti-urban islands in an urban sea. These places all have their specialized service packages, which do act as advertisements saying, in effect, "all those who like the kind of life symbolized by these services come and join us, if you can afford it."

THE INTERDEPENDENCE OF SPECIALIZED MUNICIPALITIES

What has been said thus far will enable one to understand much of metropolitan politics, but it covers only half of the situation. It is the other half that leads to many of the intense political battles. The municipalities of the metropolitan area are specialized and, consequently, interdependent. One specialized area can only exist if its complement in specialization exists elsewhere. If there is an industrial suburb, there must also be a residential one; if there is a rich man's suburb, there must also be one for the poor. The fact of interrelatedness is dramatized twice daily by glutted commuter arteries, leading not only to the core city, but criss-crossing in every direction, through any major metropolitan area.

If it were not for this interdependence, each little specialized suburb could have its political cake and eat it too. All local policies could be conceived in terms of self images. But the dynamics of the metropolis will not let that occur. These dynamics are expressed through the need to create integrating mechanisms which, though they maintain the over-all system of specialized areas, often transform the nature and character of individual municipalities in the process.

The *system maintenance* mechanisms of the metropolis may be classified into two principal categories, the communications and utility systems. Here, communication system is intended to include what is traditionally called transportation, as well as communications. Mumford's messages, so to speak, take physical as well as symbolic forms. Highways, airports, mass transit, telephone, telegraph, radio, television, delivery services, mail, and water transport facilities comprise the principal communications system.

Each of these systems must have a jurisdiction larger than any single municipality, for it is their function to integrate the specialized municipalities into an operating whole.

The utility networks supply power, water, and waste disposal services which enable the technological appurtenances of each socio-spatial unit to carry on. For technological and financial, rather than functional, reasons, the utilities are usually operated as large area networks, which supply services to more than one municipality. But strictly speaking, none of the utilities has to be larger than a given municipality in order to be functionally operative. Miniaturization of these services can take place in the form of on-site facilities and small package plants.

There is, in addition, a third set which might be considered system maintenance mechanisms—the central facilities. These are the major service facilities in urban areas which sustain and support urban life. These exist in both the private and public sectors. In the more public sector, every metropolitan area requires the presence of one or more university, museum, stadium, arena, library, hospital, and the like. These services are most often handled through *ad hoc* and semi-public arrangements which infrequently demand intergovernmental cooperation for their creation. For those that are revenue-producing, a single government, often the core city, will act as an entrepreneur in providing the service. Generally, central facilities are not major sources of political friction.

The system maintenance functions do just what those words imply: they maintain the over-all system, and in the process, insure that particular life style values are preserved or enhanced. In this sense, they are instrumental services. However, these services not only bind the specialized areas into an over-all social and economic system; they also profoundly affect the spatial distribution of specialized areas. Strategic locations are, in large part, defined in relationship to the system maintenance functions. This is particularly the case with the communications systems, of which the ground transportation arteries are the most important. Utility networks play a similar role, but to a much lesser extent, and their role varies more radically from place to place. The existence of central facilities makes the truncated service complements of small suburbs possible.

It is the central argument of this paper that the socio-spatial units resist integration of what I have called life style services, but accept, and at times encourage, integration of system maintenance services. More accurately, the response is such when the issues are perceived correctly. The consequences of structural changes in service arrangements are subject to numerous interpretations. Campaigns can be obfuscating, and adroit publicity in the context of a metropolitan referendum can at times place issues in a light which does not foretell their likely consequences. However, only occasionally will the campaign techniques alone control outcomes. The proposition about decentralized life style services and centralized system maintenance services generally holds true.

Metropolitan politics can be further understood by realizing that various systems maintenance services have quite different impacts in the course of their creation or expansion. The most essential difference lies in their feedback effect on locational advantages. Several illustrations will help to clarify this point.

The differential effects stemming from the expansion of an intra-urban expressway and a telephone system in a metropolitan area will now be considered. When a new highway is built, it alters the whole pattern of accessibility among points within the metropolis. Areas which were previously too remote for commuter homes suddenly become accessible in a time-of-travel sense. New interchanges in places which previously had no attractions for these uses, become desirable locations for shopping centers and warehouses. A new expressway causes many incongruities between social and economic values attached to locations and the existing zoning ordinances. The established life style of communities becomes threatened by the invasion of socio-spatial units whose values are at variance with those already existing in the community.

Contrast this situation with the impact of the extension of a telephone system. Within certain limits, there are no spatially strategic access points in a telephone system. Aside from a few esthetic objections to new utility poles, telephone system expansion does not disturb the ecological balance of areal specialization. This, indeed, may explain why highways are publicly owned and telephones are not.

The highway problem warrants a closer look. If highways do not comprise some semblance of a network, they are not even highways, because they are supposed to go to places where travelers want to go. To be integrated, they must be planned, not simply added to by each suburban increment to the metropolis. Therefore, there is a tacit consent that area wide governmental agencies have control of highways (usually the state, and now, more and more, the federal government). At the same time, highway construction is the most volatile metropolitan policy area. Every new expressway is fought vehemently; yet it is built! The battle is so intense and bitter because the life style of some areas must be sacrificed to maintain the life styles of most other areas. There is a wrenching conflict between the benefited and the disrupted. Frequently, the problem is solved by building highways through areas with the fewest political resources for obstructionism, or through areas that may acquire actual benefits, such as an industrial or a commercial area. Highway politics cannot be explained in any economic gains and losses fashion. Communities in which land values will be enhanced by highway construction often still oppose it.

Thus it can be seen that the integration and centralization of system maintenance functions does not always proceed with ease or without conflict. But the process does continue, though interrupted by occasional reversals. Strategies may have to be changed, but in the long run, the pattern does not.

While it is possible conceptually to classify municipal services into life style and system maintenance policies, it is more likely that the variable is continuous, rather than dichotomous. The scale on the life style side refers to the importance of the service in maintaining preferred values. Probably the most critical policy is land use regulation, with education a close second. Both of these policy areas have great potential for affecting the rate of rewarding or disruptive message exchanges. Along the continuum, such policies as housing, urban renewal, recreation, libraries, police, and parks follow in approximately that order of importance. Certain health and welfare functions may be effectively neutral, along with such minor administrative matters as joint purchasing and police radio networks.

A similar continuum exists on the system maintenance side, which is related to the importance of the service to the continued existence of specialized areas. Here, central facilities are least important, utilities next, with the communication services most vital. In addition, different socio-spatial units have different value hierarchies. It follows, therefore, that one suburb might bitterly oppose the integration of a certain service, while another would remain neutral on the issue.

INTERVENING VARIABLES

This life style theory involves an ideal type; no metropolitan area behaves exactly as the theory predicts. However, if it is correct, deviations must be explained in terms of intervening variables. Alternatively, to the extent that an actual metropolitan area approaches the ideal type, its politics will conform to that predicted. This can be stated in the form of propositions: for example, *the more specialized the political sub-units of a metropolitan area, the more political behavior in the area will conform to that predicted.* The factors which influence the development of municipal specialization are key areas for investigation.

Specialization should be considered an indicator, for it is only the precondition for a set of social actions. Specialization is the basis for a sense of community solidarity and identity which in turn leads to a protective posture. What can match the political fervor of a Grosse Point on a zoning issue or Cicero on civil rights?

The identification of the politically relevant kinds of specialization has not been developed. Some preliminary investigations have been performed by the author and associates [15] in relating demographic characteristics and policy variations among suburbs. This analysis was based largely on census and fiscal data, both of which are rather blunt instruments. However, positive relationships were established. Work needs to proceed, both in developing indicators of specialization and in establishing the critical breaking points.

Specialization has been chosen as the appropriate descriptive term over homogeneity because even the most suburban municipal units embrace a certain variety and range of socio-spatial units. There are some extremely homogeneous suburbs, but they remain as examples of specialization fully developed. Normally, municipal boundaries do not operate as sharp demographic breakpoints. Any municipality can absorb a certain degree of internal diversity and still maintain a dominant style. In fact, a certain degree of internal diversity is often required for the maintenance of daily activities. However, a scanning of the range of mean values describing any municipal characteristic in a metropolitan area will quickly establish that real diversity (specialization) exists.

If the degree of specialization is a key to the decisions made in a metropolitan area, those factors which influence the degree of specialization become relevant intervening variables. Three conditions are likely to influence the degree of specialization.

(1) *The larger the metropolitan area, the more specialized are the municipal units.* Suburban specialization in a small metropolitan area is likely to be confined to the "good" and the "other" side of town, in a rudimentary Hoyt sector fashion. Larger metropolitan areas are likely to contain the many gradations of status, class residential suburbs, as well as highly specialized industrial, commercial and other types of suburbs. It is probably also the case that specialization is somewhat related to the size of the municipality, with smaller places being more specialized.

(2) *The older the metropolitan area, the more specialized its municipal units.* The assumption here is that place identities become crystallized over time. Moves are made with a greater awareness of the life style of each place. In the burgeoning newer metropolitan areas, growth may take place so rapidly that the visibility of the life style remains low and the local

---

[15] Williams, *et al., op. cit.*

political structures are not sufficiently stable to employ effective screening policies for entering socio-spatial units.

(3) *The more permissive state incorporation laws are for local self determination, the more specialized the municipal units.* This postulated metropolitan behavior should be most fully realized when the metropolitan citizens have free choice in drawing their municipal boundaries. In fact, the opportunities for doing so vary greatly from state to state. Some states, such as Michigan and California, for years gave suburban residents wide latitude in fringe incorporation decisions. In the East, suburban boundaries are largely predetermined by traditional town and township lines. In still other states, such as Texas, the core city has had the initiative with respect to annexing fringe areas. However, even under this circumstance a vigorous outcropping of fringe area incorporations has taken place.[16]

Metropolitan area politics is a function not only of internal circumstances, but also of outside influences emanating from state and federal governments. The theory is formulated with reference to indigenous forces. There remains the possibility that accommodations within the metropolitan areas can be amended by higher levels of government. This appears not to be the case to any great extent, as higher levels seem to respect, rather than disrupt, the metropolitan settlement. Interventions from the federal government are most forceful in the system-maintenance areas. The only substantial area in which the federal government is willing to require authoritative metropolitan wide planning as a condition for receiving grants-in-aid is in the interstate highway program. Contrast its policies here with those in housing and urban renewal, where federal policy operates fully within the metropolitan framework of decentralizing decisions on life style policies.

The policies of state governments do not vary radically from those of the federal government. Mandatory county assumption of services is likely to be confined to the more neutral or low conflict service areas such as the distribution of categorical welfare payments or health benefits. In both of these areas, benefits are distributed to individuals and the policies have little affect on the life style of any community. (The county services which antedate metropolitan development may be exceptions to these observations.) In fact, state grant-in-aid programs financially underwrite the whole decentralized pattern of metropolitan areas. Particularly school aid provides a fiscal flow enabling poor suburbs to maintain autonomous school districts. This takes some of the pressure off the consolidation movement.

---

[16] Richard L. Stauber, *New Cities in America* (Lawrence: Government Research Bureau, the University of Kansas, 1965). The largest number of SMSA incorporations of any state in the decade 1950–60 was in Texas (83).

Although there may be some states which are exceptions to the above generalizations, with reapportionment placing more power in the hands of the suburbs, future development is likely to follow the predicted course.

SOCIAL CONSEQUENCES OF SPECIALIZATION

At the outset, it was stated that at present there is neither an adequate analyical model of metropolitan area politics nor a proper appreciation of the social significance of what is occurring. If the life style theory presented here describes the present state, and, more important, the future course of metropolitan development, its probable social consequences are worthy of serious consideration.

Metropolitan areas, as presently constituted, will eventually find solutions for system maintenance services. Many writers point to this trend as a proof of the ability to muddle through using present governmental structures. In the short run, it is often more of a muddle than muddling through, as some of the system maintenance services are expanded only after protracted and costly delays. A twenty year gap between need and construction of a given facility is not uncommon. Even if we accept this course of decision-making as normal, the decentralization of life style policies promises to remain a durable arrangement. It is easy to dismiss this problem. People are happier in living where they have compatible neighbors; certain forms of specialization are highly efficient. But, is the new metropolitan form the best of all possible urban political structures? There remain a number of concerns.

Little research has been done in the United States on life in a specialized community. The English sociologists have shown greater interest in this subject partly because of the new towns policies. Peter Willmott reports on life in a large, homogeneous, and mature working class suburb of London.[17] Homogeneity has removed much conflict from the lives of its inhabitants and contentment is the norm. But there were other consequences of this specialized life style. The school system was miserable. Upward mobility was positively discouraged by the culture of the community. We are now developing our working class suburbs, and the school situations are similar. What does the new metropolitan form mean for the future of social mobility?

The metropolitan form, as it is now emerging, is an ecological heaven for whites only. The most disturbing instances of racial violence in the North are not in the core cities, but in the suburbs. In the core cities, the

---

[17] *The Evolution of a Community* (London: Routledge and Kegan Paul, 1963).

police force must maintain some semblance of neutrality; at least there is political recourse when it does not. In the specialized suburbs, the whole power of law, police, and social institutions is likely to be arrayed on one side of the conflict, and this assures that the possibility for racial residential mobility will be narrowly circumscribed.

In every major metropolitan area, there are developing obsolete suburbs and satellite cities that are as dysfunctional, in terms of locational and physical requirements for contemporary urban life, as are the old prairie, wheat belt service towns. As the suburbs spiral down, they have an accumulation of tax, service, and leadership woes. Unlike the heterogeneous and diversely composed core cities, which mobilize strengths and resources from viable areas in order to cope with problem areas, the deteriorating suburb cannot employ this urban renewal strategy. When a suburb goes down, people just move away and normally there is no unit of local government that can or will assume responsibility for what happens.

There are other possible consequences of the new metropolitan form. Are we creating unemployment by decentralizing manufacturing, yet excluding low wage persons from access to jobs because of the absence of suitable housing? Few suburbs will permit public or low cost housing to be built near the very factories they seek to alleviate property tax problems. Public health departments tend to exist more in the high status suburbs than in the low status ones. Libraries, recreational programs, and government financed social services exhibit a similar pattern.

In brief, while national attention is focused on the problems of core cities as dumping grounds for the unfortunate metropolitan citizens, the country may be creating a new system, which, in the long run, will have even more unfortunate consequences for the distribution of opportunities. At least the core city has high visibility; consequently, its problems are politically salient at the state and national levels. What is emerging in the new metropolitan form may be more easily overlooked. Thus, even if the study of municipal specialization falls short of explicating metropolitan intergovernmental relations, though I believe it will not, this subject is worthy of our attention for other reasons.

21

DIFFERENTIAL PATTERNS OF
COMMUNITY POWER STRUCTURE:
An Explanation
Based on Interdependence

JOHN WALTON
Northwestern University

[Proceeding from a secondary analysis of the existing body of community power structure studies, an explanation of local power arrangements is advanced based on Warren's vertical axis of community organization or the interdependence of the local community and extra community institutions. Earlier studies indicate that the following variables are associated with competitive power structures: absentee ownership, adequate economic resources, satellite status and political party competition. Each of these is interpreted in terms of greater community interdependence. According to the theoretical argument developed here, interdependence tends to produce a fragmentation of local normative order as well as the introduction of new resources and sanctions, leading to a more competitive power arrangement. Implications of the explanation are drawn with reference to future research.]

In the relatively brief period since its inception, the study of community power structure has attracted a wide range of enthusiasts. Researchers of diverse backgrounds have found their particular interests coalesce around the assumption that local leadership processes are of central importance to the explanation of community action. The research implications of this approach have been explored in a variety of areas including urban renewal, social welfare, health and hospital services, community conflict, and ethnic relations.[1] Though often divided on issues of how the leadership

---

[1] See, for example, Amos Hawley, "Community Power and Urban Renewal Success," also included in this present volume, pp. 393–405; Warner Bloom-

process is organized and the extent to which power is effectively exercised, investigators are in agreement concerning the viability of research problems suggested by the approach.

In addition to these fertile substantive applications, much has been done to develop the research methods of power structure studies.[2] The conflict which prevailed a few years ago between proponents of rival methods seems to have subsided with the recognition that different methods tap different dimensions of the total power scene. Investigators now appear to agree on the need for methodologically balanced, comparative, and longitudinal studies. This trend is manifest in several notable works that have appeared recently.[3]

In spite of these convergences, however, there has been almost no progress in one vital respect; the development of theoretical explanations of the reported findings. Elaborate documentation of the atheoretical character of the field hardly seems necessary. One has only to peruse a portion of the literature to discover that the principal issues are almost entirely concerned with method and conflicting interpretations of how broadly power is distributed. Only rarely are some of the initial steps in theorizing

---

berg and Morris Sunshine, *Suburban Power Structures and Public Education: A Study of Values, Influence and Tax Effort* (Syracuse: Syracuse University Press, 1963) ; Ralph B. Kimbrough, *Political Power and Educational Decision Making* (Chicago: Rand McNally & Co., 1964) ; Irving A. Fowler, "Local Industrial Structure, Economic Power and Community Welfare," *Social Problems*, 6 (Summer, 1958), 41–51; Ivan Belknap and John Steinle, *The Community and Its Hospitals* (Syracuse: Syracuse University Press, 1963) ; Floyd Hunter, Ruth Connor Schaffer, and Cecil G. Sheps, *Community Organization: Action and Inaction* (Chapel Hill: University of North Carolina Press, 1956) ; James S. Coleman, *Community Conflict* (New York: The Free Press, 1957) ; William A. Gamson, "Rancorous Conflict in Community Politics," *American Sociological Review*, 31 (February, 1966), 71–81; James McKee, "Community Power and Strategies in Race Relations," *Social Problems*, 6 (Winter, 1958–59), 41–51.

[2] L. Vaughn Blankenship, "Community Power and Decision Making: A Comparative Evaluation of Measurement Techniques," *Social Forces*, XLIII (December, 1964), 207–216; William V. D'Antonio and Eugene Erickson, "The Reputational Technique as a Measure of Community Power: An Evaluation Based on Comparative and Longitudinal Studies," *American Sociological Review*, 27 (June, 1962), 362–376; Linton C. Freeman, *et al.*, "Locating Leaders in Local Communities: A Comparison of Some Alternative Approaches," *American Sociological Review*, 28 (October, 1963), 791–798.

[3] Robert Presthus, *Men at the Top: A Study in Community Power* (New York: Oxford University Press, 1964) ; Robert E. Agger, Daniel Goldrich, and Bert E. Swanson, *The Rulers and the Ruled: Political Power and Impotence in American Communities* (New York: John Wiley & Sons, 1964) ; William V. D'Antonio and William H. Form, *Influentials in Two Border Cities: A Study in Community Decision-Making* (Notre Dame: University of Notre Dame Press, 1965).

represented by conceptual considerations and the development of propositional inventories.[4]

The purpose of this paper is to develop a theoretical explanation of how power is distributed in local communities, and to consider briefly how various power arrangements may account for different forms of community action. The analysis incorporates earlier theoretical discussions of the community and a systematic review of the power structure literature. Anticipating the conclusions for a moment, it will be argued that as communities become increasingly interdependent with extracommunity institutions, changes in the local normative order ensue producing more competitive power arrangements.

Starting with a review of previous research, the argument moves on to consider the adequacy of certain theoretical approaches and, finally, to develop the propositions concerning power structure and community action.

FINDINGS OF PREVIOUS RESEARCH

In an earlier paper the findings of thirty-three power structure studies dealing with fifty-five communities were analyzed in order to determine the relationship between a number of substantive and methodological variables and the dependent variable type of power structure.[5] Subsequently that analysis was replicated using a somewhat larger number of studies.[6] The selection of studies was intended to be exhaustive of the published literature in social science devoted specifically to the study of community power structure. By dealing with the published literature some unpublished studies were excluded, especially dissertations. Confining the analysis to the social science literature excluded journalistic reports. Finally, the criterion that the research be specifically concerned with community power excluded a number of community studies dealing with stratification, local government, and related aspects of social and political life. These criteria were employed in a screening of the literature, and the resulting list of studies was checked against several lengthy bibliographies to insure its inclusive-

---

[4] For some efforts in this direction see Agger, *et al.*, *ibid.*; Presthus, *ibid.*; M. Herbert Danzger, "Community Power Structure: Problems and Continuities," *American Sociological Review*, 24 (October, 1964), 707–717; Terry N. Clark, "Community or Communities?" (this volume).

[5] John Walton, "Substance and Artifact: The Current Status of Research on Community Power Structure," *American Journal of Sociology*, 71 (January, 1966), 430–438.

[6] John Walton, "A Systematic Survey of Community Power Research" in Michael T. Aiken and Paul E. Mott, *The Structure of Community Power: Readings* (in press).

	Pyramidal	Factional, Coalitional and Amorphous	Total
Absentee Ownership			
Present	2	18	20
Absent	12	9	21
Total	14	27	41
	$Q = -.85 \quad .01 > p > .001$		
Economic Resources [d]			
Adequate	9	17	26
Inadequate	6	5	11
Total	15	22	37
	$Q = -.39 \quad .30 > p > .20$		
Type of City [e]			
Independent	14	22	36
Satellite	2	10	12
Total	16	32	48
	$Q = -.52 \quad .20 > p > .10$		
Party Competition			
Competitive	0	10	10
Noncompetitive	10	12	22
Total	10	22	32
	$Q = -1.0 \quad .02 > p > .01$		
Change in Power Structure			
Dispersion	2	17	19
Concentration	0	0	0
No Change	3	4	7
Oscillation	2	1	3
Decline Locally	1	2	3
Total	8	24	32

[a] The cell entries in the table represent communities, rather than studies, since a single study often dealt with two or more towns.

[b] The variable power structure was originally coded in terms of four categories. The categories are collapsed here to avoid small N's and to provide a contrast between more and less concentrated power arrangements.

[c] The N's in each of the subtables vary because the studies coded do not uniformly provide data on each variable.

[d] Operational definitions of the following three variables are indicated by the type of information coded under each category. Adequate economic resources—includes towns with a reportedly prosperous business community, low rates of poverty, and unemployment; inadequate economically—underdeveloped with high rates of poverty and unemployment. Independent city—includes central cities of metropolitan areas and independent manufacturing, commercial or agricultural

ness. Thus the studies are regarded as a universe, defined by the above criteria, rather than a sample.

Each study was reviewed and, when sufficient information was available, coded in terms of a number of self-explanatory independent variables (for example, region, population size, industrialization, economic diversity, and the like). Similarly, the type of power structure identified in each report was coded in terms of four categories: (1) pyramidal—a monolithic, monopolistic, or single cohesive leadership group; (2) factional—at least two durable factions that compete for advantage; (3) coalitional—leadership varies with issues and is made up of fluid coalitions of interested persons and groups; (4) amorphous—the absence of any persistent pattern of leadership or power exercised on the local level.

Table 1 indicates those few associations which were found to be significant or meaningful.[7]

In contrast to these positive findings, a large number of variables, including region, population size, population composition, industrialization, economic diversity, and type of local government, were *not* found to be related to type of power structure.

Taking these results as a summary of the present status of research, it appears that no firm generalizations are suggested. The findings fail to conform to any neat pattern such as an association between competitive power structures and greater complexity of local social and economic organization. The inadequacies of such an explanation are underscored by the negative findings. The evidence may, however, be suggestive of some less obvious explanation. In order to explore that possibility some implicitly theoretical positions in the area of community power and a major theoretical work on American communities will be examined, considering,

---

centers; satellite city—suburb or town dominated by a nearby city. Party competition—the existence of two or more local parties (or affiliates in formally non-partisan cities) which regularly contend for public office; noncompetitive—a one party town.

[e] When the zero-order level findings on economic resources and type of city are examined controlling for research method, a factor associated with type of power structure identified, the differences here do not persist. The findings are reported here because they are suggestive and because the low quality of the data may be obscuring significant associations. That is, the lower the quality of the data, the more difficult it is to demonstrate statistically significant relationships and the more likely it is that such relationships may be obscured. That is, in the present context I have gone beyond a strict interpretation of the earlier findings in an attempt to draw some meaningful generalizations.

[7] A complete summary of the findings, positive and negative, is to be found in Walton, *ibid.*

in both cases, how they square with the above findings and how they might inform the present analysis.

THEORETICAL APPROACHES

In one of the first attempts to bring some order out of the confusion of results, Rogers developed a series of propositions concerning community political systems.[8] His dependent variable, type of political system, was made up of the categories monolithic and pluralistic. In stating the relationship between these and a number of characteristics of community social structure, Rogers hypothesized that the following would be associated with a pluralistic system: a high degree of industrialization, a large population, a socially heterogeneous population, a polity differentiated from the kinship and economic systems, a local government of extensive scope, two or more political parties and the unionization, or other political and economic organization, of working class groups. The underlying theme in this series of propositions, what has been referred to as the implicit theory, centers on the effects of industrialization, and attendant processes of urbanization and bureaucratization, the outcome of these being structural differentiation which contributes to a pluralistic power situation. The approach is, of course, central to contemporary social science whether stated in terms of *gemeinschaft* and *gesellschaft* or any other of a variety of polar types.

Hawley has presented a somewhat more specific approach.[9] Here power is defined as a system property whose distribution can be measured by the ability to mobilize resources and personnel. In any total system, such as a community, this ability lies in the various component sub-systems and is exercised through their managerial functions. Hence, operationally, the greater the number of managerial personnel, the greater the concentration of power. If it is granted that success in a collective action requires the mobilization of resources and personnel, and that this ability is greatest where power is most highly concentrated, then it follows that the greater the concentration of power in a community the greater the *probability* of success in any collective action. In a recent paper, inspired in part by the Hawley piece, Butler and Pope have suggested another measure of power

---

[8] David Rogers, "Community Political Systems: A Framework and Hypotheses for Comparative Studies," in Bert E. Swanson, ed., *Current Trends in Comparative Community Studies* (Kansas City: Community Studies Inc., 1962). A similar but more comprehensive formulation is Terry N. Clark, "Power and Community Structure: Who Governs, Where, and When?" *The Sociological Quarterly*, Summer, 1967.

[9] Hawley, *op. cit.*

concentration—the number of profile or key industries and the concentration of managerial functions within these.[10]

It should be noted that the Hawley and Butler and Pope papers are concerned chiefly with community action; for each the premise is that more concentrated power situations are conducive to concerted action. Unlike Rogers they are not trying to explain patterns of power distribution but, rather, employ these to explain community action. Nevertheless, they are pertinent here because they imply a theoretical position involving the saliency of managerial functions in the determination of community power structures.

How do these explanatory schemes square with the findings culled from the existing literature? Considering first the hypotheses formulated by Rogers, the evidence runs counter to his notions of the effects of industrialization, population size, and population heterogeneity. On the positive side, his proposition about political parties, though not entirely equivalent to party competition, is supported. Unfortunately, no data are available on the remaining three propositions. What evidence exists, however, indicates that Roger's propositions do not fare very well within the present context, though they may have greater predictive power in a cross cultural or historical perspective. For our purposes the implication is that the theoretical approach implicit in these propositions is in need of revision. Perhaps it will be necessary to abandon the simplified notion of a unilinear relationship between the growing complexity of industrial society and more pluralistic local power arrangements, in favor of a more limited, yet more discriminating explanation.[11]

The evidence presented previously is not directly relevant to the Hawley and Butler and Pope approaches since these attempt to explain community action. If, however, it is assumed with these authors that concentrated power structures are associated with community action, and then the antecedent link in their chain of reasoning is examined, it is found that those community characteristics allegedly conducive to power concentration (ones engendering a large number of managerial functions)—industrialization, economic diversity, proportion of absentee ownership, and economic resources—are either unrelated or associated with the less concentrated power structures in the data. This fact can hardly be taken as

[10] Edgar W. Butler and Hallowell Pope, "Community Power Structures, Industrialization and Public Welfare Programs," paper read at the 61st annual meetings of the American Sociological Association, Miami Beach, Florida, August, 1966.

[11] This conclusion applies to similar propositional inventories based on the "evolutionary" or "continuum" notion. See, for example, Delbert C. Miller and William H. Form, *Industry, Labor and Community* (New York: Harper, 1960).

a refutation of the positions presented. What it does indicate is that the number of managerial functions appears to be a poor indicator of type of power structure (though it may indicate the number of potentially powerful people in community action).

In short, the analysis thus far demonstrates the need for theoretical statements which are both more explicit and account better for the available data.

Warren's analysis of *The Community in America* [12] provides a pertinent general framework for dealing theoretically with the specific questions of power structure. Warren's central thesis is that American communities are undergoing a drastic transformation of their entire structure and function; "(this) 'great change' in community living includes the increasing orientation of local community units toward extracommunity systems of which they are a part, with a decline in community cohesion and autonomy." [13] Although Warren analyzes these changes along seven fundamental dimensions of community life, a summary statement indicates their relevance for present purposes:

In the first place, they signalize the increasing and strengthening of the external ties which bind the local community to the larger society. In the process, various parts of the community—its educational system, its recreation, its economic units, its governmental functions, its religious units, its health and welfare agencies, and its voluntary associations—have become increasingly oriented toward district, state, regional, or national offices and less and less oriented toward each other.

In the second place, as local community units have become more closely tied in with state and national systems, much of the decision-making prerogative concerning the structure and function of these units has been transferred to the headquarters or district offices of the systems themselves, thus leaving a narrower and narrower scope of functions over which local units, responsible to the local community, exercise autonomous power.[14]

On the basis of these observations concerning the "great change" and with the simultaneous recognition that communities (that is, 'combinations of social units and systems which perform the major functions having locality reference') do persist as meaningful units, Warren finds useful a distinction between the *horizontal* and *vertical axes* of community organi-

---

[12] Roland L. Warren, *The Community in America* (Chicago: Rand McNally & Co., 1963) and "Toward a Reformulation of Community Theory," *Human Organization*, 15 (Summer, 1962), 8–11.

[13] *Ibid., The Community in America*, p. 53.

[14] *Ibid.*, p. 5.

zation. The vertical axis refers to connections between community organizations and extracommunity centers, and the horizontal axis refers to connections between community organizations. The "great change" involves an increase in the former type of connections often at the cost of the latter.

In what follows several propositions will be developed which relate Warren's approach specifically to the question of how power is distributed on the local level. His concept of a vertical axis of community organization has particular importance for this analysis.

AN EXPLANATION OF DIFFERENTIAL PATTERNS OF COMMUNITY POWER STRUCTURE

Power is defined here as *the capacity to mobilize resources for the accomplishment of intended effects with recourse to some type of sanction*(s) *to encourage compliance.*[15] This definition includes the elements of both potential and actualized power in that capacity for mobilizing resources refers to potential while the application of sanctions refers to actualized power. *Capacity* also implies a distinction from *right* such that *authority* is not confused with the definition. Following Lasswell and Kaplan, the threat of sanctions, positive or negative, distinguishes *influence* from power—influence refers only to the capacity to mobilize resources.

Power structure is defined as *the characteristic pattern within a social organization whereby resources are mobilized and sanctions employed in ways that affect the organization as a whole.*

For the sake of simplicity competitive and monopolistic power structures will be dealt with here.[16] Monopolistic power structures characterize

---

[15] This definition derives from a number of discussions of the concept of power. Some of the most relevant writings include Bertrand Russell, *Power: A New Social Analysis* (New York: Barnes and Noble, 1962); Max Weber, *The Theory of Social and Economic Organization*, trans., A. M. Henderson and Talcott Parsons (New York: Oxford University Press, 1947); Talcott Parsons, "On the Concept of Political Power," *Proceedings of the American Philosophical Society*, 107 (June, 1963), 232–262; Harold Lasswell and Abraham Kaplan, *Power and Society: A Framework for Political Inquiry* (New Haven: Yale University Press, 1950).

[16] This is not meant to imply that such a dichotomy is the most useful framework, though it tends to preoccupy the literature, for example, Presthus *op. cit.*, D'Antonio and Form, *op. cit.* Etzioni has offered four types of control structure based on the means of control available to various positions within an organization; see *A Comparative Analysis of Complex Organizations* (New York: The Free Press, 1961). Agger, *et al.*, characterize power structures with two variables, "distribution of power" and "convergence of leadership ideology," and a resulting four-fold table. Construing the

social organizations in which the capacity for mobilizing resources and recourse to sanctions are the exclusive property of a group with similar interests. In competitive situations the capacity for mobilizing resources and recourse to sanctions are possessed by two or more groups with different interests.

The basic assumption of the theoretical statement to be developed here is that a monopoly of power produces a situation in which consensus is the most important factor underlying the use of power. This consensus may, but need not, imply agreement on values and objectives. What it does imply is agreement concerning the capabilities of those holding power to realize their own intentions over a wide range of community relevant issues. In such a monopolistic situation expectations concerning the norms prescribed by the existing power arrangement tend to be widely recognized. That is, the limits of allowable (non-sanctionable) deviance and opposition are narrow and clear. As a result of these congruent expectations, potential rather than manifest power is more commonly the mechanism by which compliance is encouraged; overt conflict and coercion are relatively infrequent occurrences because compliance can be realized without them. Merriam captured the sense of this assumption when he wrote "Power is not strongest when it uses violence, but weakest." [17]

By contrast, in competitive situations the exercise of power moves from a reliance on consensus to more overt applications of sanctions. This becomes necessary to the extent that competing groups become capable of restricting the scope of each other's sanctions. Claims to power must be supported by effective action. Greater normative diversity, with attendant diversity in expectations, characterizes this situation. Such circumstances result in a greater incidence of conflict stemming from the fact that those who would exercise power are required to make evident their claim through the use of sanctions.

It should be added that each of these circumstances contains elements of the other. Monopolistic power arrangements do, at times, generate

---

second variable as an indicator of leadership cohesiveness, the formulation provides an important distinction between truly competitive systems and cases where power is shared among a number of groups but similarity of interests unites them in a monopolistic power arrangement. Many controversies in the field stem from a failure to make this distinction.

[17] In a more elaborate statement Merriam writes "In most communities the use of force is relatively uncommon in proportion to the number of regulations, and the success of the organization is not measured by the amount of violence in specific cases but by the extent to which violence is avoided and other substitutes discovered." Charles E. Merriam, *Political Power*, Collier Books edition (New York: The Macmillan Company, 1964), p. 36.

divergent norms and expectations just as they occasionally have recourse
to overt applications of coercion. More important, the role of consensual
expectations and potential power are critical to all forms of social organization and can be observed in many of the transactions carried on in
competitive power settings. In this connection conflict is probably most
characteristic of those transitional periods in which power is becoming
more or less diffused since it is at this point that the normative order is
most uncertain and expectations least clear.[18] In the event that this transition is one from monopolistic to competitive it may culminate in a new set
of rules defining community power arrangements which, while more conducive to conflict than the monopolistic situation, produces less conflict
than the transitional phase.

Because at first glance this assumption may appear to be a truism, its
nontrivial character will be demonstrated. Presthus' study of two New
York communities which differed on a pluralist-elitist continuum is valuable here. Discussing the more elitist of the two Presthus reasons;

In Riverview sharper class and economic differences and resulting disparities
in expectations, values and consensus seem to have placed a premium on more
centralized, imperative leadership. As organizational theory and studies of
group behavior suggest, social support, shared values, and common expectations
make possible the minimization of overt power and authority. When community consensus is limited, leaders tend to function in a more unilateral manner.[19]

Here the minimization of overt power and authority is equated with a more
pluralistic (competitive) power situation. The present argument agrees
with the prior notion that common expectations result in a minimization of
overt power (and conflict), but this is taken to be characteristic of a
monopolistic situation. Thus, when community consensus is limited the
leadership process tends to be more competitive.[20]

Obviously the relationship identified in my assumption may operate in
either direction; changes in the competitiveness of the power situation can
produce changes in norms and expectations and, similarly, changes in

---

[18] Although the present concern is with community conflict, this argument closely
parallels Durkheim's thesis on suicide and changes in the normative order.

[19] Presthus, *ibid.*, p. 427.

[20] A more precise treatment of this relationship would specify types of conflict and
how these are associated with various power arrangements. For example, monopolistic
power structures may suppress dissent and conflict, they may manage it within
innocuous limits or they may engender revolutionary conflict. Competitive power
structures, on the other hand, may encourage conflict which results in a stalemate or in
effective argument and nonrevolutionary change.

norms and expectations can lead to changes in power arrangements. This approach is concerned with developing an explanation of the change in power structures, that is, in the latter direction of the causal complex.

This section has reasoned that normative expectations bear a particular relationship to power structure and that conflict can be taken as an indicator of that relationship.[21] In what follows an attempt will be made to elaborate the connection between normative expectations and types of power structure in terms of the data drawn from existing community studies.

Returning to the data in Table 1, the question of how the ideas presented would account for the findings can now be raised. It will be recalled that the data indicate a relationship between competitive power structures and the presence of absentee-owned corporations, competitive party politics, adequate economic resources, and satellite status. Further, in those communities where change was studied, the trend was in the direction of a greater dispersion of power. Do these findings suggest some underlying explanation?

Upon closer examination the evidence does point to an explanation. Each of the variables associated with competitive power structures reflects the interdependence of the community and extra-community centers of power or increased emphasis on the vertical axis. For example, a high proportion of absentee-owned industry suggests that many community relevant decisions are controlled by the personnel and interests of national corporate bodies whose influence may stem from either a deliberate intervention in local affairs or from the more characteristic aloofness to local responsibility.[22] Similarly competitive political parties may often reflect the involvement of county, state and national party organizations in a struggle for control of local constituencies.[23] While it could be reasonably argued that inadequate economic resources result in substantial intervention and control by state and federal agencies which extend aid to local bodies, the position taken here is that communities with more adequate economic

[21] James S. Coleman, *Community Conflict* (New York: The Free Press, 1957) accords with this point by arguing that whenever the pattern of control is so complete that certain elements can see no way of moving into a position of power, there may be sporadic conflict but no organized opposition (nor, presumably, regular conflict).

[22] For studies documenting this see Robert O. Schulze, "The Bifurcation of Power in a Satellite City" in Morris Janowitz, ed., *Community Political Systems* (Glencoe: The Free Press, 1961), 19–80; Roland J. Pellegrin and Charles H. Coates, "Absentee-owned Corporations and Community Power Structure," *American Journal of Sociology*, 61 (March, 1956), 413–419.

[23] On this point there is little evidence pro or con and I present it only as a plausible hypothesis.

resources maintain a greater number of interdependent ties to extra-community institutions such as suppliers, markets, investors, and other economic units. Finally, in the case of type of city, the connection is apparent. Suburban municipalities and smaller towns which form satellites of larger urban centers are interdependent in a variety of economic and political activities including municipal services, jobs, consumer behavior, and the like. If, at points, the relationship between each of these variables and community interdependence is not unambiguous, the position taken here is enhanced by the pattern they suggest when taken together.

Drawing together all that has been said up to this point, the proposition which seems to account best for the findings can be stated as follows; *to the extent that the local community becomes increasingly interdependent with respect to extra-community institutions (or develops along its vertical axis) the structure of local leadership becomes more competitive.*[24]

Theoretically this proposition derives from the more general statement concerning norms and power arrangements. That is, the mechanism by which interdependence, or increasing relevance of the vertical axis of community organization, affects the distribution of community power is the disruption of the local normative order associated with the existing power structure. Development along the vertical axis involves the introduction of new interests and new institutional relationships implying new definitions of the community, and these have the effect of disrupting consensual normative expectations.

In addition to a differentiation of allegiances, these changes include the introduction of new *resources* and *sanctions* into the community. Local organizations with verticle ties to extracommunity institutions frequently share in the capital and human resources of the larger entity making it possible for them to sustain a broader scope of activities than would otherwise be the case. For example, absentee-owned corporations may receive funds and skilled personnel for a desired expansion of local opera-

---

[24] It should be noted that the inferences about change are drawn primarily from cross sectional data and thus run the risk of incorrectly inferring trends. Given the nature of available data there is no alternative other than recommending future longitudinal studies following the lead of Agger, *et al.* and D'Antonio and Form, *op. cit.* Other studies which attempt to replicate earlier work include Delbert C. Miller, "Decision-Making Cliques in Community Power Structures: A Comparative Study of an American and an English City," *American Journal of Sociology*, 64 (November, 1958), 299–310; David A. Booth and Charles R. Adrian, "Power Structure and Community Change: A Replication Study of Community A," *Midwest Journal of Political Science*, VI (August 1962), 277–296; Donald A. Clelland and William H. Form, "Economic Dominants and Community Power: A Comparative Analysis," *American Journal of Sociology*, 69 (March, 1964), 511–521; M. Kent Jennings, *Community Influentials: The Elites of Atlanta* (New York: The Free Press, 1964).

tions making them more important as local tax contributors, employers and suppliers. Such resources carry with them potential sanctions. In the above example some of these would include the threat to locate elsewhere,[25] threat of cut-backs or other actions having an adverse effect on the local economy, support or nonsupport in local elections. What has been said here of absentee-owned corporations could also be said, though perhaps in less dramatic ways, of other vertical community organizations. The point to be emphasized is that these organizations introduce new sources of power into the local picture and, being interdependent, they also have stakes in the local decision-making process which occasionally must be defended. The greater the number of community organizations with vertical ties, the more frequent and the more inclusive are contests surrounding the decision-making process.

In summary, the theoretical statement advanced here states that the introduction of organizations with vertical ties produces a greater interdependence between community and extracommunity centers of power. This interdependence brings changes in the local normative order, as well as new resources and sanctions, creating circumstances conducive to the emergence of competing power centers. Accordingly, variables which reflect the interdependence of the community and the "carrying society"—absentee ownership, party competition, adequate economic resources and satellite status—are associated with competitive power structures; whereas those variables which reflect only intracommunity change—economic diversity, population increase, etc.—are not so associated.[26]

Parenthetically, it is instructive to note certain parallels between this argument and Banfield's theoretical treatment of the exercise of power. Defining power as "the ability to establish control over another" (that is, "the ability to cause another to give or withhold action"),[27] Banfield states

---

[25] For a discussion of this ploy and other sanctions available to economic institutions see Arnold Rose, *The Power Structure: Political Processes in American Society*, (New York: Oxford University Press, 1967), Chapter 3.

[26] The point to be emphasized here is that greater complexity and specialization are not necessarily conducive to the changes under consideration, but only insofar as these developments produce greater interdependence. At some point, of course, complexity and specialization do necessitate greater interdependence but it would seem that this is not always the case at every level of community development. We would expect that some of these variables are confounded such that increasing size, for example, will be related to competitive power structures at that point in a community's development when size and interdependence vary together. According to this argument such an association would be spurious. This may be the case though the available data are too crude and provide too few observations to allow an unequivocal solution.

[27] Edward C. Banfield, *Political Influence: A New Theory of Urban Politics* (New York: The Free Press Paperback Edition, 1965), p. 348.

that any actor has a limited stock of power which he spends or invests in ways that he believes will maintain and enhance his ability to control. When "investment opportunities" change so does the structure of influence. For example, he offers the following proposition; "As the number of autonomous actors increases, control tends to become less structured. Structures of control, that is, relationships which are stable from proposal to proposal, are expensive to maintain. The value of a structure—and thus the amount that will be invested in it—tends to decline as the outcome of the process becomes less and less subject to control." [28] In the present context the number of "autonomous actors" increases as a result of changes in normative expectations and the effectiveness of sanctions. Similarly, the result here is a less concentrated structure of power.

Returning to my own explanatory scheme, one loose end can be tied up. The findings on change in Table 1 indicated that community power structures are tending to become more competitive. This trend is a predictable consequence of the spread of "metropolitan dominance" [29] and its implications for greater community interdependence. That is, if Bogue and others are correct, and there seems to be ample evidence that they are, the spread of metropolitan dominance would lead one to predict a corresponding trend toward competitive power arrangements according to our explanation. That is, in fact, what the findings indicate.

Discussing the effects of increasing interdependence, Greer summarizes the consequences for the "locality group" in terms of a loss of autonomy, exposure to conflicting norms and the fragmentation of local normative order. In connection with the latter he identifies many of the events and explanations embodied in the theoretical statement developed here.

Fragmentation of the local normative order is a predictable consequence; some of the members of the local group must conform to patterns from afar, since they are dependent upon the large, extended organization for their livelihood. Others take advantage of the local group's loss of coercive power to exploit added degrees of freedom; they experiment with new means to old ends, they exercise freedom of choice. Others, still, are dependent upon the local order for social position and rewards; their life is controlled by its norms, but with the attrition of dependence (and therefore the basis for order), they find it impossible to communicate or to enforce compliance. (The cutting edge of the sanctions depended, after all, upon the interdependence of the

---

[28] *Ibid.*, p. 318.

[29] Don J. Bogue, *The Structure of the Metropolitan Community* (Ann Arbor: Horace H. Rackham School of Graduate Studies, University of Michigan, 1949).

local group.) When individuals become committed to groups centering out-side the locality, the new dependence brings a measure of independence from their neighbors.[30]

This fragmentation of the local normative order, accomplished through changes in expectations concerning power leads, according to this theoretical statement, leads to changes in the structure of community power, and specifically to more competitive power arrangements.

METROPOLITAN POLITICS AND COMMUNITY ACTION

Recalling that the purpose of this paper was to develop an explanation of how power is distributed in local communities, *and* how power arrange-ments may account for community action, some comments on the latter question are called for. Explanation may be particularly useful for two reasons; first, the foregoing analysis bears directly on the subject of community action and, second, the discussion serves to integrate another perspective on power and decision-making into this explanation.

In his well known essay describing the local community as an "ecol-ogy of games," [31] Long argues that the concept of "power structure" suffers from misplaced concreteness, that when we look more closely at cities we find no such structured decision-making institution.

What is characteristic of metropolitan areas is the lack of overall decision-making institutions. This does not mean that there are not institutions with power in metropolitan areas. It does mean that there are no institutions with sufficient power and overall responsibility to make decisions settling metro-politan issues and solving metropolitan problems . . .[32]

Rather, Long conceives of metropolitan issues as having careers in which interested and powerful parties—governments, groups and institutions—interact and "develop a system of largely unintended cooperation through which things get done . . ." [33] In this process actors deal with metropolitan problems from a limited point of view, that is, one confined to their particular interest and institutional base.

There are at least two reasons why Long's empirically persuasive approach has stymied students of community power. One would appear to

---

[30] Scott Greer, *The Emerging City: Myth and Reality* (New York: The Free Press, 1962), pp. 50–51.

[31] Norton E. Long, "The Local Community as an Ecology of Games," *American Journal of Sociology*, 44 (November, 1958), 251–266.

[32] Norton E. Long, *The Polity* (Chicago: Rand McNally & Co., 1962), p. 157.

[33] *Ibid.*

be the fact that much of this research has been conducted in places other than metropolitan areas where decisions settling local issues are possible. Second, the well known controversy over pluralism and elitism in the literature—because it is a debate over who makes local decisions, a small, cohesive group or a large, diverse one—may have obscured the possibility that no one makes such decisions.

In the present explanation metropolitan areas are prototypes of interdependent, vertically organized communities. Here a highly fragmented and competitive power arrangement in which the scope of any group or institution would be limited to prime interest areas could be expected. That is, the competitive process would militate against generalized influence and require that actors work to maintain their position within the system. Long and Banfield concur with this prediction in the stress they put on metropolitan politics as going systems in which institutions and groups seek to maintain and enhance their power in particular areas, public policy representing the results of their cooperation.[34]

Under these circumstances one would expect to find a fragmented and competitive pattern of community action. Community action in American cities seems increasingly to fit this pattern. The most apparent illustrations are found in the activities of civil rights, anti-poverty, and peace groups which often possess resources conferred by extra community institutions and are beginning to seriously involve themselves in the local political process. Here, of course, they encounter opposition from other local and vertically organized groups. As a result coordinated community action becomes more problematic and public policy represents less a reflection of consensus than a byproduct of the competitive process in which power is differentially exercised. Discussing the resurgence of radical politics in Chicago, Cleveland, Pittsburgh, Gary, and several other cities, one author concludes "In the midwest, this tendency is general, and holds promise of becoming the outstanding fact of urban political life in America by the end of the decade." [35] In another vein, several studies which have touched on the consequences of increasing involvement of the federal government in local affairs find, contrary to political folklore, an enhancement of competitive, democratic processes.[36]

---

[34] Also relevant to this characterization is Wallace S. Sayre and Herbert Kaufman, *Governing New York City: Politics in the Metropolis* (New York: Russell Sage Foundation, 1960).

[35] Stephen A. Booth, "The New Politics Goes Local," *The Nation*, V. 204, No. 22 (May 29, 1967).

[36] Presthus, *op. cit.*; William V. D'Antonio, "Community Leadership in an Economic Crisis: Testing Ground for Ideological Cleavage," *American Journal of Sociology*, 71 (May, 1966), 688–700.

Notable among deviant cases is the Vidich and Bensman study [37] where involvement of state and county governments resulted in an abdication of responsibility on the part of local leaders. While it is significant that these changes diluted the power of Springdale's elite, it is also recognized that the consequences of extra community involvement were not those we would predict. In this regard the theory presented here may be in need of modification. Recalling that Springdale is a town of 2,500 people and that its extra community ties center chiefly around state subsidies, it is reasonable to infer that both the nature of the community and of the vertical ties are contingent elements in the theory presented here. Perhaps it is the case, for example, that changes along the vertical axis lead to greater competitiveness only in those communities which possess a certain minimum of institutional viability and that without this the same changes spell the demise of local leadership.

CONCLUSION

The explanation offered here is an attempt to push the study of community power beyond a disproportionate emphasis on technique and toward a concern for testing propositions derived from explicit theoretical statements. There seems little doubt that this alternative is best suited for resolving the controversies over how power is distributed in local communities, and for generalizing research in this area to the larger problems of social organization and change.

The theory developed in this paper states that the introduction into the local community of the institutions and influences of national-urban culture produces a "fragmentation of local normative order" or a disruption of consensual expectations concerning the norms prescribed by existing power arrangements. As expectations are altered and interests are differentiated, new resources are exploited for the creation of competing power groups.

The theory focuses on one direction of influence in what is undoubtedly a complex process. In so doing, however, it has the virtue of generating a number of testable propositions. Future comparative studies could evaluate, on the basis of first-hand data, the fundamental proposition regarding community interdependence and the advent of competitive power arrangements. A sampling of related propositions includes:

(1) Changes, other than interdependence, which challenge the local normative order lead to more competitive power arrangements.

---

[37] *Small Town in Mass Society*, (Princeton: Princeton University Press, 1958).

(2) Intra community change which does not challenge the normative order does not lead to greater competitiveness.

(3) Vertical ties which do not alter the normative order do not lead to the exploitation of new resources and more competitive power arrangements.

(4) Normative diversity within a community leads to a greater frequency of application of overt sanctions (Presthus).

(5) The greater the number of vertical ties in a community, the smaller the scope of local power groups.

(6) The greater the number of vertical ties (and competitiveness) the more difficult (less frequent) is coordinated community action.

In addition to suggesting propositions the theory implies a new direction for research in that it locates the source of local change in the relationship between the community and extra community institutions. It is expected that researchers will find this theory informative as they become increasingly aware of what it implies for the choice of an appropriate unit of analysis in future community power studies. If the theory is correct the appropriate unit of analysis is not the community per se but, rather, the relationship between the community and the institutions of national-urban culture.

IX

RESEARCH ON
COMMUNITY DECISION-MAKING

22

PRESENT AND FUTURE RESEARCH ON COMMUNITY DECISION-MAKING:

The Problem of Comparability *

TERRY N. CLARK
University of Chicago

In the last two decades, hundreds of case studies of communities have been conducted in an attempt to advance understanding of the structure and dynamics of one of the basic units of contemporary social existence. Many important conceptual advances have been made on the basis of intensive investigation of individual communities. But as the number of case studies has continued to increase, and proponents of one or another position have pointed to studies of different individual communities in support of contradictory propositions, the necessity for comparative studies of large numbers of communities has become increasingly evident.

In the last five years, several comparative studies of communities have been undertaken in an effort to generate data that can support comparative propositions in which the structural characteristics of communities are central variables.

As comparative community studies grow in number, in turn, there hopefully will be a greater concern with cumulating comparable data from one study to the next. Most directors of comparative studies initially undertook their research because of the weaknesses inherent in case studies, and one would hope that particularly they—recognizing the limitations of isolated pieces of research, and the short period of time in which even their work can become obsolete as increasingly larger studies are undertaken each year—will be more concerned to render their work comparable with other contemporary studies as well as future investigations.

---

* Parts of this paper were presented at the Session on Comparability in Community Research at the Sixth World Congress of Sociology, International Sociological Association, 4–11 September 1966, Evian, France.

It is toward the general goal of advancing comparability that this final chapter is directed. It represents an effort to facilitate cumulation of results among comparative community studies that have been completed in the recent past, that are underway at present, and that will be undertaken in the future.

The orientation here is thus largely methodological: general theoretical questions will not be dealt with except insofar as they impinge directly on the problems at hand. More specifically, the focus is on matters related to data collection: the types of variables investigated, the combinations of techniques employed toward this end, the content of specific items in questionnaires and interview schedules.

First, fourteen recent studies will be listed that have taken a comparative approach, and that have investigated four or more communities, sometimes in two or more national societies. Next, the types of data collected and procedures being used for their collection in some of the major comparative studies will be considered. Third, the Committee for Comparability in Community Research, and the relevance of its activities to the matters at hand will be discussed. Finally, there will be a brief discussion of the Community Research Data Archive.

RECENT MAJOR COMPARATIVE STUDIES

1. Robert R. Alford, University of Wisconsin, and Harry M. Scoble, University of California at Los Angeles, U.S.A., are presently studying in detail both leaders and the general population through interviews and questionnaires in four Wisconsin cities. They are also collating large amounts of demographic and political data to be fed onto magnetic tape on all cities in the United States with a population over 25,000.

2. Charles M. Bonjean, University of Texas, U.S.A., has recently completed a study of four communities in the American South, and is presently putting demographic and political data on tape for all cities and counties in the United States.

3. Jean Cuisenier, Director of the Programme Méditerranéen at the Centre de Sociologie Européenne in Paris, France, is currently directing programs with social scientists in Tunisia, Turkey, France, Yugoslavia, and perhaps Spain and Portugal. Kinship structures, economic development, and community power are being studied, and basic demographic materials collected on about twelve communities in each country.

4. William Gamson, University of Michigan, U.S.A., has collected data on eighteen small New England communities, including basic demographic materials, reputational leadership information, and decision out-

comes for water fluoridation controversies and two other issues in each community.

5. Claire W. Gilbert, Florida Atlantic University, U.S.A., has brought together materials from published case studies of 166 communities and examined interrelationships among numerous community structural variables—community power being a central one.

6. The International Studies of Values in Politics involves researchers from India, Poland, Yugoslavia, and the United States. About 30 communities are being investigated in each country, basic demographic data collected from published sources, and 1000 political leaders interviewed about their values and involvement in community activities. Although over 100 persons have been involved in the studies at some point, the leading participants include, from India, Rajni Kothari, Director, Centre for the Study of Developing Societies, New Delhi, Kailish K. Singh, Indian Institute of Technology, Kanpur, and V. M. Sirsikar, University of Poona; from Poland, Jerzy J. Wiatr, Director of the Program of Political Sociology at the Polish Academy of Sciences; from Yugoslavia, Anton Vratusa, Director of the Institute of Social Sciences in Belgrade, and Zdravko Mlinar, Institute of Sociology, Ljubjana; from the United States, Philip E. Jacob, University of Pennsylvania.

To complement the study of the values of leaders, case studies of decision-making are being conducted in two issue areas of two communities in each country.[1] In addition, in the United States a more extensive program of studies on community decision-making, which will be discussed shortly, is being carried out in conjunction with ISVP and NORC at the University of Chicago.

7. The Inter-University Consortium for Political Research at the University of Michigan is presently transferring onto magnetic tape enormous quantities of data relating to communities, although almost exclusively for the United States at this time. Included data are those from the 1952, 1956, and 1962 *County and City Data Book* of the U.S. Census on demographic, political, and economic variables for all counties and cities in the United States; from the Scammond, *America Votes* series, Vols. 1 to 4, county election data for President, Senator, Congressman, and Governor; from the

---

[1] At the time that this volume is going to press, the only case studies that I know are completed are Terry N. Clark and James W. Wagner, "Community Values, Decision-Making, and Outputs: Configurations of Inactiveness," International Studies of Values in Politics, USA series No. 83, April 1967; and Terry N. Clark and William Kornblum, "Community Values, Decision-Making, and Outputs: Configurations of Innovation and Activeness," International Studies of Values in Politics, USA series No. 84, April 1967. A volume including these case studies is planned.

1960 and 1962 *Congressional District Data Books;* from the U.S. Census, election and demographic data; and, partially completed, historical materials by county for every election in the United States since 1824 for Governor, Senator, Congressman, and President. The Consortium's archival facilities will be discussed below.

8. Cveto Kostič, Sociological Institute, Belgrade, Yugoslavia, is collaborating with M. Cuisenier in studying about a dozen Yugoslav communities. A sample of communities stratified on such variables as economic development, dominant religion, population size, and geographical region, has been investigated for general structural data and decision-making processes.

9. Henri Mandras, Director of the Groupe de Sociologie Rurale at the Centre National de la Récherche Scientifique, France, Paris, is engaged in studying French rural communities. In a preliminary enquiry about 15 communities have been studied, leaders and the population interviewed, and organizations documented.

10. John B. Mitchell, Ohio State University, U.S.A., is studying about a dozen small communities in Ohio, collecting power structure data using a modified reputational technique.

11. Ehsan Naraghi, Director, Institute of Social Science Research and Studies, Teheran University, Iran, is planning to study at least 100 Iranian communities in terms of a large number of variables.

12. The National Opinion Research Center at the University of Chicago has recently completed a study of school integration in a dozen Northern American cities, and is preparing an investigation of a representative sample of 200 American communities to be undertaken in the very near future. The 200 communities will become a Permanent Community Sample. In each community, contact will be established with an Academic Informer—a local social scientist who can be instructed to collect information—as well as with professional interviewers, so that the 200 communities will serve as a sampling frame which can be offered as a research facility to other social scientists interested in having any sort of community questions investigated in a large sample. Public opinion data on many of the sample communities have already been collected by NORC during approximately the last decade, and will be available for future historical comparisons, as well as for relating public attitudes to community structural variables.

13. Bert E. Swanson, Sarah Lawrence College, U.S.A., has been collecting data on school districts in sub-communities of New York City, and is also studying about a dozen other American cities. In each case, decision-making processes and demographic materials are being collected.

14. John Walton, Northwestern University, U.S.A., has recently completed an investigation of about 55 case studies of communities from published works, and is preparing a study of local communities in Latin America. Demographic, political, economic, and power structure data will be collected.

AREAS OF COMPARABILITY IN DATA COLLECTION

There are at least six major areas in which many of these studies are collecting data: demographic composition, economic structure, political organization, power structure, leadership values, community public opinion. Each will be discussed in turn.

(1) *Demographic Composition.* Demographic data is generally the most readily available, and the most frequently collected both by previous and on-going studies. Transferring basic demographic data for large numbers of communities onto magnetic tape will make future research a great deal more efficient. The Michigan Consortium's efforts, and those of Bonjean and Alford, are no doubt examples that will be imitated many times over in future years. The American *County City Data Book* (Washington, D.C.: U.S. Government Printing Office), being used by all three, contains information on 208 variables for every county and for every city over 25,000 in the United States.

For smaller American communities, for subdivisions of established census units, for some areas of Europe, and for most of the rest of the world, the data are not so easily available—except for the larger cities. Frequently, however, materials will be collected and recorded at a regional level, but only aggregate results sent on to higher levels. In these cases, the individual researcher must contact local officials or consult regional archives for the information.

When results from earlier governmental censuses are not available (as was the case for Cuisenier in Turkey and several other Mediterranean countries), it is necessary to interview local officials as informants for estimates, or to gather material for estimates following procedures such as those devised by the Physiocrats and political arithmeticians in the years before national censuses, or if resources are adequate and the communities not too large, to conduct a complete census of the community population.

A variety of computed variables, derived from combinations of the basic available data, can be used to establish indicators for more general concepts. Published computed variables of various sorts are available for American cities: Angell's "moral integration," with indexes of crime, welfare effort, heterogeneity, and mobility for 43 cities over 100,000; [2] Thorndike's "goodness" ratings of 310 cities with populations over 30,000,[3] and of 144 cities between 20,000 and 30,300; [4] Gillen's occupational indexes for 1,073 cities; [5] the various indexes in Duncan and Reiss; [6] and Hadden and Borgatta's factors.[7]

While these indexes were specifically constructed for American cities, it would be of interest to compute the same indexes for cities in other countries.

Particularly in a comparative study, it is often of interest to compute some of the indexes reported in these previous works for the communities being investigated; the indexes can be used as both independent and dependent variables to supplement analysis utilizing general demographic characteristics.

(2) *Economic Structure.* A good deal of economic data on local communities is generally collected at the time of a national census and published in census reports. For the United States, the *County and City Data Book* contains dozens of economic variables, for example: total bank deposits, local government revenue, total local expenditures, per cent local expenditures for education, total community employees, number covered by social security, manufacturing establishments by size, and the like. The *U.S. Census of Manufacturers* gives data on economic structure for communities over 10,000, including community population, number of establishments, average number of employees, total salaries and wages, average number of production workers, and total wages.

Numerous handbooks are also available: *Moody's Industrial Manual* (issued yearly) includes data on the officers and board members for large corporations, corporate financial history, subsidiaries, principal plants and properties, and operating statistics. *The Economic Almanac,* issued yearly by the National Industrial Conference Board, contains assorted economic data for larger cities. Labor union membership, organization, and so forth are reported in the *Labor Fact Book,* the *Sourcebook of Union Government*

---

[2] Robert Cooley Angell, "The Moral Integration of American Cities," *American Journal of Sociology,* July, 1951, supplement.

[3] E. L. Thorndike, *Your City* (New York: Harcourt Brace, 1939).

[4] E. L. Thorndike, *144 Smaller Cities* (New York: Harcourt Brace, 1940).

[5] Paul B. Gillen, *The Distribution of Occupations as a City Yardstick* (New York: Columbia University Press, 1951).

[6] Otis Dudley Duncan and Albert J. Reiss, Jr., *Social Characteristics of Urban and Rural Communities, 1950* (New York: John Wiley & Sons, 1956).

[7] Jeffrey K. Hadden and Edgar F. Borgatta, *American Cities: Their Social Characteristics* (Chicago: Rand McNally & Co., 1965).

Structure and Procedures, and the *Directory of National and International Labor Unions in the United States.*

Much of the U.S. Census data on the economic characteristics of communities is being taped by the Michigan Consortium, Bonjean, and Alford, using the *Country and City Data Book.* Data from handbooks such as those just listed could be profitably appended to future efforts of this sort.

Cuisenier has suggestively analyzed community economic structures using mainly Tunisian and Indian data.[8]

(3) *Political (Legal) Organization.* A factor that has been too frequently neglected as an independent variable in communities is the character of the local political institutions. In case studies of single communities it is easily neglected, as well as in comparative studies of a single region or country where all communities have very similar political institutions. In comparative studies involving communities with differing political institutions, it is those specific aspects of political institutions that differ from one community to the next that are most highlighted. One finds, for example, a great deal of discussion in the United States about the importance of partisan versus non-partisan elections, and of mayor versus city manager forms of government—because these are two major aspects of variation among local American governments. Cross-national studies, however, have emphasized the comparatively small number of functions performed by local American governmental units in contrast to those of England and Mexico.[9] Such general findings need to be further refined through more systematic comparative research, which can help to bring into the limelight those aspects of political institutions which are not so universal, and help to evaluate their importance.

The Municipal Yearbook, published annually by the International City Manager's Association in Chicago, focuses mainly on those aspects of American governments that vary within the United States, such as mayor versus city manager, partisan or non-partisan elections, method of electing councilmen (from wards or at large), and the size of the council districts.

---

[8] Jean Cuisenier, *L'Ansarine, Contribution à la sociologie du développement* (Paris: Presses Universitaires de France, 1963); Cuisenier, "Le systeme economique villageois," *Etudes rurales,* XIII–XIV (April–September, 1964), 132–172.

[9] See Delbert C. Miller, "Decision-Making Cliques in Community Power Structures: A Comparative Study of an American and an English City," *American Journal of Sociology,* LXIV (November, 1958), 299–310; William V. D'Antonio and William H. Form, *Influentials in Two Border Cities* (Notre Dame: University of Notre Dame Press, 1965).

Useful studies can be made based on these data, through examining interrelationships among them and general census data,[10] but analysis is limited by the relatively narrow range of variation in types of political institutions in contrast to what is possible with a cross-national study. Almond and Verba's investigation of public attitudes in England, Germany, Italy, Mexico, and the United States made an important contribution to understanding the differences in context within which political institutions in these five countries must function.[11] The International Studies of Values in Politics may be just as revealing for differences in orientation among political leaders in India, Poland, Yugoslavia, and the United States. Similarly, differences in the organization of political institutions in different countries are variables that become more salient without cross-national comparisons.

(4) *Power-Structure—Decision-Making Processes.* There have been three widely used methodologies for studying the distribution of influence in local communities: the reputational approach, the decisional approach, and the positional approach. An extensive literature has developed pertaining to the merits and demerits of the three approaches that will be largely passed over for the moment. Only a few examples of adaptations of each of the three methodologies in recent comparative studies will be taken up here.

The reputational approach.—After the pioneering work by Floyd Hunter in 1953, *Community Power Structure*,[12] dozens of community studies have made use of variations of the reputational approach to study what Hunter designated the "community power structure."

William Gamson has more recently used a basically reputational approach in studying eighteen New England communities. Persons active in three issues in each community were asked the following question: "In many communities, relatively few people are able to affect the outcomes of issues sometimes because they are in a position to make key decisions or because they have the ability to persuade others to follow their leadership. Would you tell me the names of the most important and influential leaders in this community even if they do not hold public office?"[13] About a dozen of the most frequently named persons were designated reputational leaders

---

[10] An outstanding recent example is Raymond E. Wolfinger and John Osgood Field, "Political Ethos and the Structure of City Government," this volume.

[11] Gabriel A. Almond and Sydney Verba, *The Civic Culture* (Princeton: Princeton University Press, 1963).

[12] Originally published by the University of North Carolina Press; Doubleday-Anchor paperback, 1963.

[13] "Reputation and Resources in Community Politics," this volume.

and interviewed about their activities in various community issues. Reflecting recent thinking on the question, however, Gamson did not interpret those persons who were named as actual leaders, but as individuals having a reputation for influence in their communities.

Variations of the reputational approach have been used in comparative studies by the National Opinion Research Center (NORC) and by John Mitchell.

One particularly interesting variation is what has been called here the "issue specific reputational approach." It consists of asking informants to rank or score particular individuals, groups, or organizations—community actors—in terms of their influence in a particular issue area. It may be used in a simple open-ended form with a question such as, "Who is influential in matters of educational policy in this community?" A slightly more structured variation presents a list of (presumably) leading actors for the informants to choose from. A third, and most structured, variation has the informant rank the actors in terms of their relative importance, or respond as to their importance using a graduated scale of importance—for example, "highly influential," "somewhat influential," "not very influential." This last variation of the issue specific reputational method is being used in the ISVP-NORC study of decision-making in 51 American communities.

The decisional approach.—Often associated with Robert Dahl, who popularized the decisional approach in his *Who Governs?* [14], variations of this method have been used with increasing frequency in recent years. Robert Alford and Harry Scoble have used a modified decisional approach in their comparative study of Wisconsin communities. Using two concrete decisions and two more general issues, they interviewed community leaders asking first, "Can you tell me if you were involved in any way in this decision?" Second, they established the leader's views in the matter in terms of agreement with the decision or his alternative preferences. Third, they inquired about the amount of controversy—"a little," "some," "a great deal"—and then focused on major actors in the decision with the question "Do you identify anyone—individuals or groups—with having originated the proposal which led to this decision?," and again with a question about who "worked hardest" in bringing about the decision. Sixth was an enquiry about opposing individuals or groups, and finally, another about "who benefited most" from the decision.

The same format was repeated four times, twice for decisions and twice more for general issues.

The National Opinion Research Center has joined forces with the

---

[14] (New Haven: Yale University Press, 1961).

International Studies of Values in Politics program for studying community decision-making in the United States. It seems useful to discuss this particular project in more detail, not simply because I am serving as joint study director with the two projects, but because a number of interesting advances have been made in the course of our work.

A major aspect of community decision-making that has continually interested writers on the subject is the degree to which decisions are made by a small number of persons or by a larger number of individuals and groups: the degree to which power is centralized or decentralized in local communities. In the NORC-ISVP study, data are being collected using NORC professional interviewers in a total of 51 American communities. Four issue areas are being studied in detail in each community: the election of the mayor, urban renewal, the poverty program, and air pollution. If virtually no action had been taken in a community in one of these areas, this too was a finding demanding explanation.

Instead of using a sociometric procedure of "snowball sampling" for uncovering the persons involved in each issue area and then interviewing them, a standard panel of knowledgeable community residents was interviewed as informants. For information about decisions in all four areas, interviews were conducted with persons in contact with different sectors of the community: the president of the Chamber of Commerce, the president of the bar association, the president of the largest bank, the head of the largest union, and the editor of the newspaper with the largest circulation. For more detailed information relating to the election of the mayor, structure of the political parties, and the poverty program, the mayor and the chairmen of the two political parties were interviewed; for information on urban renewal, the urban renewal director; for air pollution, the health commissioner.

A similar format was used to study each of the four issue areas. A first series of questions asked about the importance of fifteen different community groups for influencing decisions in the specific issue area (political parties, church leaders, labor unions, neighborhood groups, and the like). Then the names and positions in the community of the most important *supporters* of the issue were asked; the major reasons, in the informant's opinion, for their supporting the issue; the "resources or kinds of influence" used by the supporters; and their success in attaining their goals. A total of about 25 questions were posed to elicit information in each of these matters. The same general questions were then repeated for the *opponents* of the specific issue.

The basic procedure used for classifying communities as centralized or decentralized as concerns decision-making structure was to assign one point to every actor named as playing some kind of active role in each issue area. If, for example, only the mayor and organized labor were named as the supporters in each of the four issue areas, and only the retail merchants named as the opponents in each of these same areas, then the total score for the community would be 3. But if six different actors were named in each of the four issue areas, with no overlap from one issue area to the next, the community would be assigned a score of 24. Such a quantitative measure of centralization can easily be correlated with the other sets of variables using standard statistical procedures.

The positional approach.—The positional approach is the simplest of the three methods, consisting of simply defining community leaders as the incumbents of high positions in major community institutions— government, political parties, industry, labor unions, and the like.

The positional approach is often combined with one of the first two methods, as did Mitchell with the reputational, and Alford and Scoble with the decisional.

When the focus of a study is largely on topics other than decision-making, the positional method may be used to obtain a list of leaders about whom further information can be collected. This was initially the procedure used in the International Studies of Values in Politics, where 30 position-holders in government administration, elected posts, and political parties in each of 30 communities in each of the four countries are being studied.

(5) *Community Leaders' Values and Activities.* The International Studies of Values in Politics program is administering a questionnaire to a total of 4000 local political leaders in India, Poland, Yugoslavia, and the United States. The questionnaire consists of three major parts. The first is a value inventory of 185 items, generally agree-disagree statements scored on a four-point scale such as the following: "It is not necessary for the political leaders to be concerned about the economic development of the country," or "If there is disagreement about a program, a leader should be willing to give it up," or "National goals should not be obtained at great costs to local communities." The items have been extensively pre-tested over the past year with samples from each of the countries, and ten scales established through factor analysis: economic development, conflict resolution-avoidance, participation, selflessness, local-national orientation, action propensity, honesty, change orientation, equality, and political responsibility.

Many of the items have already been used in earlier studies, and after they have been administered to the 4000 political leaders, future studies will have in these items an excellent base against which to compare their own results. The ease of administering the items, as well as the possibility of utilizing only a sub-sample of them, makes their repeated use particularly desirable.

The second part of the questionnaire consists of leadership activities, and contains a number of suggestive items. One question asks leaders to check if they are active in ten different areas, including industrial development, agriculture, housing, health, education, and political organization activities. Another item asks the leader to rate his influence—"great," "some," or "none"—for each of these ten areas. There is also a provocative open-ended question: "In the areas where you feel you have a great deal of influence, what was the single most important recent action here in which you participated, and how did you participate?"

A further section deals with conflicts and cleavages, and establishes the relative importance of various reference groups. A major emphasis in this section is on the relative loyalty of political leaders on the one hand to traditional local groupings—such as ethnic, religious, and racial groups, local citizens, and associates—and on the other to higher level administrative and political party hierarchies. The positions taken by local community leaders in local-national conflicts are particularly crucial in countries undergoing rapid social change, often initiated from above, and these items, combined with the ideological orientation of the leader toward traditional or modernizing values, constitute a very strong questionnaire.

(6) *Community Public Opinion.* The utility of collecting data on general public opinion in a community is perhaps obvious, with the possibilities it offers for contextual analysis of political organization, decision-making processes, and leaders' values and activities. And yet, only seldom have community studies collected public opinion data. Some of the more recent comparative studies fortunately are collecting such data, however, including Alford and Scoble, Cuisenier, Kostič, Mandras, and the National Opinion Research Center. But the range of items used is so wide that it is advisable to utilize items that have been widely used in earlier studies, so that an established basis of comparison is available.

THE COMMITTEE FOR COMPARABILITY
IN COMMUNITY RESEARCH

At one point about two years ago, when in the process of planning a comparative study of community organization and decision-making, the author happened to learn of two other major comparative studies already in progress. After further enquiry, nine major comparative studies of communities throughout the world were disclosed. And it also became evident that almost none of the project directors had made contact with one another, despite the fact that they had been in the recent past, or would be in the near future, collecting data on very similar topics, using relatively similar methods. At that stage, it seemed that the most useful step would not be to start a tenth study. Instead, it appeared more useful to make an effort to bring together the various project directors, and to work toward making comparable as many sections of as many studies as possible. Without coordination, the same lack of comparability and of cumulativeness that had so plagued community studies in the last decades would simply be perpetuated on a grander and far more costly scale.

The result was the creation of the Committee for Comparability in Community Research. While the Committee attempts to maintain close contact with the project directors of major studies, the formal organization of the Committee consists simply of the author as Chairman, and an Executive Committee including: Michel Bassand, University of Geneva; Jean Cuisenier, Centre de Sociologie Européenne; Cveto Kostič, University of Belgrade; S. Nowakowski, University of Warsaw; and Margaret Stacey, University College of Swansee.

Initially the only activities consisted of our writing to and visiting various project directors, and sending out synopses of studies, preliminary reports, and questionnaires of the various studies. Some interest was expressed, but it was not until a few small, informal conferences were held between two or three project directors that any definite coordination actually began to develop. Small meetings of two or three project directors followed (four in the United States, one in England, and one in France). At the Evian meetings, a session was held under the author's chairmanship on Comparability in Community Research at which many of the persons involved in research on communities in France, England, Germany, Yugoslavia, Bulgaria, Poland, Morocco, and the United States met to discuss their work. Subsequent conferences have been held in the United States, France, and Yugoslavia.

While a number of small agreements resulted between two or three projects for standardizing data collection in a few areas, the most impressive success growing out of the Committee's work has been the coordination of three very large projects: the International Studies of Values in Politics program, the National Opinion Research Center's studies based on the Permanent Community Sample, and a series of studies conducted in five Mediterranean countries by the Programme Méditerranéen of the Centre de Sociologie Européenne. ISVP and NORC are now impressively economizing by directly coordinating their efforts from research design, to pretesting, data collection, coding, and analysis by working on a cost-sharing basis. The author is serving as joint study director with the two projects. Meetings with the Programme Méditerranéen have been held, and some arrangements for standardizing research effected, although none as important as the ISVP-NORC agreement. Contact has also been established with a number of other persons involved in research on communities with whom agreements for standardization may be concluded in the future.

The most important activities of the Committee thus far have been in diffusing information about projects and arranging small conferences that have led to standardizing research designs and questionnaire items of different studies. It has also started to bring together punchcards, print-out, codebooks, selected questionnaires, tally sheets, and other types of information from comparative community studies that can eventually grow into a Community Research Data Archive.

The quantities of data that have been collected thus far are rapidly becoming unmanageable, and in the near future a more elaborate arrangement will have to be made for its handling and storage. Some of the issues related to the Community Research Data Archive will now be considered.

A COMMUNITY RESEARCH DATA ARCHIVE

The advantages of reanalyzing, supplementing, and further reanalyzing data collected by earlier researchers have become obvious in a number of areas, perhaps especially so in the field of political behavior. The Inter-University Consortium for Political Research at the University of Michigan was specifically organized for the purpose of efficiently storing and distributing data to persons throughout the world interested in reanalyzing materials collected in earlier studies. Numerous other national and international organizations are being created for the expressed purpose of facilitating exchanges of data among interested persons, such as the recent National Council of Social Science Data Archives in the United States, and the Standing Committee on Social Science Data Archives of the International Social Science Council, UNESCO.[15]

Nothing of this sort has yet been organized for the specific purpose of

---

[15] For reviews of recent developments in data archives, see Ralph L. Bisco, "Social Science Data Archives: A Review of Developments," *American Political Science Review*, LX, No. 1 (March, 1966) 93–109; and Stein Rokkan, ed., *Data Archives for the Social Sciences* (Paris: Mouton, 1966).

collecting, storing, and distributing data on community studies, although there would appear to be a growing need for such a facility.

The technical problems are actually relatively few. A number of organizations—and in future years there will no doubt be many more of the same type—are eminently equipped to deal with the technical matters relating to data cleaning, standardization of formats, compilation of machine-readable codebooks, storage, and distribution of data to interested persons throughout the world. In the near future, it appears, open telephone lines will be established—analogous to those joining many heads of state—by which it will be possible to transfer in a matter of minutes any data stored on magnetic tape in a central archive to connected centers throughout the world.

The major problems in this area are organizational and financial. It is necessary to convince individual researchers of the advantages of such a facility, and for them to keep their data in suitable form so that they may be turned over to a central facility. It is necessary to obtain funds for the venture. It is necessary to locate and to bring together persons who will oversee activities of this sort. And finally, it is necessary to disseminate information about such activities to potentially interested persons so that they will be able to take advantage of the facility.

The specific details for the organization of a Community Research Data Archive should be integrated with efforts being made by other groups and organizations along similar lines. Toward this end, contact has been established with some of the major groups and organizations involved in the planning of data archives, and future action by the Committee will be taken in conjunction with their recommendations: Inter-University Consortium for Political Research, University of Michigan, U.S.A.; DATUM, Bad Godesberg, Germany; Zentralarchiv fuer Empirische Sozialforschung, University of Cologne, Germany; Council of Social Science Data Archives; Standing Committee on Data Archives, International Social Science Council, UNESCO; Executive Committee, International Sociological Association.

In the meantime, the Committee will continue its major activities:

(1) to collect, record, and distribute information about comparative community studies to interested researchers throughout the world;

(2) to hold small conferences for purposes of advancing comparability and cumulativeness in community research;

(3) to bring together data on comparative community studies for the Community Research Data Archive, which, as soon as suitable arrange-

ments for technical handling are completed, will be turned over to some organization specializing in data storage and distribution.

The cooperation of all persons concerned with these activities is hereby solicited; information and enquiries may be addressed to:
Terry N. Clark, Chairman
Committee for Comparability in Community Research
Department of Sociology
1126 East 59th Street
University of Chicago
Chicago, Illinois 60637
United States of America

INDEX OF NAMES

INDEX OF TOPICS

487